SARAH WINNEMUCCA

Sarah Winnemucca

BY SALLY ZANJANI

University of Nebraska Press : Lincoln and London

Publication of this volume
was assisted by The Virginia Faulkner Fund,
established in memory of Virginia Faulkner,
editor-in-chief of the University of Nebraska Press.

Library of Congress Cataloging-in-Publication Data
Zanjani, Sally Springmeyer, 1937–
Sarah Winnemucca / Sally Zanjani.
p.   cm.
Includes bibliographical references and index.
ISBN 0-8032-4917-9 cloth : alk. paper)
1. Hopkins, Sarah Winnemucca, 1844?–1891.
2. Paiute Indians – Biography. 3. Paiute Indians –
Government relations. I. Title
E99.P2 H699 2001 979'.0049745–dc21
[B] 00-060787

For my dear friends Marie and Eileen

Contents

List of Illustrations   ix

Acknowledgments   xi

Prologue   1

1. The World of the Paiutes:
   *"Many years ago, when my people were happier
   than they are now"*   5

2. The San Joaquin:
   "Rag friend"   20

3. Genoa:
   "Our dear good friend, Major Ormsby"   42

4. The Pine Nut Mountains:
   "I felt the world growing cold"   55

5. Winnemucca Lake:
   "It is a fearful thing to tell, but it must be told"   68

6. Camp McDermit:
   *"Can you wonder that I like to have my people
   taken care of by the army?"*   90

7. Winnemucca:
   *"I would willingly throw off the garments
   of civilization and mount my pony"*   114

8. Malheur Reservation:
   "I cannot tell or express how happy we were"   128

9. The Bannock War Begins:
   *"I, only an Indian woman, went and saved my
   father and his people"*   146

10. The Bannock War:
   "I had a vision, and I was screaming in my sleep"   169

11. Yakama Reservation:
   "I am crying out to you for justice"   189

12. Washington DC:
   "This which I hold in my hand is our only hope"   202

13. Fort Vancouver:
   *"For shame! For shame! You dare to cry out liberty
   when you hold us in places against our will"*   219

14. Boston:
   *"I pray of you, I implore of you, I beseech of you,
   hear our pitiful cry to you, sweep away the
   agency system"*   236

15. Lovelock:
   "Education has done it all"   255

16. Henry's Lake:
   "Let my name die out and be forgotten"   284

   Epilogue: *Sarah Today*   299

   Notes   307

   Bibliography   347

   Index   357

Illustrations

FIGURES

Truckee approaches his white brothers	15
Fort Churchill	80
"Savages" drawing	83
Camp McDermit	96
Chief Winnemucca	100
Natches Winnemucca	117
Samuel B. Parrish	130
William Rinehart	136
Gen. Oliver O. Howard	161
Sarah Winnemucca on an army mission	166
Bannock War battle scene	177
Umapine and other Indian scouts	179
Portrait of Sarah Winnemucca	198
Lewis Hopkins	227
Elizabeth Peabody	238
Sarah Winnemucca in her lecture costume	246
Indian gamblers in Reno	279
Paiute harvesters near Lovelock	282
Indian women preparing pinyon nuts	287
Sarah Winnemucca in a late photo	291

MAPS

The world of the Winnemuccas, 1858–78	xiv
The Bannock War, 1878	168

Acknowledgments

I AM GRATEFUL to Paiute tribal elders Helen Williams and Marjorie Dupée for sharing their time and memories with me. Cary Hanson and Georgia Hedrick generously made sources in their collections available to me. Guy Rocha kindly commented on a portion of my manuscript. Several colleagues provided their advice: Michael Brodhead, Phillip Earl, Jeff Kintop, and Anton Sohn.

My debt to Judy Adams, Humboldt County Library, Winnemucca, Nevada, who offered invaluable assistance, cannot be overstated. Jane Daniels, Island Park Historical Society, Idaho, shared her wide knowledge of the area. Other colleagues at libraries, museums, and historical societies furnished much aid and many courtesies. Special mention should be given to Duncan Aldrich, Patrick Ragains, and Millie Syring, University of Nevada, Reno Libraries; Jennifer Evans, University of Washington Libraries; John Mead, Oregon Historical Society, Portland; Scott Sanders, Olive Kettering Library, Antioch College; Christine Simpson, Reno Veterans Administration Medical Center Library; Sarah Theimer, Idaho Historical Society, Boise; Joy Werlink, Washington State Historical Society, Tacoma; and to the staff of the Sierra View Library, Reno. I am also indebted to Ruth Danner, deputy recorder, Humboldt County, Nevada, and to the staff of the Washoe County, Nevada, school board, all of whom made important contributions.

Mary Ellen Jones provided helpful research assistance at the Bancroft Library, University of California, Berkeley. Cartography was done by Patricia DeBunch. The generous financial support of a foundation that prefers anonymity is acknowledged with appreciation.

SARAH WINNEMUCCA

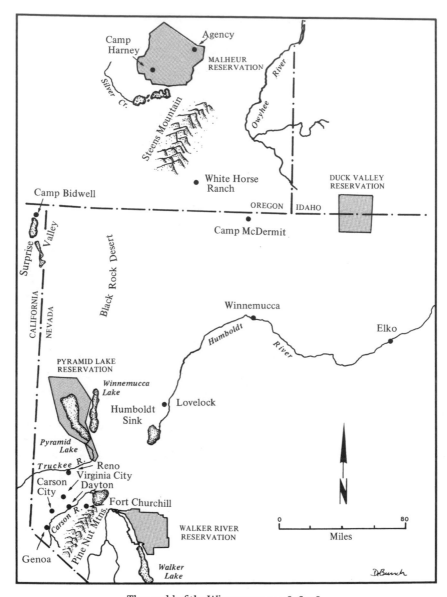

The world of the Winnemuccas, 1858–78

Prologue

O AN AUTHOR accustomed to pursuing the unknown story along the roads less traveled, Sarah Winnemucca looms above the historical landscape of the Great Basin like Mount Everest — and poses a similar challenge. Now that racism and the effort to crumple Sarah inside the cage of an alien Victorian morality have faded, her achievements stand forth more strikingly than ever, as do the qualities that made her unique and moved her father, Chief Winnemucca, to declare to his people at the end of the Bannock War, "None of us are worthy of being chief but her."

Some Indian women, such as Sarah Winnemucca, have played important roles in the saga of American history, but when Sarah is compared to her two most famous predecessors, Pocahontas and Sacajawea, significant differences emerge. Sarah began her career as one component in a broad family effort in which her grandfather, her father, and her brother Natches worked toward the same end. By contrast, Pocahontas, whose friendliness toward the British colonists was often at odds with her father's hostility, and Sacajawea, who was kidnapped as a girl by an enemy tribe and married to the French Canadian fur trader and interpreter Toussaint Charbonneau, lacked family support.[1]

Sarah, more than these earlier Indian women, created her own role. When Pocahontas was scarcely more than a child, her sympathy with and interest in the colonists led her to be a negotiator for them with the Indians. She also saved lives and on several occasions brought Indian provisions to the colonists when starvation stalked the Jamestown outpost. Still, the expansion of her role beyond these early kindnesses was

1

not entirely her own doing. When the whites abducted her and held her hostage, they hoped that her unfriendly father would agree to peace in exchange for her return. And when they sought to transform her into an English lady and an Episcopalian, she made no objection, but the idea had not been her own. Moreover, when she journeyed to England with her white husband, John Rolfe, her son, and a retinue of Indians, it appears that she was again being used by others rather than pursuing a mission of her own. Her audience with the queen and other gala affairs there came about because the Virginia Company wanted to showcase her as an advertisement for their colony. Similarly, Sacajawea did not of her own volition offer her services to the Lewis and Clark expedition; Meriwether Lewis and William Clark evidently hired Charbonneau in part because they foresaw Sacajawea's future usefulness as a Shoshone interpreter. In short, others chose both Pocahontas and Sacajawea for the roles they played. Sarah chose herself. She volunteered — alone — for service in the Bannock War, and she made herself a spokeswoman for her people by becoming a popular lecturer with a mission to sway public opinion. In the felicitous phrase of literary scholar LaVonne Ruoff, Sarah became "the mightiest word warrior of her tribe."[2]

Important differences between Sarah and the other two Indian heroines also stem from the drastically altered power relations that they faced. Both Pocahontas and Sacajawea were concerned with easing the entry of a small, weak group of whites into an Indian world. In addition to rescuing John Smith and a number of other colonists and sharing life-saving provisions, Pocahontas taught the Indian method of growing tobacco to her future husband, who would develop the Virginia tobacco industry. Sacajawea, as well as interpreting, advised on routes in her native country and showed Lewis and Clark Indian plant foods.[3] Thus, both taught whites some Indian ways to help them survive.

Sarah, by contrast, faced a white world from a shrinking Indian outpost and recognized that Indians needed the white man's skills in order to survive. She spoke tirelessly for her people in lectures on both coasts and in pleas to army officers and politicians in Washington DC and Ne-

vada. As the eloquent voice of the Paiutes, she brought a small and obscure Indian tribe into public view. Believing that an early end to the
Bannock War, a war the Indians were doomed to lose, would be the best
outcome for her people, she served the U.S. Army as scout, messenger,
and interpreter. Her bravery in the face of great danger — at one point
leading her father's band from the enemy camp into safety — and her
epic rides for long distances over harsh terrain are the stuff of western
legend. At other times, she served peace as vigorously as she rode her
galloping horse across the desert with a general's message, and mediated between settlers and Paiutes on more than one tense occasion.
Yet she made her greatest contributions in the intellectual realm. She
wrote a book — the first by an Indian woman, the first by any Indian
west of the Rockies, and the first to record the customs of the Paiutes.
Without government assistance, she started an Indian school and created a model for Indian education that was far ahead of its time.

As a result of her position as the daughter of a chief and of the public
role she had created for herself, Sarah became something of a celebrity.
Newspaper reporters interviewed her, covered her lectures in detail,
and wrote about her doings; Indian agents with whom she clashed
excoriated her in their reports; army officers and others reminisced
about their contacts with her; and in her later years, her eastern supporter, Elizabeth Peabody, wrote two reports on her school and many
letters on her activities. Although these varied sources far exceed the
information normally available on an Indian woman of Sarah's day, the
heart of any chronicle of Sarah's life must inevitably be her book, *Life
among the Piutes: Their Wrongs and Claims*, written when she was thirty-
nine, eight years before her death in 1891. *Life among the Piutes* is at once
an ethnohistory of her tribe, a tract urging justice for them, and an autobiography intended to vindicate the author. Not unnaturally, these
purposes shape the narrative, and anything that reflects badly on the
Paiutes or on Sarah has been omitted. At the same time, Sarah's vivid
and emotional account of many incidents recorded nowhere else from
an Indian point of view endow her book with enormous value as a historical document.

3

Because Sarah's is an autobiography written almost entirely from memory years after the fact and largely intended for the political purpose of winning justice for the Paiutes, questions concerning its accuracy have been posed. After carefully cross-checking incidents in Sarah's book against other sources whenever possible, I found that her memory for people and events was extraordinarily correct, as has been widely recognized. However, Sarah sometimes erred on chronology, dates, and numbers, mistakes perhaps understandable for someone not trained early in the white man's chronological mode of thinking and calendar. These errors I corrected through other sources. Although the accuracy of the wording, if not the sense, of the dialogue directly quoted by Sarah may seem doubtful, I have considered spoken words an aspect of her verifiably remarkable memory for events and have used much of the dialogue given in her book in direct quotations. As historian Stephen Ambrose observes, apropos of words attributed to Crazy Horse, "Illiterate people everywhere are noted for their excellent memories. The early Greeks passed on the long Homeric tales from one generation to the next with hardly a phrase out of place, a phenomenon that occurs again and again among primitive cultures." Sarah, of course, had made herself literate, but her early training occurred in a culture where memory served in place of the written word. Moreover, among the Indians of the Great Basin, the daughter of a chief would have been specially trained to memorize.[4] It is also true that the moments most deeply felt are least likely to be forgotten. No doubt Sarah's intense emotions over the wrongs suffered by the Paiutes seared both words and deeds in her memory. Many may linger in our memories as well.

1
The World of the Paiutes

"Many years ago,
when my people were happier
than they are now"

A S A CHILD Sarah Winnemucca's name was Thocmetony, meaning "shell flower" in the Paiute tongue. Her memory began with terror and flight. In the late fall (possibly of 1848), her band camped by the Humboldt River, where the men fished and the women gathered grass seeds for winter food. When they heard that a party of white men were approaching, everyone began to run. The Paiutes knew that white men often killed Indians on sight. Worse still, they had heard that white men were cannibals. In the winter of 1846–47, a party of white travelers stranded and starving in the high mountains on their way to California had turned to eating each other and their Indian guides.

Knowing what they knew, and fearing worse, the Paiutes ran for their lives, the gray brown of their rabbit-skin tunics barely visible in the gray blue of the sage plain and the gray purple of the mountains beyond. But little Thocmetony was too frightened to run. Her mother, Tuboitony, with Thocmetony's younger sister on her back, urged the child onward, but Thocmetony's small brown legs seemed frozen and refused to obey. Thocmetony's aunt, also struggling with a terror-stricken little girl, suggested burying the two children in the earth and returning for them later. If the girls slowed their flight, the whole band might be killed and eaten. Frantically, Thocmetony's mother scooped up the sandy earth and smoothed it back into place over her daughter, leaving the little face exposed but hidden and shaded from the sun by sagebrush. So small a child, so little disturbance in the earth. If she made no sound, the white men would never find her. The two women cautioned Thocmetony and her cousin that if they heard noises they must not cry out lest they be killed and eaten. Then the two mothers raced away to catch up with the rest.[1]

"With my heart throbbing and not daring to breathe, we lay there all day. It seemed that the night would never come," Thocmetony later remembered. We can readily imagine the terror of that child immobilized in the sand. Afraid to make a sound. Afraid that she felt the thunder of galloping hooves vibrating through the earth. Afraid that her parents would never return ("Oh, father have you forgotten me. Are you never coming for me?"). Afraid that they had hidden her too well to find her again. Afraid of all the creatures that prowled and slithered over the desert, but most of all of the dreaded white men. When night came she finally dared to cry, and she sobbed as though "my very heartstrings would break." Sounds of footsteps and whispering reached her ears. Death or life? More frightened than ever, Thocmetony lay still as a stone, except for the heart that beat so wildly she thought it would "leap from my mouth." At last she heard her mother's voice. Strong hands hurriedly dug away the earth that surrounded her and lifted her from burial to be happy once more in the arms of her parents.[2]

Not only would fear of white men mark the beginning of her memory but Thocmetony's life would be lived in reaction to them. She would endlessly ricochet between terror and attraction, fury and admiration, rebellion and acceptance, hope and despair. In her eyes, "They came like a lion, yes, like a roaring lion, and have continued so ever since." She would always revolve around them as she struggled to find a place for herself and her people in the world they had snatched away.

Thocmetony was born on the cusp of the white invasion. In 1844 — the probable year of her birth — the white owls, so called by the Paiutes for their bearded faces and pale eyes, had scarcely penetrated her homeland. For a short time, Thocmetony would know traditional Indian life, and she would write an invaluable primary source on the old ways of the Paiute people in the Great Basin. That it was the first

6

book to be written in English by an Indian woman shows the extraordinary height of her achievement.[3]

For some four thousand years, the lives of the Paiutes had been shaped by the harshness of the Nevada desert. Little rain falls in the land between the Sierra Nevada and the Great Salt Lake. For many months, a merciless sun bakes this arid world, and the traveler unversed in desert survival can easily dehydrate and die. By custom, Paiutes meeting on the trail greeted each other not with the equivalent of "hello" but with *uduta hada* ("It's hot"), an observation valid for much of the year. In winter, when icy winds whistle and snow often mantles mountain and valley, few travelers met on the trails because the Paiutes stayed close to the fires in their lodges. Theirs was a universe where dust devils twirled and mirages shimmered on the horizon, a place of sage and greasewood plains, burning white alkali flats, and ranges of juniper- and pinyon-studded mountains. Nowhere could one travel beyond the sight of the mountains, and Thocmetony's people traveled far indeed in their seasonal wanderings in search of food.[4]

In the aboriginal period, they seem to have had little sense of themselves as a single people, an Indian nation of Paiutes. Yet they knew well where the boundaries lay between their territory and the lands of other nearby Indian peoples: Washo Indians, speaking a language entirely different from theirs, clustered in the Carson Valley and Truckee Meadows at the base of the Sierra; California Indians on the other side of the great mountain range, where a few of the more daring Paiutes sometimes traveled to trade; Bannocks, sharing a common speech with the Paiutes, in southern Oregon and southwest Idaho; Shoshones, in northeastern Nevada, living much as the Paiutes lived, and speaking a language similar to theirs and yet impossible to understand. Farther south, beyond the Shoshone and near the Colorado River, lived another people who were similar yet not the same. White men, whose ways were ever mysterious, would call these people the Southern Paiutes, although their language was different from the Paiutes of northwestern Nevada.[5]

Relations between the Paiutes and these other peoples seem to have been peaceful as a rule. They rarely had time for such luxuries as raids or warfare, being much engaged in the struggle for survival. Unfamiliar with the ceremonies, the campfire stories, the laughter, and the sweeter side of Paiute life, explorer John Charles Frémont, in an early encounter with the Paiutes, saw only the struggle: "In this wild state the Indian lives to get food. This is his business."[6]

The names and organization of the Paiute bands reflected the primacy of survival. Because life depended on the joint efforts of a group working together cooperatively, the family was the essential unit, and families often shifted their allegiance from one band to another. Each band derived its name from the principal food source in the area where most of the year was spent. The Kammidika-a (Jackrabbit Eaters) lived north of Pyramid Lake; the Kuyuidika-a (Cui-ui Eaters), so named for the prehistoric black sucker fish they ate, clustered around the delta where the Truckee River flows into Pyramid Lake. This region, together with Honey Lake to the northwest, was the homeland of Thocmetony's band. Eastward lay the domain of the Kibidika-a (Ground Squirrel Eaters); farther south were the Toidika-a (Cattail Eaters) and several other bands. All together, an estimated twenty-three Paiute bands roamed the vast territory from the Owens Valley in California through most of western Nevada and into southern Oregon and Idaho.[7]

Necessity kept these bands small in size and flexible in their responses to shifting conditions. The amount of grass seeds or ground squirrels at any given spot was not enough to feed a large concentration of people — or a small one — if the group stayed too long in one place. Thus the bands remained loose clusters of families, perhaps one hundred to two hundred individuals, that followed seasonal food supplies. They convened in larger gatherings only on special occasions when the desert's infrequent bounties could feed a large number at once: the annual fish spawning in the Truckee Delta, the mud hen hunt at the Humboldt Sink, an antelope hunt, or the pinyon nut harvest in the mountains in a good year.[8]

As survival dictated the size and naming of the Paiute bands, it also influenced their leadership. Anthropologists Julian Steward and Erminie Wheeler-Voegelin have observed, "There are few native people in the world who were so unorganized as the Northern Paiute . . . ," and scholars agree that the concept of chieftainship was alien to the Paiutes, only developing when whites demanded a central authority they could deal with. The bands did, nonetheless, have a respected male figure, a headman, whose authority depended upon the force of his personality and his ability to persuade others to agree with his proposals. The elders, sitting in a circle and smoking with the headman, reached some decisions, but in general councils, the entire band participated in decision making, including women, who sat in the second circle but were permitted to voice their opinions.[9]

Authorities other than the headman led some of the band's activities. For instance, a rabbit boss took charge of the rabbit hunt, in which the Paiutes stretched long nets across the plain and drove rabbits into them to be clubbed to death. The dance boss, "He Who Knows Many Songs," supervised ceremonial dances; the shaman healed the sick and spoke his visions. Sometimes functions overlapped. Old Winnemucca, Thocmetony's father, who had the power to charm antelope to their death in a hunt, served as headman and antelope shaman. He also prophesied on occasion and related myths to his people that explained their troubles. Some said he could heal bullet wounds. More than fifty years after his death, old men still spoke of his extraordinary shamanistic powers.[10]

If she had been born a century earlier, Thocmetony's life would have been very different. When she reached maidenhood, she would have stopped playing with the naked children modeling little animals from the clay of the riverbanks and hunting them with toy bows and arrows, mimicking the work they would soon grow up to do. Wearing a skirt of grass or shredded sagebrush bark or a winter tunic made from woven strips of rabbit skins, she would learn the work of a woman — first, how to gather fuel. A large pile of wood demonstrated a young woman's desirability as an efficient wife. How to make a shelter

9

for the family of sagebrush and pine boughs in the mountains and a round lodge of woven cattails (a *kahnee*) at the edge of the marshes where the desert rivers died. How to split fish with a stone knife and dry them in the sun. How to dig roots for food and collect the eggs of water birds along the shore. How to cook a cattail pollen cake and sieve buckberries into a sharp flavorful paste. How to collect ripe, black Indian rice grass seeds, separate them from their husks, and grind them. How to harvest and roast pinyon nuts when the band made their annual autumn journey into the mountains. And how to weave baskets of reed and willow beside the fire while winter winds tore at the fragile tule lodge: fine-woven narrow-necked water jugs sealed with pitch; cooking baskets, also pitch-sealed, in which the women stirred hot stones from the fire to heat the food within; broad flat baskets for collecting seeds beaten from the tall rice grasses; large conical burden baskets in which the women carried household necessities when the band moved thirty to fifty miles in search of a new food source. Baskets of many shapes and kinds for a multitude of tasks.[11] The skill Thocmetony developed as a glove maker suggests that had she been born in an earlier time she would have woven admirable baskets.

Physically mature and accomplished in the skills of a woman, the girl became the special charge of her grandmother until she married. Looking back many years later, Thocmetony wrote of the spring courtship ritual, the "Festival of Flowers." Each day the girls would walk together in the hills to see if the wildflowers after which many of them had been named had started to bloom. The young men shared in the atmosphere of expectation until, at last, the headman would indulgently announce: "My dear daughters, we are told that you have seen yourselves in the hills and the valleys in full bloom. Five days from today your festival day will come. I know every young man's heart stops beating when I am talking. I know how it was with me many years ago. I used to wish the Flower Festival would come every day."

On the appointed day, each girl gathered her namesake flowers and wove them into wreaths and crowns. Then they marched along and danced, each girl singing about herself in the persona of her flower while her swain danced and sang by her side: "I am so beautiful! Who will come and dance with me while I am so beautiful? Oh, come and be happy with me! I shall be beautiful while the earth lasts. Somebody will always admire me; and who will come and be happy with me in the Spirit-land? I shall be beautiful forever there."[12]

Other aspects of courtship were less romantic and laced more with the symbolism of practical necessity. A young woman might offer a man she favored a gift of food. Seizing her wrist instead of taking the food was the sign that he preferred her. No higher mark of favor among a people ever intent upon survival could be imagined. If a young man sought to win a girl, he demonstrated that he was a good provider by bringing game he had killed to her family's dwelling. All night he sat outside the lodge. If the girl changed from her usual sleeping place beside her grandmother to make her bed beside her mother, his suit had been rejected and he came no more. But if she continued to sleep in the same spot, he came back each night, bringing his kill and moving his vigil a little closer until at last she opened her arms to him and took him into her bed. Without public ceremony, the marriage was sealed.[13] In her great-grandmother's day, the energy Thocmetony brought to every task she undertook would no doubt have produced large piles of fuel that demonstrated her desirability as a bride. Whether she would have encouraged the courtship of a good provider is more difficult to guess, for she showed a certain weakness for the ne'er-do-well with a handsome face.

Thocmetony's unusual capabilities would have led her to become extraordinary in any time period in which we can imagine her. Not a headman, for that position was closed to women, but she surely would have spoken out eloquently and persuasively in council. She would have made a marvelous teller of tales to children, hypnotizing them with her burning black eyes and the music of her words, as they sat around the evening fire. They would see Itsa, the trickster coyote, prance through firelight and shadow and learn from his misdeeds, for among her many accomplishments, Thocmetony was a gifted teacher. She might have become a shaman, as women could do, drawing her power from a spirit animal, chanting, raising eagle feathers over the sick before their souls traveled too far to be retrieved. The shaman's powers were sometimes inherited, and Thocmetony's father had been a great shaman, as well as a headman. Even in her own time, Thocmetony dreamed visions of things to come.[14]

When the years turned her at last into a *tubitson*, a bent, old woman with white hair, mahogany skin wrinkled as a walnut, and eyes dimming from the smoke of many lodge fires, she might have been the aged woman of unusual powers sent by the band with an advance party to their traditional pinyon grove. While green pinyon cones roasted in a pit, she would cast handfuls of dirt to charm away the ghosts of the East, the West, the North, and the South so that the pinyon nuts would ripen and the people would not hunger. Then she would descend from the mountains with the others, bringing these first nuts and a small tree so that the pinyon-nut prayer dance could begin. When an old woman grew too feeble to keep up with the band on their necessary peregrinations, they abandoned her, letting her die. The more fortunate elders died among their people and were buried in unmarked graves.[15]

So it had been, season after season, year after year. But this was not to be Thocmetony's life. The world of the Great Basin Indians was about to change forever with the coming of white people, beginning with the early trappers and explorers. Fur trapper Jedediah Smith made the first passage in 1826, traversing the tip of what is now southern Nevada on his way to California, returning by present Ebbetts Pass over the Sierra and crossing the desert with great difficulty. Peter Skene Ogden, a Hudson's Bay Company trapper, stripped the Humboldt River of its scanty beaver in 1828–29 and made friendly contact with the Indians. Trapper Joe Meek, by contrast, ventured into the Great Basin in 1832 and casually shot an Indian (probably a Shoshone) on the mere suspicion that the man intended to rob his traps. The kind of cultural ethnocentrism that equated different with dangerous and bred misunderstanding operated on both sides. Annie Lowry, a half-Paiute woman, related that an Indian hunting party had stoned two white travelers to death near the Forty Mile Desert for no better reason than "knowing it was not right for men to be so different from themselves."[16]

Violence on a larger scale erupted when the Indians confronted frontiersman Joseph Reddeford Walker in 1833 during his journey to California. As Annie Lowry heard the story, confirmed by sources in the Walker party, Captain John, a Paiute leader, had persuaded the Indians to treat the white men with friendship. Young men from all the bands in the vicinity gathered in a holiday mood and, according to Lowry, had no intentions more hostile than making a bold show and trying on the white men's hats. Many of the young Indians had never been away from their families overnight. They spent the time playing games, telling stories, and painting their bodies with bright geometrical designs. When the young Paiutes approached the next morning, Walker and his men mistook them for a party of Shoshones they had previously frightened away with a display of marksmanship — shooting at ducks and peppering a beaver-skin target. Misinterpreting the advance of the throng Lowry described as the "smiling, prancing, high-stepping Paiutes" for an attack, thirty-two of Walker's men surrounded the Paiutes and opened fire. The Indians, who had never heard guns before, at first mistook the noise for thunder. Thirty-nine Paiutes died, and the rest ran away howling through the tall marsh grass.[17]

When the Walker party passed through the Humboldt Sink the following summer on their return trip from California, another bloody encounter with the Paiutes ensued, but on a smaller scale, this time with fourteen Indians dying. Apparently, the large number of Indians, the uncertainty as to their intent, and the uncontrollable fears of the men in Walker's party produced these massacres. Yet the long-term effects of Walker's passage far outweighed the deaths of the young Indians. The harshness of the terrain and the paucity of beaver had insulated the region from all but a few white contacts, but Walker established the feasibility of an emigrant trail across the Great Basin to California.[18]

Although Thocmetony's band, the Kuyuidika-a, probably heard of these unhappy incidents when bands gathered and exchanged news at the Pyramid Lake fish spawning or the Humboldt Sink mud hen hunt, her grandfather Truckee and her father, Winnemucca, both pursued a policy of peace and friendship with white men. Thocmetony described Truckee's first encounter with them as it had been related to her. When news arrived that a party of white men traveling east from California was nearing his encampment on the Humboldt Sink, Truckee expressed delight that his "long-looked for white brothers" had finally come. With a small group of his leading men, he approached the white men's camp and was sharply ordered to stop at once. Truckee cast down his rabbit-skin robe and raised his arms to show that he had no weapons, but the white men would not allow him to come near. Truckee gazed at them sorrowfully. For several days he and his men followed the party, camping near them by night and traveling within their field of vision by day, in an effort to gain their trust. "But he was disappointed, poor, dear old soul," observed Thocmetony.[19]

After this rebuff, Truckee remained hopeful that his "white brothers" would soon return, but he felt obliged to repeat a traditional tale to his people to explain white men's cold behavior. In the beginning, he told them, the first man and woman had four children, a dark-skinned boy and girl and a white pair. Soon the children began to quarrel, and their fighting made the household so unhappy that their parents realized they must be separated. First Man had great powers. He had no need to hunt because he could call the game to him. He could also transport his children to another place with mere words. "Depart from each other, you cruel children," he said. "Go across the mighty ocean and do not seek each other's lives." The white boy and girl disappeared; the dark-skinned pair remained to become the progenitors of the Indians.

Truckee ended the tale by repeating his wish to love the white men as he loved each member of his own band and by exacting a vow from his people: "I want you one and all to promise that should I not live to

Truckee approaches his white brothers. Reprinted from Howard,
Famous Indian Chiefs I Have Known.

welcome them myself, you will not hurt a hair on their heads, but welcome them as I tried to do." The people agreed and returned to their work. In the hard times to come, many may have wished that First Man would appear once more to reinstitute the separation.[20]

During the 1840s Truckee succeeded in establishing the relationship he had sought with white men. He became a "famous guide," in the words of one anthropologist, when, in the late autumn of 1844, he showed the way to the Stevens party — the first to successfully cross the mountains with wagons. Without Truckee's help the party might have frozen or starved to death in the Sierra. He served as guide for several other emigrant parties and acquired from them the name by which we know him. Truckee, according to Thocmetony, means "alright, very well," quite possibly the answer the emigrants frequently heard from the old chief in response to their requests. The emigrants named the Truckee River in his honor and presented him with a tin pie plate, which he greatly prized and wore as a hat. When they learned the plate's intended use, Thocmetony and her grandfather saw this as a good joke. The members of another band, who evidently resented the growing prominence of the Kuyuidika-a leaders above their headman, ridiculed the pie-plate hat as an example of the old man's naivety.[21]

In January 1844 an important traveler arrived in the Great Basin and expressed the horror at the barren desert landscape that many emigrants later felt. Approaching Pyramid Lake from the north with his exploration party, Frémont wrote, "The appearance of the country was so forbidding that I was afraid to enter it." Frémont camped beside the reed *kahnees* of the Kuyuidika-a, highly praised the taste of the two- to four-foot-long "salmon trout" they gave him ("superior, in fact, to that of any fish I have ever known"), and tried unsuccessfully to recruit an Indian guide for the mountain crossing. Since Thocmetony relates that Truckee and Frémont met at present Wadsworth, a distance upstream from the lake, their encounter probably occurred during Frémont's second journey across the Great Basin in the autumn of 1845, when he did not visit Pyramid Lake — if it took place in

Nevada at all. Although Frémont usually related his Indian contacts with considerable interest, he makes no mention of this meeting.[22]

An initial meeting in California is also possible. When Frémont launched the Bear Flag Revolt in 1846 to take California from the Mexicans and advance his own position, Truckee had traveled to California with an emigrant party. Truckee and several other Paiutes, along with some recruits from other tribes, joined Frémont's motley army for the march to conquer Los Angeles. When Truckee returned to Nevada in the autumn of 1847, he had seen wonders far exceeding the tin pie plate that he had once gathered his people together to admire. He had made important friends, and he had come to understand the true source of white men's power. Shortly afterward, he returned to the "beautiful country" of California.[23]

Although Truckee refused to deviate from his policy of peace and friendship toward whites, the condition of the Paiutes rapidly grew more desperate. In 1845 the Humboldt Trail leading across present Donner Pass was already so well traveled that Frémont called it the "emigrant road," but with the discovery of gold at Sutter's mill in 1848, emigrant traffic over the trail increased to a flood. In 1849 traders established Nevada posts during the travel season to sell fresh animals and necessary goods to the emigrants. Soon the posts became permanent, and ranchers began laying claim to the Great Basin's few watered and fertile valleys.[24]

This white intrusion seriously disrupted the ways by which the Paiutes had wrung a precarious living in an arid and inhospitable environment over the millennia. Whites' livestock consumed the grasses the Paiutes depended upon for seed food. Whites burned Indian food caches. Whites, seeking fuel and timber, began cutting down the pinyons from which the Paiutes harvested nuts. Whites killed the game and sometimes the Paiutes themselves. An estimated two-thirds of the Paiutes died in this way during the period of white contact. When he headed the Kuyuidika-a during Truckee's absences in California, Winnemucca had foreseen all this and more in a terrible prophetic dream. After the same dream came to him for three nights, Winnemucca knew the spirits had spoken and he must tell his people. According to Thocmetony, he called a convocation at the Carson Sink in the spring of 1847. She would have been nearly three, rather young to remember the event so clearly, which suggests a later date for the convocation, an earlier birth date for her, or a description related to her by others (a device she sometimes uses in her narrative without differentiating from events she witnessed herself). Thocmetony later recounted how the men of the band rode out singing a welcoming song to greet Winnemucca and his family. Winnemucca decreed five days of games and entertainment before he would speak, for the number five had a talismanic significance to the Paiutes. He may have also seen it as a kind of final fling.[25]

The people enjoyed themselves more than they ever would again. They hunted rabbits, fished, played games, raced horses, danced, and ran footraces.[26] When the allotted time for these diversions had passed, Winnemucca told his dream. He said, "I dreamt this same thing three nights, — the very same. I saw the greatest emigration that has yet been through our country. I looked North and South and East and West, and saw nothing but dust, and I heard a great weeping. I saw women crying, and I also saw my men shot down by the white people. They were killing my people with something that made a great noise like thunder and lightning, and I saw the blood streaming from the mouths of my men that lay all around me. I saw it as if it was real."[27]

Winnemucca advised his people to flee to the mountains — far from the emigrant trail — where they could live on fish, rabbits, and pinyon nuts. All day the old women spoke among themselves, turning over Winnemucca's warning. That night one of the other shamans called a council, and the men gathered. Five times the pipe they smoked passed to the right. Next they sang five songs taught to the shaman by the spirits. Then the shaman went into a trance while the men continued to smoke in silence. After a little time had passed, a sound from the shaman's lips like faraway crying broke the stillness. When he emerged from the trance, the shaman sobbed and confirmed Winnemucca's terrible dream. Whites would kill a great many Paiutes with their guns. Hundreds more would die from a "fearful disease" that would come from the white men. But some Paiutes would survive.

"We all wept," Thocmetony related, "for we believed this word came from heaven."[28]

2

The San Joaquin

"Rag friend"

THOCMETONY thought she was born about 1844. If her birthplace was the Humboldt Sink, it may have been summer or early fall when the Kuyuidika-a gathered at the place where the Humboldt River ended in a broad, shallow lake, dotted with marshy islands and ringed with green reeds, for the annual mud hen hunt. At molting time, when lost feathers left these small black ducks unable to fly, the Paiutes stretched long nets across the mouth of the river. Women and young people stationed along the edge caught any mud hens that came ashore, while men in boats made from tules tied together with cattail ropes poled across the still blue waters at dawn, driving birds into the nets to be killed. Then the Paiutes feasted on roasted mud hens, saving the excess birds for a leaner time by splitting and sun-drying them.[1]

Thocmetony's mother, Tuboitony, would have taken no part in these crucial activities. By Paiute custom, the mother who had just given birth rested for twenty-five days while her husband and her women relatives waited on her. Roasted mud hen would have been denied to her and her husband, for they could eat no meat during this period. Instead they might have been offered another summer delicacy: cattail pollen cakes baked between two layers of cattail leaves. Tuboitony would have been busy preparing necessary things for the baby because nothing could be made in advance lest such confidence bring ill luck to the newborn and jeopardize its survival. Foremost among the new baby's needs was its basket — a small, narrow, loosely woven boat of unpeeled willow in which Thocmetony could ride while her mother walked or rocked her baby on her knees while sitting on the ground with legs stretched straight before her in the Paiute way. Tuboitony would line the basket with feathers, ideally the soft, downy breast feathers of a swan and wrap the little one in sagebrush bark rubbed soft or in a mat of dried algae. In colder weather the baby would need a little rabbit-skin blanket. Every five days, Tuboitony bathed herself and made a new basket until the allotted time had passed and all the discarded baskets could be bundled together in a tree, along with the baby's umbilical cord. Tuboitony then secured the baby with crisscrossed thongs in a finer, ornamented basket, where she would remain until she grew too big. When the time came for the Kuyuidika-a to travel again on their seasonal peregrinations, Tuboitony would walk with the rest of the group, carrying on her back the large burden basket that contained her family's possessions and on her arm her baby's little basket.[2]

Thocmetony's parentage conferred some distinction upon her. Her mother was Truckee's daughter, and her father, Winnemucca, who had three or four wives and whose name "the giver" suggests his generosity, appears to have been a man of substance. Moreover, he was a shaman with the gift of prophecy and was readily accepted as headman of the Kuyuidika-a in Truckee's absence. But Thocmetony was a middle child, just one among many, with three older brothers, an elder sister, and a throng of cousins. Had there been nothing to set her apart, she might have been just another little girl, lost in the crowd. Before dying in a massacre, Tuboitony would bear at least two more children. Thocmetony could barely remember the birth of her younger sister, a time when the world around her had greened with the coming of spring. Her mother handed her some pretty beads and asked her if she wanted to buy something with them. Thocmetony replied that she would like to buy some pinyon nuts.

"Would you like something else you can love and play with? Would you like to have a little sister?" asked Tuboitony.

Thocmetony responded enthusiastically to this idea but specified "a little, little sister; not like my sister Mary, for she won't let me play with her. She leaves me and goes with big girls to play." Thocmetony was about to offer her beads when Tuboitony's new baby cried so loudly that it frightened her, and she, too, began to cry. Her mother comforted her in her arms, explaining that the clamorous crying came from her new baby sister. This baby was probably Elma (her Indian name has not been disclosed).[3]

Other early memories were less pleasant than Elma's birth. Thocmetony's burial in the sand must have been the worst, but other dreadful remembrances darkened her early years. The burning of the Kuyuidika-a seed caches brought both winter hardship and tangible evidence of white people's ill will. As Indian food supplies dwindled, the Indians began stealing from emigrant camps, a practice that increased the likelihood of violent confrontation. It was said that whites killed with "something like thunder and lightning," as Thocmetony put it. After the desperate Donner party turned to cannibalism in the snowbound Sierra, Indians became convinced that whites not only killed people but ate them. Truckee would have learned of this horror upon his return from California in the spring of 1847, and, if he traveled with Frémont and Stephen W. Kearny, he might have even witnessed the burial of the grisly remains. When Paiute parents warned their children that if they behaved badly whites would come and eat them, too, the terror increased. Each time the children looked down from their mountain refuge and saw dust in the valley, they imagined that white people were pursuing them.[4] After Truckee returned from a sojourn to California with guns of his own, he realized his firearms horrified the children and ordered the guns removed from the Kuyuidika-a camp. He made no mistake. The children screamed with panic each time one of the new guns fired in the distance. They sobbed so long and hysterically that some of the women finally requested that Truckee and his companions cease firing guns before the children died of fear.

After the firing stopped, Thocmetony screamed and fought and even bit her mother as Tuboitony tried to bring her back to the family *kahnee*. Finally Winnemucca bundled her into his arms and carried her to her grandfather. As the child hid her face against her father's chest, Truckee tried to coax her out of her panicky sobbing: "So the young lady is ashamed because her sweetheart has come to see her. Come, dearest, that won't do after I have had such a hard time to come to see my sweetheart, that she should be ashamed to look at me."

Her brothers assured their grandfather that they were glad to see him, and Truckee continued to coax and tease Thocmetony. Perhaps, though he had many grandchildren, she was a favorite of his even then. "See that young lady; she does not love her sweetheart anymore, does she? Well, I shall not live if she does not come and tell me she loves me. I shall take that gun, and I shall kill myself." This brought on a fresh outburst of tears that continued for several days, and quite some time passed before Thocmetony reconciled with her grandfather.[5]

All through the winter Truckee told the people about the wondrous works of the white men that he had seen in California, creations more astonishing even than the houses on wheels they drove along the emigrant trail. With his own eyes, he had seen "big houses" that traveled faster on the ocean than "any horse in the world." When the people expressed amazement that a house as large as the hill to which Truckee pointed would not sink, Truckee insisted that it was so. He spoke of the beautiful clothes the white people wore. He told of a thing still more marvelous than the floating house: a gun that could shoot a ball the size of his head as far as a mountain twenty miles away. He recounted battles and the conquest of a great city of Mexicans. Largely by imitation, not always knowing the meaning of the words, he had learned a little English, and he taught his people the "Star-Spangled Banner" and the army roll call. He treasured his gun and caressed it by the hour, saying, "Goodee gun, goodee, goodee gun, heap shoot."[6]

But even the gun was not the most precious among the possessions he brought back from California. His treasure was his "rag friend," a letter from Frémont requesting that all who read it should treat him well. Thocmetony remembered how he took his rag friend out and talked to it. He explained its miraculous powers to the people: "This can talk to all our white brothers, and our white sisters, and their children. . . . The paper can travel like the wind, and it can go and talk with their fathers and brothers and sisters, and come back to tell what they are doing, and whether they are well or sick." This talking rag, he believed, was the true source of white men's power.[7]

As Truckee's account of the Bear Flag Revolt and all its wonders took a place, after many retellings, beside older legends such as "When Rabbit Killed the Sun" and the "Battle with the Saidukas," not everyone drew the lesson that Truckee intended. Truckee might insist that whites and Paiutes were brothers, descended from a common progenitor, but the Kuyuidika-a shamans declared that those who could create such marvelous works must be "pure spirits," not human beings: "None but heavenly spirits can do such wonderful things. We can communicate with the spirits, yet we cannot do wonderful things like them." No matter how Truckee averred that the whites were a beautiful people, good and kind to everyone, the shamans, with Winnemucca's terrible dream in mind, believed otherwise: "Your white brothers will yet make your people's hearts bleed . . . for we can see it. . . . The dead are lying all about us, and we cannot escape it. It will come. . . . Dance, sing, play, it will do no good; we cannot drive it away." Thocmetony observed that these warnings "did not go far with my grandfather."[8]

Not much time passed before Truckee's faith in white people was severely tested. Men of the Kuyuidika-a often came down from their place of refuge in the mountains to fish on the Humboldt River. During one of these fishing expeditions, white men from an emigrant party fired at them, killing one of Truckee's sons and wounding nine other men. Five of these men died of their wounds. The people buried the dead in the Paiute way, crouched and facing the East in shallow graves, with their bows and arrows, drinking cups, and other personal possessions. Their faces were covered so they could not be seen by those who dreamed of them. The Paiutes had long believed that a look from the eyes of a dead man would draw the spirits of the living away with him. Elders of the band said prayers, cast a handful of dirt into each grave, and spoke the traditional words to the dead on their passage to the Spirit Land: "We loved you, but your place is no longer here. Go now, don't come back in the dreams of your children. Leave them alone, you have a good place to go." Thocmetony's parents and her uncle's widow cut off their long hair and slashed such terrible bleeding gashes on their arms and legs in mourning that the little girl feared they too would die.[9]

After rocks had been placed on the unmarked graves, where no one would ever go again, and the *kahnees* of the departed ones had been burned so their spirits could not return, many among the Kuyuidika-a wanted to take revenge by killing the white people who had settled permanently at the Humboldt Sink. In one council after another, Truckee absolutely refused to allow this. With tears streaming down his face, he reminded the people of the promise they had made him to do no harm to the whites. He declared that the vows of peace and goodwill that he and his people had made meant even more to him than the life of his "dear beloved son." His own loss undoubtedly enabled him to speak with added authority. He argued that the whites who remained at the Humboldt were not the same ones who had committed these unprovoked murders. "After your promise, how dare you ask me to let your hearts be stained with the blood of those who are innocent of the deed that has been done to us by others?" Although the first victims to fall among the Kuyuidika-a must have seemed a confirmation of the darkest prophecies, Truckee's powerful influence prevented more violence. He told them "they could do nothing of the kind while he lived," related Thocmetony.[10] And so it was for years to come, until the outbreak of the Pyramid Lake War.

Confident that his peace policy would hold, Truckee moved forward with his plan to educate his people in the ways of white society. Already, after his return from the Bear Flag Revolt, he had taken thirty Paiute families with him for a sojourn to California. Now he determined to bring his own family, once more leaving Winnemucca in charge of the Kuyuidika-a. Truckee wanted his elderly wife and most of his kinfolk to accompany him. Tuboitony wept and begged to stay with her husband, but Truckee remained adamant. Thocmetony, as usual, sobbed loudest of all. The date of this trip cannot be easily determined because Thocmetony could not always correctly date events that occurred when she was a child, and her chronology is sometimes confused. Although 1850 has been suggested by one of her biographers, 1851 seems more likely because Truckee described a "red stone" (probably brick) house in Stockton, where the first brick houses date from 1851. Thocmetony would have been seven years old.[11]

On the first day of their journey on horseback, the group camped at the Carson Sink, a place south of the Humboldt Sink that was probably familiar to Thocmetony. The next day's route — upstream along the Carson River — probably took Thocmetony into territory that was new to her but not unlike the landscape she had always known: a sage plain with juniper- and pinyon-studded mountains to the north and low gray hills shaded with rose and cream to the south. That night they camped beside the river. On the third day, as they continued to follow the river, advance scouts rode back with the news that some white men's houses were ahead. (By this Thocmetony apparently meant emigrant wagons, which she also called houses.) With his rag friend in hand, Truckee rode ahead to introduce himself and returned with some crackers, which he divided among the people. Thocmetony does not appear to have been much impressed by her first taste of white people's food, choked down between fits of sobbing and perhaps less tasty than seed gruel, let alone roasted squirrel. Truckee declared that the friendly reception accorded to him and the gift of crackers demonstrated the powers of his rag friend. "Just as long as I live and have that paper which my white brothers' great chieftain has given me, I shall stand by them, come what will," he declared, kissing his rag friend and holding it aloft. "Oh, if I should lose this, we shall all be lost. So, children, get your horses ready, and we will go on, and we will camp with them, or by them tonight, for I have a sweetheart along who is dying for fear of my white brothers." This last was aimed at Thocmetony, who continued to cry and hid under the rabbit-skin robes.

When nothing calmed Thocmetony's hysterics over the possibility of actually meeting the dreaded white men, Tuboitony, her older children, and several other women pleaded with Truckee not to camp beside the white people. Seeing that the women spoke "two words for themselves and one for me," in Thocmetony's phrase, Truckee, for once, capitulated to their fears. As the Indians passed the white men's camp, Thocmetony, riding behind one of her brothers on a horse, covered her face.[12]

Their journey continued through the Carson Valley, where the river wound through natural meadows. At this point, they were passing through the territory of their traditional enemies, the Washo Indians, but Thocmetony mentions no encounters with the Washos. Truckee may well have taken his party east of the hills below present Carson City to avoid the hollow on the western side where the Washos often camped. No doubt this was Thocmetony's first close view of the mountain barrier of the Sierra, which she often glimpsed on the far western horizon. The prospect of traversing these towering peaks that thrust straight toward the sky from the valley floor had alarmed many emigrants, especially so late in the season with the winter snows at hand, but old Truckee had crossed these mountains many times.

Encounters with white people continued. During the next, while Thocmetony cowered under her mother's robe and screamed, "Oh my sister! Don't let them take her away," Truckee took little Elma and showed her to the white people, with one of Thocmetony's brothers tagging along. The old chief wanted his people to see for themselves white people's kindness to children. Thocmetony stopped crying long enough to take a peep and saw them give something white to the children. One of the white women walked over to offer some to her. Thocmetony held out her hand without looking when her grandfather ordered her to take it. It was sugar. Though Thocmetony liked the sweet taste and related that this first gift from a white person "made my heart very glad," sugar failed to sweeten her feelings. When Truckee called her to him and told her not to be afraid of white people because they were very good, Thocmetony stubbornly responded that "they looked so very bad I could not help it."[13]

The Indians traveled with this wagon train until the beatings the captain gave to the blacks who drove his team upset Truckee so much that he preferred to part company with them. The most likely route from Carson Valley to California would have taken the group over Carson Pass. It may have been in Hope Valley, where the last golden leaves clung to the trees in the ghostly white aspen groves on the slopes of the mountains, where they came upon a large emigrant encampment. Thocmetony, clinging to her brother's back, asked him to hide her under his rabbit-skin robe, then she scratched and bit him when he made no move to do it. After being invited to spend the night with the emigrant party, Truckee returned the next morning with wonderful gifts: red shirts for the men, calico for the women, and a dress for Mary, Thocmetony's pretty older sister. Nothing for Thocmetony, who had hidden herself so well under the robes this time that no one could find her. Her mother began to lament, fearing the worst, "Oh, father, can it be that the white people have carried her away?" Thocmetony, cross because no gift had been brought for her, stayed hidden. When she heard her brothers and sister crying over her disappearance, she finally crawled out from her hiding place.

Too displeased to coax his little sweetheart into better humor, Truckee scolded her sharply. The white people loved good children, he told her, not "bad ones like me." Thocmetony responded with a new freshet of tears and went to sleep in the cold mountain night still crying and wishing she had been allowed to stay home with her father. Paiute children were well known for seldom crying because their parents taught them from an early age that the cry of the horned owl came from a witch woman in the sky looking for children to eat; if she heard a child cry, she would toss him into her big spiked basket. Nonetheless, for the tearful Thocmetony, dread of white men far surpassed her fear of the witch woman in the sky.[14]

At the next encounter, Truckee and some of his men walked back with boxes from the white men's camp. Tuboitony saw two white men coming with him. When Thocmetony heard this, she begged her mother to hide her. "I just danced around like a wild one, which I was." As Tuboitony made a place for the visitors to sit down, with Thocmetony clinging behind her, the little girl took a cautious peep and screamed, "Oh, mother, the owls!" Visions of their large white eyes and hairy faces haunted her all through the night. It would have taken a shaman of unusual powers to see in this sobbing, terror-stricken child the future spokeswoman of the Paiutes.

Truckee had not despaired of converting her to his way of thinking, however. As the Indian party traveled on through a forest of tall pines, very different from the short junipers and rounded blue-green pinyons familiar to Thocmetony, Truckee continued to talk to his granddaughter about the goodness of his white brothers. Heavy snow fell the night they camped at the summit, and Truckee ordered his people to ride on quickly before the deepening snow made movement impossible. Thocmetony does not seem to have minded the snow. Perhaps she hoped to see the mythic Toya Numu, the mountain pygmies who dance on the snow and raise the snowy mists with their tiny, whirling feet.[15]

That night the Paiutes overtook some emigrants camped to rest their oxen, and Thocmetony witnessed the power of her grandfather's rag friend. She watched Truckee ride over to the emigrant camp. "Quite a number of white men came out to him. I saw him take out the paper he called his rag friend and give it to one of the men who stood looking at it; then he looked up and came toward him and held out his hand to my grandfather, and then the rest of the white men did the same all round. Then the little children and the women did the same." Nothing frightening had happened, and the Indian children stopped being afraid, all but Thocmetony. The sight of her grandfather with the white owls sickened her. The next morning she could not eat, and she pleaded with her mother to take her home to her father. Her mother said: "We can't go alone; we would all be killed if we go, for we have no rag friend as father has. And dear, you must be good, and grandpa will love you just as well as ever. You must do what he tells you to do."

Thocmetony covered her face and cried as though her heart would break. At that moment, Truckee arrived. "Well, well, is my sweetheart never going to stop crying?" he said. When he called her to him, Thocmetony came sullenly, with her head hanging down, but as soon as he told her he had "something very beautiful" for her, she brightened. He gave her a little cup, explaining that it was meant to drink water from, not to wear. Then he asked his wife to bring his pie plate and merrily related to Thocmetony the story of how other soldiers in the Bear Flag Revolt had laughed when he wore it as a hat. He told his people that the white men had even prettier things to eat from than the pie plate but cautioned them never to take anything lying around outside the white men's houses. He explained that clothes they might think had been discarded had only been hung out to dry after washing. The gift of the cup, combined with Truckee's unrelenting pressure, finally led Thocmetony to take the first hesitant step along the path her grandfather had so clearly laid out for her. She decided, "I will make friends with them when we come into California."[16]

Shortly afterward, they rode into the Sacramento Valley. Truckee explained to his people that they would bypass his many friends in this area and ride on to Stockton, where they would camp for ten days or so before continuing on their way to a ferry on the San Joaquin River. He also gave them a preview of the wonders they would see in Stockton. One of his white brothers there had a "red stone" house so tall that one had to climb three times to reach the top. At this, the Indians laughed incredulously. There was more: "A big house that runs on the river, and it whistles and makes a beautiful noise, and it has a bell on it which makes a beautiful noise also." When one of his sons asked how big the water house was, Truckee answered that they would soon see for themselves.

One night a large number of men camped nearby. After visiting them, Truckee explained that these were Mexicans who might kill them if they knew he was an enemy who fought against them with Frémont's forces. He had kept his rag friend concealed so it could not reveal his identity. Thocmetony's response was predictable: "I cried so that one could have heard my poor heart beat. Oh, how I wished I was back with my father again!"[17]

Darkness fell before the Paiute party reached Stockton, and Thocmetony saw "something like stars ahead of us" — her first sight of a city lit up at night. Stockton had grown from a tent city to a bustling entrepôt of perhaps twenty-five hundred inhabitants, with an even larger floating population of visitors bound for the gold regions and miners wintering in town. To serve the surrounding agricultural region and the mines of the southern Sierra, a constant stream of wagons and pack mules plied the road between Stockton and the mines, while steamboats and other vessels unloaded goods at the docks. As the Paiute party rode toward the city, a bell from one of the steamboats rang out, and Thocmetony thought it "the prettiest noise we had ever heard in all our life-time." All the same, she arrived crying.[18]

That night tears and excitement mingled so that she could not sleep. She could hardly wait to see the water house the next morning as Truckee had promised. She finally fell into such a deep sleep that she did not hear the steamboat's loud whistle nor awaken in time to visit this wonder with the others. When she opened her eyes, her mother told her that her brother saw the water house. He said that it had many looking glasses all around it and that it was so tired when it reached the dock that its deep breaths nearly deafened him. Thocmetony begged to go see it for herself, but Tuboitony refused because her son had also said so many white people crowded near the water house that "one could hardly get along," a prospect that obviously appalled her. To assuage Thocmetony's disappointment and forestall another bout of sobbing, she offered the little girl her first taste of a novel treat — "sweet bread," white people's cake.

After devouring the cake greedily, Thocmetony became very sick. Her head ached, her face swelled so that she could not open her eyes, her skin reddened and erupted in an itchy rash, her body shook with chills. Her mother held her in her arms, while her brothers and sisters wept and prayed over her. In keeping with the Paiute belief that the sorcery of a malicious person causes illness, Tuboitony blamed the cake. "The sugar-bread was poisoned which your white brother gave us to eat, and it has made my poor little girl so sick that I am afraid she will die," she said to her father. Although Truckee pointed out that everyone else had eaten the sugar bread without ill effects, he too blamed it for Thocmetony's illness. He suggested that Tuboitony had failed to bless the food in keeping with Paiute tradition before giving it to her little daughter.

Both were mistaken. Thocmetony had suffered a severe allergic reaction to poison oak, a nasty relative of poison ivy that is foreign to the Great Basin but widespread in California. In late fall, when its clusters of three thin, shiny leaves turn bright red, poison oak would have been especially tempting to touch. While she lay in misery, unable to open her eyes, Thocmetony felt a gentle hand smoothing something on her face while a sweet voice said, "Poor little girl. It is too bad," words she soon learned without understanding them. She thought the voice must belong to the spirit her father had told her would one day take her to the Spirit Land.

When she began to feel better, she asked what the spirit's words meant. The ever-anxious Tuboitony, scarcely less fearful of white men and all their works than Thocmetony — an attitude her daughter may well have sensed and absorbed from her — at once leapt to the conclusion that a little girl who talked to the spirits must be dying. Truckee, brushing aside his daughter's latest alarm, told Thocmetony that his "good white sister" came each day to put medicine on her. After she could open her eyes again, Thocmetony waited eagerly to see the face that belonged to the words and thought the white woman beautiful, not a white owl. Every day while Thocmetony recuperated, the white woman brought her something good to eat. One day she came with several pretty dresses for Thocmetony and wept while she spoke with Truckee. The old chief later explained that the dresses had belonged to his white sister's dead little girl and gave orders that they must be burned in keeping with Paiute customs on the possessions of the dead. Thocmetony, whose desire for the pretty dresses easily outstripped her fear of a visitation from a ghost, reacted in the usual way. She cried.[19]

After Thocmetony recovered, the Indian party made their way along tule marshes, where elk grazed and shiny black-and-white magpies flew, to the crossing at the San Joaquin River, beyond which lay a broad golden plain. Here, Jacob Bonsall and Hiram Scott operated a highly profitable ferry — a heavy, flat boat hauled across the river by a rope — as well as a launch, an inn, and a grazing area to serve the heavy traffic between San Francisco, Stockton, and the southern Sierra mines. Bonsall and Truckee had probably met during the Bear Flag Revolt in which Bonsall also served with Frémont. Bonsall and Scott welcomed the Indians in what Truckee surely regarded as proper style, with the slaughter of a beef and a feast.

Truckee later told the others that he would take a herd of the ferrymen's cattle and horses to the mountains to graze while the rest — Tuboitony, her children, and two of her brothers and their families — stayed behind to look after the remaining stock and learn the ways of white society. Tuboitony sobbed and passionately protested: "Oh, father, don't leave us here! My children might get sick, and there would be no one to speak for us; or something else might happen." What that something else might be became clear when she begged Truckee to take Mary with him. Tuboitony may have understood little English, but she could interpret the looks that some white men gave her oldest daughter, the beauty of the family. Truckee would not be moved. If he took Mary to the mountains, she would not "learn how to work and cook" as he wished. Tuboitony and the children would not be alone, since her brothers and their families were staying at the ferry also. Moreover, Bonsall and Scott had promised to take "the very best care of you and the children." And Truckee always believed the promises of his white brothers.[20]

The kind of care they took soon became all too clear. What followed Truckee's departure for the mountains with the herd was the attempted rape of Mary. In Thocmetony's words: "The men whom my grandpa called his brothers would come into our camp and ask my

33

mother to give my sister to them. They would come in at night, and we would all scream and cry; but that would not stop them." The would-be rapists are not identified, though they were probably hired men working at the ferry. Nor is Mary's age revealed, but since Paiute girls often married soon after they became physically mature and she was still unmarried, she may have been as young as thirteen or fourteen. Her uncles and brothers dared not protest, for fear of being shot.

At length the Indians hit upon a stratagem. Each night they fled from their campground and hid, probably in the tule marshes. On one confusing night, five white men came after the fire had died. Loud noises ensued in the darkness, and Thocmetony found herself with others inside the inn, probably the first time she ever slept under a roof. Except that she did not sleep. Wanting assurance that Mary was still alive and safe, she asked to sleep with Mary, and all through the night, cuddled beside her, she felt Mary's heart thumping wildly with fear. Fear crested into panic in the morning when they went downstairs to a room crowded with white people and believed themselves trapped. "There is no outlet to the house. We can't get out," exclaimed Mary frantically, with tears in her eyes. Thocmetony began crying and ran to Mary. Scott, quickly understanding, opened the door, walked outside with the Indians, and motioned them to the cookhouse. He squeezed Thocmetony's hand and said three words she understood, "Poor little girl."[21]

While the Indians sat on the floor in the cookhouse, the pretty objects around them enchanted Thocmetony. Mary explained that the long, high thing was a table used by whites when eating, that the cups on it were used for drinking hot water, and that the red things around it were chairs to sit on. Thocmetony thought the red chairs particularly fascinating. When she asked if she might sit on one, her mother told her that she must not or the white people might whip her. The cruelty of whites who spanked their children or pulled them roughly by the ear often shocked the Indians, who used no corporeal punishment on their children. Thocmetony continued to stare with rapt attention at one of the red chairs. One might call it a symbolic moment:

34

for most of her life she would be seeking a place at the white men's table for herself and her people. A white woman came in and lifted her little girl into the chair. In response to Thocmetony's inevitable question, Tuboitony told her that the little white girl would not be whipped because the chair belonged to her father. After white people had eaten at the table, places were set for Tuboitony and her children, and Thocmetony gained the object of her desire: she was allowed to sit in the red chair. Disliking the coffee in her cup, she kept twisting around to look at the picture on the back of the chair. Her mother warned her that if she did not sit nicely and eat her food the whites would whip her, a threat that may have been taking its place in the Paiute catalogue of unpleasant fates along with the witch woman and her spiked basket.

After the meal, one of Thocmetony's brothers told Tuboitony that Scott wanted them to sleep inside the inn, where the women would learn dishwashing, sewing, and other household work. Tuboitony's brothers would accompany Scott on a trip to the mountains to check on Truckee and the herd. As he spoke, Tuboitony and Mary began to sob. Tuboitony tearfully said, "Dear son, you know if we stay here sister will be taken from us by the bad white man. I would rather see her die than see her heart full of fear every night." Mary would only be safe, she felt, if the whole family went to the mountains with Scott. For once, Thocmetony did not cry. All her hopes were focused on sitting again on the red chair.

Following a long session with Scott, the boy returned to tell them that permission to depart together had been refused. Tuboitony and her daughters would be allowed to join Truckee, but the boys must stay at the ferry. The thought of splitting her family tore Tuboitony in two. Although she could save Mary if she went to the mountains, she feared for the lives of her boys if they were left behind at the ferry. Helpless to protect her children in this alien land and furious with the man who dared to tell her where to go and what to do, her grief overflowed: "I cannot see for my life why my father calls them his white brothers. They are not people; they have no thought, no mind,

35

no love. They are beasts. . . . They tried to take my girl from me and abuse her before my eyes and yours too, and oh, you must go too."[22]

When Scott came near, she held out her hands to him in pitiful entreaty and begged to be allowed to depart with all her children, while the children cried. Although Scott probably understood none of her words, he knew well enough from her son's previous request what she wanted. When her pleading hands grasped him and could not be torn away, he finally nodded his head.

Grief instantly turned to happiness. The red wagon in which they would ride to the mountains so charmed Thocmetony that she jumped around like a cricket in her excitement. Mary was less easily pleased. When Thocmetony asked her sister if she wasn't delighted by this chance to ride in the "beautiful red house," Mary bitterly replied, "Not I, dear sister, for I hate everything that belongs to the white dogs. I would rather walk all the way." She must have trudged beside the wagon for many miles. As they traveled, Tuboitony reached a decision and warned her children that Truckee must not be told why they had left the ferry. Apparently she feared that her father, whose trust in his white brothers seemed unshakable, would be angry with his family for mishandling their opportunity and send them back to the ferry. How she longed for the protection of her husband, Winnemucca, whom she believed would have killed any white man who tried to violate Mary.

Although Thocmetony did not overhear the long talks that ensued between her mother and her grandfather after they were reunited in the mountains, Tuboitony seems to have kept silent about Mary. In all likelihood, the "mountains" meant the Sierra foothills, where grass for pasturage grew abundantly in a rolling, parklike landscape sprinkled with dark green live oaks. Truckee told the boys that their work with the stock had pleased Scott and that Scott wanted them to continue at the ferry. They readily agreed to accept three horses apiece and some money for their labor. Although Thocmetony saw her mother and Mary crying from time to time, Truckee gave them permission to stay in the mountains with him. He insisted, however, that the boys must return to the ferry. On seeing her mother weeping as she readied her sons' horses, Thocmetony threw herself on the ground in a storm of tears and raged at her grandfather: "Oh, brothers, I will never see them anymore. . . . Oh, you naughty, naughty grandpa, you want my poor brothers to be killed by the bad men. You don't know what they do to us. Oh, mother, run — bring them back again!" Others feared to cross the old chief, but not Thocmetony.[23]

A long separation from her brothers ensued. From time to time, white men came from the ferry to the mountains. After they departed, Truckee would display his rag friend and declare that it said the boys were well. (Thocmetony does not indicate whether this news arose from the magical powers he ascribed to the original letter or whether more recent notes from the ferrymen also became rag friends.)

At last Truckee declared that the snows had retreated sufficiently in the high Sierra for them to return home. The joy of Tuboitony and her daughters knew no bounds. The women sang as they worked and sewed dresses from the calico that had been given to them. They made the morning of their departure a kind of thanksgiving festival, with prayers, songs, and dances. First they went to the ferry to collect the rest of the family, and they spent several days there. Scott, exceeding his promises, gave Tuboitony's sons eight horses apiece, and the same number to Truckee, while other men in the Indian party received only two or three. Truckee saw their horse herd as generous payment for little work, an added proof of the white men's goodness. In the not-so-distant past, the Paiutes had been "foot Indians" and horses had been seen as competitors that ate the grasses they depended upon for seed food. When they captured a mustang, they did not ride it. They ate it. Although the exact date when they became "horse Indians" — sometime after 1845 — remains a matter of dispute, the possibility of using horses for raids on emigrant wagon trains and settlements spurred the transition. The Paiutes' love affair with the horse had begun. In Annie Lowry's words, "From the minute the Paiutes first saw a man on a horse, his whole life was dedicated to owning and riding such an animal. It was as easy for a Paiute to ride a horse as for him to breathe. He did not have to learn how. He already knew." As Truckee's family drove their herd of horses toward the mountains and home, they believed themselves wealthy indeed. The Paiute word for a rich man translated as "many horses have."[24]

Nonetheless, they did not depart without anxiety for the women. The ever-watchful Tuboitony saw the men who had tried to take Mary talking to Truckee and looking at the girl. Mary at once grew fearful that her grandfather might give her away, and Thocmetony watched with a thumping heart. They need not have worried. They saw Truckee shake his head and walk angrily away from the men. After this incident, Mary was placed in the special care of her grandmother, the traditional Paiute guardian for a girl of marriageable age.[25]

What had the family gained during the winter that Truckee intended as a learning experience that would start them along the path they must follow? The children had seen many wonders such as the steamboat and the red chairs that they would later describe when everyone gathered around the evening fire and the traveler related every detail of his journey many times over. Although Thocmetony's special linguistic abilities still lay dormant, at least one of her brothers had learned enough English to translate between his mother and Scott. They also may have acquired their English names that winter. One of Thocmetony's brothers was dubbed Natches, "boy" in Paiute, the term the white men heard Truckee use repeatedly when he spoke of "my boy." Thocmetony nowhere tells us at what point in her life she became Sarah, but if white people's tongues stumbled over her Indian name, they may have planted Sarah upon her early. (On this assumption, she will henceforth be called Sarah.) Even though the women had acquired neither English nor domestic skills because they had spent most of their time in the foothill pasturelands with Truckee, they left with some sense of the way that white people lived. They learned that white people could be as kind as the woman who ministered to Sarah when she lay suffering and gave the child her dead daughter's clothes, or as wicked — later a favorite word of Sarah's — as

the men who pursued Mary. It is evident that Mary's experience left
Sarah with a lifelong fear of rape, but when she blossomed into womanhood, she would neither retreat to the mountains nor seek safety
by remaining inconspicuously among her people. Instead she would
pack a knife.

Truckee's party returned to greater sorrows than they had yet
known. It may have been in Hope Valley, among aspen groves shimmering with new green leaves, where they met other Indians who
told them that great numbers of Paiutes had died during the winter.
First one would sicken, then the entire family would die. White men
had poisoned the Humboldt River and bewitched all the land. Without waiting to hear more, Tuboitony cut her daughters' long, shining
black hair and her own in mourning. When Truckee asked after Winnemucca, they told him that Winnemucca still lived, as did all who
had remained with him in the mountains. Truckee sent one of these
men to summon Winnemucca to Mormon Station, where they would
camp and await him.

At last, Winnemucca and a number of the Kuyuidika-a rode in
from the north, all with the shorn hair and gashed limbs of mourning. Puidok ("deep eyes") was one of Winnemucca's several names,
and he may already have taken on the appearance of a late photo, with
broad cheekbones, a long nose, creases running down from the nos-
trils to a wide, thin-lipped mouth, and the half-closed, sorrowful
deep-set eyes of one who has grieved too much. Winnemucca told a
story similar to that told by the men on the mountain trail. As soon as
someone drank from the poisoned river, he died. White people had
surely caused this, for everyone knew that disease springs from the
doings of malevolent people. The prayers of the shamans had been of
no avail against the white men's evil powers. They had tried everything they knew: telling the people what designs to draw on their
faces with white paint, singing, circling counterclockwise around the
fire while the patient lay on the west side of it, sucking the painful
place on the patient's body, spitting the bad blood away, falling into a
trance, rising when the willow stick with the sacred eagle feather was

39

passed above, and repeating the singing, the sucking, and the circling all through the night. Even with all this, the patients had died, and also the shamans themselves. Two of Tuboitony's sisters, their husbands, and all their children save one little girl were among the dead.[26]

Truckee refused to accept the poisoned water explanation. "My dear children, I am heartily sorry to hear your sad story; but I cannot and will not believe my white brothers would do such a thing," he said severely and pointed out that if the whites had poisoned the river, they too would have died when they drank from it. Instead he believed the deaths had been caused by "some fearful disease" previously unknown among the Paiutes and unrelated to witchcraft. In this theory, he was more right than he knew: the fearful disease that ravaged his people is now believed to have been the eastward spread of the Asiatic cholera epidemic that accounted for the deaths of an estimated one in every seventeen inhabitants of Sacramento in 1849–50 and for large numbers in the Sierra mining camps. Truckee then cautioned his people against any vengeful acts toward the white men: "Some of you may live a long time yet, and don't let your hearts work against your white fathers; if you do, you will not get along. You see they are already here in our land; here they are all along the river, and we must let our brothers live with us. We cannot tell them to go away. I know your good hearts. I know you won't say 'Kill them.' Surely you all know that they are human. Their lives are just as dear to them as ours are to us."

As before, at the murder of his son, the loss of two of his own children and their families gave added weight to Truckee's words. He then launched into a long oration intended to comfort his people — and perhaps to assuage his own aching heart — by describing the joys of the Spirit Land where their loved ones had now passed by way of the starry path of the milky way. Many were so deeply moved that as he spoke they cried out in affirmation like an audience at a revival meeting. But not Sarah: "He talked so long [that] I for one wished he would stop, so I could go throw myself into my father's arms, and tell him what the white people were." Truckee sealed his speech with another paean of praise to the rag friend upraised in his hand: "This is my friend. Does it look as if it could talk and ask for anything? Yet it does. It can ask for something to eat for me and my people. Yet, it is nothing but a rag. Oh, wonderful things my white brothers can do. I have taken it down to them, and it has asked for sacks of flour for us to eat. Come, we will go and get them." Finally Truckee stopped talking, and Sarah ran with her mother and the others to her father. With Winnemucca at his side, old Truckee went to the little settlement at Mormon Station and returned with a red shirt and blanket for Winnemucca and flour for everyone.[27]

Once more, Truckee had succeeded in staying the hand of vengeance. The peace he worked so hard to maintain would hold for nearly a decade. But after the magic of his eloquent words faded and the travelers beheld a camp with blackened empty spaces left by the burned *kahnees* of the dead, many must have felt that the terrible visions of the shamans were coming true before their eyes.

"The dead are lying all about us, and we cannot escape it," they had prophesied. "Dance, sing, play, it will do no good; we cannot drive it away." None could doubt any longer. Now the dying had begun.

3

Genoa

"Our dear good friend, Major Ormsby"

THE WHITE MEN'S COUNTRY beyond the great wall of mountains had charmed Sarah even though its people terrified her, but the austere desert was the homeland she longed for. White travelers in the Great Basin saw the desert very differently than she. Frémont wrote of its "dreary and savage character," its burnt appearance, and the sense of dread he felt upon entering it; Edwin Bryant, who traversed the Great Basin on mule-back in 1846, found it "sufficiently cheerless and desolate to depress the most buoyant temperament" — with "sable and utterly sterile mountains" and arid plains "incapable of sustaining either insect or animal"; James H. Simpson, exploring in 1859 for the Army Corps of Engineers, reported in the same vein on "dark and dreary" mountains — "fit monuments of the desolation which reigns over the whole desert" — "wretchedly sandy and barren" country and vistas "exceedingly forbidding in appearance." In Sarah's eyes, however, the desert was her "dear country," re-entered not with horror but with joy, its secrets of sustaining life well known to her people. Though Sarah was not one to rhapsodize about the scenery in her writings, she no doubt also considered Pyramid Lake, the startling blue-green oblong set among gray sands and pastel desert hills, a beautiful place.[1]

Sarah has little to say about the period following her return from California. Indeed, she dismisses it in a single short sentence: "I will jump over about six years." Obviously, nothing from these years could compare to the memorable events that preceded. The placement of a chapter on Paiute customs following her account of the California journey suggests that the time was chiefly occupied by a return to as much as could be salvaged of her old way of life. The mouth of the Truckee River at Pyramid Lake still teemed with fish in the spring, the mountain pinyons still brought forth nuts, but much had been lost. Settlers had claimed the Humboldt River as the river route became part of a major emigrant trail, thus depriving the Paiutes of the river's fish and waterfowl. Even though the cholera epidemic may have reduced the number of mouths to feed by as much as half, diminished food supplies in a subsistence economy meant starvation. Frederick Dodge, an early Indian agent, sympathetically observed that "the encroachments of the Emigrant have driven away the game upon which they depend for subsistence. They cannot hunt upon the territories of other tribes, except at the risk of their lives. They must therefore steal or starve."[2]

As the Indians increasingly turned to raids upon white settlements and wagon trains, relations with whites deteriorated. The specific role of the Kuyuidika-a in these raids is not known (and is not revealed by Sarah, who writes nothing uncomplimentary to her people). Nonetheless, in an effort to reduce the tensions, settlers at Honey Lake, northwest of Pyramid Lake, made a treaty with Winnemucca in 1856. Under its provisions, if Indians stole, the settlers should complain to the chief and "not take their revenge indiscriminately upon the Indians," and if a settler stole cattle or horses from Indians or molested their women, the chief should take his grievance to the settlers, and they would "redress his wrongs and punish the offender." The Honey Lake agreement was notable for another reason: long before Sarah could be accused of aggrandizing her family's position at the expense of the headmen of other bands, white men had started to recognize Winnemucca as a leader and show their preference for dealing with a hierarchical authority — a chief — instead of the assorted headmen of many fluid bands.[3]

Mining for gold on a small scale by individual prospectors commenced in 1850 in Gold Canyon, adjacent to the Comstock, but prior to the great mining rush for Comstock silver that ended the decade, the ranchers and traders around Genoa (previously Mormon Station) in the Carson Valley wielded more political influence. Though miniscule in number throughout the 1850s, the early settlers more than compensated with the enormity of their ambitions. As the name Mormon Station implies, Utah Territory initially exercised jurisdiction over the area that would become Nevada. One group of Carson Valley settlers strove to alter this state of affairs by winning separate territorial status for the region. Public arguments for the change centered upon the familiar refrain of establishing law and order and eliminating difficulties of communication with a government more than five hundred miles away in Salt Lake City or with crossing the Sierra if the region should instead be annexed by California. At the same time, the settlers must have known that territorial status would bring political office and power to a new elite or, in the more pungent phraseology of a California newspaper, to "broken down politicians, land grabbers, and office hunters."[4]

Loose factions began to form in the Carson Valley. The first centered on "Lucky Bill" Thorington, a wealthy gambler and entertaining raconteur with varied interests in the area. His sidekick, William ("Uncle Billy") Rogers, his Washo Indian allies, and a handful of Mormons and "old settlers" shared his distaste for a newcomer in the opposite camp. This recent arrival was Maj. William Ormsby, a man with a dark, neatly trimmed mustache and beard, a long nose, and a determined stare, whose title derived from the rank he had held in the Pennsylvania militia. Forty-three years old at the time of his arrival in the Carson Valley in the spring of 1857, Ormsby was descended from an English family that had emigrated first to Ireland and later to Pennsylvania in the eighteenth century. At thirty he had married a sixteen-year-old Kentucky girl, Margaret Trumbo, who bore him a daughter they named Lizzie. In 1849 Ormsby joined the rush to California with several male relatives, leaving his wife and baby behind. Soon convinced that his future fortunes lay in the West, if not on an even more distant horizon, he briefly returned to Kentucky in 1852 to bring his family. He then occupied himself with running a stage line from Sacramento to Marysville. This, however, was one of his more mundane activities. In 1856 Ormsby is believed to have joined the forces around the mad dreamer William Walker, who attempted to conquer Nicaragua, make himself an emperor, confiscate large tracts of land, and sell them to the motley group of Americans around him, with the ultimate aim of admitting several Central American countries to the union as proslavery states.[5]

After Walker's Nicaraguan adventure collapsed, Ormsby found a new arena for his aspirations in the Carson Valley. With a keen eye toward future developments, he acquired a variety of interests. These included land holdings near Gold Canyon, where he anticipated greater mining activity, and in Eagle Valley, a promising site for the future state capital. In the process, he made friends among those who shared his vision of the future and enemies among the old settlers. Ormsby was the major thrust behind the effort to make Nevada a territory separate from Utah Territory. Indeed, the *Territorial Enterprise* observed that "everything of moment" in the region, whether political or financial, had Ormsby in the thick of it.[6]

What his larger aspirations were we can only guess, but if he shared any part of the fantasies of some of his associates, they were large indeed. Some southerners, including an important congressional supporter, envisaged Nevada as a slave state that would serve as a southern wedge in the West to reconfigure the uneasy balance between North and South in the pre–Civil War period. Judge James M. Crane, an intimate of Ormsby and an unofficial delegate to Congress, looked beyond the rewards of statehood and articulated the dream of a "Pacific Republic," formed from perhaps twelve states. It was in the household of this ambitious man, William Ormsby, that Sarah gained her first real knowledge of the white world.[7]

Not long after the Ormsbys moved from California to Genoa in the spring of 1857, Sarah and one of her sisters (probably Elma) came to live in the Ormsby home. In this we may well suspect the guiding hand of old Truckee, ever anxious for his people to learn the language and skills that would enable them to "get along" in the altered world he saw before them, and especially solicitous of his favored grand-daughter. Their placement with Ormsby, rather than another settler, confirms Ormsby's friendly relationship with the Paiutes. Sarah relates that they came as "playmates" for the Ormsby's daughter, Lizzie Jane. While the lively and intelligent Sarah, then thirteen, and Elma, several years younger, would have made good companions for nine-year-old Lizzie, it seems likely that the Indian girls came primarily as servants, a condition that Sarah's pride would not allow her to admit in later years. Since Sarah relates that her family took her home after she had learned to "talk very well," it may well be that the Winne-muccas had made an arrangement with the Ormsbys: Sarah and her sister would help with household tasks in exchange for learning English.[8]

Whatever criticism might be made of the Ormsbys, their attitude toward Sarah and her sister places them among the more enlightened settlers. Sarah wrote of their great kindness to her in an era of extreme prejudice against Indians. It was a time when many believed that "the only good Indian is a dead Indian" and when arguments could be waged over whether Indians belonged to the human race. Among those with less rancorous views, the Great Basin Indians, lacking the dangerous glamour of the mounted Sioux warrior in full regalia, ranked rather low in the Indian hierarchy. Simpson, in the Utah phase of his exploration, found the Indians "worse in condition than the meanest of animal creation"; Frémont, expressing a similar impression as he approached Pyramid Lake, called them the "nearest approach to mere animal creation."[9]

Events rapidly refuted these ugly stereotypes. The adaptable Paiutes, schooled by a harsh environment to turn to another food source when an old one failed, gained an early reputation as desirable employees. Richard N. Allen, a Genoa resident and author of the dispatches signed "Tennessee" in the *San Francisco Herald*, called them "peaceably disposed and industrious" and added that ranchers preferred to employ them as hired hands instead of "Americans" (to be sure, they also cost less). They received further approval in another

1857 California newspaper as being the "best servants in America" and as "excellent cooks, farmers, herdsmen, and mechanics."[10] The speed of the transition is startling: ten years earlier the Kuyuidika-a were hiding in the mountains, and only a bold adventurer like Truckee and a few boon companions had any acquaintance with the white world. Truckee unquestionably viewed the successful adaptation of the Paiutes to the new ways as the only alternative to an increasingly desperate and marginal existence, and the change must have given him great satisfaction.

At the base of the towering, sharp-peaked Sierra, where the mountain shadow falls by midafternoon, was Genoa. The town sat on a slope overlooking the curving course of the willow-lined Carson River and ranches where large herds of cattle and horses grazed in meadows enclosed by pine log fences. The settlement consisted of an old fort, surrounded by a ten-foot stockade of upright pine logs, and several structures that visitors described as "pleasant modern tenements," in contrast to the "dingy apartments" at old Mormon Station. One observer counted 107 inhabitants at the settlement in 1857. The Ormsbys lived in a former tin shop at the old fort, a residence they undoubtedly saw as a way station on the path to grander things. But to Sarah, who generally admired the edifices of white people, the home in the former tin shop must have seemed a fine one.[11]

While living in the Ormsby household, Sarah learned a multitude of things about white people, but the most momentous was the English tongue: "While with them we learned the English language very fast." Indeed, the Paiutes became noted for picking up English quickly. One Virginia City resident observed, "The most of them talk good English, and some of them swear like pirates." Sarah, with her unusual linguistic aptitude, would have learned even more quickly than most. If she heard any swearing in the Ormsby household, it must have puzzled her because she later declared that curses had no counterparts in her native language; Paiute condemnations extended no farther than calling someone "coyote" or "bad." Margaret Ormsby, a fashionable woman with heavy dark hair, very white skin, and

47

small, pretty features, despite the touch of severity about her prim, pursed lips, probably corrected Sarah's verbal errors until they disappeared.[12]

The Ormsbys must have also introduced her to books. Because there was no school in the Carson Valley — an early school in Israel Mott's home apparently did not survive — Margaret Ormsby may have taught her daughter to read and write, and the Indian girls might have been allowed to learn along with Lizzie. Later it would be not only the fluency and correctness of her English that set Sarah apart from other Paiutes but also her ability to read and write. In view of his sophisticated perception of literacy as the true source of white men's power, greater even than guns, Truckee must have been delighted when Sarah became able to both decipher and create rag friends.[13]

What else she learned in the Ormsby household remains conjectural, since Sarah reveals nothing more. Perhaps English and household skills were as much as a young teenager plunged into an alien world could absorb. Yet she may also have gained a sense of woman's place in white society. In fact, Margaret Ormsby was an atypical example of Victorian womanhood. Although she lived in an age when proper ladies were supposed to confine themselves to the domestic sphere, Margaret appears to have been well acquainted with business and politics. Following her husband's death in 1860, she lobbied the Nevada legislature for a toll road and conducted real estate and mining transactions so successfully that at her own death in 1866 the *Carson Appeal* called her "one of the most extensive property holders" in Nevada.[14] From Major Ormsby Sarah may have learned something about ambition and the means of gratifying it; and from Margaret Ormsby, she may have learned something about the important role a strong-minded woman could play. Perhaps she also acquired a sense of white perceptions of the Indians along with her English lessons. Not many years later she would play upon these expectations in her theatrical performances.

Though her fluent English and her expanded understanding of whites shaped Sarah's life in profound ways, a horrifying event dominated her memories of life in the Ormsby household. In early September 1857, pack train operators John McMarlin and James Williams were returning with supplies from Placerville, California. After McMarlin's riderless horse appeared at a trading station, searchers found their murdered and stripped bodies in the high Sierra above present Lake Tahoe. The placement of arrows in their bullet wounds, clumsy as it was, succeeded in the apparent objective — laying the blame for the murders upon Indians.[15]

Determined to punish the crime, Ormsby sent for his Paiute allies to identify the tribe that had made the arrows found in Williams's and McMarlin's bodies. Sarah's brother Natches and her cousin Young Winnemucca (also known as Numaga) arrived with a large party and recognized the arrows as Washo. Agreeing to bring in the culprits, they held a war dance that Sarah notes was the only one she ever saw. Little Lizzie Ormsby, among the many white onlookers, kept asking Sarah which dancer was Natches. If Sarah's older brother had painted himself for war, with half his face white, the other half red, and wide bands of paint around his limbs and body, he would have been hard to recognize. At the conclusion of the dance the onlookers sung the "Star-Spangled Banner," surprising Sarah with their rendition, because white people sang it so differently from the way she had been taught by her grandfather. A Paiute party then rode forth in search of the Washo miscreants.[16]

Thus far, accounts on the crime from varied sources substantially agree, but beyond this point, the truth remains problematic, in part because Nevada had no printed newspaper that provided regular detailed reports on events as they occurred. The brief and occasional dispatches sent to California newspapers hold the advantage of contemporary composition over Sarah's recollections, written many years after the fact; at the same time, Sarah's deep involvement in Indian matters may have made her aware of undercurrents hidden from others. According to the *San Francisco Herald*, Uncle Billy Rogers encountered several Washo workmen in Genoa and noticed that one was wearing a shirt that had been recently stolen from his Hope Valley cabin. At gunpoint, he demanded the names of the murderers and robbers. When the Indians refused to answer and tried to run away, Rogers shot and wounded one of them. In a separate incident, a Washo headman, "Captain Jim," lured one of his tribesmen to a barn near Genoa. Whites led by Rogers surrounded the barn and captured the man, who wore trousers they recognized as McMarlin's. Questioned the next day, the tribesman admitted having witnessed the murders but blamed them on two other Washos. His captors shot and killed him during an escape attempt.[17]

In Sarah's more fully elaborated version, the Paiute party returned with about ten Washos, including Captain Jim. When questioned by Ormsby, Captain Jim admitted the arrows were Washo but denied that any member of his band could have committed the crime. He said he could account for the presence of everyone (an improbability, with a band that numbered around 342). Numaga threatened to make war on the Washos if Captain Jim failed to deliver the murderers. A few days later Captain Jim brought in three prisoners, evidently without regard for probable guilt, instead choosing those with the fewest dependents to support.[18]

Lynching fever spread through Genoa. Sarah heard men speak of hanging "the red devils right off"; boys threw stones at the prisoners and berated them with the "most shameful language." A group of armed men arrived, possibly the military guard Rogers had requested from California authorities, and escorted the prisoners from the small house where they had been confined. The terrified Washos broke free, attempted to run away, and were shot. Though one was merely wounded, he too eventually died. The Washos grieved over their dead so as to "make the very mountains weep." Sarah ran sobbing to Margaret Ormsby and protested that the slain prisoners were innocent. Mrs. Ormsby sternly replied, "How came the Washoe arrows there? and the chief himself has brought them to us, and my husband knows what he is doing."[19]

The Indians did not absolve themselves of guilt so readily. Sarah overheard Captain Jim telling Natches that he believed the blood of his slain tribesmen was on his hands and their spirits would haunt him while he lived. The mother of one of the dead Washo called down a curse upon the Paiutes from the Maker, "You may all live to see the day when you will suffer at the hands of your white brothers, as you call them." Later that winter Captain Jim visited Natches at his camp in the Virginia Range, told him erroneously that the white killers of McMarlin and Williams had been caught, and demanded payment for the lives of the Washo prisoners. Natches placed responsibility for the tragedy on Captain Jim and the white men. Nonetheless, when he set forth to look into the matter, he gave Captain Jim a horse on which to accompany him. "The poor Washoes had never owned a horse in their lives," observed Sarah, with the newly acquired superiority of a horse Indian.[20]

Whether it happened as Sarah recollected or as the California newspapers reported, the incident revealed a significant aspect of Sarah that would become more evident in time. Despite the position of the Washos as ancient tribal enemies of her people, she drew no satisfaction from their loss. Instead her sympathies lay entirely with the "poor, poor Washoes." In her worldview, the main dichotomy she saw was Indian versus white.[21]

The date Sarah left the Ormsby household remains unclear. She placed it shortly after the Washo episode, and the absence in her autobiography of the lynching of Lucky Bill Thorington by vigilantes in Genoa suggests that she departed before June 1858. Surely the doomed gambler who sang "The Last Rose of Summer" beneath the gallows would have made a considerable impression. After riding away from Genoa, Sarah lived for the rest of the winter with Natches and Mary at Johntown in the Virginia Range, where a small number of miners worked claims prior to the discovery of the Comstock Lode in the spring of 1859. It is likely that the Paiutes hired to work Henry Comstock's claim at American Ravine included her brothers Natches and Tom.[22]

Dan De Quille, later a well-known journalist and the author of *The Big Bonanza*, relates that Sarah attended the Saturday night dances in

"Dutch Nick's" Johntown saloon during those early days: "As there were but three white women in the town, it was necessary, in order to 'make up the set,' to take in Miss Sarah Winnemucca, the 'Piute Princess.'. . . When the orchestra — a 'yaller-backed fiddle' — struck up and the 'French four' was in order, the enthusiastic Johntowners went forth in the dance with ardor and filled the air with splinters from the puncheon floor. When a Johntown 'hoss' balanced in front of the 'Princess,' he made no effort to economize shoe-leather." Along with his condescending attitude about including an Indian girl at the dances, De Quille suggests that the Johntown "hosses" made special efforts to impress her. Sarah would have been almost fourteen, broad-featured with lively black eyes, short in stature, perhaps already developing a voluptuous figure, and garbed in a dress of the kind she would have learned to wear under Margaret Ormsby's tutelage.[23]

Two extremely harsh winters, 1858–59 and 1859–60, took a heavy toll among the Paiutes. During the first, the *San Francisco Herald* reported "great suffering" among the Indians and "a great many deaths" from starvation and cold. When Indians killed some cattle, newspaper correspondent Allen urged the settlers to be tolerant because the Indians had been exposed to such "unusual severities," in addition to the loss of their accustomed food supplies.[24]

Because her father took his family to the San Joaquin to hunt and fish for the winter, Sarah escaped the first season of famine. Probably it was during this sojourn in California that Sarah heard a fire-breathing Methodist minister preach that those who did wrong burned in hell forever while their friends in heaven watched their sufferings, unable to help. His graphic image of damnation frightened her so much that she wept and longed to be "unborn." Her mother and others comforted her by assuring her of the verities of Paiute belief: she would go to the Spirit Land when she died and hell did not exist. "It was only here that people did wrong and were in the hell it made." Given Sarah's experiences, the reality of hell on earth would have needed little explanation.[25]

The following winter blew in even worse than 1858–59. Heavy

snows blanketed the valleys and the mountains, with pines ink blue in the distance against the whiteness. The bitter cold turned the Carson Valley into a "great boneyard," where cattle and horses froze to death in the fields. Humans suffered too: "Many persons have been frozen, more or less." And still the icy winds rolled more pewter gray clouds, heavy with snow, over the Sierra. Of the Indians, the *San Francisco Herald* observed, "the poor miserable wretches are suffering very much."[26] In their thin reed *kahnees* and flimsy brush shelters, the Indians froze more, not less.

The *Territorial Enterprise* reported in graphic detail: "The Indians in Truckee Meadows [the site of present Reno] are freezing and starving to death by scores. In one cabin the Governor [Provisional Territorial Governor Isaac Roop] found three children dead and dying. The whites are doing all they can. . . . They have sent out and built fires for them, and offered them bread and other provisions. But in many instances the starving Indians refuse to eat, fearing that the food is poisoned. They attribute the severity of the winter to the whites." After all, the Indians had always known that calamities came from the hatred of a malevolent person. And the hostility of many whites could not be mistaken. Further, hadn't Indians died from eating beef that whites later said had been poisoned with strychnine and left out to kill wolves?[27] So they said. Would they not have known that the poisoned meat would be found by the hungry people scouring the land in search of food?

In Sarah's eyes, the charity of the settlers came too little and too late. Among her people, a band with little food turned to another with more abundant supplies. Food was usually willingly shared because the Paiutes honored charity, and the bands knew that in their time of need the favor would be returned. To ask for desperately needed food — even though the whites saw it as shameful begging — never dishonored the supplicant. In Sarah's own family, the traditions of charity and hospitality were especially strong. Her father had been given the name Winnemucca, "the giver," for good reason.[28]

Sarah saw only one cause behind the starvation and suffering of her people while the whites stayed warm and adequately fed: white selfishness. Later, with bitterness that the years had never erased, she recalled the time when the Indians had helped some stranded emigrants: "During the winter my people helped them. They gave them such as they had to eat. They did not hold out their hands and say: 'You can't have anything to eat unless you pay me.' No, — no such word was used by us savages at that time."[29]

4

The Pine Nut Mountains

"I felt the world growing cold"

T HE STARVATION WINTER of 1859–60 had a good deal to do with the bloody battle that followed. The hardships of that season conclusively demonstrated that the Nevada desert had insufficient resources to support two peoples. And as more whites streamed in with the Comstock rush, many Indians were arriving at the belief that they must "starve or fight."[1]

At the same time, tensions among the settlers escalated to such a pitch that many also anticipated war, despite Winnemucca's efforts to promote the peace that Truckee had upheld. Winnemucca rode to Genoa in 1858 to report the presence of two white fugitives who sought refuge with his band. He kept in touch with Maj. Frederick Dodge, Indian agent for the area. Nonetheless, public suspicions of the Indians during an era of scattered violence could not be easily allayed. The mysterious death of Peter Lassen, a Danish-born blacksmith in Honey Lake who had befriended the Indians and was generally admired for his honesty and character, aroused dark suppositions. A sharpshooter with a rifle shot and killed Lassen and his companion on a prospecting trip near Pyramid Lake in April 1859. Although many white renegades infested the region, settlers automatically blamed Indians for any act of violence. When Dodge inspected the murder scene, however, he voiced doubts that Indians were responsible. Whiskey, blankets, and beef, which Indians would normally have taken, remained intact at the site, and the surviving member of the Lassen party reported the tracks of a shod pony nearby (Indians did not shoe their horses). Agent Dodge discussed the murders with both Winnemucca and Numaga at Pyramid Lake, but their inquiries among the Paiutes failed to uncover any information. The Lassen murders remained unsolved, and many dismissed Dodge's denial of Indian culpability as blindness arising from his sympathy for those he liked to call his "children."[2]

That fall, near the Walker River, *San Francisco Herald* correspondent Allen confronted "about one hundred red skinned devils" who questioned him insolently, and a rancher reported that Indians had stampeded some stock. Again, Dodge arrived to speak with Winnemucca, who calmed tempers. Allen described the chief as "the most peaceful quiet old fellow in the world." Indeed, insofar as they were capable of admiring an Indian, whites admired Winnemucca, now gray-haired but still standing tall at more than six feet. "His appearance is venerable," wrote Allen, "and indicative of his high character, as an Indian, for integrity and honor." At the christening of the burgeoning city of tents, shacks, and dugouts on the Comstock Lode in the autumn of 1859, one faction favored naming it "Wunnemucca" after the chief. The name "Virginia City" took hold, but the effort to honor Winnemucca showed the miners' esteem for him.[3]

During the terrible winter of 1859–60, relations between the settlers and the Indians worsened. Indian suffering seems to have aroused a certain guilty paranoia among the settlers. They might have said the Indians had grown too "enervated" to survive, but they knew where the responsibility rested: "The occupancy of their wonted hunted grounds by the whites, with their accompanying herds, has driven the game from the country." Settlers leapt readily to the assumption that Indians would react to their desperate situation much as they would have done — with military action.[4]

In January 1860 an incident occurred that confirmed the settlers' worst fears. After a young man named Dexter Demming was found murdered in his ransacked Honey Lake cabin, a posse of soldiers and settlers followed the murderers' trail from the cabin and attacked the fortified Indian camp where the tracks ended. There they found Demming's violin, books, and other possessions — apparent proof of Indian guilt. When the settlers rode to Pyramid Lake and demanded that Winnemucca accompany them to Honey Lake to answer for the crime, the chief responded with unaccustomed temerity. Not only did he refuse to come to Honey Lake, then or at any future time, but he demanded sixteen thousand dollars in payment from the settlers for the Honey Lake Valley. The settlers learned then that Winnemucca had been levying rent on ranchers who grazed stock in his Pyramid homeland and characterized such assertiveness on the part of an Indian as "blackmail." Ethnologists Martha C. Knack and Omer C. Stewart have suggested that the Demming murder was committed by the Smoke Creek band of Paiutes (Jackrabbit Eaters), over which Winnemucca exercised no authority beyond his relationship to the headman, reputedly a brother-in-law. Settlers drew no such distinctions. To them, Paiutes were Paiutes, and Winnemucca was responsible for all of them.[5]

War fever spread. Provisional Territorial Governor Roop called for troops and ammunition on the grounds that "We are about to be plunged into a bloody and protracted war with the Pau-Ute Indians." He issued a proclamation requiring all citizens to sleep with their weapons. A false nighttime alarm of Indian attack brought the residents of Susanville into the town square rubbing their eyes and clutching their guns. Rumors swept through the settlements, including a preposterous tale that Indian beggars in the Virginia City streets were actually spies scouting out the defenses of the city preparatory to an invasion. When the Paiute bands congregated at Pyramid Lake for the spring fish run, settlers interpreted the gathering as a council of war.[6]

In truth, the assembled bands had been discussing war as well as fishing. Qudazoboeat, a Shoshone headman married to a Paiute woman, declared himself ready for war. Moguanoga (known to the settlers as Captain Soo) of the Humboldt Meadows band did the same, as did Saaba of the Smoke Creek band, Sawadabebo from the Powder River, Yurdy from the Carson River, and Nojomud and Hozia of the Honey Lake Valley Paiutes. Sequinata, also known as Chiquito Winnemucca, of the Black Rock Desert country, was later described by the

Indians who listened to him as "impatient for the strife to begin." Hazabok, a headman and shaman from the Antelope Valley, spoke in favor of war and promised he would turn the warriors' tobacco into lead to supply them with bullets, kill the whites with raging hail storms, and cause the earth to swallow them. Truckee, who had twice turned back the anger of his people from war, appears to have sunken too far into old age to speak. At least, no one mentioned him. Winnemucca was believed to favor war but kept silent.[7]

One voice rang out for peace — that of Sarah's thirty-year-old cousin Numaga — a tall, straight, powerfully built man of quiet dignity, with keen, black eyes and high, jutting cheekbones. He rode from family to family, urging his friends not to make war and bring destruction upon themselves. Seeing that his efforts to persuade had no effect, he went away by himself and lay down in silence with his face to the ground. On the third day, the people came to the place where he lay and mocked him. One suggested scornfully that he should go live among the white men because "your skin is red but your heart is white." Others threatened to kill him unless he got to his feet. "Do it if you wish," said Numaga, "for I don't care to live." When the council convened, chief after chief stood to relate the wrongs his band had suffered and to call for war. Then Numaga entered the circle, looking like the ghost of one already dead, and made what may be the most eloquent plea for peace ever voiced by an Indian leader:

You would make war upon the whites. I ask you to pause and reflect. The white men are like the stars over your heads. You have wrongs, great wrongs, that rise up like those mountains before you; but can you, from the mountain tops, reach and blot out those stars? Your enemies are like the sands in the bed of your rivers; when taken away they only give place for more to come and settle there. Could you defeat the whites in Nevada, from over the mountains in California would come to help them an army of white men that would cover your country like a blanket. What hope is there for the Pah-Ute? From where is to come your guns, your powder, your lead, your dried meats to live upon, and hay to feed your ponies while you carry on this war? Your enemies have all of these things, more than they can use. They will come like the sand in a whirlwind and drive you from your homes. You will be forced among the barren rocks of the north, where your ponies will die; where you will see the women and old men starve, and listen to the cries of your children for food. I love my people; let them live; and when their spirits shall be called to the Great Camp in the southern sky, let their bones rest where their fathers were buried.[8]

If the time he laid with his face upon the earth had been a power quest, Numaga's prayer for the power to move his people had been answered. As he spoke for an hour, the tide seemed to be turning in favor of peace, until a messenger rode in on a galloping horse with news of the outrage and the slaughter at Williams Station, a trading post on the Carson River. It is the outrage that Sarah dwells on in her book. Not the speeches in council, which she passes over in silence. Not the victorious battle, which she scarcely mentions. But the outrage that, like all the wrongs to her people, bled like a wound that could never heal. It must have recalled to her the terror and the tears of that first winter on the San Joaquin when the white men came after Mary. As Sarah tells the story, two little girls about twelve years of age went out to dig roots for food. When they failed to return, their parents and other members of their band combed the country in search of them. No trail remains long concealed from an Indian tracker. They quickly found signs of the girls and followed them to Williams Station. The Williams brothers denied having seen the youngsters and invited the Indians to search their cabin. Finding no sign of the lost girls, the Indians left in a state of perplexity. The girls' footprints could not lie. Yet where were they?[9]

Some days later the Williamses offered an Indian who stopped at the station a gun and some ammunition in exchange for his horse. Strong condemnations of those who trafficked in guns with the Indians had not stopped the Williamses from engaging in such a profitable business. This trade went badly, however. Believing that the traders drove an unfair bargain, the Indian went to the barn to retrieve his horse, and the Williamses sicced their dog on him. When the dog bit him, the Indian cried out in pain. The muffled voices of the girls answered him.[10]

The man returned to his band and related his story. A party of nine that included Natches, Moguanoga — the headman of the Humboldt Meadows band — and the girls' relatives burst into the Williamses' cabin just before dark. Once more the Williamses denied any knowledge of the lost girls. A brother of one of the girls knocked down one of the Williams men with his gun and raised it to strike the other when one of the brothers bent down and opened a trap door beneath his feet. "This was a surprise to my people, who had never seen anything of the kind," observed Sarah. Descending into the cellar hole, the father found his daughters lying on a little bed, their mouths gagged with rags. When he brought them up into the light and the other Indians saw their condition, they killed both Williams brothers, along with three other men at the station, and set the place ablaze. A third Williams brother, camping farther up the river, survived. When he returned to the cabin, instead of burying the dead, he rode hard to spread the alarm of Indians on the warpath. At his heels — so he said — rode five hundred Indian warriors, the first of many exaggerations of the Indians' numbers.[11]

When the messenger arrived at Pyramid Lake and hastened into the council circle with news of the bloody events at Williams Station, Numaga at once broke off his plea for peace and said with sorrow, "There is no longer any use for counsel. We must prepare for war, for the soldiers will now come here to fight us."[12]

As in all he had spoken that day, Numaga saw the future with the eyes of a prophet. Yet he had counterparts among the settlers — men of peace and moderation who argued that the Williams Station killings should be carefully investigated and punishment should be restricted to those responsible. One newspaperman suggested that the murderers might not have been Indians. *San Francisco Herald* correspondent Allen poked fun at Genoa's alarmists in his dispatch and laid the blame upon the misdeeds of the Williamses. The trouble, he wrote, "originated in the gross outrages of the whites themselves, and will end with the destruction of those who caused it. There is a set of fellows ... who keep little grog shops called trading posts, along the great immigrant road, scarcely one of whom is too good to commit the worst of crimes. These are the people whose injustice exasperates the Indians."[13]

Unfortunately, for all concerned, the moderates were trampled in a stampede to war. Foremost in the rush appeared a man later characterized as "impetuous as a torrent" — Sarah's dear good friend Major Ormsby. Sarah herself dryly suggests that Ormsby should not have been "so hasty." Why Ormsby, despite his friendship with the Winnemucca family, turned so violently and suddenly against his Paiute allies is difficult to fathom. Perhaps the answer lay in his political ambitions: returning as a military hero from an expedition to chastise the "bloodthirsty savages" might boost his chances for high office in the new territory of Nevada just over the horizon.[14]

Like Ormsby, many who volunteered in Carson City, Virginia City, and other communities clustered near the Comstock had little conception of the dangers ahead. As Dan De Quille observed, they anticipated that war with the Paiutes would be "a sort of pleasure excursion." The motley force that set forth under the slogan "an Indian for breakfast and a pony to ride" numbered a little more than one hundred men — disorganized, untrained, and ill-equipped. Because the contingents from communities other than Carson City refused to accept Ormsby's leadership, they also lacked a unified command.[15]

After pausing at Williams Station to bury the dead, the men continued toward Pyramid Lake, some sixty-five miles north of Virginia City. On a tableland beside the Truckee River late in the afternoon of 12 May 1860, they spotted a group of mounted Indians, and Ormsby ordered his men to attack. The Indians fell back and disappeared, pursued by the volunteers. After one of the volunteers fired the first shot, Indians suddenly emerged from behind every sagebrush. As a murderous crossfire rained down on them, the volunteers realized, too late, that the Paiutes had cleverly trapped them within the wings of a crescent formation. In the distance they saw an Indian chief, mounted on a black horse and strikingly garbed in a white-plumed headdress with a red-and-white sash thrown over his shoulder, calmly giving orders with motions of an indistinct object in his hand. Unfamiliar with the Paiute custom of appointing different leaders for special functions, the volunteers supposed that Winnemucca directed the battle, but in fact it was Numaga, whose plea for peace had ended in his acceptance of the role of war chief. His conflicted attitude toward the war was aptly symbolized by the object he held — a combination peace pipe and battle ax.[16]

A disorderly and panic-stricken retreat toward Virginia City ensued, complicated by the narrowness of the trail. The volunteers first fell back to a meadowland fringed with cottonwood trees beside the river, only to find that Sequinata and his warriors had concealed themselves there and started to fire. Even in the midst of battle, Numaga made a last attempt at peace, but Sequinata and his men could not be restrained. The fleeing volunteers could take pride in a few instances of heroism, such as when one-legged Capt. Richard Watkins stood on his crutches and blazed away with his guns to hold a narrow stretch of trail until others had passed.[17]

Watkins escaped; Ormsby did not. As Sarah tells the story — and it is all she has to say of the battle — Natches, riding ahead of the other warriors, came upon Ormsby already wounded. When Ormsby begged for his life, Natches told him he would fire a bullet over his head, after which Ormsby should lie down as though he had been killed. Nonetheless, while Ormsby continued to implore his Indian friend, a bullet from another warrior killed him. The Indian combatants later said that if darkness had not intervened and allowed some volunteers to escape, they would have annihilated every last man. Survivors continued to straggle into Virginia City over the next several days, and casualty counts varied widely, but as many as 70 men may have been killed in a force of 105.[18]

Allen may have exaggerated when he called the battle the bloodiest disaster for white men in the past century, but it loomed large in 1860, when such routs as the Fetterman massacre and the Battle of the Little Bighorn (a comparable instance of rash bravado) still lay in the future. He also expressed admiration for the "consummate generalship" of the Indian chief, a demonstration of white men's tendency to relate more readily to the military leader than to the peacemaker. At a time when panic prevailed and women and children were being gathered behind barricades in a stone building, not every settler possessed Allen's coolness. De Quille reported "a grand stampede, many men suddenly remembering that they had business on the other side of the Sierra Nevada mountains."[19]

Although a "thrill of fear" rippled over the Pacific Coast at news of the disastrous battle, Californians responded generously to the settlers' call for men and arms, as Numaga had believed they would. On 2 June a force of at least 750 regular soldiers and volunteers under the command of Col. Jack Hays set out to satisfy the public outcry for "immediate chastisement of the savages," as the *San Francisco Steamer Bulletin* phrased it. Numaga's warriors resisted during a prolonged engagement that ended indecisively, with only light casualties on both sides. The Paiutes vanished into the shimmering white playas and myriad canyons of the Black Rock Desert, and Hays soon abandoned the attempt to pursue them. Just as Numaga had foretold, the white men had come like sand in a whirlwind and driven them into the barren rocks of the north. Intermittent fighting in the northern deserts would resume in future years, but the Winnemuccas would take no part in it.[20]

Both Indians and volunteers conducted certain gruesome postwar rituals. After the first battle, the Indians danced around the bodies of two particularly mettlesome volunteers and cut bowstrings from the sinews in the back of one of the men as a mark of honor. They mutilated and stripped other victims but took no scalps. Although Hays strictly forbade scalping in the second battle, at least one volunteer disobeyed and paraded from one Virginia City saloon to another, where the scalp dangling at the end of his rifle brought him free whiskey.[21]

The troops moved from a temporary encampment to establish Fort

Churchill some distance to the east of Virginia City, where they remained to deter further hostilities. The more meaningful deterrent may have been an informal armistice arranged between Numaga and Frederick W. Lander, an engineer constructing an army wagon road through the Black Rock Desert, where he lost one of his men in a skirmish with the Indians. Numaga agreed to restrain the Paiutes for a year, provided the unprovoked killings of Indians and the rapes of Indian women ceased and the Indians received compensation for the loss of their homeland. He also spoke of the famine among the Paiutes and their willingness to learn farming in the style of white people. Lander, lacking authority to negotiate a peace treaty, promised to inform Washington authorities of the Indian grievances.[22]

Winnemucca took no part in this discussion. Allen reported that he had "absquatulated, taking with him his baggage and women and children." Dodge believed that Winnemucca, smarting from the defeat, had taken his family north beyond the Black Rock Desert to safety in Oregon. Sarah may have ridden north with her father, but she is silent on the subject of this journey to the region where she was to spend some of the most eventful years of her life.[23]

Although some anxious settlers objected to locating the Indians so near at hand, the Pyramid Lake War, as it became known, did not stop the Pyramid Lake area from becoming a reservation. Indeed, the Paiutes' enhanced reputation as a military force to be reckoned with may have won them greater consideration. In 1859 at the request of the Office of Indian Affairs, Dodge had recommended two reservations for the Paiutes, one at Pyramid and the other at Walker Lake. The commissioner of Indian Affairs requested the president to establish these reservations by executive order in 1859. Fifteen years passed before a president issued the order, but, in the meantime, authorities treated Pyramid Lake as a de facto reservation, withdrawing the lands from settlement, assigning Indian agents, and surveying the boundaries Dodge had roughly described.[24]

Encroachments beyond those boundaries by white settlers became a persistent problem, lending a certain force to Allen's observation that the root of the trouble with Indians lay in "the morbid thirst for Indian blood and Indian Territory, which, like a pestilence, has taken possession of the minds of the unlettered, half-civilized, but Anglo-Saxon *sans culottes* of Western Utah." Whether Sarah and her father saw the establishment of a Pyramid Lake homeland as a positive development is rather doubtful. Winnemucca, who claimed all the land from the Carson Valley to the Oregon border for the Paiutes, scorned the idea of "being limited to the reservation," and Sarah would become one of America's most vocal critics of the reservation system.[25]

The sojourn in Oregon lasted only briefly. By mid-August the Winnemuccas returned to their usual haunts at Pyramid Lake. Winnemucca told a visitor that the Paiutes had done no more than defend themselves against Ormsby's attack in the Pyramid Lake War. Allen reported that Winnemucca was "not in the best humor" because he believed the government had broken all the promises that had been made to him. Nonetheless, he resumed the policy of peace that he and his father-in-law had upheld for so long. In September he paid a visit to the military contingent at Fort Churchill. There, in a parley with army officers, he blamed the recent hostilities upon the Bannocks, Shoshones, Pitt River Indians, and a few renegade Paiutes. He reiterated that the settlers should have brought their grievances to him instead of attacking and strongly affirmed his desire for a permanent peace with the white men.[26]

Early in October the Paiutes lit the signal fires of death upon the mountains. The sorrow that outweighed all the other tragedies of Sarah's life was upon her. Truckee was dying. De Quille relates that the old chief had been bitten by a tarantula, but his advanced years, and perhaps despondency over the breakdown of the peace he had championed since the first white men entered his world, may have contributed to his decline. Paiutes from far and wide gathered to see Truckee. They met at an encampment at the northern edge of the Pine Nut Mountains — southeast of Virginia City, and across the river valley where the unwilling Sarah had once traveled behind her grandfather on her first journey to California. As they sat solemnly around him, Truckee sent for a white man named Snyder, known as "the white Winnemucca," and asked him to take Sarah and Elma to Scott in California to be placed in a convent school. Snyder took Truckee's hand and vowed that he would.[27]

Truckee then told Winnemucca he must be a "good father" to the Paiutes as head chief. The dying chief broke down and wept, and all those around him also sobbed. When a large contingent of Indians rode in the next morning, he still clung to life. The shamans chanted and tried their charms, all to no avail. Afternoon passed, another night fell, and in all this time Sarah had not dared to close her eyes for fear that her beloved grandfather might die while she slept. At midnight the shaman said, "He is dying. He will open his eyes in a minute."[28]

It was as the shaman said. Truckee's gaze seemed as bright as ever, and he asked his son-in-law to raise him up, calling for the children. He told Winnemucca that he hoped he would "live to see as much as I have, and to know as much as I do" and adjured him to do his duty to his own people and his white brothers. Truckee then closed his eyes and lay down. Tuboitony, believing him dead, threw herself upon her father's bosom, but the shaman drew her away. Once more Truckee opened his eyes and made his last request: his rag friend must be placed upon his breast when they buried him. The shaman told the people Truckee would speak once more before he entered the Spirit Land, and indeed, his lips seemed to move again as if he whispered just before he died. The people sobbed wildly and flung themselves upon his body. Sarah was grief-stricken. She remembered: "I crept up to him. I could hardly believe he would never speak to me again. I knelt beside him, and took his dear old face in my hands, and looked at him quite a while. I could not speak. I felt the world growing cold; everything seemed dark."[29]

Captain John, one of Truckee's sons-in-law and a rival of the Winnemuccas for leadership, spoke the eulogy over Truckee's grave: "A good man is gone. The white man knows he was good, for he guided him round deserts and led him in paths where there was grass and good water. His people know he was good, for he loved them and cared for them and came home to them to die. All know that Truckee was a good man — Paiutes and Americans." Truckee's burial combined white and Indian practices. With the assistance of Snyder and other white men, the people buried Truckee according to his instructions beneath a cross on which his name had been cut. Captain John explained, "Truckee was much with the white men, he liked their way and learned much of them that we don't understand." The people interred all his possessions with him, burned his hut in the Indian way, and, as a mark of respect, killed six horses.[30]

Although Sarah had resisted him every step of the way — weeping, raging, railing, and storming — Truckee had been the predominant influence in her life. Her adored grandfather was a bold adventurer who dared to step out of the prehistoric world into the white world. He was not only a man of wisdom and curiosity who saw beyond guns and steamboats to the true source of the white men's power but also a leader who more than once had turned his people away from war. As Captain John said, "Not many are fit to lead in the path where Truckee walked." Truckee had pushed, pulled, and prodded his reluctant granddaughter along the path of the white people, somehow seeing in this stubborn child the fiber of a future leader. Often Paiute children formed stronger bonds with grandparents than with their parents, as did Sarah with Truckee. Now she grieved for him as she would never grieve again: "The great light had gone out. I had father, mother, brothers, and sisters; it seemed I would rather lose all of them than my poor grandpa. I was only a simple child, yet I knew what a great man he was. I mean great in principle. I knew how necessary it was for our good that he should live. I think if he had put out his hands and asked me to go with him, I would gladly have folded myself in his arms."[31]

5

Winnemucca Lake

*"It is a fearful thing to tell,
but it must be told"*

·

SARAH'S WHEREABOUTS during the years immediately following Truckee's death are difficult to determine, a problem compounded by her occasional inconsistencies and erroneous dates. Snyder apparently kept his promise to the dying chief. Sarah relates that Natches and five other men took her to California with Elma and that Scott enrolled them in the San Jose convent school. It has been established that the school has no record of the two girls, but the reason may be the brevity of their attendance. Sarah bitterly recalled that because the wealthy parents of other pupils objected to the presence of Indians in the school, they were forced to leave after only a few weeks. At times, Sarah found it expedient to represent herself as "convent educated" to establish her bona fides in white America and once even declared (unless misquoted) that she had spent three years in the convent school. The truth reflected greater credit upon her: with energy and determination, she educated herself, learning Spanish as well as English. Truckee would have been enormously pleased by her progress.[1]

It seems likely that Sarah and her brothers lived for some time near Santa Cruz, where game abounded in the coastal hills. She later spoke of this period in an interview and recalled living with a Mrs. Roach in Stockton at some point. In any case, she returned to Nevada by stagecoach. Clearly, the white world had lost the wonder it held for her in the days when a steamboat panted from exhaustion and a red wagon could enchant. The stagecoach aroused no comment.[2]

A period of relative peace followed the Pyramid Lake War and the

68

informal treaty between Numaga and Lander. Indeed, mutual trust had been restored to the point that Winnemucca and four hundred of his warriors, wearing their finest regalia, gave Territorial Governor James W. Nye a ceremonial welcome to Pyramid Lake in 1862. According to historian Myron Angel, "the whole band of savages kept up a continuous war-dance for the edification and entertainment of their pale-faced visitors, dancing on live coals to show their disregard for pain, and performing other feats of Indian character." Gifts were exchanged, and Warren Wasson, the well-liked Indian agent who had arranged the meeting, received Numaga's combination tomahawk and peace pipe, as well as his eagle-plumed war cap, his bow and arrows, and an offer of Sarah for his bride. Although Wasson accepted the tomahawk, he "graciously declined" Sarah's hand. One imagines the frontiersman Snyder standing behind her. His voice is low in her ear, "I'd have taken you and left the tomahawk." He may have been her first lover.[3]

How Sarah felt about being offered as a gift along with the tomahawk to the handsome, black-bearded young Indian agent of twenty-nine years (and rejected) has never been revealed. The compliments and good fellowship concluded with a "grand dance" in which soldiers, Indians, and officials all participated, a notable contrast to the bloody battles of 1860. Nonetheless, fanatical hatred still persisted in some hearts. The *Gold Hill News* called powwows, "with a horde of naked, painted devils whose only religion is murder, theft, and arson," a ridiculous notion. Occasional cattle thefts in Honey Lake Valley and raids on stations along the edge of the Black Rock and Smoke Creek Deserts by Smoke Creek Sam and his band of renegades kept white grievances alive.[4]

Sarah makes no mention of her alleged marriage to Snyder in any of her writings or interviews, but De Quille, who was a generally accurate witness and was well acquainted with the Winnemuccas, states that Sarah married him. It is possible that an attachment developed between them during the trip to California in 1860, if not before, since the "white Winnemucca" had lived with the Indians for some time. Sarah would have been sixteen, a girl of marriageable age according to Paiute reckoning. She did not share the good looks of her ill-fated sister Mary or the height of her father, tending more to the short and stocky build characteristic of her people — so characteristic, indeed, that the Paiutes told a myth about it. When Coyote and his wife were bringing the first people down from the north in a narrow-necked water jug, Coyote, naughty as always, removed the top from the jug to peek inside. The tall, slender people escaped and became the Indians of the Northwest; the Paiutes, however, were too short and stocky to follow, and they did not emerge until Coyote poured them out of the jug into the Great Basin. Sarah also shared the blunt features common to her people, as well as the fine black eyes and the smooth black hair, which she often wore loose and curled in the Anglo manner. She showed a flair for the dramatic in her style and dress. With her full-bosomed figure, her sparkling black eyes, and her vivacious, charismatic personality — transforming what might have been plainness in a duller girl into something akin to beauty — men had found her attractive from the time of the Johntown dances.[5]

We know nothing of Snyder's appearance, except that he had lived so long with the Indians that two visitors mistook him for one of them. Nor have his first name or other particulars about him come to light. Although a number of Snyders appear in the early records, a man living so far beyond the pale is unlikely to be among them. Aside from Sarah's brief mention of Snyder's presence at her grandfather's deathbed, he exists only in the pages of De Quille's *Big Bonanza*, and even there it is not clear whether Snyder, the "white Winnemucca," and the German who lived with the Indians are all the same man. De Quille relates a story of two German prospectors who spent the night in Winnemucca's encampment shortly after the Pyramid Lake War. One of them awakened in the night when an old Indian woman seized him by the hair and nearly cut his throat. A man he mistook for one of Winnemucca's warriors saved him. Identifying himself as a German living with the Indians, the stranger warned the young prospector not to complain to Winnemucca about the old woman who tried to kill him because she was one of Winnemucca's wives (presumably another wife than Tuboitony, since neither the age nor the violence sound much like Sarah's mother).[6]

When the prospectors left the camp, Winnemucca gave them a string of twisted sinews knotted in several places to guarantee their safe passage back to Virginia City. It worked like the magic in a fairy tale. Each time a party of Indians stopped them, the display of the knotted sinews changed menacing looks to friendly smiles, and the Indians undid one of the knots. An Indian beside the Carson River untied the last knot and reclaimed the sinews, then rode away singing softly in German. The prospectors belatedly recognized him as their unnamed German benefactor.[7]

If Sarah indeed married Snyder, Truckee, who told the white man, "I have always loved you as if you were my own dear son," would have surely approved. After 1861 a formal marriage by Nevada civil or religious authorities would have been impossible because the first territorial legislature passed miscegenation laws forbidding marriage or cohabitation between Indians and whites under penalty of fines and imprisonment. Unless Sarah's relationship with Snyder was an informal liaison, she must have married him — if she married him at all — according to Paiute custom. De Quille, much of whose information came from Sarah's brothers Natches and Tom, may have been misinformed about Snyder. Alternatively, Sarah may have kept silent about him because in later years she was criticized for her many marriages. Admitting to an additional marriage would have given ammunition to her enemies. According to De Quille, Snyder died on a return visit to Germany after living with Sarah for several years.[8]

The year Sarah turned twenty marked an important stage: her emergence as a public personality. "Princess Sarah," as she would be called, sometimes with derision and sometimes with genuine respect, started to break out of her chrysalis. This development was made possible by the prominence of her father and her fluency in English. The condition of the Paiutes remained desperate. Niggardly reservation provisions, fruitless attempts to collect rentals and payment

for Indian lands, conferences with white officials, raids, and even warfare had not brought them subsistence enough to compensate for
all they had lost. Another starvation winter loomed ahead. Could a
means be found to secure money for the food and blankets they
would need?

The Winnemuccas first attempted a public appeal. In late September 1864, Winnemucca, one of his sons, and two of his daughters paraded through the Virginia City streets to the Wells Fargo express office, where a large crowd gathered around them. Winnemucca gave a
speech, translated by Sarah, in which he disavowed responsibility for
the Pyramid Lake War, described the privations suffered by his people
since the white men took over their land, and said simply, "I came
to ask white man to give us something, but I do not want white man
to give unless he is entirely willing." After passing the hat, Sarah
counted contributions amounting to twenty-five dollars, and Winnemucca bowed in gratitude and gave an Indian whoop. The crowd
responded with what a newspaper called "three hearty, rousing
cheers — all seemingly well pleased with the Chief and his daughters,
'especially' with the daughters." "Especially with the daughters"
hints that Sarah continued to excite the same kind of admiration accorded to her at those dances in Dutch Nick's saloon several years earlier.[9] All the same, twenty-five dollars would not begin to cover Paiute
needs. Something more effective than a simple public appeal must be
devised, and perhaps a novel idea began to buzz in Sarah's head. Long
before most Indian leaders, she understood that white people's curiosity about Indians could be turned into a source of revenue. Another
twenty years would pass before Sitting Bull appeared on the eastern
stage in a series of highly popular tableaux, later joining Buffalo Bill's
Wild West Exhibition. The Winnemuccas went on stage much earlier,
and the concept may have been Sarah's, for at twenty she knew the
white world much better than her father, her personality was more
forceful than her siblings, she shared Truckee's receptiveness to inno-
vation, and, throughout her life, she was something of a performer.
Although she would later become a solo lecturer, in these initial ap-

pearances she relied on her family in the Paiute way. The family had always been the essential unit in Paiute culture, outweighing all other relationships and allegiances.[10]

The Winnemuccas' theatrical enterprise commenced in Virginia City at a time of economic depression and political ferment. No new ore bodies had been uncovered, high operating costs and extravagant management consumed profits from the mines, and a sizable proportion of the population that the previous year crested at an estimated fifteen thousand had decamped. During the last phase of the Civil War, dispatches from the battlefront crowded newspaper columns, and torchlight processions by partisans of the Union cause marched through the streets. Moreover, despite the questionable veracity of Nevada's claims to a sufficient population and a flourishing economy, statehood was about to be granted, thanks to the exigencies of Washington politics.[11]

Such distant issues made little difference to the Indians living on the edge of town in shanties domed in the traditional shape but made from canvas and flattened tin cans. These Indians had become a familiar sight to Virginia City residents. The men cut and sold wood and did odd jobs; the women worked as laundresses and did domestic chores, and sometimes they begged or scavenged, as they had once gathered buckberries or cattail pollen. Yet the Indian sifting refuse for usable items did not enjoy the prestige of a chief, and when Winnemucca, tall and dignified as always, rode through the streets with one daughter behind him on his horse, Sarah riding abreast, and Natches with a small party of warriors holding a decorated crescent above the chief's head, it created a considerable stir.[12]

The parade halted in front of the imposing brick International Hotel, where Sarah translated Winnemucca's speech proclaiming his friendship for the whites and his refusal to join in warfare against them despite overtures made to him by "plains tribes." This probably alluded to the Bannocks, whom Winnemucca had visited at the request of a white official seeking safe passage for prospectors en route to the new Idaho mining excitements. Soliciting contributions from the crowd for Indian relief yielded some results. Sarah expanded on her father's theme of friendship during a subsequent interview, the first of many that would place her ideas before the public. Her words made clear that, like Numaga's attempt to avert the Pyramid Lake War, the Winnemuccas' policy of peace and cooperation with white men had aroused opposition from some Indians. She claimed that an uncle of hers had recently been cut in pieces and burned by Paiutes in the Walker River country when he tried to dissuade them from warfare.[13]

This last was a reference to the death of Winnemucca's brother Wahe, a tall, imposing figure and a spirit chief. Myron Angel relates a story probably told to him by Agent Wasson that is diametrically opposed to Sarah's. In Angel's version, Wahe conspired to murder Wasson and gradually infiltrate Fort Churchill with small parties of Indians who would slaughter the garrison. Wasson punctured this plot by boldly entering the encampment where fifteen hundred Paiutes and Bannocks had convened and making a powerful plea for peace. Wahe, disgraced by the collapse of his plans, fled to Oregon. This conspiracy account conforms so neatly to literary formulas of the day — and so poorly to usual patterns of Paiute warfare — that it appears suspect. Upon Wahe's return, two Paiute chiefs killed him and disposed of his remains in a manner meant to ensure that the spirit chief would not resurrect himself and take revenge. So strong was his medicine, as his descendants tell the story, that even after his head had been severed his body continued to battle his assailants. They also believe that Wahe had gone to the Walker River country to court a second wife, a story that suggests a different reason for his murder. Although Winnemucca refused a picture of Wahe, saying "Me see him too much all the time" (perhaps a hint that the spirit chief returned in dreams to haunt the living), his brother's murder greatly upset him.[14]

Whatever the truth of Wahe's death, Sarah's interview served to publicize Indian performances. Entertainment on the Comstock had grown more varied since the days when the only amusement was the Saturday night dance in Dutch Nick's saloon. The free-spending, pleasure-seeking mining camp crowd turned out to see everything from opera and Shakespearean drama to vaudeville and minstrel shows. But Indian performances were something new.[15]

Nevada journalist Sam Davis credits the Winnemuccas' theatrical appearance to theater owner Max Walter and relates that when Sarah first walked onstage her uncanny ability to arouse an audience already showed:

The old chief betrayed no embarrassment as he walked to the footlights and commenced what was probably a good talk; but the princess, overcome by stage fright, got all tangled up in her attempted interpretation, and finally sat flat on the stage, and, putting her hands before her face, said:

"I'm so ashamed! I can't tell you what Winnemucca is saying."

If she had artfully designed to make a hit she couldn't have succeeded better. There was a storm of applause, and thereafter it was nothing but applause, though the audience learned little of what the old chief was saying.[16]

This initial lecture developed into a more theatrical performance in which, as literary scholar Noreen Grover Lape has observed, the Winnemuccas used white stereotypes about Indians to create entertainment. Following a minstrel act, the Winnemucca show at the Sutliff Music Hall presented several tableaux vivants, a popular nineteenth-century theatrical form consisting of various scenes with no plot. These included "The War Council," "Taking a Scalp," "Grand Scalp Dance," and "The Coyote Dance." In a bow to public sentiment, the scalpers lifted the hair of a "copperhead" sympathizer of the Confederacy, which no doubt roused the audience to patriotic fervor. With memories of the Pyramid Lake War still fresh, the scalp dance should have been bloodcurdling, if authentically depicted. Traditionally, warriors waving branches of brush danced in a circle around a scalp placed atop a pole, and the one who had taken the scalp pantomimed biting motions at the spot where the victim's neck would have been while chanting "so that is how your blood tastes."[17]

In the audience was a man sporting a large, showy gold watch who wore a coonskin cap Davis described as "of ultra Davy Crockett style."

James Miller, who became the Winnemuccas' agent, had been "a stage-man, or a horse-man, or something else of that sort" in the remoter reaches of eastern Nevada, but it took him little time to appraise the "speculative value" of the Paiute performance and turn himself into a theatrical impresario. When he promised the Winnemuccas fortune and glory if they let him arrange performances for them in San Francisco, they readily agreed, hoping that the money needed for Paiute relief would follow.[18]

In San Francisco Indians were a greater novelty than on the Comstock — perhaps as great as San Francisco was to Indians. Nonetheless, if *Alta California*'s review reflected general sentiments, the Winnemuccas' first San Francisco performance — a Saturday matinee at the Metropolitan Theater on 22 October billed as a "ROMANTIC ENTERTAINMENT" — was less favorably received than in Virginia City. On the Comstock, where Winnemucca commanded respect, the *Virginia Daily Union* had called him the "formidable aborigine" and the "great Winnemucca"; *Alta* mocked the Winnemuccas as the "Royal Family" and ridiculed Winnemucca's speech in the Paiute language for sounding like "Rub-a-dub, dub! Ho-dad-dy, hi-dad-dy; wo-hup, gee-haw. Fetch-water, fetch-water, Manayunk!"[19]

Alta's reservations about the authenticity of the tableaux had some foundation. The Metropolitan's forest scenery had little to do with the "world of sand drifts, sage clumps, and alkali waters." The buckskin clothing worn by the troupe instead of more realistic rabbit-skin tunics had probably been chosen because the Paiutes increasingly looked to the Plains Indians as their models — Sarah might have also learned that white people expected Indians to dress in buckskin. Evidently, the Winnemuccas lengthened their act for the San Francisco stage. They added a lecture on Indians, which *Alta* found overly long and riddled with clichés, and several scenes showing Pocahontas saving the life of Capt. John Smith, which may have represented a canny effort to purloin the popularity of "Po-ca-hon-tas; or Ye Gentle Savage," a stage classic that had recently played the Nevada mining towns with great success. While sympathizing with the need for Paiute relief, one old friend of the Winnemuccas essentially concurred with *Alta* and called their theatrics "degrading exhibitions."[20]

Alta had only two positive comments. Their reporter admired Sarah's "sweet English voice," as all who encountered her usually did, and he found the Indians' ability to remain immobile "as if carved of bronze" quite striking. The Winnemuccas would have learned that skill early because it was useful during hunting and warfare, but immobility meant that they lacked the showmanship of riders on galloping horses and of the reenacted battles that enlivened Buffalo Bill's Wild West Exhibition. The Winnemuccas' success in show business came nowhere close to Sitting Bull's, and after a few San Francisco performances, they abandoned the plan (probably Miller's) to take the show to Washington DC. Still, the theatrical venture had shown Sarah how she could affect white audiences, a lesson she would one day put to good use.[21]

Although they played to packed houses on the Comstock for nearly a week, their expenses in San Francisco must have been considerable, and Davis relates that their earnings disappeared into the pockets of Miller, who then "abandoned the poor devils and left them penniless and ponyless among strangers in a distant land." They made their way home as best they could, walking, working, and begging, with nothing tangible to show for their theatrical effort.[22] Through her interviews, Sarah may have reached some with her message on the Paiute commitment to peace, but events would demonstrate that she failed to convince those who most needed convincing.

In March 1865 trouble between Indians and whites erupted anew when Indians killed two white men on the Walker River. The circumstance that one of them had flogged the Indians who took revenge on him did little to allay fears among the settlers that the killings signified something more dangerous than an isolated incident. As dispatches to Governor Henry G. Blasdel show, these apprehensions escalated to a high pitch when two white men were killed in separate incidents on the road between Honey Lake and the Humboldt. (Although Indian responsibility for one of these murders has never been proven, blame fell upon the Indians.) Settlers in Star City and Unionville, claiming that "Indians hold the entire route, and small parties dare not travel," called for provisions, arms, and troops. Settlers in Honey Lake complained that Indians had stolen some cattle. The *Humboldt Register* declared that killing Indians on sight was the "only sane" policy, and the *Gold Hill News* advocated a "final solution of the great Indian problem: by exterminating the whole race, or driving them forever beyond our frontier." In response to Blasdel's prompt request for troops, Maj. Charles McDermit, commander at Fort Churchill, sent a contingent from Company D, a volunteer company commanded by Capt. Almond B. Wells, a young and inexperienced officer who may have been eager to make a name for himself fighting Indians.[23]

Unaware of impending danger, a number of the Kuyuidika-a camped east of Pyramid Lake near Mud Lake (also called Winnemucca Lake), which was fed by a deep narrow channel from the Truckee River before it entered Pyramid. To the east thrust the Sahwave Mountains, dark cleanly sliced triangles with fluid markings of dull green and slate blue, strangely different from the broken rose and cream-colored peaks to the south. March was a lean time of year, with winter ending and spring foods not yet on hand, and the migratory birds that often alit in the reeds and tules of the shallow lake proved insufficient. Winnemucca and the men set forth on a hunting expedition. Sarah was then living in Dayton at the mouth of the canyon south of the Comstock.[24]

Before dawn on March 14, having received word that Indian cattle thieves had camped at Mud Lake, Captain Wells marched his command to the site, divided them into three squads, and attacked, killing twenty-nine Paiutes. Just one escaped, a sister of Sarah's who sprang onto a horse and galloped wildly across sagebrush and sand outdistancing her pursuers.[25]

Although the volunteers suffered no more than a slight wound in one man's shoulder, Wells's report described the event as a tough battle involving hand-to-hand combat with veteran Indian warriors. Sarah's description, no doubt received from her sister, the sole survivor, differed considerably: "The soldiers rode up to the encampment and fired into it, and killed almost all the people that were there. Oh, it is a fearful thing to tell, but it must be told. Yes, it must be told by me. It was all old men, women and children that were killed. After the soldiers had killed all but some little children and babies still tied up in their baskets, the soldiers took them also, and set the camp on fire and threw them into the flames to see them burn alive. I had one baby brother killed there."[26] Tuboitony was among the dead. Sarah related that her father almost died from grief, and her anger and outrage sear the pages of her book.

The Mud Lake massacre received applause in many quarters. The *Humboldt Register* approvingly observed that Wells "understands the business" of fighting Indians, the *Territorial Enterprise* staunchly upheld him, the *Virginia Daily Union*, on the basis of initial reports, issued the clarion call: "let loose the dogs of war, and cry havoc," and no evidence suggests that the military reprimanded Wells for wrongdoing. The *Virginia Daily Union*'s subsequent call for a military investigation nonetheless underscores the circumstance that certain unpleasant rumors and curious facts had started to surface concerning Wells's supposed battle with the veteran warriors. The *Union* wondered why a fierce fight involving hand-to-hand combat had produced only a slight wound in one volunteer's shoulder. It also appeared odd that the military had not followed normal procedure and confiscated the weapons belonging to the vanquished enemy. The volunteers had reportedly scalped the Indians, which was, in the eyes of the *Union*, "a burning disgrace to the service." Moreover, a rumor began to circulate about the drowning of infants. Two hundred frightened Indians congregated at Murphy's Station near Humboldt Lake. They sent women and children into white men's towns in the apparent hope that they would not be killed there. When fires burned on the mountain tops, the residents of Virginia City feared a retaliatory Indian attack. In fact, the Paiutes had lit the signal fires of death.[27]

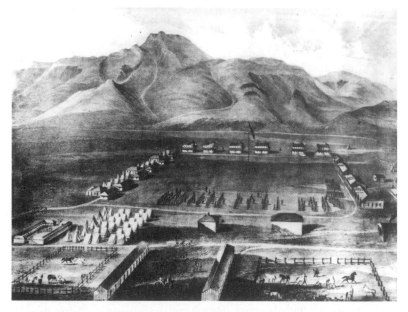

An early lithograph of Fort Churchill. Courtesy of the Nevada Historical Society.

In his first report to the legislature, Blasdel, the first elected governor of the new state of Nevada, later declared that the Mud Lake massacre "caused a great excitement among the Piutes, and a general war seemed inevitable." Blasdel faced influential newspapers calling for blood and a legislature that would soon be heatedly debating whether "extermination," "subjugation," or "scalping" would be the most suitable word to use in a resolution on how to deal with the Indian question. Much to his credit, Blasdel sought to pacify the Indians and listen to their grievances.[28]

At Blasdel's request, McDermit convened a conference with the Paiute chiefs at Fort Churchill. Many Indians had already arrived before Winnemucca made a ceremonial entrance wearing full war paint (which he removed the next day). When Governor Blasdel, impressively tall at six-feet-five-inches, with a black beard and dark, piercing eyes, rode toward the adobe compound with a military guard and a detachment of troops, the infantry stood in formation to receive him, their bayonets shining in the late afternoon sun, and sixty-six Paiute chiefs and leading men awaited him. Apparently aware that smoking usually prefaced serious Indian discussions, the governor and McDermit passed out after-dinner cigars, which some chiefs accepted and smoked with evident curiosity.[29]

The conference the next morning began with a statement from the chiefs, read by an interpreter, on their desire for peace. Numaga reported on the Mud Lake massacre. He confirmed that Winnemucca's wives had been killed and all except three or four in the camp had been women and children, the cattle thieves having departed before Wells's arrival. Some women had jumped into the water, where the volunteers shot those who did not drown. Numaga also made clear that violence had been unnecessary because he would have surrendered the culprits if a request had been made to him.[30]

The remainder of the conference centered on lesser grievances: the theft of Indian horses, the murder of a Walker River Indian, the white man who defrauded Natches of five hundred dollars. Joaquin Ben, of the Walker River country, and Big George, a heavyset Indian almost as tall as Blasdel, asked the most searching questions. Why, they wanted to know, could white men testify against Indians in trials while Indians were not permitted to testify against white men? And why were Indians always executed by white men's courts while white men were never convicted of their crimes against Indians? The governor and the commander could provide no satisfactory answers.[31]

Winnemucca, who said little during the discussion, rose at the end to speak. The ability to express oneself movingly and persuasively was an essential component of leadership among the Great Basin Indians — indeed, the Shoshone word for chief meant "talker." As once Truckee had stood over the body of his dead son and turned his people away from war, now Winnemucca summoned all the eloquence at his command to bring them to peace. The *Virginia Daily Union* admiringly observed: "His voice was full and strong, and the language of his nation flowed as rapid and uninterrupted from his lips as the torrents of his mountain home. His gesticulations were graceful, and, altogether, he looked the orator, and a man to command."[32] That he could bring himself to make this speech less than two weeks after the slaughter of his wives and the burning of his infant son testifies powerfully for his commitment to peace. The renaming of Mud Lake as Winnemucca Lake remains an ironic testament to his losses.

After the conference, the Paiutes accepted gifts of calico and blankets and appeared "well pleased." The bloodshed had not yet run its course, however. During the next year, as author Sessions Wheeler has rightly pointed out, "the Black Rock Desert region became the principal battleground for a conflict which, in respect to its ferocity, probably had no equal in Nevada history." Sarah saw it in much the same way: "They went after my people all over Nevada. Reports were made everywhere throughout the whole country by the white settlers, that the red devils were killing their cattle, and by this lying of the white settlers the trail began which is marked by the blood of my people from hill to hill and from valley to valley."[33]

Some skirmishes were small enough to nearly escape notice in the white world. Take, for instance, a brief item in the *Humboldt Register*: "[Lieutenant] Wolverton came upon one of the thieving bands at dusk of Thursday evening. Killed all the bucks — number not exactly known — and took the squaws and children prisoners." Other battles were larger in scope. The Battle of Fish Creek Valley on a wintry day in late January 1866 left every Indian on the field dead — thirty-five in all. Even the rabidly anti-Indian *Humboldt Register* admired the bravery of the fallen warriors: "The Indians had fought with a heroism that astonished everyone who witnessed it. They made no offer to surrender; uttered no sound but yells of defiance; and continued to fire their poisoned arrows until they were so weak that they could throw them but a few feet."[34]

The army fought another major battle with the Paiutes at Rock Canyon barely more than a year after the Mud Lake massacre. Although the soldiers shot "everything that wore paint," killing eighty Indian men and thirty-five women, they were denied what the *Humboldt Register* termed "the satisfaction of exterminating the entire

This etching from De Quille, *The Big Bonanza*, was ironically labeled
"Savages" by the author.

band" because some Indians had hidden in the rocks of the canyon walls and fired at the retreating soldiers. Unless the commanding officers falsified their account to excuse shooting women, the Paiute women had worn male garb and fought beside their men. The horses took part as well. In later years the Paiute elders told a story of a warrior horse: a Paiute man had lifted his family onto the horse's strong back, and though flying bullets shot his mane and tail to bits, the horse fought his way to the top of the mountain, carrying the family to safety in the rocks.[35]

Prior to these victories at Fish Creek Valley and Rock Canyon, the army had fared rather poorly. Indians at an encampment east of Clover Valley repeatedly repulsed the attacks of Wells's seventy-man force, finally compelling Wells to retreat under cover of darkness, and McDermit was killed when Indians ambushed a small scouting party. The situation changed when Captain Soo (Moguanoga) of the Humboldt River band decided to assist the army, evidently in the belief so eloquently voiced by Numaga just before the Pyramid Lake War that continued resistance would result in disaster for the Indians. Captain Soo became a scout, led the army to the Paiute encampment at Fish Creek Valley, and fought with his men alongside the soldiers. He also spied and informed on Indians sought by the military. The men he fingered were peremptorily shot, an act that won warm applause from the *Register*. This eager cooperation signified a considerable change of heart for Soo, who took part in the attack on Williams Station that ignited the Pyramid Lake War.[36]

Starvation increased the number of predatory bands of Paiutes, Bannocks, and Shoshones in the Black Rock. In 1866 Blasdel saw their desperation clearly. During his visits among various bands in 1865, "I found them, in several instances, with nothing to subsist upon but rabbits, mice, grasshoppers, ants, and other insects." They spoke of how the white men had cut down the pinyon trees that were their orchards and put cattle to graze upon the grass that had provided their seed food. Blasdel found their arguments "unanswerable." Agent Wasson estimated that half of all the Paiutes had died from famine, disease, and warfare during the years 1859 to 1865.[37] Although the number of murdered Indians far exceeded settler casualties, atrocities by Indians aroused palpable horror. In her white-hot anger, Sarah never mentions the northern Nevada settler burned alive by Indians or the ranches deserted by settlers fearful of murder at Indian hands. She wrote to convince others of the justice of the Indian cause, and she refused to admit any justifiable reason behind the call for military action by the isolated and frightened settlers in the northern deserts. In her eyes, the sole cause for the battles in the Black Rock was white greed: "The only way the cattle-men and farmers get to make money is to start an Indian war, so that the troops may come and buy their beef, cattle, horses, and grain. The settlers get fat by it."[38]

Sarah relates that in 1866 she left the Comstock to live with Natches and his wife at the Pyramid Lake Reservation. There, through a winter of hardship during which they had little to eat beyond some flour occasionally given to her sister-in-law by the Indian agent in exchange for doing his laundry, Sarah experienced the cruelties of the reservation system and found the basis for a crusade that was to become a consuming passion for much of her life. She would not withdraw as some did, nor would she accept in silent misery what she had no power to change. Before her spirit finally broke, she would rage with all the eloquence at her command in print and in lectures against the injustices of the reservation system, and she would carry her appeals to men of power.[39]

With a pen dipped in fury, she later indicted the Indian agents she watched come and go: "This is the way all the Indian agents get rich. The first thing they do is to start a store; the next thing is to take in cattle men, and cattle men pay the agent one dollar a head. In this way they get rich very soon, so they can have their gold-headed canes, with their names engraved on them." The Indian agents at Pyramid (originally called "farmer in charge") found so many opportunities for gain that they connived to get the position. According to Sarah, one agent received his appointment by bribing his superior, but he did not remain long because another aspirant, Calvin Bateman, hired some Indians to frighten him off the reservation. Then Bateman "got rich in the same way."[40]

An issue of goods for the Shoshones arranged by the Nevada agent failed to silence Sarah's complaints. Anything but mollified, Sarah sarcastically attacked the miserly allowances given each family: "Oh, such an issue! It was enough to make a doll laugh. A family numbering eight persons got two blankets, three shirts, no dress-goods. Some got a fish-hook and line; some got one and a half yards of flannel, blue and red." In tacit protest, some Indian men appeared the next morning with just one leg dressed in flannel.[41]

After Agent Bateman presented a generous amount of flour to the Shoshones, Sarah upbraided him in front of his superior for being a hypocritical Christian: "You come up here to show off before this man. Go and bring some flour to my people on the Humboldt River, who are starving, the people over whom you are agent. For shame that you who talk three times a day to the Great Father in Spirit-land should act so to my people." Bateman may have thought this outspoken young Indian woman had learned English too well. He would not be the last Indian agent to feel the sharp side of her tongue.[42]

Sarah thought James Spencer, who became the agent at Pyramid in 1879, was an improvement over his predecessors. Spencer issued blankets to the old and the blind, provided some wagons for Indian use, and brought his daughter to teach school. Spencer soon died, however, and his replacement claimed a portion of every Indian crop but did not provide seed or instruction in farming. Sarah raged and railed unceasingly against such treatment: "Oh, my dear good Christian people, how long are you going to stand by and see us suffer at your hands? We shall never be civilized in the way you wish us to be if you keep on sending us such agents year after year, who do nothing but fill their pockets, and the pockets of their wives and sisters, who are always put in as teachers, and paid from fifty to sixty dollars a month, and yet they do not teach. The farmer is generally his cousin, and his brother is a clerk."[43]

At the same time that Sarah began involving herself so hotly in reservation affairs, Winnemucca had chosen another path. After the Mud Lake massacre he refused to return to Pyramid Reservation. Just as Sitting Bull, some years later, would take his people north to Canada, Winnemucca took to the northern mountains with a small band of devoted followers. Far from the reservation agents who tried to dictate every move, they found a refuge where they could live as they had always lived. In the vast solitude of Steens Mountain, Winnemucca could pursue the spiritual quest through which he tried to understand the meaning of the cataclysmic events that had altered his world and led him to question his beliefs.

It has been suggested that Sarah largely created Winnemucca's place as chief. She knew he was merely the headman of a loosely organized band, yet she asserts his primacy at every opportunity. But settlers on the Comstock had known and respected Winnemucca when Sarah was a youngster with no means of aggrandizing her father's position. It has further been remarked that when whites, who preferred to deal with a hierarchical leader, concocted the role of chief, the men they elevated often lost authority among Indians.[44]

Still, the settlers continued to believe in chieftaincy as an office that could be awarded and removed by white men rather than Indians, and, in 1866, the citizens of Humboldt County petitioned to have Winnemucca replaced as chief by Captain Soo. This surely had a geographical dimension: settlers looked to the Indian leader in their locality, just as the influential Comstockers had long elevated Winnemucca. It also reflected the political ambitions of a rival band leader, since Captain Soo actively campaigned to be "chosen Chief of the friendly Piutes; to be known by the title of 'Winnemucca'; and to have supreme command of the Piute Nation," as the petition put it. At the same time, the petitioners accused Winnemucca of having "turned traitor to his tribe, deserted his Country and joined the hostile Indians of the North." The dominant force behind the petition, however, was undoubtedly a move to reward Soo for "his fidelity to his white brethren on the battlefield." No evidence indicates that Soo succeeded in gaining recognition as supreme commander of the Paiute nation, and several years later he was killed during a struggle for su-premacy in his band by his brother, who saw him as a traitor. Indiffer-ent to the matter of who the white men cared to call chief, Winne-mucca stayed in the mountains.[45]

Instead of withdrawing with him, Sarah, Natches, and various other relatives continued to live at Pyramid Lake Reservation, with the possible exception of Elma, who, at an undisclosed date, married a white rancher and went to live with him in Montana. In theory, the reservation should have given the Paiutes a sanctuary where they would be safe from the warfare raging in the Black Rock. But settlers showed no respect for the understood boundaries of a reservation that would remain unsurveyed for years, and even the occasional well-intentioned Indian agent had scant success in halting their en-croachments. Without compensation to the Paiutes, settlers sent their cattle to graze on the reservation, where the animals consumed feed needed for Indian stock; settlers preempted a considerable part of the fisheries that had long been the Kuyuidika-a staff of life; and even though the barren surroundings of Pyramid Lake provided little arable land, settlers took over much of that meager amount.[46]

Despite the general unsuitability of Pyramid for agriculture, the Office of Indian Affairs firmly upheld the ideal that in order to civilize the Indian he must give up the old nomadic way of life, the life to which Winnemucca so stubbornly adhered, and become a farmer. One of the Paiutes who attempted to comply with this effort was Sa-rah's uncle Truckee John (the name suggests that he may have been a brother of Tuboitony's). He built a house and established a fenced farm on the Truckee, where he kept horses and raised hay, grain, and vegetables. He prospered so well that a nearby rancher named Gates began to covet his land. A plot between Gates and his confederates Alec Fleming and Edward Payne soon ensued. Fleming and Payne celebrated the Fourth of July 1867 with heavy drinking, which cul-minated in the murder of Truckee John in what has been called "a par-ticularly ugly way which even offended the sensibilities of rather hard-bitten Nevadans." Fleming and Payne departed for the Comstock, killing two more Indians along the way and boasting of plans to raise a company of men to exterminate Indians. They then disappear from local history, unpunished for their crimes. Gates gained possession of Truckee John's farm.[47]

This outrage brought Winnemucca down from the north to threaten Fort Churchill with a force of two to three hundred warriors. Another war was averted, but ethnologists Knack and Stewart have found that Paiute anger over Truckee John's murder lasted for generations. In a council meeting seventy years later, Indians still spoke of how Truckee John had "lost his life and his land." He was the second of Sarah's uncles to be murdered by white men, another turn in the long trail marked by the blood of her people.[48]

6
Camp McDermit
*"Can you wonder that I like to have my people
taken care of by the army?"*

IN THE BEGINNING, before the sun and the moon were created, was the night. Only shamans can see through the darkness to the night beneath, but for curings and dances night is the time when power may be captured, especially around midnight or in the hour before dawn. Night is powerful and immortal, and the night spirit is capricious. It may choose you — or it may not. Even if you are not a shaman who can see the night beyond the blackness, the spirit of the primordial night may send you animal messengers or speak to you in dreams.[1]

None of the children of Winnemucca became shamans, nor did they follow the Ghost Dance messiahs and the Dreamer chiefs who rose from the agonies of a desperate people. When others flocked to hear Wodziwob preach the new Ghost Dance religion at Walker Reservation in 1870, they stood aside. They did not paint themselves and dance with the others in concentric circles, chanting of a spirit journey by the path of the milky way. Nor did they look for the coming of armies of the dead pouring out of the rising sun. Yet sometimes the power of the night brought Sarah or Natches prophetic dreams of disasters. These vivid forebodings blended seamlessly into days of terror and crisis lived at the frenetic pace of a galloping horse.

In 1868 a series of events began to unfold that would result in Sarah's departure from her Pyramid Lake homeland for northern Nevada and Oregon. According to Sarah, it started when Pyramid Reservation Agent Hugh Nugent sold some gunpowder to an Indian, an illegal transaction despite widespread use of guns by the Paiutes for nearly a decade. Shortly afterward one of Nugent's men shot and killed the Indian for possessing gunpowder illegally. The uneasy peace that had prevailed south of the Black Rock since the Pyramid Lake War hung in the balance. "All our people were wild with excitement," Sarah remembered. And they wanted to kill Nugent.[2]

Worried by this volatile situation, Sarah and Natches decided to warn Nugent. As they rode hurriedly across the Truckee River, deep and gushing with spring snow melt, Sarah's horse fell on the slippery stones, dumping her into the water; Natches, always there for her, jumped into the water and helped his bedraggled sister to remount. Far from appreciating their concern, Nugent reacted furiously to their warning. He declared that he had plenty of men with guns and said, "we will show the damned red devils how to fight." He summarily sent Sarah and Natches away. Still fearful that an attack resulting in the deaths of white men might bring a campaign of extermination against the Indians, Natches decided to station ten young men at the river crossing with orders to stop any Indians bent on revenge. He instructed them to use deadly force if necessary.[3]

That night, at the hour when the power of darkness speaks, a terrible dream came to Natches. He rose at midnight and called the people together. Then he told of the dream that showed him how Nugent's would-be killers had instead attacked white men in Coffman's Station at Deep Wells on the Idaho Road. "I see only one dead; one is not dead, but he will die. I see a great many horses taken by them." Natches then rode into the darkness with thirty men in an attempt to head off the attackers.[4]

He had scarcely departed when an alarm sounded. Sarah sprang onto her horse and rode bareback to meet an approaching horseman. "We shall all die this very day," he told her and confirmed that there was much truth in Natches's dream: brothers of the murdered Indian had attacked Coffman's Station and mortally wounded a white man. A second messenger arrived and he also confirmed Natches's dream. Meanwhile, Nugent decided to call upon the army, a weapon agents often used against Indians who disagreed with them. Aside from the

U.S. marshal, the army provided the only method of enforcement on the federal lands of the reservations. Reports of several violent incidents involving Indians had already brought soldiers on detached service from Camp McDermit to quell the unrest at Pyramid. This time, however, events did not unroll as Nugent intended. Even though he of course neglected to mention the matter of the gunpowder transaction and the murdered Paiute that had instigated the attack on Coffman's Station, the officers declined to follow his script. Instead, they decided to investigate the Indian side of the matter before taking action.[5]

Late the next night two Indians brought a message for Sarah. She puzzled so long over the penmanship that the other Indians began to doubt that she really knew how to read ("I was very poor, indeed, at reading writing; and I assure you, my dear readers, I am not much better now"), but eventually she deciphered it. As best she could recall, the message signed by Lt. Aaron Jerome read: "Miss Sarah Winnemucca, — your agent tells us very bad things about your people's killing two of our men. I want you and your brother Natchez to meet me at your place to-night. I want to talk to you and your brother." When she told the Paiutes who gathered around her the purport of the message, they asked her to "speak on paper" to the soldiers.[6]

Sarah protested, "I have nothing to write with. I have no ink. I have no pen."

This aroused derision. "Oh, take a stick — take anything. Until you talk on that paper we will not believe you can talk on paper."

Thus challenged, Sarah called for a sharp pointed stick and fish blood with which to write an answer agreeing to the meeting. The result may not have met the high standards of penmanship that drew favorable comment from those who saw Sarah's letters, but it was evidently legible. Soon after the messenger rode back to Lieutenant Jerome, Natches came in. On hearing the news, he called for fresh horses, and Sarah and he rode off with an escort of twenty warriors. ("We went like the wind, never stopping until we got there.")[7]

Jerome and Nugent were waiting for them. As soon as Sarah dismounted, she poured out the whole story of Nugent's nefarious deed. Sarah's passionate words and flashing black eyes silenced Nugent as completely as though she had transfixed him with a Paiute bone spear. Jerome, clearly convinced, briefly questioned Natches about the stolen horses. Sarah and Natches agreed to meet with the officer again the next day and returned to reassure their people that the soldiers would take no reprisals against them. At the next meeting, this time at the Indian encampment, Jerome offered the Paiutes army protection. Seeing obvious signs of starvation among the Indians, he asked them what provisions they had. They told him that they had "nothing just then, but we hoped the fish would soon run up the river so that we might catch some." The compassionate lieutenant obtained three wagons of provisions for them from Fort Churchill. Sarah was overjoyed: "Oh, how glad we were, for we were very poorly off for want of something to eat. That was the first provision I had ever seen issued to my people!" When Nugent then offered to sell the army some beef for the Indians, Jerome curtly told him to "be off."[8]

Shortly afterward Jerome summoned Sarah and Natches to tell them he had received a message from his commanding officer inquiring as to the whereabouts of Winnemucca. Usually Sarah's anger propelled her as surely as the west wind blew, but at this moment the sorrows she had endured overwhelmed her and she dissolved in tears: "I told him father had not been in since the soldiers killed my little brother. I told him that he sent word to us that he had gone to live in the mountains, and to die there. I was crying all the while I was talking with him." This outburst from the usually strong and able Sarah frightened the Paiutes around them, and Natches had to explain.[9]

Jerome then urged Sarah and Natches to bring Winnemucca and his band into Camp McDermit on the northern Nevada border with Oregon, where the army would issue provisions to them. Sarah, too overcome for once to press her opinions, left the decision to Natches. He agreed that they would go to McDermit and try to persuade Winnemucca to join them. The other Indians feared for Winnemucca's safety: "Maybe they will kill him. You and your sister know what liars the white people are, and if you go and get him and he is killed by the soldiers, his blood will be on you."[10]

Good reasons underlaid these fears, since hatred of the chief still burned brightly in some quarters. The *Winnemucca Argent* expressed no regrets over a report of the "treacherous old rascal's" death (which proved false). In 1867, during one of Winnemucca's occasional visits to Susanville, a lynch mob formed to hang him. He was saved by the daughter of former Territorial Provisional Governor Isaac Roop, a diminutive but determined young woman named Susan, who hid Winnemucca in a bedroom and, with a gun in her hand, ordered the leader of the lynch mob away from her door.[11]

Although Natches knew the dangers facing his father, Jerome had gained his confidence. He told the others: "Because white people are bad that is no reason why the soldiers should be bad too." By refusing to call the soldiers white people, Natches paid them a high compliment; "white man" (*taibo*) had become a term of opprobrium among the Indians. Sarah and Natches set off with the army detachment on a twenty-eight-day journey to Camp McDermit, a trip long enough for Jerome to have had time to scout along the way for roaming bands of Indians.[12]

Jerome's effort to bring Winnemucca and his followers into Camp McDermit was part of a larger campaign waged by the army in which the warfare in the Black Rock Desert had constituted the southern theater of operations. Eastern Oregon and western Idaho were the homeland of the Bannocks, a Paiute-speaking people similar to the Paiutes but more warlike. Buffalo Brush (often called Paulina), one of the famous Bannock chiefs of the period, broke out from the Klamath Reservation in 1866 and embarked upon raids that spread terror through the sparsely settled region. Far from railroads and major travel routes, the arid landscape of eastern Oregon remained relatively empty of white settlement, and some Paiutes, driven north by the loss of their homelands to white ranchers and the cruelties of the reservation system, found refuge there and joined the Bannocks to form hostile, nomadic bands.[13]

In 1866 the army dispatched the brilliant commander Gen. George Crook to subdue these bands and place them at Camp McDermit and several other army posts pending their permanent settlement on reservations. General Crook came, saw, and liked very little of what he beheld: he found the whole region "in a state of siege" with hostile Indians "dealing death and destruction everywhere," he believed that "bad men from the south, refugees, deserters, etc. — all against the government" had infested the country, and the army officers stationed there impressed him as dissipated and ineffectual. No doubt the fierce stare beneath winged eyebrows that were reminiscent of a Mongol warrior grew fiercer as Crook speedily took matters in hand — marching through blizzards, besting the Indians at the Battle of the Infernal Caverns, and finally sitting down with Chief Weawea and others to make a wise peace.[14]

A. B. Meacham, who was present at the council in early July 1868, relates that the assembled chiefs refused to make decisions without Winnemucca, which delayed the proceedings for sixteen days. When Winnemucca finally arrived, Crook granted his request to live outside the reservations, despite the circumstance that government policy at the time mandated settling the Indians on reservations — or else. Winnemucca reciprocated by renewing his promise not to join the Bannocks in hostilities. These two leaders may have reached a meeting of minds rather easily, for Crook believed the reservation system engendered idleness and mischief among the Indians. Since most of the chiefs shared Winnemucca's unwillingness to live on the distant Klamath Reservation, Crook agreed that the bands represented at the council might pursue a nomadic life in their homeland, provided they surrendered and committed themselves to peace. Instead of stealing from the settlers in times of hardship, they should request emergency rations from the army, and in the event of trouble with the settlers, they should seek protection at the army posts. After the council, Winnemucca always wore an army jacket that he said Crook had given to him.[15]

By the time Sarah and Natches reached McDermit, Crook had

Camp McDermit. Courtesy of the Nevada Historical Society.

largely completed his mission, although mopping up operations continued for some time. The camp had been erected in the broad, flat Quinn River Valley near the mouth of the canyon where the southern branch of the river flows from the Santa Rosa Mountains in northern Humboldt County near the Oregon border. The plan was standard for army posts of the period: a rectangular parade ground with officers' quarters — one of adobe and two of stone — on one side and on the side nearer the river, stone quarters with earthen floors for the men. The efforts of various officers to beautify the northern sagebrush desert with trees, shrubs, and a garden met with scant success. Beside the fort lay an encampment of Quinn River Indians, housed at first in traditional *kahnees* and later in tents issued to them by the army.[16]

Although Camp McDermit had its beauties, when rosy light illuminated the sculptured mesas in the distance, those stationed there found it "joyless and lonesome" and a "colorless, forbidding sort of place," in the words of Martha Summerhayes, an officer's wife. Feeling herself condemned to life in a primitive place beyond the edge of the civilized world and initially deprived of the company of other women (she did not, of course, count Indian women), Summerhayes soon sank into depression. The absence of bird song, insect hum, or animal sound, except when the howl of a coyote joined the sentry's night call of "all's well," created a well of silence that seemed oppressive to those unused to it. But to the Indians, Camp McDermit offered a sanctuary beyond the petty tyrannies of reservation agents. The army issued rations to them that supplemented their usual hunting and gathering, and they peddled game and wild edibles or worked as servants to the soldiers ("All the work we do is only child's play. We would do more if they would only ask us to").[17]

The Quinn River Paiutes already encamped beside McDermit greeted Natches and Sarah warmly and spread robes on the ground for them to sit on. They said "many beautiful things" about the kind treatment they had received at the camp. It was agreed that five people would accompany Natches to tell Winnemucca about life at McDermit. The old men told Sarah they could understand Winnemucca's bitterness over the Mud Lake massacre and other wrongs he had endured at the hands of white people. The *taibo* seemed to enjoy their suffering, and "we have to stand it like a little mouse under a cat's paws." Once these old men had been masters of their own fates, smoking in council as they made decisions for their people, and providers to their families, drawing power from the bear and killing the charmed antelope. Now they could hope for nothing more than sanctuary from the guns of white men who shot them like coyotes, and kindness from "our soldier fathers."[18]

Sarah's first important mission at Camp McDermit occurred when the army decided to abandon Camp Smith and move the Paiutes subsisting there to McDermit. In the Oregon region on White Horse Creek, north of the Quinn River Mountains, these Indians, who had neither game nor arable land, faced starvation when army rations ended, and settlers pressured the army to remove them so they would not poach the stock. And stock raising was becoming big business in eastern Oregon, with an 1879 sale from a single rancher's herd reportedly totaling $650,000. Lt. Col. James N. McElroy, commander at McDermit, asked Sarah how many companies of soldiers would be needed to escort the Paiutes to the post. "I told him none," Sarah recalled. Although McElroy found this difficult to believe, Sarah eventually convinced him, and a small party consisting of the lieutenant colonel, his servant, Sarah, and her half-brother Lee Winnemucca rode north. Twenty years older than she, Lee was probably the son of one of Winnemucca's more senior wives.[19]

At Camp Smith, Sarah and Lee sat up all night talking in council with their people without McElroy's participation. It was unusual for a woman to take a leading role, instead of voicing her opinions from the outer circle when the chief and the elders sat and smoked in council. Apart from this break with tradition, the council at Camp Smith was conducted in the old way, with the leader as the "talker" who persuaded until voluntary agreement was reached. As Sarah put it, "We Indians never try to rule our people without explaining everything to them." After McElroy furnished wagons for the children at Sarah's request, the evacuation was accomplished in two days. The Indian encampment at Camp McDermit grew larger.[20]

The commanding officer expressed concern that pressure from the militant white settlers would compel Crook to battle any Indians he encountered outside the forts and reservations. Thus he strongly urged Sarah and Natches to persuade Winnemucca to come into the camp. He offered provisions, clothing, and protection to Winnemucca and his band. Natches finally agreed: "If you will give me your heart and hand, I will go and try to get my father to come to you." He nonetheless declined the offer of a cavalry escort because if Winnemucca saw soldiers he might believe they came with hostile intentions. Instead, Natches would travel alone, bearing a letter (another rag friend) that explained his mission to any white man he encountered and making "the son's signal fire" as he approached his father. Although their meeting may have been delayed by difficulties in locating the elusive old chief, Winnemucca finally rode into Camp McDermit with a small band of companions. Some evidence suggests that his arrival did not occur soon after Sarah's own, as she remembered, but in February 1869.[21]

Before long, Winnemucca resumed his nomadic ways, but those who later reminisced about their service at Camp McDermit remembered him vividly. He often visited them, sometimes to converse in his broken English, occasionally aided by Sarah's fluent translation. Martha Summerhayes found his garb a "curious mixture of civilization and savagery." In addition to the army coat presented to him by Crook, he wore an army officer's hat, a ring in his nose, a medal given him by Gen. Oliver O. Howard, a buckskin shirt, leggings, and moccasins. He tied his long black braids with strips of red flannel. Dr. George Kober, a young German-born physician at Camp McDermit, would write about Winnemucca's "magnificent physique" and "noble carriage."[22]

Winnemucca was curious about *taibo*'s mysterious ways. While one army wife was writing a letter, she became aware that Winnemucca had been standing close behind her for some time, watching in complete silence. On occasion, when something puzzled him, he would pursue an inquiry for several days until he was satisfied. He had a good sense of humor and impressed those who knew him as dignified, courteous, and sensitive. When the child of one of the army officers died, Winnemucca expressed his condolences as soon as he heard the news. The old chief knew how it felt to lose a child, ever since his infant son was cast into the flames of the burning Indian camp.[23]

Much of Winnemucca's conversation with his white friends reveals a philosophical quest to understand *taibo*'s beliefs and to reconcile them with his own traditions. He often mentioned to Martha Summerhayes that General Howard told him good Indians would ascend to heaven. He may have interpreted this as an assurance that even if *taibo* proved right about the afterlife, Indians would still reach the Spirit Land. With Sarah translating, he engaged in long discussions with Kober, who thought him "not only a great chief, but also a

Chief Winnemucca in 1880. Courtesy of
the National Archives.

philosopher, a man with a soul, who thirsted for knowledge regarding
the life beyond." Winnemucca and Sarah told the doctor some of the
Paiute history about early white contacts and the battle between the
Paiutes and the red-haired cannibals that Sarah later recounted in
her book.[24]

But Winnemucca also had questions that Kober found "by no
means easy to answer." He wondered what evidence white people had

on life after death. He wanted to know why God allowed such hardships to fall upon Indians that their very existence was jeopardized. He had come to believe that Indians were a vanishing race and that "nothing short of a miracle could save them from complete extermination." When they finished talking, Winnemucca courteously thanked the doctor for his kind words and expressed the hope that the Indian and *taibo* would go to separate heavens. God had "mixed them up on this earth, and white man got everything and Indian man got nothing." How much Winnemucca valued his talks with Dr. Kober was shown at his death when he left his gold ring to the doctor.[25] No evidence suggests that Sarah shared her father's spiritual concerns. Perhaps that was the way of the world: the old searched for truth while the young fought for justice. Some, like the angry men, fought with guns while others, like Sarah, fought with words.

At the same time, Winnemucca remained, as Kober phrased it, "most solicitous about the future of his people." With eloquent oratory, he made frequent appeals for aid to the Paiutes, which kept the army rations coming, at least most of the time. Yet the possibility that his people would sink into listless dependency as wards of the government clearly troubled him. To receive rations while doing nothing seemed to him an imposition. The women should gather roots and seeds in the old way, he told them in council. He sought and received permission for the men to hunt game with ammunition supplied by the army. This agreement rested on the mutual trust that Winnemucca had established, as well as on a disregard for legal niceties. The army officers appear to have had no misgivings about how the Paiutes would use their firepower.[26]

The emergence of "one Indian interpretress" in Camp McDermit post returns in December 1869 reveals that Sarah was working in her first paid position for the U.S. government — and in a position of no small importance. Since colonial times, interpreters had played a crucial role in Indian-white relations, exercising functions that often extended beyond translation into diplomacy. The effective interpreter needed not only linguistic facility but also an understanding of the cultures of both peoples, a requirement Sarah was admirably fitted to fulfill. As she noted, trouble often resulted when Indian interpreters had an imperfect grasp of English or a lack of scruples about misrepresenting a document at an agent's behest ("I know this, for some of them are my relatives"). Sarah's difficulties would be of a different character. She would rage at the injustices she saw, storm into conflict with powerful men regardless of the consequences, and, finally, lose the confidence of Indians who blamed the messenger for white men's unkept promises. But Sarah had learned her lessons in the Ormsby household well. Never would she misunderstand.[27]

One minor incident in June 1870, which might have riffled the smooth relationship between the Paiutes (no longer technically "prisoners of war") and the army, worried Sarah. One night someone stole the herd of cattle maintained as a beef supply for the camp. Intensive search by the soldiers failed to locate the herd. "At last," related Sarah, "the commanding officer thought the Indians, who knew how to track a trail, would do better at such business than white men, who do not know how to find a trail of anything." Lee Winnemucca and five other Indians volunteered. After following the trail for two days, they found the herd hidden in a deep canyon. Soldiers then accompanied the Indians to arrest the thief and help drive the herd back to the camp. Sarah felt greatly relieved because she had feared that if the herd was not recovered the theft would be blamed on Indians.[28]

In the spring of 1870 Sarah sent her first letter pleading the cause of the Paiutes. Although she wrote at the request of the Camp McDermit commander with the immediate purpose of providing information about her people to Maj. Henry Douglas, the superintendent of Indian Affairs for Nevada, she succeeded in educating a broader public, for several newspapers also printed her letter. It impressed Douglas so much that he forwarded it to the commissioner of Indian Affairs in Washington, acknowledging that he found her criticism of past practice at the Nevada reservations "appropriate and just." The letter won recognition as a classic statement of the Indian plight. *Harper's* magazine reprinted it, and Helen Hunt Jackson included it in her powerful and popular polemic *A Century of Dishonor*, published in 1881.[29]

As usual, Sarah blasted the Pyramid Lake Reservation agents, who provided neither rations nor instruction in agriculture: "If we had stayed there, it would be only to starve." She went on, "If this is the kind of civilization awaiting us on the reserves, God grant that we may never be compelled to go on one, as it is much preferable to live in the mountains and drag out an existence in our native manner." She acknowledged that the Indians at military posts received good treatment, but the future troubled her: "How long is this to continue? What is the object of the government in regard to Indians? Is it enough that we are at peace? Remove all the Indians from the military posts and place them on reservations such as the Truckee and Walker River Reservations (as they were conducted) and it will require a greater military force stationed round to keep them within the limits than it now does to keep them in subjugation." She called for a guaranteed permanent home for the Indians on their "own native soil," education, and protection from white encroachments, ever a serious problem at Pyramid.[30]

The celebrity Sarah received from newspaper coverage of her letter and the *Harper's* reprint, along with an article that praised her sagacity, might have aroused local pride. Instead, it stirred a disposition to put "*our* Sally" in her place. The *Humboldt Register* printed her letter, and expressed doubt that she could have written it herself. Shortly thereafter, the *Humboldt Register* reprinted a vicious burlesque from the *Boise City News* that demonstrated the racism that Sarah so often faced:

We made a slather at Miss Sarah's age by the number of scales of greasy dirt which naturally accumulated on the ridge of her comely countenance during the lapse of years. She was about four or five feet high — how is that for "Lo?" — and not quite as broad as she was narrow. Her raven tresses, which had been permitted to coy with the sportive breeze, unbound, unwashed and uncombed, from her earliest childhood, stood out in elegant and awry confusion from her classically shaped cabesa, *which contributed to her contour an air of romantic splendor. Her style of dress, though primitive, closely assimilated that worn by her more fashionable sisters in Paris and other big towns. It was the fashion of the day, slightly exaggerated, consisting of an elegant scarf about a foot wide, cut from an ancient horse blanket, which was gracefully girded round her delicate waist, the circumference of which, owing to the scarcity of clover and fresh crickets at that season, had materially diminished, over which hung a beautiful set of skeleton hoops. . . . Her feet were encased in moccasins, and showed evident indications of hard service and long walks over the rocky hills and sagebrush plains, the mud of her native heath, crisp and dry, clinging tenaciously to her toes.*[31]

It is likely that Sarah never saw this baleful mockery. If she had, she might have challenged the editor to a duel and landed in court — as she did on a future occasion.

As Sarah increasingly became the voice of the Paiutes in the white world, she carried on her father's traditions of eloquence and solicitude for his people. In August 1870 she wrote to the commissioner of Indian Affairs urging that Camp McDermit not be abandoned. Evidently assuming white authorities felt little concern for the welfare of the Indians, she turned to arguments that she thought might carry more weight — the safety of the settlers and government expense. She suggested that the army presence prevented Indian violence and provided the Indians with supplies they would never receive on the reservations from "*dishonest officials.*" She warned that if the Indians were forced onto reservations they would "commence a series of depredations" upon the settlers and that the expenses of restoring order would far exceed the cost of maintaining Camp McDermit. However cogent her logic, Sarah failed to understand that in the turf war then in progress between the army and the Interior Department any argument to the commissioner on behalf of the army would hardly receive a favorable reception.[32]

Regardless of the wishes of the Indians, Washington attempted to prod them into the reservations through a series of conferences. At one of these at Camp McDermit in May 1870 between fifty Indian men and Major Douglas, Sarah and Natches served as interpreters. Winnemucca was notable by his absence; his vow after the Mud Lake massacre never to return to the Pyramid Reservation to live left nothing to discuss. Although Douglas told the Indians that Camp McDermit would definitely be abandoned, the Indians refused to agree to probable starvation on the reservations. They felt that their chances for survival were far better in their homeland, even if they were reduced to eating grass and ants after army rations ceased ("I won't starve. Lived here before whites came and don't care"). Said one Quinn River Paiute: "I will stay here and lay my bones here with my dead children." If Sarah was the one who spoke for him, we can be sure his words lost nothing in translation. Sarah also used the occasion to passionately protest the unpunished murders of five Indians by settlers during the previous two years: "White men kill Indians and all right — nothing is done with them, they are not hanged or hurt at all. Not so with Indians — they kill white man and they are killed right off." As the commander of the Pacific Division's report for 1870–71 shows, she in no way overstated the crisis.[33]

In 1871, a drought year when Indian food sources dwindled still further, the Paiutes sent Sarah to San Francisco to plead with the army commander of the Pacific Division for more provisions. She described the desperate condition of the Indians at Pyramid and the lack of help from Indian agents: "We would all much rather be slain and put out of our misery than to be lingering here — each day bringing new sorrows — and finally die of hunger and starvation. We know full well that the Government has been, and is still willing to provide us with all we need, but I must inform you that it never gets past these Agents hands, but they reap all the benefit while we have all the suffering." She certainly convinced the army officers, as shown by Gen. John M. Schofield's endorsement of her plea and some increase in provisions for the Paiutes. Nonetheless, as author Jack Forbes observes, her burning criticism earned her the hostility of the Office of Indian Affairs.[34]

Despite her concern over the uncertain future of the Paiutes, the years at Camp McDermit may have been among the happiest of Sarah's life. She was a young woman in her prime enjoying the admiration accorded to her as belle of the ball. In the purple prose of one newspaper writer: "They who had unflinchingly withstood the onset of the fiercest redskins now fell helpless victims to the charms and witcheries of the proud native beauty. Figuratively speaking, the hearts of most of the young commissioned and non-commissioned officers at the camp soon dangled like so many bleeding scalps at her belt."[35]

Fanny Corbusier, an army surgeon's wife at the post, observed, "She was fully aware of her charms and lost no opportunity to display them." Sarah rode sidesaddle on a fine horse and wore a black velvet waist and skirt, a large, black hat with red plumes, and gauntlet gloves. When Sarah, mounted on her horse, came dashing into the post with red streamers from her hat and wrist flying in the wind, her appearance was "always very dramatic and spectacular." Usually Sarah gave these exhibitions right after dress parade: "With a flourish which I have never seen duplicated in any show, she would gallop across the parade ground — supple, but erect and in perfect balance — her quirt hand lifted in a queenly salute. Between the barracks and across the parade ground again, and she would be gone amid the lusty cheers of the men. Or, on occasion she would dismount just long enough to receive their plaudits — be remounted by some gallant soldier, and be off."[36] Perhaps the man who cheered the loudest and doffed his hat the highest was one Lt. Edward Bartlett.

Although she courted male attention, Sarah feared rape. Upon her arrival at Camp McDermit, she decided that she would be safest living with the Quinn River Indians, and the commander acceded to her request to have the Indian camp placed off limits to both soldiers and settlers. Molesting Indian women was a widely acknowledged problem at the military installations, and Paiute women had been particular targets since the early settlement period, when a newspaper article noted that they could not go out to gather food "without some

of those beasts in human shape dogging their steps for lewd purposes."[37] The recollection of what had happened to her sister Mary on
the San Joaquin remained forever seared in Sarah's memory.

Nonetheless, Sarah apparently felt confident enough in her ability
to defend herself with her knife to indulge in a good deal of gambling,
drinking, and carousing with the soldiers. Winnemucca heartily disapproved, remarking at one point to Fanny that he considered his
daughter "no good." A famous gambler himself, known to have gambled away all he possessed down to his breech clout on occasion, Winnemucca could hardly condemn the gambling. Indeed, gambling was
an amusement for both men and women thoroughly embedded in
Paiute tradition. Success in gambling, even with a vision of "winning
the whole world," sometimes became the legitimate object of a Paiute
power quest. The stick game, in which opposing teams try to guess
who holds the stick and wager on the results, had been played for centuries, and *taibo*'s card and dice games quickly gained favor.[38] It seems
more probable that Winnemucca opposed his daughter's evenings of
revelry with white men. If he knew of her growing fondness for Edward Bartlett, he may have felt that the lieutenant's propensity for
hard drinking would fuel one of his daughter's unfortunate weak-
nesses.

One of Sarah's more innocent amusements was Paiute football. She
played this game with the other Indian women on the parade ground
before a large audience, both white and Indian. Noted Fanny Corbusier: "The score seemed to be determined by the number of times each
side had, or touched the ball during the mad scramble between the
points or goals. Every one was screaming at the top of their lungs and
the game ended when no one had any voice left — or so it seemed to
me." In the Paiute way, wagers were laid on the outcome.[39]

A curious piece of fiction about this period (though not published
until ten years later in the *Youth's Companion*) reveals how Sarah had
captured the imaginations of those at Camp McDermit. Although author E. E. Hamilton declares at the outset that his story is "strictly
true," this seems highly doubtful. The hero of the piece is the com-

mander Capt. Henry Wagner, who, in real life, was a stern, dark-bearded, German-born Civil War veteran who had seen service in many major battles. In a strange reprise of the Wahe-Wasson affair, Wagner strides alone into the Indian camp at moonrise and courageously foils a plot to massacre the garrison, proclaim Sarah queen, and commence a war of extermination against the whites. The villains are, of course, the Indians and "Lieutenant Nemo," who, "carried away by his infatuation for the Indian girl, agreed to join the savages." Nemo meekly surrenders his sword to Wagner and the rebellion collapses "by the quick wit and wonderful nerve of a single man."[40] Some years later when a reporter related this fanciful tale to Sarah — apparently the first time she had heard it — she burst out laughing and said, "That's a dreadful story!" The shred of fact that apparently inspired the author was the disturbance when Bartlett (aka Nemo) fired blanks from a howitzer into the Indian camp while drunk. One wonders if elements of truth may nonetheless have surfaced in some details. The author writes that "with all the arts of her wily nature" Sarah ensnared the lieutenant's affection and that he declared his intention of marrying her. On hearing this, Captain Wagner "argued against this strange mesalliance" — as he may have done. This teller of tales surely erred on Sarah's wily nature; she was, if anything, too frank and straightforward, too much inclined to damn the torpedoes and sail straight ahead. But he accurately recorded the usual impression of Sarah when he wrote that she "possessed wonderful beauty and a fine mind."[41]

Sarah relates that in 1871 conflict with Wagner lost her the position as Camp McDermit interpreter. Others also found Wagner difficult to get along with. Fanny Corbusier observed that the commander "seemed to enjoy objecting to everything on general principles." His objections to Edward's proposed marriage to an Indian woman may have been particularly severe and the cause of his sharpened conflict with Sarah. Although she acknowledged her bad luck at gambling and she suffered a considerable loss in the autumn of 1870 when her dwelling was robbed and burned and her horse and saddle stolen,

Sarah had other ways of making a living. She sewed and sold buck-skin gloves and fur-trimmed overcoats and worked as a matron in the McDermit hospital. Nor was the "Paiute Princess" too proud to take up the job by which many Indian women earned a living — laundress.[42]

When Sarah and Edward asked a Catholic priest at McDermit to marry them, he refused on the ground that the union would be illegal under Nevada's miscegenation laws. This setback failed to deter them, nor did an unsuccessful attempt to secure a Nevada marriage license. The intended groom was then a very young man, twenty-two to Sa-rah's twenty-seven, tall and dashing, with blue eyes, dark brown hair, olive skin, and a tattoo of a woman on his arm, which may have sur-prised Sarah. Appointed to a lieutenancy at age nineteen, he quickly turned into the black sheep of a distinguished military family: his fa-ther was a professor at West Point; two brothers were well on their way to becoming high-ranking military officers; and his sister was married to Gen. John Schofield. Kober called him a "flighty young man," a kindly description for one who apparently conceived the idea of marrying the Indian princess as an amusing escapade.[43]

Shortly after receiving his promotion from second to first lieuten-ant, Edward narrowly missed disgrace for defrauding the govern-ment in collusion with contractors. His military records suggest that only his father's influence saved him from court martial ("My dear General, My unfortunate boy is again in trouble"). He was allowed to resign from the army in November 1871. None of these developments marred his reckless charm in Sarah's eyes. She braved the unyielding disapproval of her father, and the couple eloped to Salt Lake City to be married by a justice of the peace on 29 January 1872.[44]

Predictably, the wedding brought ridicule from the press: "It will be remembered that about two months ago Miss Sallie and a young Lieut. who has since become her liege lord applied in this county for a marriage license. They were informed by the Clerk that the people of Nevada, entertaining such an exalted opinion of the noble red man, with his manifold virtues, and desiring to protect poor Lo and his race, from the evils of miscegenation, had solemnly prohibited such marriages by law, and he must therefore, refuse the license."[45] Although Sarah's growing prominence brought her attention and often admiration, it also bred a disposition to cut the Paiute princess down to size because she was Indian.

Unfortunately, those who had opposed their union proved right. Within three weeks the faithful Natches was in Salt Lake City insisting that Sarah must return with him to her people, though she could not hope to win her father's forgiveness. Sarah obeyed. Although she gave the impression that her family had ended the marriage, a woman so forceful as Sarah probably would have resisted unless she had grown disillusioned with Edward or he had already decamped. She later accused him of excessive drinking, repeatedly importuning her for money, selling her jewelry, and deserting her — if so, she was not the first Indian woman to be abandoned by a white man who considered their marriage a matter of temporary convenience. Nor do her other charges ring false. During his brief service on the plains, Edward had been arrested for drunkenness and bad debts, among other charges. "His example would ruin the best company in the service," observed his commanding officer. It is likely that family influence had gained him a posting to Camp McDermit instead of a cell in the brig.[46]

We do not hear Edward's side of it, but we may surmise that when the charming rider in black velvet turned into a woman with strong opinions who was on her way to becoming a crusader, he became equally disillusioned. He may also have found it more painful than he had anticipated to be repudiated as a "squaw man," apparently a matter of some gossip among the military. Sarah may have hoped for a reconciliation, and only after the passing of several years and the arrival of a new love did she finally divorce him.[47]

An unsettled period ensued for Sarah. As she told a reporter, "I have really no particular home, but spend most of my time in Winnemucca." In June 1872, Indians from far and wide — Sarah among them — convened for a large fandango by the Humboldt River. Apparently, old Winnemucca was not alone in condemning Sarah's fondness for revelry. When another Paiute woman cast aspersions on her virtue, Sarah went after her tooth and nail. The scratching, biting, hair-pulling brawl ended with Sarah bouncing triumphantly on top of the woman. With each bounce, she gave the fallen enemy another swat in the face and exclaimed, "There, talk so about me to white folks, will you!" An insult to Sarah's reputation invariably received an instant — and often violently physical — response.[48]

Only two weeks later, Sarah again figured in what a *Humboldt Register* headline called "A BLOODY COMBAT," this time more probably in defense of her flesh than her reputation. The incident occurred in the dining room of a Winnemucca hotel, the Travelers Home, empty except for Sarah and the waiter with whom she fought. She gave him a black eye; he gave her a bleeding split lip. Determined that this time justice would be done for an Indian by the white man's law, Sarah went forth to swear out a warrant for his arrest, but before she could do so, she began to tremble with spasms and sank into a coma. The *Humboldt Register* speculated on several possible causes — among them the suspicion that she had been drugged — but it seems likely that Sarah had received injuries less visible than the bleeding lip. The Paiutes carried her away to their camp to care for her, but the settlers, having no faith in the shaman's chants and charms, fetched her back to the Frenchman's Hotel to be nursed in what they believed was the proper way. After two days of terrible stillness, during which her survival seemed improbable, she recovered to become once more her usual vibrant self.[49]

While Sarah was visiting in Reno in February 1873, a reporter from the *Nevada State Journal* sought an extensive interview with her, which appeared under the headline "THE PIUTE PRINCESS." For once, the reporter's approach showed genuine respect: "The high position you hold among the lodges of the Piutes, and the active interest you have taken in Indian affairs, have from time to time brought you into enviable notoriety, and a further knowledge would no doubt interest a great many." Sarah obliged with a history of herself and her people and spoke frankly about her father's anger over her marriage to Edward. Nor did she neglect this opportunity to vent her spleen against the Indian agents as "too anxious to keep the people down, or from doing anything to help themselves, for should my people raise their own provisions his place would be worth but little." Promised farming implements never arrived, and the agent at Pyramid rented out the reservation to stockmen, pocketing the fees for himself instead of using them for the benefit of the Indians.[50]

Much of the interview centered on Winnemucca's current activities, a matter that called for a good deal of explanation just then. According to the *Idaho Statesman*, Sarah's father had incited the Bannocks to rob and murder during the preceding summer. Winnemucca had reportedly turned to the Ghost Dance religion, sending runners to the various tribes to tell of his prophecy that one day Indian warriors would rise from their graves and collect on the plain in a powerful army that would wipe out the white men. When settlers around Steens Mountain began preparing for war that fall, Winnemucca repeatedly went to their camp to declare his determination to keep the peace, but the settlers refused to believe him.[51]

War came instead in the "land of burnt out fires," the lava beds near Tule Lake, Oregon, where a handful of Modoc warriors succeeded in holding the U.S. army at bay for months, and the battle continued to rage at the time of Sarah's interview. Questioned about her father's disappearance from his usual haunts, Sarah appeared to give some credence to the rumor that he had gone to join the Modocs: "I cannot say that I know my father and his braves have gone to the Modocs, but that seems to be the general impression among us." She spoke of the "bitter feeling" among her people over the alleged murder of a Paiute in Oregon and Winnemucca's call for the "best young men" to join him in looking into the matter.[52]

The reporter inquired whether Sarah could use her influence to prevent the Paiutes from making common cause with the Modocs. Sarah demurred. She explained that when the Paiutes believed themselves insulted "they seem to lose all reason." She said that she had tried to play the peacemaker, warning her people of the army's superior firepower and attempting to convince them of the "utter foolishness" of another war. Although she appeared doubtful that her words had much effect, she may have been more successful than she knew. Neither her father nor any other Paiutes joined the Modocs. Indeed the Modoc War remains chiefly notable in the annals of frontier conflict for the small number of Indians involved. Fifty Modoc warriors successfully fought an overwhelming number of soldiers. When the army finally subdued them after several months — through the treachery of captured Modocs — the victory cost the U.S. government an estimated ten thousand dollars per warrior (in 1873 dollars). Though she was too diplomatic to say so, Sarah secretly admired the Modoc resistance.[53]

The interview ended with praise for Sarah's "very attractive appearance," her grace, her sparkling black eyes, her black curls, her tasteful suit of black alpaca trimmed with green, and her "excellent conversational powers." The reporter expressed the hope that other Indians would follow her example to reach "a higher sphere of civilization" and concluded by writing, "an hour spent in her company cannot fail to be attended with pleasing remembrances."[54]

Such acclaim for an Indian woman could not pass without contradiction in Nevada in 1873. The next issue of *Reno Crescent*, a rival newspaper, pronounced Sarah's every word a falsehood and called her "a common Indian strumpet."[55]

7

Winnemucca

*"I would willingly throw off the garments
of civilization and mount my pony"*

THE YEAR 1874 began with one of the worst crises the Winnemuccas had yet endured: the arrest and imprisonment of Natches. Having heard that blankets would be issued by Indian Agent Ingalls at Walker Reservation, Paiutes living in the Humboldt region went to claim their share. Issuing supplies only at the reservations was one of several methods by which agents tried to induce the Paiutes to live there, a move that most continued to resist. Ingalls told them to collect their blankets at Pyramid Reservation from Agent Calvin Bateman, who declared that he had nothing to do with the matter and suggested that they appeal once more to Ingalls. Natches demanded an explanation on why the Paiutes should be "shuttlecocked" back and forth from one agent to another and receive nothing.[1]

Angry words passed between Natches and Bateman, but a larger matter concerned Natches far more than the agent's threats to have him sent away, never to return. After the Paiutes departed from Pyramid empty-handed, Natches went to the editor of the *Humboldt Register* to discuss a disturbing rumor. It was not possible, was it, that all his people were going to be taken away to the Fort Hall Reservation or the Indian Territory? In fact, the rumor had some foundation. Secretary of the Interior Columbus Delano had been obsessively at work upon a master plan to abolish the smaller reservations and consolidate all the western Indians in a single large reservation in the Indian Territory.[2] This was the Paiutes' worst nightmare: exile. Being torn away from the mountains of home to become strangers in a strange land. Well, they knew what had already happened to the Modocs.

While Natches worried, Bateman, one of the missionary agents whose presumed religious and moral character was supposed to distinguish him from less professionally Christian predecessors, busied himself at executing his revenge upon the Indian who had dared to argue with him. Years of public criticism from Natches's outspoken sister may have sharpened his enmity toward the Winnemuccas. First, he complained to General Schofield that Natches was inciting the Indians against him and urging them to leave the reservation. Next, he obtained a letter that accused Natches of causing unrest and requested that he be sent away. According to Sarah, Bateman had secured the "X" mark signatures of several Indians on the letter by misrepresenting it as a request to Washington for clothing. Schofield responded by sending an investigator sometimes critical of the Winnemuccas — Captain Wagner. That officer arrested Natches and took him to San Francisco, where the army imprisoned him at Alcatraz.[3] Sarah's uncharacteristic silence during this emergency suggests her absence.

This may have been the period of what a newspaper termed Sarah's "morganatic alliance" with Charles B. Hamilton, another of the handsome cads she loved unwisely but too well. Canadian-born, thirty-seven years old, dark-haired, gray-eyed, and well dressed, with "unmistakable marks of dissipation" on his face, Hamilton had worked as a deputy county assessor in Winnemucca, where Sarah probably met him. She reputedly lived with him for a while in Wyoming. Tax assessment was not, however, the only form that Hamilton's interest in other people's property assumed. A newspaper report from Reno in December 1875 charged that "through sharp practice and false pretenses he has succeeded in swindling a number of our citizens out of divers sums of money and decamped to parts unknown." By that time, Sarah had surely grown indifferent to his whereabouts and disinclined to ever acknowledge any connection with him.[4]

It must have disconcerted Bateman to see Natches emerge from prison with his standing enhanced at the agent's expense. White citizens in the Humboldt area sent a letter testifying to Natches's sterling character and urging his release — startling evidence of his support among settlers. The press heartily condemned Bateman's conduct. The *Humboldt Register*, for instance, commented sarcastically on the Reverend Bateman's "christian character" and suggested that he "bag his head and leave the country." When Schofield interviewed Natches after eleven days of imprisonment, only a few moments of conversation sufficed for the general to see who was in the right. Schofield ordered Natches immediately released, criticized Bateman severely, and declared his intention to report the agent to headquarters. When Natches returned to Winnemucca, Indians from near and far, including a band of Shoshones from Battle Mountain, gathered for a celebration.[5]

It may be that the broad support accorded to Natches emboldened him to instigate a novel undertaking. When he learned that Washington officials would be coming to Nevada to investigate the condition of the Indians, he decided that instead of passively allowing the nefarious Bateman to provide information about them, the Paiutes should take their own census and report upon their condition themselves. He visited every locality in the Nevada realm of the Paiutes and convinced each headman to make a careful count of every member of his band and determine how many lived on the Walker River and Pyramid Lake Reservations and received government assistance. Then, in August 1874, he convened a grand council at Winnemucca attended by some 500 Indians. The Indians' own census had been completed: 2,455 Paiutes in all, only 253 on reservations; the largest single group was the 950 Humboldt Paiutes led by Natches. If the agent's 1868 count of 4,200 was correct, this signifies a population decline of more than 40 percent, tragic evidence of the continuing ravages of disease, starvation, and loss of hope among the Paiutes.[6]

The chiefs, Buena Vista John of Winnemucca, Breckenridge of Stillwater, Johnson of Carson Sink, George Curry and Jim of Pyramid Reservation, George of Battle Mountain, Grass Valley Bob, Nick of Walker

Natches. Courtesy of the Nevada Historical Society.

River, and John of Big Meadows, among others, unanimously condemned Bateman for his corrupt administration of their affairs and his practice of allowing white men to forcibly take over Indian ranches on reservation lands. With one voice they declared that they would not be forced onto reservations and demanded to know why Indians should not be allowed to live where they pleased, as white men did. Whether Natches and the assembled chiefs obtained an interview with the visiting officials from the Office of Indian Affairs is not clear. That they had no effect on Indian policy is beyond dispute.[7]

The Paiutes were not ready to acknowledge defeat, however. Necessity had schooled them in patience and perseverance from an early age. Neither the hunter unwilling to trail the deer for days nor the woman disinclined to scour the desert sands for an edible root until the light grew dim get anything to eat. Instead of meekly accepting their fate, the Winnemuccas began preparing for the largest political effort they had undertaken, this time on several levels. They had learned a few things about *taibo* in the ten years that had passed since the public appeals and the theatrical appearances. Unlike the Paiute, *taibo* did not value generosity nor share his riches with the needy. Instead of hoping to awaken his beneficence, they would try to influence the decisions of his chiefs.

At the end of December, the Winnemuccas assembled with other Paiute leaders in the town of Winnemucca. Upon the arrival of Winnemucca from the North, the *Territorial Enterprise* opined that respect should be shown to the recognized leader of the tribe that once held sway over the lands of northwestern Nevada. Although Winnemucca had aged — he is estimated to have been eighty — and his clothing was ragged, his tall, proud carriage and his firm step impressed the reporter. Sarah arrived by train from Salt Lake City, where she had spent some time in the spring of 1873. (A fellow traveler reported her "almost talked to death by a lot of New York and London red-cravat gentry," possibly fascinated by the novelty of meeting a real live Indian.) Her 1874 return may have signaled the end of her purported affair with Hamilton in Wyoming. When she stepped off the westbound train in Winnemucca, she embraced her father warmly, but he responded with cold indifference — perhaps a sign that he had not yet forgiven her marriage to Edward, and her liaison with Hamilton had only increased his disapproval.[8]

As a first step, Sarah, Natches, and their brother Tom took Winnemucca to San Francisco for an interview with Schofield. The general had requested this conference, and the younger Winnemuccas undoubtedly believed their father's prestige would give added weight to their plea. The Paiute delegation made two requests of Schofield. The first was not to abandon Camp McDermit. Winnemucca argued that without the shield of the military at Camp McDermit the settlers would not permit Indian rabbit hunts because they frightened the cattle. Rather than starve, the Indians would be forced to forage from the settlers; this would result in war. Schofield apparently gave this veiled threat little credence and forbore from mentioning that because the Paiutes had been at peace for some years, government economizing dictated the closure of McDermit. That might have sounded too much like an incentive for warfare. Secondly, the Winnemuccas sought relief for the poverty-stricken condition of the Paiutes through farming implements, seed grain, and an instructor to show them how to farm. The general, while sympathetic, suggested a meeting with Sen. John P. Jones and referred them to their Indian agent. The Winnemuccas vainly protested that experience had shown the agents would provide no help.[9]

Detesting the bustle and noise of the city and unable to sleep outdoors on his blanket in the way he preferred, Winnemucca returned to Nevada as expeditiously as possible. Sarah and Natches followed more slowly. Sarah had become such a well-known figure that when they paused in Sacramento for a few days many people recognized her as she walked past them in the street. She willingly spoke of the Paiute cause to a reporter from the *Sacramento Record*, but the reporter appeared more interested in Sarah herself. He admired her speech ("she made use of the very best English, clothing her thoughts in words pure, expressive and classical") and her good looks ("the handsome, well formed, intelligent looking petite young lady with dark flowing hair, Spanish eyes and complexion").[10]

Although their appeal to higher authority in the army had produced no results, the Winnemuccas next turned to Nevada politicians. They journeyed to Carson City, where Sarah tried to drum up public support for their cause and sought an opportunity to testify before the legislature. She was disappointed that the interview she granted to a *Virginia Chronicle* reporter never appeared in the newspaper, but the *Carson Appeal* ran an article advocating the continuation of Camp McDermit and urging the legislature to give Sarah a "full and respectful hearing."[11]

McDermit provided an issue on which settlers and Indians could agree, even though land ownership divided them. Western frontiersmen strongly believed that the land over which these barbarous nomads roamed, without establishing ranches, towns, or industries, was theirs for the taking. Moreover, they saw developing it for the ultimate benefit of the nation (and themselves) as a patriotic duty. Cultural issues also divided Indians and whites. The more racist settlers dismissed the Indians as a nuisance at best and a menace to be exterminated at worst, and even the more enlightened could not conceive of the Indians they encountered (often ragged beggars living under destitute conditions) as anything but part of an inferior culture that ought to be remade in the image of white society. On the less fundamental issue of Camp McDermit, however, Indians and settlers could come together. Indians saw it as a refuge of safety under the aegis of the army and as a possible source of renewed rations; settlers sought its continuation as a protection against Indian unrest and as an economic asset where local produce could be marketed.

The journals of the Nevada senate and assembly do not indicate whether the legislators permitted Sarah to testify on Camp McDermit. Nonetheless, the initial success of the Camp McDermit resolution suggests that her moving words may have given it extra thrust. Introduced by Humboldt County State Sen. C. S. Varian and bolstered by a petition from residents in the area, the resolution sailed through the senate on 22 January without a dissenting vote, only to founder a few days later in the assembly, with a vote of nineteen to twenty-two. The resolution had been sandbagged by legislators who calculated that retaining Camp McDermit would jeopardize their chances of gaining an army post in their own counties. It had been a near miss.[12]

Then, as now, a U.S. senator who took an interest in a cause could have a powerful effect on Washington officials. Unluckily for the Paiutes, Sen. James Nye, who as Nevada governor had shown concern for the Indians, lost his office in 1873 to John P. Jones. Still hopeful, the Winnemuccas sought an interview with Senator Jones. A large Welshman, long of beard and chin, with a genial face, Jones had made an overnight fortune in the Crown Point Mine on the Comstock. He received the Winnemuccas sympathetically, promised to help them, gave Sarah a twenty-dollar gold piece, and did absolutely nothing. That gold piece, a bone tossed to the hounds, was the only tangible result of their political offensive.[13]

Immediately after this latest failure, Sarah fell seriously ill. The nature of her malady has not been specified, but, fortunately, she had not succumbed to the "paralyzing sickness" (possibly polio) then spreading among the Paiutes west of the Humboldt. Perhaps Sarah was above all sick at heart. All the same, she rallied sufficiently to serve as interpreter at a 16 February conference at Camp McDermit between Wagner and Winnemucca, accompanied by at least sixty of his leading men. Winnemucca declared that keeping the peace had been his "constant purpose" for many years and that he had rejected recent overtures from the Bannock and Shoshone to join them in warfare against the whites. In the treaty he made with General Crook, the general had promised food if the Paiutes remained at peace. Yet the army had fed them only when they were classified as prisoners of war, and the reservation agents had given them nothing. His people held him responsible for the unfulfilled promises made to them. With the old eloquence that had so often moved a council gathering, Winnemucca pled for his starving people and demanded an unequivocal answer: Would the captain provide for them or not?[14]

Although moved by the suffering of the Paiutes, Wagner, felt obliged to go by the rules. The army's role was to punish and protect, not to provide. He had informed Schofield of the Indians' desperate condition and received permission to issue pork to them. At this point, Sarah asked the assembled Paiutes if they would eat pork, which they vociferously rejected, declaring that they would instead raid the camp's cattle herd. Sarah reminded the captain that the Paiutes had earlier discarded the pork issued to them. Wagner stiffly responded that if the Paiutes were really starving, they would eat pork as the soldiers did. The captain's bafflement can be readily understood, since among white men the Paiutes bore the reputation of eating every disgusting creature that moved or crawled, including insects. This was not strictly true. The Paiutes drew the line at that totemic animal — coyote — and at the carrion-eating magpie. Perhaps they saw the pig as a similar scavenger. Or an issue of spoiled meat that sickened them may have turned them against pork — Dr. Kober wrote of cases in which Indians fell ill from eating insufficiently cooked meat from diseased animals. Whatever the cause, they remained adamant: no pork.[15]

Sarah added her pleas to her father's. She said her people were starving, having failed to collect roots and seeds in the autumn under the false impression that provisions would be issued. As a matter of humanity, the government should feed them for just a few months to help them through the winter. In years past her people had helped the hungry white men who came among them. Seeing that Wagner would not bend from his position of pork or nothing, Sarah wildly — and perhaps unwisely — turned to threats. She declared that if the Paiutes failed in their appeals they would be forced to turn to raids. She would willingly "throw off the garments of civilization" and "mount her pony" to join them. Bitterly, she recalled that when hostile Indians had swarmed over the area the officers had "talked very sweetly" to her. She reminded the captain of the army's great difficulties in subduing a mere fifty Modocs and allowed him to imagine how much more difficult it would be to conquer over a thousand Paiutes. A "talker" she was, in the best traditions of Paiute leadership, but Wagner could not be moved from his mission to protect the settlers and their stock and nothing more.[16]

Sarah next took the Indian cause to the press, demanding to know why the off-reservation Paiutes had received no provisions from the fifteen thousand dollars appropriated by the government for their benefit and why even those on reservations had fared little better. Much as he would have liked to, Bateman did not dare arrest and send her to Alcatraz in chains, but he did send runners to frighten the Indians. The message was that unless they came in to reside at Pyramid Lake Reservation soldiers would drive them away to Wyoming, a threat (and a falsehood) that aroused great alarm. The *Humboldt Register*, one of several newspapers that fully supported Sarah's charge, saw this as an effort to "create a muss among the Indians" in order to "cover up his stealings." Instead of submitting to Bateman's control at Pyramid, many frightened Paiutes fled north. The standoff continued: Bateman remained in office, issuing no provisions; but he lacked the power to silence Sarah by intimidating her people.[17]

As a last resort, the Winnemuccas appealed to public charity. A delegation composed of Sarah, Natches, Winnemucca, and several headmen called at the Winnemucca newspaper office of *Silver State* and asked editor E. D. Kelley to publish an article on the destitute condition of the approximately one thousand Paiutes in Humboldt County. Although some subsisted by working at odd jobs and by scavenging garbage, many would be forced to "steal or starve" in order to survive the winter. After Sarah described in moving and pathetic terms the desperation of her people, Kelley obliged with an article. *Taibo* could be generous. The Indians had seen over one hundred thousand dollars collected on the Comstock alone for the relief of Civil War veterans. But, as they had known since Winnemucca's first appeal to the public eleven years earlier, charity for Indians was a frail hope. Blocked in all they had tried to do for their people, Winnemucca withdrew to the solitude of Steens Mountain, and Sarah remained in the town of Winnemucca.[18]

Meanwhile, Indian policy in distant Washington evolved unaffected by the ideas of the Indians themselves. In the 1870s, President Ulysses S. Grant's new "peace policy" entailed placing the Indians on reservations, eradicating their culture, and turning them into English-speaking, Christian farmers suitable for assimilation. Frances Paul Prucha, an expert on Indian history, rightly observes that it might better have been termed the "religious policy," since the government essentially abdicated its responsibilities and turned authority on the reservations over to religious societies. The troubled reign of Agent Bateman — "you who talk three times a day to the Great Father in Spirit Land" and cheat the Indians, in Sarah's scorching words — unforgettably illustrates the results of the new order, the old corruption with a hypocritical religious gloss.[19]

Moving as she did between the Indian and white worlds, Sarah's attitude toward the peace policy reflected her experience and her ideas. Although she never advocated the eradication of traditional Indian languages, she strongly favored learning English, as had her grandfather Truckee before her. Her success as a spokeswoman and an interpreter had shown her the value of communication in the only language most white men understood — their own. In an era when some racists still saw the Indian as subhuman and unteachable, her efforts in Indian education would become one of her highest achievements. Agent Douglas, recognizing her potential as a teacher, had fruitlessly urged the Commissioner of Indian Affairs in 1870 to establish an Indian school at Pyramid Lake Reservation with Sarah as the teacher. He argued that her education and her "knowledge of the Indian language and character" would make her "invaluable as an instructress." Sarah's own effort to start an Indian school at Camp McDermit had fared no better. Apparently, *taibo* had not responded to her appeal for used school books.[20]

Perhaps — though she never said so — the religious conversion demanded by *taibo* was another arena in which she envisaged her people acquiring the new way without abandoning the old. She later declared herself a Methodist and participated in large meetings aimed at converting the Indians. Yet it is difficult to tell how much *taibo*'s new religion coexisted in her mind with the ancient beliefs, a common compromise for Indians. Indeed, in one well documented case, a Pyramid Lake shaman who practiced peyotism also served as an Episcopal deacon.[21]

Having bowed to the inevitable loss of the hunting and gathering way of life, Sarah repeatedly said that with appropriate implements and instruction the Indians would learn to farm. If the unsuitability of the Nevada reservations for farming large portions of land troubled her, the pressing need to escape the tyranny of reservation agents outweighed it. On one point she clearly diverged from the reformers of her time: never would the English-speaking Paiute farmers of the future working their own parcels of land be assimilated to the point that they ceased to be Indian. Sarah prided herself on refusing to forsake the Indian world for the white one, as her sister Elma and others had done. Her book *Life among the Piutes* lovingly details Paiute customs and does not fail to point out certain respects in which she thought Paiute culture superior to *taibo*'s. How deeply she would have felt the loss if there had ceased to be an Indian world to which she could from time to time return.[22]

The Paiute world compelled no pretenses to ladylike deportment. It was that same Sarah whose tasteful garb and modest demeanor so impressed reporters who drank and brawled with the Modoc woman known as Snake River Sal and attempted to burn down her enemy's *kahnee* in the Indian encampment in the sagebrush behind the courthouse. Accounts varied as to the cause. In one version Sarah attacked the younger and prettier Modoc woman out of jealousy over a Paiute man desired by both; in another, Sarah resented Snake River Sal's insults, a reprise of her previous fracas with an Indian woman who maligned her. Given Sarah's touchy pride and her many amours, both versions are plausible. All agree that Sarah fared the worse, and the sheriff declined to make arrests. For several nights, liquor reportedly obtained from the Chinese continued to flow into the Paiute encampment, and several *kahnees* of sacks and canvas stretched over willow poles burned down in suspicious fires. Newspapers, ever eager to belittle the Paiute princess, seized on the brawl with glee. "ROYALTY ON THE RAMPAGE" read one of the headlines.[23]

Winnemucca in 1875 was a town of about five hundred, and a major staging and teaming center for traffic to Idaho from the Central Pacific Railroad, completed in 1867. It had also developed into a rather dangerous place. An early historian observed that due to its location at a spot "where persons of all nations and character come in contact [it] has an extensive record of homicides." Winnemucca obviously shocked Kober, who feared going to sleep in such a "bad town" on his journey to Camp McDermit. He called it "a veritable den of thugs or a bedlam of drunken cow-boys, sheep-herders, miners, and prospectors." It must have been one of these roughs, Julius Argasse, who tried to force his way into Sarah's dwelling.[24]

If Julius Argasse thought Sarah would lie back trembling, begging, and weeping beneath his assault, he thought wrong. With a penknife, she cut a terrible gash in his face from eye to neck. Local authorities jailed her on the charge of "assault with intent to do great bodily harm." Apparently, prosecuting Argasse was not considered. Deep concern spread among the Paiutes over Sarah's fate in *taibo*'s courts, where any Indian transgression against a white man, no matter how well deserved, had always been severely punished. After all, no more than angry words had sent Natches to Alcatraz.[25]

Deliverance came in the form of an influential lawyer of forty-two, with strong, clear-cut features, large, light eyes, a short-trimmed beard, and liberal sympathies. Born in West Virginia, McKaskia (Mac) Bonnifield had headed west to Kansas, where he became a prominent Free Soil politician. He reached the Humboldt County mining camp of Unionville in 1862 and later moved on to Winnemucca. Few major cases went to trial in Humboldt County over the next fifty years in which he was not involved. He became a strong advocate of woman suffrage in an era when conservative resistance continued to block enactment in Nevada. He had arrived in time to see some of the ugliest atrocities of Indian-white warfare in the northern deserts, but this did not prevent him from taking up the cause of an Indian woman.[26]

While Sarah languished in jail, Bonnifield began assembling an array of sterling character witnesses on her behalf (as sterling, at least, as Humboldt County society in 1875 afforded). Several physicians and "prominent church members" agreed to stand up and be counted for Sarah. Faced with such formidable opposition, the district attorney moved to dismiss the case. Outside the red brick courthouse, with elongated windows, gabled front, and a small balcony supported by columns, the Paiutes gathered, anxiously awaiting news of Sarah's fate. When they learned she had been freed, the assemblage erupted in general rejoicing. First Natches, then Sarah, addressed the crowd. The penknife with which the Paiute princess had halted Argasse was regarded as an object of such great public interest that it was presented for exhibition at the American centennial.[27]

After this incident, Sarah headed north as her father had done, first to Camp McDermit, later to a dwelling at Summit Springs on the Idaho Road. There, her fondness for spirited horses of the kind she used to ride so dashingly into the Camp McDermit parade ground resulted in an accident in which her horse threw her and dragged her through the sagebrush. She emerged injured and badly bruised but not converted to tame, plodding horses. The next month she had healed enough to travel to Camp Harney for a meeting with her father.[28] Then came an unexpected summons from Malheur Reservation.

8

Malheur Reservation

"I cannot tell or express how happy we were"

A N EARLY PIONEER in southeastern Oregon wrote of being impressed by the "bigness" of everything: "The country was alive with cattle, horses, sheep and wild animals surpassing anything in size and numbers we had ever seen. Beeves were being driven to market by the thousand, the roads were blocked with big six-horse wool wagons and we sighted great herds of deer and antelopes." Malheur Reservation was on the same scale, a generous domain of lavender hills studded with sage and juniper and of secluded green valleys along the three branches of the Malheur River and several creeks. Set aside by executive order in 1872 for "all the roving and straggling bands in Eastern and Southeastern Oregon, which can be induced to settle there," it comprised about 1,778,560 acres, 12,000 of which were arable. Perhaps the immense sweep of the landscape generated outsized dreams. Indians dreamed of sanctuary. The slow pace of settlement in this corner of the West had spurred the hope that some of their lost world might yet be salvaged. Cattlemen dreamed of empires, such as the one Peter French was building that would eventually encompass 200,000 acres and 30,000 head of cattle. It did not take the cattlemen long to consider how much these empires would expand if they could swallow Malheur Reservation.[1]

Sarah was visiting with Winnemucca at Camp Harney, on the western edge of the reservation, when Lee brought a request from the agent in charge, Samuel B. Parrish, to serve as interpreter. Although she needed work and the agent would provide her with a place to live and pay her forty dollars a month ("a great deal of money," in Sarah's eyes), she demurred at first, but Lee insisted that she take the post, and her father agreed to accompany her. Unless they took a short cut through the hills — and Sarah would learn every trail over the next three years — they may have ridden east, then turned north to follow the canyon of the north fork of the Malheur River as it gurgled noisily over its rocky bed among scattered pines and junipers. The trail emerged into a narrow valley, green with spring grasses, where the western hills ended in curved, bulging rock formations striated with purple. The reservation agency, a cluster of five newly built wooden buildings, lay on the west side of the river south of Castle Rock, a gray peak with a sheer rock thumb pointing skyward.[2]

Although Sarah did not formally assume her post as interpreter until November, she quickly involved herself in reservation affairs. At the agency office, the Paiutes assembled to talk with Agent Parrish. Winnemucca and his followers joined the group, as did Oytes, the Dreamer chief who claimed the power to make his enemies sicken and die, and Egan (the Anglo version of Ehegante), tall, handsome, and athletic — his hair cut short at the neck. Born a Cayuse, Egan had been adopted by the Paiutes after his parents were killed in a raid, and he rose to become the leader of an Oregon band. Parrish told them: "I am a bad man; but I will try and do my duty, and teach you all how to work, so you can do for yourselves by and by."[3] He meant only that he would devote himself to work rather than ostentatious prayer, a jab at his predecessor.

Far from being a bad man, the mustachioed, heavyset Parrish became the first agent to receive Sarah's approbation. The son of a Methodist missionary, Parrish arrived in Oregon as a child in 1840. His years of experience on the northwest frontier could hardly be faulted; nor could his honesty or his concern for the Indians. As commissary, he had supervised the construction of the agency buildings. After the Christian Church of Oregon secured the position of agent for its favored candidate, he departed, only to be called back within three months. The elderly, inexperienced agent, Harrison Linville, had panicked and called on the military after being threatened by Oytes.

Samuel B. Parrish as a young man. Courtesy of the Grant County
Historical Museum.

Maj. Elmer Otis, commander at Camp Harney, recommended Linville's immediate replacement by Parrish as the best means to avert serious trouble. Worried enough to act with unusual speed, the commissioner of Indian Affairs complied.[4]

At this meeting with the Indians, Parrish outlined his plans for planting, building a dam, digging an irrigation ditch, and constructing fencing. He promised that all the produce raised by the Indians would be theirs, a sore point because at Pyramid Lake Reservation the agent treated the Paiutes as sharecroppers and took a large percentage for himself. Parrish had a different conception of his role. "The reservation is yours," he told them. "The government has given it all to you and your children."

Winnemucca asked the others, "What do you think of what this man, our new father, says?" Egan, in his deep, resonant voice, expressed approval tempered with doubt that the new agent would live up to his words. Oytes the Dreamer announced his refusal to work on the reservation and declared he would go hunting with his men. Parrish told him to "do just as you like."[5]

"So my people went to work with good heart, both old men and young women and children," Sarah remembered. "We were as happy as could be." Egan's band cut timber for fencing; Winnemucca and his followers began digging the ditch. Parrish proudly wrote to the commissioner, "The Indians show such a willingness to labor that even those who have no tools will go into the ditch and throw out dirt with their hands." Sarah delighted in their progress, an unarguable refutation of the critics who claimed Indians were lazy by nature and unwilling to work. Within six weeks, the ten-foot-wide irrigation ditch advanced more than two miles, a pace that exceeded the rate of progress Sarah had observed on the Pyramid irrigation ditch over many years. The Paiutes cleared and planted 120 acres that year. They also constructed a schoolhouse, a smithy, and a carpentry shop. The success of Parrish's humane administration showed in the chiefs' response to his appeal to bring their people onto the reservation. By the end of 1875, 742 Indians had come to live there, with more expected.[6]

Only two problems marred this happy state of affairs. The first was an ominous dispute with settlers over the reservation boundaries on the creeks in the east. A settlement fair to all parties emerged, but Parrish's strong stand probably made enemies for him among the whites. Parrish's second major difficulty entailed what he called Oytes's "bad heart," a problem that was never fully resolved. In keeping with the beliefs of the cult led by Smohalla, the Dreamer chief had warned the Indians that they should not tear the breast of Mother Earth with farming, and some listened. He scornfully condemned the reservation Indians as whites who obeyed a white man and pointed proudly to his own blackness. When sickness raged in the *kahnees* of the Paiutes during the previous winter, Oytes declared that he had caused it and that they must pay him or all would die. They paid, but Sarah related that "many died anyhow," especially the children. Oytes continued to reject reservation work and spent his time with renegade Columbia River Indians, with whom he urged the Paiutes to gamble and trade their meager possessions. Because he had refused work, Oytes received nothing when Parrish issued clothing, blankets, and yard goods to the Paiutes that autumn ("It was the prettiest issue I have ever seen in my life, or have seen since," observed Sarah). After everyone else had left, Oytes came over to Sarah and said, "You and I are two black ones. We have not white fathers' lips."[7]

Sarah answered feistily, "No, we are two bad ones. Bad ones don't need pity from anyone," bringing a laugh to the lips of the ugly Dreamer chief. But, in fact, she feared him. Oytes even alarmed her father, who believed in witchcraft to the last day of his life. The Dreamer chief's power to terrify Sarah showed that despite her mastery of *taibo*'s tongue and his way of life she remained deeply rooted in Paiute culture. She had earlier expressed her fears to Egan when they were riding together and Oytes appeared in the distance. Egan tried to comfort her. "He is nobody. Don't you mind him. If he can make you afraid of him that is all he wants, but if you are not afraid of him he will be one of the best men you ever saw."[8]

Although Sarah linked the crisis between Oytes and Parrish to the clothing issue, other evidence suggests that it occurred at an earlier date preceding her arrival. Warned that Oytes planned to kill him, Parrish wisely decided on a showdown with the Dreamer chief. When Egan brought Oytes to the agency office the next morning, Parrish took his gun and declared that Oytes had been telling everyone his powers were so strong that bullets could not touch him. Therefore, if he fired his gun at Oytes and no bullet struck him, he would give Oytes three hundred dollars. This challenge immediately changed Oytes's dark threats to cringing servitude. The two shook hands. "We were all good friends," Sarah related, "and our agent liked my people, and my people loved him."[9]

A disquieting letter arrived from the Office of Indian Affairs in Washington, however. After Parrish called the men together, he told them the letter said they had enemies in Canyon City, a mining town a short distance beyond the northwest boundary of the reservation. A petition endorsed by the governor of Oregon, Judge George B. Currey, and others claimed that the Paiutes had neither a use nor a hereditary right to the western end of the reservation. They wanted to open settlement on the Harney Lake basin and the Sylvies Valley, a mountain meadowland that had become valuable as a stopping place. Large herds of cattle being driven to the Central Pacific for shipment to market could be fed and watered there. These valleys assumed particular importance to the Indians because, despite its rugged beauty, the reservation offered little pastureland — so little that an Indian agency inspector riding through in 1874 called it "destitute."[10] Egan and Leggins, a subchief in Winnemucca's band, asked Parrish to "talk for us" in his response to Washington. They sarcastically suggested that whites who felt they needed more land should go whip the Sioux and take some of theirs. They also observed that it made them feel "bad and dispirited" to hear that when they had bent every effort in learning to live under the restrictions imposed upon them "our white brothers are trying to take away what little we have left." Vigorous opposition by Parrish and Maj. John Green at Camp Harney halted any diminution of reservation lands — this time.[11]

When Sarah's cousin Jerry Long ("Riding Down Hill with Hair Standing on End") returned after receiving medical treatment, Sarah pitied his near blindness and requested that he resume the position he once held as interpreter. She began work as an assistant to Parrish's sister-in-law, Annie (called "our white lily mother" by the Indians for her beauty and gentleness), at the new school, which opened on 1 May 1876. Because many of the Indians did not yet speak English, Parrish thought the multilingual Sarah played a vital role at the school. Although the pupils found some ideas hard to grasp — the ocean's vastness, the map colored yellow, red, and green on places that did not really have those colors — Sarah was delighted by their rapid progress: "They learned very fast, and were glad to come to school. I cannot tell or express how happy we were!"[12] Here her story might have wound into a succession of halcyon years, with Sarah contentedly ensconced at Malheur, celebrating each new stretch of ditch, each crop harvested, and each advance by her pupils. An admirable woman, to be sure, educated by sheer force of will, accomplished, and outspoken on behalf of her people but not the heroine, fired in the crucible of terrible events, that history remembers.

This future of peace and contentment was not to be hers. A letter arrived from Washington announcing that Parrish had lost his position. When he gathered the Paiutes in the schoolhouse to tell them, they refused to accept this decree or believe that their wishes carried no weight. Egan urged any who had criticized Parrish to correct the misunderstanding. None had. Oytes declared, "We will not let our father go. We will fight for him." He wanted to send for Winnemucca, then visiting at Pyramid, in the hope that somehow the old chief would summon the power to keep Parrish in his post.[13]

After Sarah had translated these heartfelt testimonials, Parrish explained that the reason for his removal was that he was not a Christian, and the reservations had been placed under control of the religious societies. Although Parrish may not have been aware of it, complaints from the settlers had also been lodged against him. They accused him of treating the Indians too well: he gave them too much

food and clothing, he overpaid his workers, and he failed to economize on his system of farming to sustain the Indians. Parrish attempted, with scant success, to convince the Paiutes that the new
agent was "a better man" whom they would like and then turned the
discussion to spring planting.[14]

Winnemucca must have ridden hard from Pyramid. As soon as he
arrived, he went with Sarah to Parrish, took the agent's hands in his,
and said, "My good father, you shall not leave me and my people. Say
you will not go."

"It is not for me to say," Parrish told him. Winnemucca sat in silence for a long time. When Parrish took him to the storeroom for a
clothing issue, Winnemucca stood in a corner of the room "like one
that was lost" and refused to accept it. According to Sarah, Paiute custom forbade gifts from departing friends because reminders of them
brought such grief. She explained to her father that *taibo*'s customs
were quite different; white men wanted mementos to remind them of
faraway friends and even kept pictures of the dead. Eventually, she
persuaded him to accept.[15]

Without delay, Winnemucca determined to appeal to the only
white men who had helped him in the past. A delegation of Sarah, her
father, Egan, and Oytes set off for Camp Harney the next morning. At
the camp, Winnemucca made a powerful plea to Major Green and his
officers to help the Paiutes in their "great trouble" and persuade
Washington to reinstate Parrish. Green faithfully reported Winnemucca's words to Washington and added his own, "It seems to me
strange to remove an agent who is doing so much for the Indians, and
one whom they are so unwilling to lose." Significantly, in view of future events, the old chief declared his belief that if Parrish had been in
charge, the Indian fights with Crook in the late 1860s would not have
occurred. The Paiutes also appealed by letter to General Oliver O. Howard, who had recently visited Malheur Reservation and expressed admiration for Parrish's "noble spirit and kind ways" and the progress
made under his administration. Howard also wrote, affirming that
his own thorough investigation had disproved charges of wrongdoing

William Rinehart. Neg. no. 56820, courtesy of the Oregon Historical Society.

by Parrish. But the army, with all the military might so visible to the Indians, lacked the power to deflect the Office of Indian Affairs from its course. When Sarah later told Parrish of their mission to Camp Harney, the bitterness so thoroughly hidden surfaced for a moment, and he laughed.[16]

"I am not of the *sentimental school*" on the Indian's behalf, the new agent, William V. Rinehart, later wrote. Indeed, none could accuse him of soft-heartedness toward Indians, or even of common humanity. Then forty, Rinehart was a pale man, clean-shaven, with a thin, cruel mouth and hard, distrustful eyes. He had crossed the plains to California before he was twenty, mined unsuccessfully, and moved to Oregon, where he clerked in stores and joined the Oregon volunteer cavalry in 1862 in time to participate in army operations against the Indians. He did not emerge from this experience with the humane attitudes of Crook and Howard. He was a man of violent temper and black hatreds and at heart probably continued to regard Indians as the enemy. After his stint in the military, Rinehart kept a saloon (according to Sarah) and became a storekeeper in Canyon City, where he did a good deal of business supplying the Malheur Reservation. Egan and Oytes claimed he also did a good deal of business selling liquor to them. Of course, Rinehart never admitted to this and instead wrote disparagingly of the worthless class of "grog venders" who traded with Indians.[17]

Trouble began soon after Rinehart's arrival. He called Egan and Oytes and their men together and directed Sarah to tell them that the reservation belonged to the government and that they would be paid a dollar a day if they worked. While the Paiutes joked among themselves about Rinehart's apparent fear of them, Egan protested that he could not understand this reversal in policy. Parrish had told them that the land was theirs and everything they raised would belong to them.

Rinehart angrily told Egan, "You can all go away if you do not like the way I do." (Indeed, Winnemucca had already departed, and Sarah must have felt very much alone without his support.)[18]

Oytes suggested that they should all go to work and find out if Rinehart would pay as promised. They did so, mowing hay, cutting wood, and working on fences. When they went to collect their pay at the end of the week, Rinehart's methods of calculation became clear. Busily writing in a ledger, he declared that after deductions for past rations and clothing issues only a small amount could be collected by the Indians. Many walked out immediately. Egan again protested: "Why do you want to play with us? We are men, not children. We want our father to deal with us like men." He said that his people would willingly work for nothing but payment had been the agent's idea. Infuriated by anything less than that "thorough and complete" submission he thought proper in Indians, Rinehart repeated that those who did not care for his practices should leave Malheur.[19]

That night the headmen gathered in conclave. The women worried that if Rinehart would not allow them to keep their crops they would not live through the winter. Oytes wanted to appeal once more to the army officers. Egan voiced concern that his people had no means of making a living if they left the good lodges they had built and the lands they had developed at Malheur. Sarah probably knew that the hereditary homeland of his band lay in the valley area east of the agency. Having no solutions to offer, she said simply, "We must wait."[20]

Her chronicle of Rinehart's cruelties, large and small, continued. When a new group of hungry Paiutes arrived to make their home on the reservation, Rinehart refused to issue any rations to them. When Rinehart erroneously thought that a little Indian boy had laughed at him, he kicked and beat the "little devil" so severely about the head that the child's mother feared this last survivor among her four children would die. The agency doctor, an alcoholic, proved useless, so Oytes brought his shamanistic powers to bear. Seeing how deeply the troubles of her people affected Sarah, Jerry Long suggested to her that they should ignore the problems of the others and simply collect their wages. Sarah indignantly refused to be silent.[21]

Matters at Malheur worsened. Rinehart threatened to shoot an Indian boy who spoke impertinently to him. Lee Winnemucca, recently arrived with several others from Pyramid, attempted to intervene: "We have come a long way to hear good things from the Good Spirit man. Why talk of killing?" Perhaps his words shamed Rinehart. The agent settled for putting the boy in handcuffs, threatening to send him to Camp Harney to be hanged by the soldiers, and locking him in the storeroom over night. Sarah, like Lee, repeatedly expressed shock over the contrast between Rinehart's hypocritical lip service to Christianity and his violent and cruel behavior.[22]

The previous year the Paiutes held an autumn dance in celebration of hunting and harvest. After the 1876 harvest, Egan reached the conclusion that Rinehart was deliberately attempting to drive his people away from Malheur. Together with Oytes, he came to make one more appeal to the agent. With Sarah translating, Egan asked for the wheat his people had raised to feed their hungry children. "Nothing here is yours. It is all the government's," Rinehart responded. Sarah protested that Rinehart should have made this clear earlier instead of allowing the Paiutes to believe that the crops they raised would belong to them. Rinehart repeated that for them to take their own wheat would be robbing the government. Egan turned to Sarah and cautioned her to translate everything he was about to say exactly as he said it. We can be certain that she did:

Did the government tell you to come here and drive us off this reservation? Did the Big Father say, go and kill us all off, so you can have our land? Did he tell you to pull our children's ears off, and put handcuffs on them, and carry a pistol to shoot us with? We want to know how the government came by this land. Is the government mightier than our Spirit-Father, or is he our Spirit-Father? What have we done that he is to take all from us that he has given us? His white children have come and have taken all our mountains, and all our valleys, and all our rivers; and now, because he has given us this little place without our asking him for it, he sends you here to tell us to go away.... Tomorrow I am going to tell the soldiers what you are doing, and see if it is all right.

Rinehart doggedly insisted that his practices were government policy and suggested they should "all go and live with the soldiers."[23]

Contention between Sarah and Rinehart had reached the breaking point, however. She claimed to have written a petition to Washington, signed by all the headmen, denouncing him (no copy of such a document has been uncovered). In any case, Rinehart indisputably held her solely responsible for having "counselled and encouraged disobedience" to his rule: "She induced two of the chiefs to accompany her to Camp Harney where they lodged complaints (so I am informed) against the agent in charge. She also procured to be written several letters to different persons all of like character — such as would naturally be prompted by a bitter spirit of revenge. The want of supplies at the agency and the protracted delay in procuring more was easily turned to account by her in the effort to engender dissatisfaction among the Indians. . . . Most of the real trouble and all the reported or imaginary threats of the Indians are believed to have originated with this unfaithful employe." Rinehart fired her, for which she observed she did not blame him. Both knew they were now enemies.[24]

She certainly did lodge complaints against him. In mid-November, Sarah traveled with Egan and others sixty miles westward through the mountains to Camp Harney, a cluster of one- and two-story wooden buildings around a rectangular parade ground, where Rattlesnake Creek emerged between gray-tipped mesas into a broad valley yellowed with autumnal grasses. To the south, beyond the valley and Malheur and Harney Lakes, rose Steens Mountain — Winnemucca's place of refuge — a mighty presence more felt than seen. When they told their troubles to Green, he promised to investigate. Egan was especially upset by Rinehart's latest outrage: a threat that no rations would be issued unless the Indians found who among them had stolen beef and then turned over the culprit to be executed. Green's visit to Malheur temporarily smoothed the conflicts. The Indians believed his calm and reasonable explanation of government policy on rations for labor. Rinehart evidently controlled his temper for the duration of Green's stay, and the major could find no fault with him beyond the Indians' obvious dislike of him.[25]

Rinehart may have had reasons for ridding himself of Sarah beyond her insubordination. He plainly saw her great influence among the Paiutes at Malheur — where she was known as "the princess" — as a challenge to his authority. Moreover, Rinehart's poisonous hatred of her father may have further disposed him against her. In his writings, Rinehart characterized Winnemucca as a "beggarly imbecile" and condemned his gambling, his "excessive vanity," and his "life of worthless vagabondage." The last charge offers a hint on the source of Rinehart's enmity. From the outset, Winnemucca had refused to remain on the reservation and submit to Rinehart's dictatorial powers. The lengthy effort to turn the wandering Winnemucca into a Malheur Reservation Indian suggests that even in old age the chief retained his political skills. Sometimes he complained that the other bands at Malheur would not acknowledge him as head chief or that the agent forced him to work with the women; sometimes he expressed fear of Oytes's black arts; sometimes he simply neglected to appear as promised; but the end result was always the same. He would not remain on the reservation.[26]

The old chief appeared at Malheur so rarely that when Rinehart embarked on an effort in 1877 to bring the outside bands into the reservation he was obliged to seek Winnemucca at Camp McDermit, where the chief was visiting. Winnemucca refused to return to Malheur. He had a new plan, which Rinehart called his "hallucination." He wanted to create a reservation on the Owyhee River where his people might live without the supervision of an agent. The key provision of Winnemucca's "hallucination" — no agent — apparently provoked neither self-examination on Rinehart's part nor alteration in his dogmatic views. In his report to the commissioner of Indian Affairs, Rinehart pressed for the closure of the army posts where Winnemucca and Chief Ochocho's bands preferred to live. Or at least the Indians could be deprived of army rations so they would be starved into submission and the nation would be rid of the "dreaded pressure of straggling Indians." Frustrated by the refusal of Chief Ochocho at Camp Bidwell, Winnemucca, and other chiefs to bring their bands to Malheur, Rinehart's allegations grew uglier. He characterized the Paiute fandangos as a "species of brothel-dance" and accused the Indians near Camp McDermit of living by prostitution — charges angrily refuted by the post commander. The Winnemuccas' belief that Indians should live where they pleased as free men was anathema to him. As he wrote to the commissioner, Indians must learn that they cannot "continue to roam the country at will in defiance of the wishes of the whites."[27]

Sarah lingered on the reservation little longer. Her last confrontation with the agent occurred when she tried to restrain him from beating a Paiute man with a stick. The man had responded to his orders too slowly. When she tried to revisit Malheur some months later, Rinehart forbade her to set foot inside its borders.[28] "The experiment of last winter proves that even if poorly fed these Indians can and will go naked," observed Rinehart in a letter to the commissioner of Indian Affairs. In an area where deep snow drifts made the mountains impassable for much of the winter except on snowshoes, Howard found such experiments hard to countenance, and he arranged an emergency issue of blankets at Camp Harney for the Indians "to prevent serious suffering." Unable to subsist at Malheur under Rinehart's regime, Egan and the others soon followed Winnemucca's example and spent much of their time in the mountains. Rinehart acknowledged that hunger had driven the Indians away. This he ascribed to inadequate government appropriations rather than his own tyrannical ways. One critic's call for an investigation of Rinehart's "rascally treatment" of his charges brought no response.[29] For the Indians the hope that Malheur had stirred for so brief a time had ended. Ominously, Rinehart had made them a people with nothing to lose.

As events at Malheur played out to their tragic conclusion, a new romance blossomed for Sarah — perhaps more than one. The first sign appeared when she at last filed for a divorce from Edward alleging desertion after less than a month of marriage. She also accused him of excessive drinking, pawning her jewelry, and failing to support her. She received her divorce and resumed her maiden name on 21 September 1876 in the Grant County Courthouse in Canyon City, the gold mining town in the mountains northwest of Malheur Reservation. So far as we know, Sarah was wholly unaware that Edward had returned to New York and, in December of the same year that he exchanged vows with her, married sixteen-year-old Louisa Butler. Unless he obtained an annulment or divorce without Sarah's knowledge, Edward must have considered his marriage to an Indian woman inconsequential. His effort to gain reinstatement in the army failed. The Bartlett couple had two children and moved to Florida, where he eventually died of tuberculosis in 1892. In Edward's new life, his three-year stint in the service expanded dramatically, while his marriage to Sarah disappeared. He told his bride that he had spent seven years fighting Indians in Wyoming, Montana, and Utah (he did not mention Nevada) and that he had never been married before.[30]

Shortly after her divorce on 3 November 1876, the year she turned thirty-two, Sarah married Joseph Satewaller in the Canyon City home of Annie Parrish, once the beloved schoolteacher at Malheur, and her husband, Charles, the brother of former agent Sam Parrish and the lawyer who had handled Sarah's divorce. Of all Sarah's husbands, confirmed and otherwise, Satewaller remains the greatest mystery. He is a husband of record, his name forever linked to hers in the marriage records at the Grant County Courthouse, but she omitted him from her history. The tax records that might have provided a clue to his identity have not been preserved, and Satewaller's absence from the Oregon censuses suggests mobility — possibly a miner who followed the rush to Canyon City and later went on to other excitements, or perhaps a cowboy trailing the vast herds of the southeast Oregon cattle empires. Snyder, though not mentioned as a husband by Sarah, at least takes on substance through a tale or two. Who Satewaller was and whether he departed from Sarah's life through death, desertion, or divorce remain unanswered questions.[31]

Another possibility is that Sarah's shadowy Indian husband was Satewaller. She herself once acknowledged in an interview that she had briefly been married to an Indian who mistreated her. Rinehart related that after his last showdown with Sarah, she married and went to live at the Warm Springs Reservation in north-central Oregon. His account of Sarah's movements gains credibility from her praise for the Warm Springs agent ("The only agent who can truly say, 'I have civilized my Indians'") — perhaps the result of first-hand knowledge of his success in helping them to be self-supporting through farming.[32]

Another candidate for the role of the Indian husband surfaces briefly. Less than four months after the Satewaller wedding, the *Silver State* reported Sarah's marriage to Bob Thacker, an Indian. She must have known Thacker a long time. He was a member of Winnemucca's band, an interpreter at Camp McDermit for a while, and sometimes a buckaroo at the McColley ranch. Apparently, Thacker possessed such large and mysterious powers of seduction that when he persuaded an Indian woman to run away with him nine years later, deserting her husband and her small son, the abandoned husband blamed her flight upon "love medicine." Although the newspaper reported that Sarah and Thacker rode from Camp McDermit to Canyon City for their wedding, no such marriage appears in county records. Unless the *Silver State* was simply misinformed about the bridegroom, the wedding may have taken place by Paiute custom, if it took place at all, and dissolved informally. Sarah's father had had several wives, Natches then had two, and polyandry and extramarital affairs were fairly common among the Paiutes, but she conformed to *taibo*'s marital practices — more or less.[33]

A newspaper story, over a year after the alleged marriage to Thacker, hinted that the maltreatment that Sarah later alluded to occurred while she was living with her Indian husband at the Warm Springs Reservation; only by force could her husband dissuade her from welcoming a white man's frequent visits. The chief result of the quarrel was not a chastened wife but a defiant Sarah riding off on her pony. The Indian husband's principal role in her life was his contribution to the number of her purported marriages (at this point four not counting Hamilton) and thus to the suspicions of sexual promiscuity that would bedevil her in the future. Sarah's own account virtually skips this period, an indication that she preferred to avoid trying to explain her conduct to her white supporters. When not with her new husband (or husbands), she evidently did housework for a rancher's wife in the John Day Valley.[34]

While Sarah temporarily withdrew from the fight for Indian rights in hope of finding happiness in the ordinary private world of husband and home, Winnemucca and Natches still strove to shape the future. In response to the persuasive powers of attorney Mac Bonnifield, Central Pacific Railroad tycoon Leland Stanford promised Natches eventual ownership of some property from the railroad land grant on the Big Meadows near the Humboldt River. In early 1877, Natches and a workforce of Paiutes began clearing the land and planting. Not only did the farm offer a livelihood for his two wives, his children, and those who worked for him but also it might demonstrate that an Indian, living where he chose among white settlers outside a reservation, could succeed. Indeed, a measure of tolerance had started to emerge in the region around Camp McDermit once bloodied by the Black Rock War. The camp commander concluded that the settlers had come to value Indian labor and Indian purchasing power as a vital part of the local economy. Far from wanting the Indians rounded up on a reservation as Rinehart insisted, the settlers preferred to have the Indians remain.[35]

Now seamed with wrinkles and blackened by many suns, Winnemucca spoke of having grown too old to continue as chief. Yet no matter how heavily his many years weighed upon him, he kept on. With Natches serving as his interpreter, he journeyed once again to San Francisco to see Gen. Irvin McDowell and press his plan for a reservation with no agent on the Owyhee and plead for winter rations for his people. Winnemucca had spent much of 1877 in Idaho, still following the ancient ways of the nomad. When Indian unrest erupted in June of that year, he rejected Governor Mason Brayman's order to withdraw from his camp on Cow Creek, while at the same time assuring the governor that he would keep the peace.[36] Once his eloquence and his powerful influence might have swayed the other bands. But a series of events that the aged chief could not control would soon sweep the Northwest.

9
The Bannock War Begins
"I, only an Indian woman, went and saved
my father and his people"

ACROSS THE GRAY SAGE DESERT of southern Oregon, past mesas and low, rounded hills faintly tinged with the green grasses of spring, thundered a herd of six hundred stolen horses. Beside them on brightly decorated pinto ponies rode the Bannock warriors, each wearing a single eagle feather in his braided hair or a headdress of porcupine skin and dyed, trimmed horses' tails. If a man had proven himself in battle, he colored the instep of his moccasin red to show that he had stepped in the blood of an enemy. On this day, their faces and bodies were painted for war.[1]

The Bannocks (also known as the Snakes) spoke the Paiute language, yet they looked different from Sarah's people. They were taller, more slender, and lighter skinned. They had myths of their own, taking for their guardian spirit the swift, darting, brilliantly colored dragonfly. They dressed in fringed buckskin, the men's shirts decorated with quills, scalps, and red, yellow, and black paint, and they lived in buffalo hide tepees. Besides digging camas roots and other vegetable foods on the broad prairie near their Fort Hall homeland, they made an annual buffalo hunt. They crossed the continental divide through the Yellowstone country and into Montana on the Great Bannock Trail. They had turned themselves into horse Indians more than a century before the Paiutes, a people they tended to scorn as "rabbit hunters." Although much fewer in number, at an estimated one thousand, the Bannocks were far more aggressive. Their detractors called them "the meanest, most treacherous, most savage and most bloodthirsty of all the Indians west of the Mississippi," and even so reasonable a historian as Brigham Madsen has observed that they looked on all whites as "fair game for raids." For years, the Paiutes had pointed to their refusal to join the Bannocks in hostilities as proof of their strong commitment to peace. It may be that the Bannocks had long hovered on the brink of war.[2]

In the late spring of 1878, a confluence of circumstances pushed the Bannocks over the brink. General Howard, who commanded the Department of the Columbia during the war, believed that the disaffection of Bannock chief Buffalo Horn had considerable influence. Buffalo Horn had served Howard as a scout of outstanding abilities during the Nez Percé war in 1877. The general's refusal to allow him the small favor of murdering three Nez Percé herders annoyed him. He returned from the war knowledgeable on the military methods of the army, "puffed up with pride," as Howard put it, and convinced that he could outdo the Nez Percé in war. Sarah, unlike Howard, saw the catalyst in the rape of a Bannock girl who had gone out to dig roots (an uncanny parallel to the events preceding the Pyramid Lake War). The matter escalated into the killing of a white man and a demand by white authorities for the arrest of the guilty party, Tambiago. The Indians promised to turn him over, but when they procrastinated, the whites arrested him themselves and confiscated Bannock arms and ponies. This infuriated the Bannocks and led a considerable faction to align itself with the combative Buffalo Horn.[3]

Winnemucca and General Crook, and even Tambiago, in a statement made before his execution, traced the war to a more fundamental cause — starvation. The Bannocks, under the thumb of another hated Indian agent of the Rinehart stripe at their Fort Hall Reservation, had received inadequate rations at the same time that their traditional food supplies dwindled. On the Camas Prairie, where they had dug camas roots for centuries, large herds of hogs brought by the white settlers, in defiance of the Fort Bridger Treaty, rooted and destroyed everything before them. Crook believed the Bannocks concluded that they must rebel before they lost the strength to fight. Later, a reporter interviewing him commented, "It is rather hard that men and officers should have to be sent out there to be killed by the Indians, when all the trouble has been brought about by thieving agents." Crook responded, "That is not the hardest thing. A harder thing is to be forced to kill the Indians when they are clearly in the right."[4]

As the situation turned more ominous, Winnemucca and Natches strove to repair the peace. Natches had resigned as chief of his band in early May, planning to devote himself to his ranch and become an American citizen. Yet he could not stop the Indians and whites from turning to him over every difficulty that arose. When the commander at Camp McDermit called on him to meet with Winnemucca, he offered his services as a peacemaker. The two hatched a plan together: the disaffected Bannock chiefs should make a trip to San Francisco. Once they had seen for themselves the full power of the white man, they would understand that war was useless. Winnemucca and Natches did not realize, as they started for Malheur with Winnemucca's followers, that it was already too late for an instructive demonstration.[5]

At Malheur, Winnemucca vainly summoned all the eloquence at his command. The wife of the agency blacksmith remembered that "Old Chief Winnemucca and three other Chiefs had their big talks in my kitchen, as they didn't want the other Indians to hear them. Chief Winnemucca tried to get them not to go on the war path, but couldn't do anything with them." No argument could prevail against Oytes's vision, for the Dreamer chief prophesied that the day had dawned when the Indians would destroy the white men and reclaim their homeland. A party of forty-six Bannocks arrived to speak of Buffalo Horn's plan: a snowball gathering more and more Indians onto itself as it rolled west and north, Paiutes, Shoshones, Umatillas, Cayuses, and many others — finally, a grand confederacy of the tribes that would drive whites from the Inland Empire. Not long after these talks, Egan, Oytes, and their bands joined the Bannocks. Sarah's subsequent analysis, cited at the highest levels of the army, blamed this defection on the starvation experienced under Rinehart's regime. It appeared that Buffalo Horn's dream of tribal confederation was coming to pass.[6]

Winnemucca and Natches rode into the hostiles' camp at their own peril to speak for peace and to save as many as they could. To illustrate his argument, Winnemucca would heap a large pile of sand representing *taibo* beside a tiny one. He would then point to the little mound saying, "This Indian. No use to fight." The inflamed warriors would not listen. As the Bannocks moved westward, burning ranches and killing the hated white encroachers as they went, Winnemucca and Natches persuaded them to spare the place belonging to Greenwood Crowley and his son James. But the urge to destroy quickly overcame mercy. Soon afterward the Winnemuccas rode back to Barren Valley with a warning to the Crowleys to flee at once. When the Bannocks set their ranch house aflame, the Crowleys had made good their escape — at least, for the moment.[7]

During the months that preceded these events, the suffering Indians at the Malheur Reservation had gone to see Sarah several times at the Cooley ranch in the John Day Valley, where she was working, to appeal to her: "We are really starving there, and we don't know what to do. . . . Go with us to Camp Harney and see the officers there. See if they can help us in some way, or go to Washington in our behalf." Sarah responded that she had no money to make a trip to Washington and that her previous report to the officers at Camp Harney had only resulted in the loss of her post at Malheur. "I will do all I can, but that is very little."[8]

They came again, and yet again. Sarah suggested that they appeal to Malheur interpreter Jerry Long. They dismissed him as a Rinehart flunky. "You are the only one who is always ready to talk for us. We know our sister can write on paper to our good father in Washington if she will." At length, Sarah promised to defy Rinehart's ban and go to Malheur. She would also transport three paying passengers, including a Mr. Morton and his twelve-year-old daughter, Rosie, in her wagon.[9]

Egan called Sarah into council the night she reached the Malheur Agency lest Rinehart should force her to leave. The Bannock party, assured by Egan that Sarah was a friend who would help them, asked her to "talk on paper" to Washington and request the return of their confiscated ponies and guns. Egan made a speech recalling the good times under Parrish and the many misdeeds of Rinehart. The uncertainties that plagued him showed in his admission, "We don't read, and therefore we don't know what to think." In the end, unable to refuse his appeal, Sarah agreed to go to Washington to talk with the "Great Father." Although the twenty-nine dollars Egan collected for her would not be enough for the journey, she planned to augment it with the sale of her wagon and team and the payment from the Mortons. Newspaperman Frank Parker, also present at the reservation, ever after declared that Sarah had saved his life with an introduction to Egan and a warning to depart with all possible speed.[10]

Sarah and her passengers set off the next day, probably narrowly missing Winnemucca and Natches. For three days they traveled toward Silver City, Idaho — the Mortons' destination — after which Sarah intended to continue to Elko and catch the train for Washington. By the journey's end, both Morton and little Rosie grew to love Sarah. He proposed to her, but she declined in proper nineteenth-century style: "You honor me too much by offering marriage to me, Mr. Morton. I thank you very much for your kind offer, but I cannot marry a man that I don't love."[11]

As the wagon rumbled over the bumpy road, they noticed something strange: "We saw houses standing all along the road without anybody living in them; and we talked about it, and did not know what it meant." They did not realize that war had started, Capt. Reuben Bernard's cavalry had gone galloping through the streets of Boise by night to pursue the Indians, and scarcely a white man remained in a vast tract of southeastern Oregon.[12]

Sarah's first news of the outbreak came from a man in a state of wild alarm whom she encountered along the road. He told her "the greatest Indian war that was ever known" had broken out. He urged her to head for Stone House on the Connor ranch, where settlers were fleeing for refuge. Another group of travelers Sarah met along the way gave the same warning and added that the Bannocks "want nothing better than to kill Chief Winnemucca's daughter." This admonition may have held some truth, because the inflamed warriors had killed two Paiutes for the crimes of living with white men and working for them. Sarah urged her team to a faster pace.[13]

When she reined in her horses at Stone House, men with guns came running out. As soon as she identified herself, one of them, an army officer, warned her that she was "in great danger" — nor did he mean from the Bannocks — and drew her inside.

She scarcely had time to deny all knowledge of the hostilities beyond the warnings heard on the road when one of the most significant events of the war became known. Several Paiute scouts entered Stone House. Although their leader, Paiute Joe, who spoke little English, mistrusted Sarah at first, he eventually told his story through her. A contingent of volunteers and Indian scouts had engaged a Bannock raiding party near South Mountain, a small mining camp south of Silver City. The volunteers retreated from the field, leaving him to be killed. Paiute Joe realized that his only chance was to kill the chief, whom he saw bearing down on him in all his painted splendor, with his warriors behind him. Paiute Joe dismounted, taking cover behind his horse, aimed his gun across the saddle, and shot Buffalo Horn. When the chief fell from his horse and his warriors halted to gather around him, Paiute Joe made his escape. Recalling the conduct of volunteers in the Pyramid Lake War and believing that citizen-scouts "take good care not to go too near Indians," Sarah would scarcely have doubted that the volunteers had abandoned Paiute Joe. The Battle of South Mountain had occurred on 8 June, prior to the Bannocks' sweep westward across southern Oregon, but it appears that the news that Buffalo Horn had been mortally wounded only became known to the army when Paiute Joe told his story to Sarah. The loss of their war chief at the outset of the war was a crippling blow from which the Bannocks would never recover, and several tribes on the brink of joining them may have drawn back in consequence.[14]

Now whirled away in the maelstrom of war, her mission to Washington superceded, Sarah never doubted her course of action. She would follow the path on which Truckee had propelled her since she was a small child. She believed that acting for the army to bring an early peace was the best way to serve the Paiutes ("I had to work for my people"). But the white men to whom she immediately offered her help distrusted her. A rumor of unknown origin that she was smuggling ammunition to the Bannocks gained such credence that the *Silver State* even published a report of her arrest on this charge. When Captain Bernard and his cavalry arrived at Stone House, Sarah was shocked to see that "all the soldiers looked at me as if I was some fearful beast." After a few moments conversation with the others at Stone House, Bernard asked Sarah about the ammunition "these citizens" told him she had stashed in her wagon. "My heart almost bounded into my mouth," Sarah remembered.

"Go and see for yourself, Captain," she answered passionately, "and if you find anything in my wagon besides a knife and fork and a pair of scissors I will give you my head for your football. How can I be taking guns and ammunition to my people when I am going right away from them?"[15]

She went on to explain her presence to Bernard, to inform him of Buffalo Horn's death, and to declare herself "at your service" for the duration of the war. The big, black-bearded captain found her words so convincing that he declined to search her wagon. He also immediately realized what a useful scout she would be but wanted to consult Howard before engaging her. The cavalry rode on to Sheep Ranch, the rendezvous point where they would meet the general, and Sarah spent the night at Stone House, scarcely less endangered by the citizenry than by the Bannocks. The citizens set a guard around her wagon. Their unfounded suspicions in the face of her unwavering loyalty wounded her so sharply that she wept. In the morning she demanded a search of her wagon. Ashamed, the officer of the volunteer guards asked her forgiveness.[16]

Just then a party of Indians accompanying a white man arrived with a dispatch from Camp McDermit, as the Bannocks had cut the telegraph wires. Bidding a hasty goodby to the Mortons, Sarah volunteered to accompany the riders to Sheep Ranch. The group galloped off for a ride of some thirty miles, with Sarah, who prided herself on her ability to ride in the same style as white women, perching sidesaddle in a proper riding habit. They arrived at a pleasant little valley bounded by steep bluffs on the south and rolling hills of sagebrush and bunchgrass on the west. To the northeast stood Lookout Butte, the vantage point from which the soldiers scrutinized the surrounding terrain for Indians. Within the valley, a high stockade enclosed ten or fifteen acres where cavalry horses grazed. Inside the stockade Sarah saw a two-story stone "hotel" beside a formidable one-story building made to withstand attack. This structure was made of three-feet-thick quarried gray sandstone walls with rifle portholes, and it had an earthen roof. Darkness was falling as Sarah presented the dispatch. She slept that night in the hotel, noting with satisfaction that the soldiers now treated her with "the highest respect."[17]

When morning came, Bernard asked her to persuade the Paiutes in the McDermit party to take a dispatch to Camp Harney or to the Malheur Agency to determine the whereabouts of the Bannocks. He promised them good pay. The Paiutes, George and John, refused to go anywhere near the Bannocks. As proof of the danger, they suddenly revealed a piece of news mysteriously withheld until this time: Natches was presumed dead. His horse had given out while helping three white men escape from the Bannocks, and his people at Camp McDermit were mourning him. When Sarah heard this, "my heart was dead within me." But instead of gashing her arms and cutting her hair in the old way, she behaved more recklessly than ever. Why, after all, should she prize her own life when her beloved brother lay dead? She told Bernard she would take the dispatch herself. Indeed, she proposed a more daring and ambitious plan: she would find the Bannocks, secretly contact her people in the Bannock camp, promise them protection and rations if they would come over to the army, and lead them away. "There is nothing that will stop me," Sarah declared, and, as always, to hear her was to believe her.[18]

In a telegram sent over the still uncut line from Boise, where Howard had arrived to take personal command of his forces, the general approved Sarah's plan and directed Bernard to offer her a reward if she succeeded. Given the dangers of the mission, the chance of Sarah's survival was considered slight. "I have little idea she will succeed," wrote Maj. Edwin C. Mason, an officer on Howard's staff. George and John, ashamed to see her ride off alone, decided to accompany her. Sarah needed only two things: a good horse and a rag friend much like the one her grandfather had carried so long ago. Bernard wrote: "To all good citizens in the country—Sarah Winnemucca, with two of her people, goes with a dispatch to her father. If her horses should give out, help her all you can and oblige." Then she was off, with a din of galloping hooves. Howard later praised her epic ride of over one hundred miles from Sheep Ranch to Steens Mountain, over some of the roughest country in the West.[19]

At the Owyhee River–crossing known as Fletcher Trails, they found a party of volunteers sleeping soundly. "Is this the way you all find the hostiles?" Sarah contemptuously inquired. "We could have killed every one of you if we had been they." Despite this sharp rebuke, the volunteers provided dinner and fresh horses for Sarah and her companions. About a mile beyond the Owyhee, they struck the Bannock trail and followed it to a deserted campsite where broken beads and other signs told Sarah that the Bannocks had cut their hair and torn their clothes to mourn the death of Buffalo Horn, who had succumbed to his wound two days after the South Mountain battle. Here, too, the warriors had danced around the scalps of slain white men to restore their flagging spirits.[20]

The Paiute party rode some fifty miles that day over rocky, waterless country. Their horses stumbled so badly on the rocks after darkness fell that Sarah finally said, "Boys, let us stop for the night, for our horses will surely fall over us and kill us, and then the hostile Bannocks will not have the pleasure of killing us." George and John laughed at this witticism. They made a dry camp and laid plans to take turns standing guard. Sarah lay down with her head upon her saddle but slept little. The horse she had tied to her arm kept jerking, and nervous excitement kept her wakeful. Above all, her heart must have ached for Natches.[21]

At daylight, Sarah jumped to her feet and said, "We will go. I am almost dead for water." As they rode "on the full jump" across Barren Valley toward the Crowley ranch, Sarah puzzled over the absence of the ranch house, usually visible from afar. The reason soon became clear: a few wisps of smoke still wafted from the ashes of the ranch. Fearful that the Bannocks might be close, Sarah's companions wanted to hasten away, but her reading of the signs convinced her that the Bannocks had burned the ranch the previous morning. "If they kill us, we have to die, and that is all about it," she said lightly, "and now we must have something to eat." All the same, she asked George to keep watch while she made coffee. Even in this emergency, Sarah refused to kill any of the chickens pecking about the blackened ruins. She knew well that *taibo*'s private property was sacred to him.[22]

While they ate a hurried breakfast, Sarah offered her companions a final chance to alter her perilous plan and made a tactful effort to assuage the pride of men unaccustomed to following a woman. "You are men," she said in conclusion. "You can decide better than I can."

George and John heartily affirmed their acceptance of her leadership, "Whatever you say, we will follow you."

They rode on, past pale mesas and through broad, gray sagebrush valleys. To the south, the sands of the Alvord Desert. To the north, Malheur and Harney Lakes, loud with wildfowl, trumpeter swans, Canada geese, pelicans, sandhill cranes, egrets, gulls, and more. Ahead, Steens Mountain, its snow-tipped, cloud-catching height rising in a smooth sweep from the desert floor. In its grassy, hidden valleys, bright with wildflowers, Winnemucca had sought peace after the Mud Lake massacre and posed questions that had no answers. Now the valleys sheltered the Bannocks. Near Juniper Lake, a small, mirror-like pond at the base of a purple brown basalt cliff, they spied another burned ranch and some bighorn sheep, one of which John killed and cached.[23]

Several miles farther they saw two Indians on the slope. George called to them while Sarah waved her handkerchief. Even at this distance she recognized her brother Lee. After they embraced, he told her that the Bannocks had taken Winnemucca and his band prisoners and confiscated most of their guns, horses, and blankets. His only good news was that Natches, though condemned to death for his aid to white men, had escaped. The Crowleys had gone back into the jaws of the lion when they rode with Camp Harney contractor Jack Scott into the Indian camp for a parley held at the Davidson ranch near Steens Mountain. The ambassadors from Camp Harney quickly found themselves captives slated for execution that evening. Pleading illness, Natches left a council with the Bannock leaders and stole away to his horses with the three white captives. After his horse foundered during the ensuing pursuit, he survived by wading along a stream, where he would leave no tracks.[24]

Anxiously, Lee warned Sarah that she was in great danger because the Bannocks had posted lookouts everywhere. He told her she must unbraid her hair, wear a blanket instead of her white woman's clothes, and paint her face with the colorings he thrust upon her. She did so and insisted that she must go to Winnemucca at once with Howard's message.

Lee attempted to deter her, "Dear sister, let me pray you not to go, for they will surely kill you." Sarah protested that she would not be recognized, but Lee reminded her that Oytes would know her at once — and surely betray her.

Sarah refused to be dissuaded: "I must save my father and his people if I lose my life in trying to do it, and my father's too. That is all right. I have come for you all. Now let us go."[25]

The mountain they needed to climb to reach the Indian encampment was "very rocky and steep, almost perpendicular." Sometimes they had to dismount and crawl on their hands and knees, with their exhausted horses scrabbling behind them, but at last they peered over the escarpment at the Indian camp below. The scene both thrilled and frightened Sarah. She estimated 327 lodges and 450 warriors (others'

156

estimates ran even higher). The words that later tumbled thoughtlessly from her pen — "It was a beautiful sight" — betrayed her riven heart. This doomed war meant danger to the future of her people, a danger she felt compelled to combat with every fiber of her being. Yet this was the grandest gathering of Indians she had ever seen. None knew better than she the weight of oppression and demeaning cruelties that had made them rise. And none felt more deeply their longing to live free from reservation tyranny.[26]

Although the Bannocks appeared largely occupied with butchering stolen cattle for an evening feast, Sarah admitted that the warriors swarming among the lodges below them made her feel "a little afraid." Nonetheless, she told Lee that they would leave their horses, run down into the valley on foot, and "trust to good luck." Lee entered Winnemucca's lodge first, then whistled for her to follow. Her father greeted his "dear little girl" with an outpouring of emotion, "Have you come to save me yet? My little child is in great danger. Oh, our Great Father in the Spirit Land, look down on us and save us!"[27]

Sarah hurriedly told them of Howard's promise and of her plan. The women must go out from the camp pretending to gather wood and make their escape. "Whisper it among yourselves. Get ready tonight for there is no time to lose," she cautioned them. She had hardly spoken when they began to slip out, one by one, with ropes in their hands, until only Sarah, Winnemucca, Lee, her companions, and several other men — all Winnemucca cousins of hers — remained in the lodge. By then darkness was falling, and the time had come to start. Winnemucca told Lee to gather as many horses as he could and meet them at Juniper Lake.[28]

As they climbed the mountain in the dusk, lack of sleep, the long, hard journey, excitement, and imminent danger took their toll on Sarah, but now she had Winnemucca to rely on when her strength and resolution faltered: "It was like a dream. I could not get along at all. I almost fell down at every step, my father dragging me along." When they heard a running horse close by, they all dropped to the ground and waited breathlessly. The horse stopped. Seemingly interminable moments passed before they heard a whistle they recognized. The rider was Mattie, Lee's young wife, bringing a horse from Lee for his exhausted sister. Gratefully, Sarah rode up the mountain, a faint shadow in the gathering darkness. Then, while the men led the horses down the steep slope, Sarah and Mattie ran down hand in hand. They would remain boon companions until Mattie's death.[29]

Beside the black mirror of Juniper Lake, the women of Winnemucca's band were cooking the mountain sheep meat Sarah and her companions had cached earlier. Sarah belatedly realized that she had given little thought to food during her headlong rush to Steens Mountain. "I did not know what hunger was all that time — I had forgotten all about eating." Nor could she take the time for it now. She told the women to mount their horses, tie their children to their backs, and eat as they rode, "for we must travel all night." When Lee declared that he wanted to go back after the near-blind Jerry Long, Sarah urged him to gather as many more as possible and meet them at Summit Springs. Winnemucca gave the order to ride, two by two, with six men in the rear as guards, and the cavalcade set off in the darkness.[30]

At daybreak they reached Summit Springs. Having ridden long and hard, with scant sleep, for two nights, Sarah lay down in exhaustion. No sooner did she close her eyes, however, than Winnemucca ordered her to first eat some of the sheep meat. She obeyed and inquired whether guards had been posted. Just then the alarm sounded and everyone leapt for their horses. Sarah and Mattie galloped out bareback to meet an incoming rider, who told them the Bannocks were following. When the rider's horse foundered, Sarah told him to jump onto her horse behind her. When they reached the camp, he related his news, "I looked back and saw Lee running, and they firing at him. I think he is killed. Oytes is at the head of this. I heard him say to the Bannocks, 'Go quickly, bring Sarah's head and her father's too. I will show Sarah who I am. Away with you, men, and overtake them.'"[31]

Winnemucca, stricken, declared, "If my son is killed, I will go back to them and be killed too."

"Father, it is no time to talk nonsense now," Sarah told him in desperation. "Be quick. Let us go. For my part, my life is very dear to me, though I would lose it in trying to save yours."[32]

Mattie and Winnemucca's latest wife began to sob. Apparently, Sarah prevailed on Winnemucca to start the cavalcade in motion once more, but the group did not move fast enough to suit what Howard called her "impatient spirit." She decided to ride rapidly ahead and asked him what message she should carry to the general. Winnemucca said that she should ask him to send soldiers to protect his people. Her exhaustion forgotten, Sarah mounted her horse immediately. Mattie called out to her, "Dear sister, let me go with you. If my poor husband is killed, why need I stay?" The two women set off together on a wild ride Sarah would never forget:

Away we started over the hills and valleys. . . . No water. We sang and prayed to our Great Father in the Spirit-land, as my people call God. About one o'clock we got to the crossing of a creek called Muddy Creek. We got off our horses and had a drink of water, and tied our horses till they got cooled off while we gathered some white currants to eat, for that is all we found. Now we watered our horses and found a narrow place to jump them across, and off again towards the soldiers as fast as our horses could carry us. We got to the crossing of the Owyhee River at three o'clock; stopped twenty minutes to eat some hard bread and coffee while they saddled fresh horses for us. We jumped on our horses again, and I tell you we made our time count. . . . We whipped our horses every step of the way till we were met by the officers.[33]

With a thunder of drumming hooves, they passed the bluffs and entered the stockade at Sheep Ranch late in the afternoon of 15 June. Bernard himself came forward to help Sarah from her horse. She burst into tears, too fatigued and excited to speak. In three days she had ridden 220 miles, a journey so remarkable that some of the officers could scarcely believe it. Sarah took justifiable pride in what she had done: "I went for the government when the officers could not get an Indian man or a white man to go for love or money. I, only an Indian woman, went and saved my father and his people." Since Howard's headquarters had moved to Sheep Ranch, she hastened to recover her composure and make her report to the general, who dispatched some troops guided by Paiute Joe to bring Winnemucca and his band to safety. Time would show that the Bannocks had not in fact killed Lee — indeed, he would outlive Sarah by many years. According to Howard, Sarah had saved seventy-five of her people; Winnemucca reckoned even more.[34]

Howard had already been impressed by Sarah on his visits to Malheur and would long remain one of her staunchest supporters. Then forty-eight, one-armed as a result of a Civil War wound, bearded, and handsome, with wavy brown hair, Howard was known as the "praying general" by his fellow officers — and somewhat scorned for his excessive attention to Christian ritual. He had headed the military Department of the Columbia since 1874 and conducted much of the pursuit of the Nez Percé in their flight toward Canada in 1877. Sometimes condemned for military movements "slower than cold molasses," he suffered by comparison with so brilliant a commander as Crook, but he had solid virtues of patience, persistence, and competence, and never risked his troops by placing them needlessly in perilous situations.[35]

If his military record was unspectacular, his record as a humanitarian toward both blacks and Indians reached a much higher level. This was the man who had headed the Freedmen's Bureau, the man in whose honor Howard University had been named, the man who persuaded Cochise to make peace, and the man who treated the Indians his profession sometimes compelled him to battle as human beings worthy of respect. A cultural imperialist he may have been, eager to civilize and Christianize the Indian, but as historian Robert Utley points out, we can scarcely expect him to espouse concepts beyond the range of the nineteenth century's most liberal thinkers. While Sarah made her excited report on the strength of the Bannocks and the escape of her band, Howard had other matters on his mind than civilizing the Indian. He had a war to fight.[36]

Howard immediately engaged Sarah and Mattie ("these brave women") as guides and interpreters. In fact, Sarah had just performed the functions of a scout in military intelligence. She located the en-

Gen. Oliver O. Howard, c. 1865. Courtesy of the Library of Congress.

emy, determined his strength and tribal identity, and found his trail. Although the army had long relied upon Indian scouts in the West, it was a highly unusual role for a woman. Whatever her official title, Sarah served as scout, guide, and interpreter and also left a vivid chronicle of the war. It was to be a short but complicated conflict in which the need to guard exposed settlements and block possible enemy escape routes obliged Howard to divide his forces. But the war as Sarah experienced it in the Oregon theater of operations is the matter that concerns us here.[37]

While Howard admired Sarah's competence, strength, and resolve, Mattie, her comrade in arms, charmed him with her "sweet manners and loving spirit." Mattie was then about twenty, and Sarah's references to her as "dear little Mattie" suggest that she was small and slight. Although she had attended the Malheur school where Sarah taught for a while, she lacked Sarah's fluency in English. She spoke it rarely and hesitantly, "with a pretty musical tone, each sentence sounding sometimes like a song," as Howard remembered. After her father, Paiute chief Shenkah, died from battle wounds when she was so small that she could scarcely remember him, Mattie was raised with loving kindness by her uncle, Egan. In time, she became the young bride of Sarah's middle-aged brother Lee. Like Sarah, she must have ridden for the army with a divided heart.[38]

Howard's revised battle plan centered upon sending his cavalry forward in separate columns to trap the Indians in their camp at Steens Mountain, a decision in which Sarah's report on the number and location of the Indians played a critical part. He had previously thought the enemy consisted of a comparatively small raiding party encamped in the area of the Camas Prairie and the Lava Beds. In his own words, "I had sufficient confidence in her story to change my whole plan of movement — a change which afterward proved to be for the best." At this juncture, he briefly shifted his headquarters east to old Camp Lyon, an outpost on upper Cow Creek near the Idaho-Oregon border that had been sold several years earlier to a local rancher.[39]

Thus an angry Sarah found herself jolting slowly along in a wagon away from the looming battle, when she would have much preferred to be flying forward with the cavalry. But Howard had ordered her to remain with his headquarters, and she obeyed. When some cavalry units rode past them, the soldiers thought Sarah had been taken prisoner. Sarah and Mattie laughed, but they would soon see how rampantly the rumor of Sarah's disloyalty had flourished. Finally, the general and his staff arrived at Camp Lyon, which consisted of a pole-and-log corral in a meadow and, on a gravel bar south of a creek, a rudimentary outpost of hand-hewn cottonwood and pine log buildings with earth-covered pole-and-willow roofs. Howard began negotiating with a stage owner who demanded a large price for transporting the party north to Stone House.[40]

Outraged, Sarah cut into the conversation, "That is the way with you citizens. You call on the soldiers for protection and you all want to make thousands of dollars out of it. I know if my people had a herd of a thousand horses they would let you have them all for nothing." The general looked at her oddly and said, "Yes, Sarah, your people have good hearts, better ones than these white dogs have." Nevertheless, the stage owner got his price.[41]

In hot, dry weather they made a two-day journey through barren alkali and sagebrush country amidst clouds of thick dust. The hired stage finally drew up before a two-story inn of thick, rectangular, gray stone blocks with tall arched windows beneath a wooden balcony. Here, at Stone House (in present Vale), families and travelers from the surrounding countryside had fled for refuge. Soon after their arrival, the rumors of Sarah's disloyalty came to a head. Frank Parker, the traveler Sarah had encountered at Malheur, told Howard that Sarah had incited the Indians at the reservation to make war. The general called Sarah to confront her accuser. This monstrous falsehood made her weep, and she related the events of that journey with passionate emotion interspersed with tears. Not only did she convince the general that she spoke the truth but also Parker realized that he had been misinformed and asked her forgiveness.[42]

Although Sarah never suggested it, one suspects the fine hand of Rinehart in the suspicions that snapped at her heels. After all, he had blamed her rather than his own corruption and mismanagement for the troubles at Malheur, and now he badly needed a scapegoat. The embarrassing circumstance that the Indians, under what one army officer derisively called his "tender loving care," had deserted the reservation to the last man had not gone unnoticed in the press. The *Sil-*

ver State bluntly observed, "We believe that his mistreatment of the Indians under his immediate supervision at Malheur, has caused them, one and all, to leave the reservation and join the Bannocks." Why not again blame Sarah?[43]

The next day, 19 June, the general and his entourage proceeded about twenty-five miles north toward Malheur City. When Howard asked Sarah for her assessment of a frightened settler's report that the Indians lurked close at hand, her opinion that none had moved near provided reassurance. No doubt the rumor sprouted from the nervous atmosphere that Major Mason perceived around them: "The people over about Harney are so scart they can't think straight." Nonetheless, alarming tidings that Captain McGregor's force had been annihilated and that massacre threatened Camp Harney could not be discounted. Whether reinforcements had reached Bernard remained unknown, and the general wanted immediate communication with the camp, a mission he saw as one of "great importance." Sarah, her impatient spirit straining at the bit, would have preferred to carry his dispatch with no other companion than Mattie, for she knew that Indians riding alone could travel faster, but the general, evidently mindful of the dangers Indians faced from terror-stricken white men along the way, sent his aide-de-camp Lt. Melville C. Wilkinson and two other soldiers with the Indian women.[44]

If the general thought vengeful settlers might endanger his Indian couriers, events soon proved him right. When the party stopped for a meal at the last stage stop before entering the no-man's-land where all had fled, the settlers' hatred scalded Sarah. The woman who brought their coffee had evidently heard the rumors of her disloyalty and presumed her to be a prisoner—as had others.

"Well, I never thought I should feed you again. I hope they will not let you off this time," she said while the protesting lieutenant vainly tried to silence her. "Why do you take so much trouble in taking her to Camp Harney? Why don't you take her and tie one part of her to a horse, and the other part of her to another horse, and let them go? I would see the horses pull her to pieces with good grace."

"You don't know what you are talking about," said Wilkinson. "This is Sarah Winnemucca."

"I don't care. Rope is too good to hang her with."

Wilkinson told Sarah not to mind this crazy woman. But Sarah did mind. The woman's hatred affected her so much that she could not eat, even though she badly needed sustenance for the long ride ahead. Like every insult she ever received, the woman's venomous words remained graven in her memory. Years later she wrote, "Dear reader, this is the kind of white women that are in the West. They are always ready to condemn me."[45]

They rode on, taking many shortcuts known only to the Indians, and reached the Malheur Reservation agency as the midnight blue sky above the dark silhouette of Castle Rock darkened and the first stars appeared. The agency buildings were deserted — a place for ghosts, a graveyard for past hopes. Sarah remembered: "Everything was dark and still, as if every living thing was dead, and there was no living thing left. This is the way it felt as we passed."[46]

On through the night they rode, for even in the darkness the women knew the way, guided by the stars above the black mountains. Lieutenant Wilkinson showed signs of giving out after so many hours in the saddle. Indeed, not many white men developed Indian endurance. One newspaper correspondent, after a shorter ride, complained of being "completely worn out," with the seat of his saddle "badly demoralized" and "every pound of my flesh in a complete jelly." One white courier even died of the strain after bringing a dispatch to Boise. An army officer admiringly wrote of Sarah, "She has been constantly in the field, enduring hardships that strong men succumbed under." Yet when they finally passed the mesas rimmed with gray rock and in midmorning reached the wooden buildings of Camp Harney, even Sarah felt so exhausted that she went to bed without eating.[47]

She would not rest long, however. Important news had to be taken back to Howard. Although reports repeatedly surfaced about Egan's lack of enthusiasm for war, Sarah's kind friend had accepted the position of Buffalo Horn's replacement as war chief of the hostiles, per-

A newspaper drawing of Sarah on an army mission. *Sunday Oregonian*,
5 Aug. 1906. Courtesy of the University of Washington Libraries.

haps from an awareness of the disasters that would ensue if the more
bloodthirsty Oytes took control. The Indians escaped from Howard's
maneuver to entrap them with converging columns at their camp at
Steens Mountain and traveled rapidly northwest over rough, broken
canyon and mesa desert country to reach Silver Creek, in a broad valley some forty-five miles southwest of Camp Harney.[48]

Their flight, then and in the weeks to follow, remains one of the
most remarkable untold epics in the Indian wars because women and
children traveled with the men. Egan's band, in the last census at Malheur, consisted of 54 men, some surely too old to fight, and 119 women
and children; Oytes's band counted 38 men and 104 women and children. Together, the Malheur Reservation Indians (not including Winnemucca's band of 144) totaled 598. This suggests that the reports of
700 to 2,000 Indian warriors may have been exaggerated — perhaps by

166

the tendency to inflate the enemy's numbers in order to add credit to one's own performance. Though how many Bannocks joined the uprising remains unknown. The entire tribe counted only about 1,000, and the 2 to 1 ratio of women and children to men probably applied to them as well. Howard, who never dehumanized his Indian enemies or succeeded in moving his troops as quickly as they did, admired their ability to flee so rapidly with small children and elderly folk in tow: "Their march was phenomenal. No white caravan of like size could stand such tremendous strain and fatigue."[49]

Nonetheless, on 23 June, Bernard's three companies of cavalry caught the Indians unaware in their camp near a stream flowing between banks thickly overgrown with willow bushes. Like some other engagements in the Indian wars, the victory at Silver Creek hailed at the time appears more ambiguous in retrospect. Bernard, a seasoned veteran of ninety-eight fights and scrimmages during more than twenty years in the army, instructed his men, "We came here to whip them and we are going to do it. I want you all to keep good order and no running. If anyone runs, I will have him shot, so he might as well die by the enemy as by friends. Forward! Not too fast!"[50]

The bugle sounded the charge, and the cavalry pounded pell-mell upon the Indian camp. By then, most of the Indians had managed to evacuate to positions in the nearby bluffs, where the cavalry could not follow. The Indians resisted with vigor. Both sides fought bravely in several hand-to-hand encounters and both suffered some casualties. After galloping through the deserted camp twice with blazing guns, the cavalry decided to await reinforcements, and withdrew. That night the Indians lit sagebrush fires to make the soldiers believe they were still ensconced in the bluffs and melted away into the mountains to the north under cover of darkness. Although this engagement bears little resemblance to a glorious victory, the army had inflicted serious damage: they had deprived the Indians of the supplies, including ammunition, hastily abandoned in the camp; they had captured an old blind woman, who proved to be Buffalo Horn's aunt; and they had badly wounded Egan, who sustained bullets in the wrist, chest, and groin.[51]

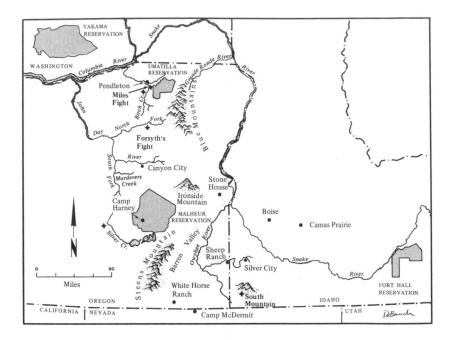

The Bannock War, 1878

10

The Bannock War

"I had a vision, and I was screaming
in my sleep"

THE BATTLE OF SILVER CREEK was the news that Sarah, Mattie, and the soldiers brought late at night to General Howard at his camp about fifteen miles from the Malheur agency. The arrival of his couriers completed what the general termed in his report "a very hazardous enterprise." Howard would have liked Sarah to turn around immediately and head back to Camp Harney with his orders, but she had already ridden two hundred miles on this mission, by his calculations, and she needed a few hours of sleep before she could swing back into her saddle again and ride on. The general and his troops breakfasted at one in the morning and moved on for a twelve-hour ride of fifty miles over mountains and rocky roads. After Sarah and Mattie arrived at Camp Harney, soldiers brought Buffalo Horn's aunt, an old blind Bannock woman, to their tent for questioning. They cared for her kindly, but, at first, she refused to talk. It was Mattie, that same sweet, gentle Mattie whose words usually sounded like songs, who threatened the woman so severely that she told all. The woman mistakenly believed that Oytes had taken the place of Buffalo Horn. She said the Indians intended to head north to the Umatilla Reservation, where Oytes expected the Umatillas to join them. And she wept for her dead nephew, Buffalo Horn.[1]

As Sarah told the old woman's story to Howard, she emphasized that a great deal depended upon the Umatillas. Beyond the Umatilla Reservation, the fleeing Indians may have hoped to reach Chief Moses, the leader of disaffected elements north of the Columbia River, and they may have ultimately sought to join Sitting Bull in Canada. Howard expected to catch the Indians within the next few days, but he took precautionary measures. He positioned gunboats on the Columbia River to prevent them from crossing and ordered intense suasion and surveillance at the Umatilla Reservation. White volunteer scouts continually reported that the Bannocks were close by and about to give battle. When the general asked Sarah's opinion, she assured him that the Indians had moved on.[2]

As Howard and his staff, accompanied by the two Indian women, rode north across the valley and into the mountains, following the Indians' trail, Sarah and Mattie spied something on a high hill. They immediately recognized it as an Indian subterfuge but decided to keep quiet and "have some fun" at the expense of the white scouts. Sure enough, the bugle sounded a halt, and the captain of the volunteer scouts rode up to report Indians on the hill. Howard, unconvinced because he saw no movement among these apparent Indians through his field glasses, asked Sarah what she thought about it.

"I see nothing but rocks put there to deceive you," she replied.

When the scouts persisted in believing they saw Indians, she spurred her horse to ride up the hill to demonstrate that no danger lurked there. Howard called her back and sent some troops instead. The officers and "the girls," as Major Mason started calling Sarah and Mattie, had a good laugh at the white scouts over the campfire that night. Sarah explained, "It is a way by which we Indians do deceive the white people by piling rocks on each other and putting round ones on the top to make them look like men. In this way we get time to get away from our enemy."[3]

On 28 June, observed Sarah, "we took up the trail in good earnest," pressing into the mountains with the general's force of 480 men. In contrast to the hot, dusty ride north of Camp Lyon, during this journey it rained. Before long, the rain turned into a heavy driving snowstorm, through which they marched all day. That night they struck a large, abandoned Indian camp, where Sarah thought the signs suggested 1,500 to 2,000 Indians. She explained that the Indians stripped the pine trees around their camps because they ate the inner bark and used the outer bark as both fuel and as a covering on the snowy ground where they slept. The pursuit slowed, due to the extreme difficulties of moving supply-wagons — some drawn by plodding, straining oxen — over a rough mountain trail. "What a diversified country!" wrote Howard. "Jagged rocks, precipitous slopes, knife-edged divides, deep canyons with sides steep and difficult, the distance from a crest to the mountain stream that tumbled over the rocks far below being sometimes four or five miles." Egan had evidently chosen an escape route that he knew white men would find difficult to follow.[4]

The advice of two white miners Howard had engaged as guides when the pursuit party passed into country unfamiliar to Sarah and Mattie contributed to their dilemma. As the mountains grew steeper, the forest thicker, and the path more tortuous, one guide deserted, and the other confessed he was lost. Although waiting for pack animals to arrive would have further delayed the army, Sarah thought trying to overtake Indians with slow-moving wagons a ridiculous notion. Mason, dark-haired and bearded, with large, mournful eyes, agreed, "This thing of following an Indian trail with wagons won't do." The frustrated general sent Captain Bernard and the cavalry ahead in hot pursuit. His pursuit proved not so hot, however. Sarah noted rather critically that the cavalry advanced only a short way before camping.[5]

Meanwhile, panic reigned at Canyon City. The fierce reputation of the Bannocks and public horror over the annihilation of Custer's command at the Little Bighorn only two years earlier undoubtedly tinged the atmosphere, and alarms from the white volunteers did their part. Rinehart, himself no stranger to panic, described it well. After returning for his records and encountering Howard at Malheur, where the general ordered him to serve the army as a guide or be imprisoned — and might not have minded an excuse for imprisoning him — Rinehart briefly obliged before fleeing the agency for Canyon City. A small group of volunteers skirmished with some Indians and rode in with a false report that the Indians were sweeping up the valley toward the town. "The panic which followed beggars description," wrote Rinehart. The "long-roll" sounded from the courthouse; men yelled; dogs barked; and women and children screamed. "Over one hundred families left their homes and clambered hastily up the steep bluff west of the town" to take refuge in the old mine tunnels. News of another skirmish with the Indians that supposedly left two volunteers dead and the rest "flying before the enemy" brought renewed panic. Some time passed before the residents of Canyon City realized that the Indians had no intention of massacring them and crept out of the tunnels.[6]

The army struggled on through the mountains, but at least the snow had stopped, and they rested when they reached a pleasant, grassy spot with sweet water and tall pines. Mason was much impressed by Sarah: "Sarah is a remarkable woman — a full-blooded Piute Indian, yet well educated, speaks the best of English, and can read and write as well as anybody. . . . She is very much more of a lady in her manner and address than many white women I know." Clearly, she had lost none of the style that had made soldiers cheer and lift their hats in the air when she rode her galloping horse into the parade ground at Camp McDermit. "It would interest you to see them [Sarah and Mattie] go anywhere with a dash few men could excel," Mason wrote to his wife.[7]

Sarah and Mattie shared a tent at headquarters and always took their meals with the general and his staff. During these trailside dinners, Sarah often spoke bitterly against Oytes and others who had led her people into war. Another topic of conversation arose when the officers probed to satisfy their curiosity about Sarah's former husband Edward Bartlett, his family well known in the service. It surprised Mason to learn that *she* had divorced *him*. Sarah, unaware that her former husband had been married to another woman for nearly six years, explained to the general that Edward was "too bad a man for any woman to live with." Mason's letter relating this juicy gossip to his wife is laced with exclamation points.[8]

It may be that Howard, through acquaintance with Edward and his family, knew more about Sarah's marriage than he said in the presence of the other officers. Later, in his reflections in *My Life and Experiences among Our Hostile Indians* on the sad outcomes of interracial marriage, he wrote of "the son of a leading citizen, in the wild days of his youth, [who] thought it would be an amusing surprise to his friends, and certainly gratifying to himself, to marry an Indian girl." The Indian bride, though not named, bore an uncanny resemblance to Sarah: she spoke fluent English and Spanish, had been educated by the Sisters of Charity (as Sarah claimed), was "bright and handsome," and felt "flattered and delighted with her prospects."[9] After marriage, Howard related, the young man drank heavily and induced his wife to drink with him. Whiskey made her "wild and unmanageable." When the couple "overturned all the staid customs of society" in a large unnamed city (Salt Lake City?), "it took much ready money and all of its influence to keep these young people out of the clutches of the law." The young man gave his wife what Howard termed an "Indian divorce," then married a white woman and raised a family — as Edward had indeed done. Although the general's account reveals aspects of the marriage that Sarah never disclosed, he still came down solidly on her side. He declared that he knew both the abandoned Indian wife and her former husband for years and, in his opinion, she was "far superior" to him.[10]

The ordeal in the mountains had not yet ended. Sarah later wrote: "Oh, such a time as we did have! On 1 July, great difficulty was encountered in getting the wagon train into the deep valley of the South Fork of the John Day River, the hill being five miles in descent and so steep as to cause constant sliding of the wagons. It took from two o'clock P.M. until after ten o'clock at night to worry the train down the hill into the camp." When they reached the point where Murderer's Creek flows into the South Fork, Sarah and Mattie saw signs of a skirmish between Indians and volunteers and pointed out the graves of two herders killed by Indians. They rode on through juniper and sagebrush country, past mountains thinly seamed with horizontal rock outcroppings. Mason, however, saw only the difficulties of the terrain ("the most broken country I have ever seen wagons taken over"). At that point, Mason's initial assessment of the outbreak as a "big spree" among the Indians that would be quickly crushed must have seemed wide of the mark.[11]

After thirteen hours in the saddle, they reached a deserted ranch house at present Dayville, where the South Fork joins the John Day River in a narrow, pleasant, grassy valley. Despite many hours of riding, Sarah remained as fresh and energetic as ever. Mason related that "In a few minutes Sarah Winnemucca and her sister were in the kitchen putting things to rights, and in due time a good supper was on the table — coffee, biscuits, spring chicken, eggs. Sarah is a good cook, and as bright and cheerful as possible." Though no special ceremony commemorated the occasion, it was the Fourth of July. Somewhere in the rear, the soldiers continued their struggle with the wagons, while the Indians, with the cavalry behind them, had moved three days ahead, burning ranches, pillaging, murdering, and terrorizing the countryside.[12]

Throughout northeastern Oregon, settlers fled to the towns, and pandemonium on par with Canyon City's seized Pendleton, a loose square of one-story shacks that housed about 150 inhabitants and an equal number of refugees from the countryside. A company of Pendleton volunteers skirmished with Indians nearby and beat a rapid retreat. One observer later said that the men defending Pendleton were such a small group — poorly armed, incompetent, and utterly demoralized — that the town would easily have fallen to a fairly small force of Indians. But the Indians made no such move. A local history attributed this to Egan's poor military tactics: indeed, his "imbecility." After all, it was what many white men would have done in his place. However, as historian George Brimlow has pointed out, the Indians avoided battle in their sweep to the north, except at the Umatilla Reservation, and attacked no towns. It may be that Egan had no wish to massacre the people of Pendleton and that it was not military imbecility but simple humanity that led him to spare the town.[13]

After sending a flurry of dispatches, Howard and his entourage pressed hurriedly onward to catch up with Bernard and the cavalry. In one day they covered sixty-seven miles (which Mason thought quite a feat and Sarah probably saw as an ordinary day's work), passing through a forest of tall pines into the open, billowing contours of the Fox Valley, rimmed in the west by a low, level ridge of mountains, blue with heavy timber. Catching up with Bernard at last, they pressed on through higher mountains that made Mason complain of the cold even while he admired the scenery of "this wild and picturesque country, so high in the air." The night of 6 July found them about fifty miles from Pendleton.[14]

By the evening of 7 July, they had caught up with the Indians near Pilot Rock. Howard toyed with the idea of sending Sarah to the Indian camp to negotiate a surrender but finally decided the danger to her was too great. "If you should get killed, your father will blame me," he told her. Sarah warned the general that the Indians would have "the best of it" in a battle on this terrain because the cavalry would have to fight their way to the crest of a bare, rocky slope and the Indians could escape into the timber. "He would not believe it," and the next day the army and the Indians met once more in the Battle of Birch Creek.[15]

Again we catch sight of Sarah's divided loyalties toward those she sometimes alluded to as "the enemy" and at other times as "my people": "What a feeling I had just before the fight came on! Every drop of blood in my veins went out. I said to sister, 'We will see a great many of our people killed today, and soldiers, too.'" Mattie shared her emotions. She had told Howard, "I am no coward-girl, and I am not afraid even when the guns fire; but I do not want war." One of the soldiers watching Sarah mistook her agitation for intense anger over the imminent battle. The bugle sounded, and Sarah whipped her horse forward to stand beside the booming Gatling gun. She heard the chiefs singing as they ran along the front line, leaping up in their defiance. She recognized Oytes's voice calling, "Come on, you white dogs — what are you waiting there for?" "All my feeling was gone," Sarah remembered. "I wanted to go to them." At the same time that a part of her longed to run to her people, Sarah admired the bravery of the cavalry in their steady advance up the hill under fire.[16]

The battle ended much as Sarah had foreseen, with the Indians disappearing into the forest. She could tell they had suffered less damage than at Silver Creek, since they had managed to move their women and children and their herds of good horses to the rear in advance of the battle, while abandoning some two hundred jaded mounts. After it was over, Sarah saw Birch Creek as a bit of a farce ("Sometimes I laugh when I think of this battle"). Although spent cartridges littered the ground, casualties on both sides had been very light. The suspicion arose that the battle had been a holding action by the Indians, intended to delay the army while the main body made their escape. Again, Howard had missed the decisive victory that would have brought an end to the war. "I felt that night tired and chagrined," he wrote. "This experience reminded me of a hunter chasing an antelope all day with several beautiful chances in his favor, but the animal's quick ears and native fleetness divined the hunter's approach and enabled it to elude all his shots."[17]

The fleet antelope would soon be brought to ground. Suspecting that the Indians were headed south, Howard, with Bernard's cavalry, moved toward Idaho by way of Fort Walla Walla. Gunboats had prevented the Indians from crossing the Columbia River. When they again veered north, Capt. Evan Miles repulsed them near the Umatilla agency on 13 July. It was a small engagement but a highly significant one, which decided the allegiance of the Umatillas, who observed the outcome from a nearby hill. That night, the Umatillas requested permission to ally themselves with the army, a major breakthrough because, until then, Howard had met with "unusual reluctance" when he tried to persuade Indians to join his forces in suppressing the Bannocks. Natches had tried and failed to persuade the Nevada Paiute chiefs to fight with the army in this campaign, and the Indians at the Warm Springs Reservation, who played a part in the Modoc War, also refused to participate. As historian Thomas Dunlay points out, the

A Bannock War battle scene. Reprinted from Howard, *My Life and Experiences among Our Hostile Indians.*

army relied heavily on Indian allies to control the vast territory of the West with a relatively small force.[18]

These new allies had methods of their own. Sarah believed it was the shaman power of the Winnemuccas to see visions that woke her in the darkness. "On the night that Egan was murdered I saw it all in my sleep. I had a vision, and I was screaming in my sleep when Mattie waked me and asked what was the matter. I told her that Egan was murdered, and I saw it all, saw his head cut off, and saw him cut in pieces." It was true. Though sources differ on whose hand did the deed and what institution became the final repository of Egan's head, all agree on the essentials. In order to avoid punishment for having initially joined the hostiles and to collect the bounty (never paid) that a settler had placed on Egan's head, Umapine, a Cayuse chief cooperating with the Umatillas, decoyed the grievously wounded chief to a meeting to discuss the alliance of which Buffalo Horn had dreamed. There, they treacherously murdered and mutilated Egan and the handful of men who accompanied him and captured eighteen Paiute women and children who ran to the scene when they heard gunfire. When an army officer told Umapine that the scalp he displayed provided insufficient proof that he had killed Egan, Umapine brought in the chief's severed head and left arm, a bloody deed that may have afforded the Cayuse perverse pleasure. Howard thought as much, "In war he displayed profound treachery and positive enjoyment of murder. Even his mates shuddered at his brutality. After committing atrociously wicked acts he would strut with pride and boast of his brutal prowess."[19]

In a letter published in the *Silver State*, Sarah wrote to Natches about the tragic death of their good friend from Malheur. At this point she knew that "the hostiles are sure to be whipped" and declared herself "much distressed about our friends." She was anxious to persuade the Indians to surrender, if Natches or Lee could arrange a meeting. Indeed, no Indian, however harmless, was safe. In her book, Sarah relates at length the story of an old Indian leading his blind wife through the woods. White men set upon them, scalped the blind woman, and cut her husband in pieces. Hearing his dying groans, "she felt so thankful that she could not see." In another incident, a burly settler took Howard to task for failing to kill his Indian prisoners, a breach of military conduct that the general heatedly rejected.[20]

The murder of their leader and the collapse of their plans completely demoralized the hostile Indians. They broke up into small bands and headed southward once more, intending to hide in the mountains until the crisis passed or lose themselves among the Indians who had taken refuge at army posts. In the wake of Birch Creek, Sarah had voiced disagreement with other scouts, who believed the hostiles would head eastward toward the Grande Ronde River. Events proved her right. After receiving news of the decisive engagement at the Umatilla Reservation, Howard, with Sarah at his side, changed course and headed up the Grande Ronde with Major Sanford's unit, while dispatching Bernard's cavalry (now commanded by Col. James Forsyth) to the Umatilla Reservation. As Howard continued to pursue Indians southward through the Blue Mountains toward Malheur, his stated object was "to bring in the Indians as prisoners, and, if possible,

Umapine, seated in the center, with other Indian scouts. Neg. no. 9536, courtesy of the Oregon Historical Society.

allay the wild fears of the ranch people and settlers, who never felt sure of protection until they saw the troops." Mason nonetheless suspected him of hoping for the conclusive victory that had repeatedly eluded him.[21]

At the same time, Forsyth chased a fleeing group of Indians near the headwaters of the John Day River up and down steep canyons, over high mountains, and through "a perfect network of fallen timber," a route he believed the Indians had chosen to slow their pursuers and gain time for their wounded, their women, and their children. Nonetheless, on 20 July, Forsyth finally caught up on a canyon of the North Fork of the John Day, where an estimated forty warriors had ensconced themselves on top of a hill. While ascending the steep canyon walls, soldiers slid down the zigzagging trail and pack animals fell backward into the stream below. According to the *Idaho Statesman*, a number of the men stampeded down the hill when the first shots rang out. By the time Forsyth rallied and redeployed his force, the Indians had escaped — as usual.[22]

Twenty-one July found Howard's contingent once again in snow in the high mountains near Canyon City. Mason's letter to his wife mentions "a grand game of snowball," probably involving the officers and "the girls." On 23 July they joined Forsyth's force at the Burnt River Meadows, where a small tree-lined river meandered through a grassy valley surrounded by low hills dotted with an occasional juniper or pine. With supplies temporarily short, Mason noted that the men "must live in the recollection" of their last meal.[23]

A soldier brought Sarah a six-month-old baby girl found when the Indians fled an attack (which attack remains unclear). Sarah identifies the attack as Forsyth's fight, and the baby may have been given to her three days later in Burnt River Meadows, when Forsyth and Howard conjoined. As Sarah took the baby in her arms, she may have remembered the time when she was buried in the sand while her parents fled. Her moment of motherhood lasted only briefly, however. She turned the baby over to an Indian woman just captured, adjuring her to keep the baby's shirt and beads so her parents would recognize her at once. Many weeks would pass before the reunion took place. Another reminder of the past appeared when the army reached Little Creek and Sarah encountered Sam Parrish for the last time. He held out his hands to her, and both wept for the tragedy of the Malheur Indians.[24]

The next camping place that Sarah recalled lay southward on the sagebrush plain at the base of Ironside Mountain, a twin-peaked outcropping with steep, bare flanks and a black cap of heavy timber. Howard decided to send Sarah, with Mattie, Lieutenant Wilkinson, and several others, directly south to the Malheur agency to see if any Indians had returned there to negotiate their surrender. Perhaps absences such as this one gave rise to a rumor among the soldiers that Sarah sometimes rode with the Indians. Seeing the agency still deserted, Sarah and her companions stayed the night and rode back, only to find that Howard had moved on toward the agency by a different route. Sarah declared herself too tired to continue without rest. Wilkinson worried about her safety but agreed to go on without her. Sarah and Mattie had rested only briefly when three men rode near. Sarah heard one say, "Come, boys, here are the girls, and the lieutenant is not with them."[25]

Sarah told Mattie to get her horse quickly, and "over the rocks and down the hill we went without stopping." The men pursued them, calling out to each other, "Catch them, boys, let's have a good time." Julius Argasse, with the long knife scar on his face, could have told them a bit about the likelihood of having a good time with Sarah, and many could have told them how little chance they had of catching Sarah once she had mounted her horse. Around six o'clock, Sarah and Mattie reined in their galloping horses at the agency, where Sarah told all to Howard and he immediately discharged the would-be rapists. Though Sarah does not identify them, they may have been volunteers, a category of humanity that Sarah despised as consistently as she praised the regular army ("The officers know well enough what they are good for").[26]

By this time, the hostiles had dispersed so widely that a general surrender could no longer be negotiated. All the same, at the general's behest, Sarah sent a captured Indian woman to her people with this promise: "Tell them I, their mother, say come back to their homes again. I will stand by them and see that they are not sent away to the Indian territory." A band of twenty-seven warriors and seventy-two women and children surrendered as prisoners of war. Before the year was done, Sarah may have regretted her promise.[27]

At the end of July, after nearly two months of campaigning, Howard and Sarah parted, bringing to an end a period of close association not seen in the West since Sacajawea accompanied Lewis and Clark. No doubt there had been many evenings along the trail like the one Mason described to his wife, with "the General and the girls standing around the campfire, laughing and talking." Howard had often turned to Sarah for advice — perhaps regretting it when he did not — relied upon her as a swift courier and a guide in unfamiliar country, protected her from the dangers she so casually ignored, and reined in her impatient spirit when he could. He later wrote of her, "She did our government great service, and if I could tell you a tenth part of all she willingly did to help the white settlers and her own people to live peaceably together I am sure you would think, as I do, that the name of Toc-me-to-ne should have a place beside the name of Pocahontas in the history of our country."[28]

Howard reached Boise on 7 August, having assigned Sarah and Mattie to accompany Forsyth on a hunt for Indian bands in the desert between Steens Mountain and the Owyhee River. Although Sarah guided the soldiers to every water source, they sometimes had to trek across forty- or fifty-mile stretches of waterless land, and men and horses suffered intensely from the midsummer heat. Hardened to the desert since childhood, Sarah pitied their misery ("my heart used to ache for the poor soldiers"). When Mattie's horse gave out, the two women took turns walking and riding Sarah's horse. They found no sign of Indians.[29]

After traveling nearly 150 miles since Malheur, they camped at White Horse Ranch (former Camp C. F. Smith). At last they spotted an Indian signal fire on the mountain in the night. When the officers asked Sarah to interpret, she explained that it signified "loneliness and distress." Just one Indian had lit it as a call for help to anyone in that vast emptiness who could understand the language of fires. Forsyth refused to believe her. She swore, in her usual impassioned way, that if they found more than one Indian on the mountain, "I have never told a truth in all my life." The subsequent capture of just one Indian, who proved to be a friend of Sarah's from Malheur, proved her right.[30] This was how the Bannock War ended — not in mass surrender, not in a decisive battle, but with a lone Indian lighting a signal fire of despair in the desert where the painted warriors had thundered by beside their great herd of horses.

Once they reached a point only seventy miles from Camp McDermit, Sarah's wish to visit her father and brothers became overwhelming, and Forsyth allowed her to go. He insisted, however, on a small military escort. Sarah agreed with reluctance, as she had envisaged a swift overnight ride. They moved at a brisk trot through the darkness, but when the lieutenant paused to repair his saddle, Sarah, too impetuous to brook delay, could no longer restrain herself and gained permission to ride ahead. "Oh, what a relief it was to gallop my horse!" The liquid rose light of dawn was washing over the mesas to the west of Camp McDermit as she rode in, giddy with exuberance, to the area where several hundred Indian refugees had encamped. Reaching Natches's *kahnee*, she teased him, "Haloo! Get up. The enemy is at hand!"[31]

Natches wrapped her in a blanket, brought her close to the fire, and called the people to gather in words that showed his pride in her. "I have here in my camp a warrior who has just arrived. Come, one and all, and see for yourselves."

Winnemucca, who had feared her dead, embraced her with tears running down his cheeks. Many had tears in their eyes as she told them all she had seen: the flight, the pursuit, the battles, the abandoned baby, the roster of the Indian dead and how each had died. Thus, time out of mind, had the returned Indian hero told his tale to the people by the campfire. When she spoke of how the evil counsel of Oytes had led Paiutes into this folly, they swore they would kill him if *taibo* failed to do it. On hearing of the treacherous murder of Egan, they immediately determined to kill Umapine, whom Sarah had told them was with Forsyth, along with several Umatilla scouts. Natches

condemned Umapine and the treacherous Umatillas as "barking coyotes" — the worst insult in the Paiute language — but he feared a violent act might jeopardize the return of women and children captured
by the Umatillas. Chief Homeli, with a mainly Umatilla force, had attacked a group of fleeing Paiutes on 17 July near Baker City and taken
more women and children, in addition to those seized after Egan's
murder. The people agreed to Natches's proposal that a small party
would accompany Sarah and himself to Forsyth's command. They
would publicly excoriate Umapine and his companions in front of the
officers, and they would concentrate upon what mattered most: the
return of the captive women and children.[32]

At this point, Winnemucca, who had so often held the people spellbound with his eloquent words in council, rose to pay the highest trib-
ute to his valorous daughter. He exhorted the Paiutes to maintain the
Winnemuccas' long commitment to peace and chided their refusal to
aid the army during the war. Sarah he praised: "How thankful I feel
that it is my own child who has saved so many lives, not only mine, but
a great many, both whites and her own people. Now hereafter we will
look on her as our chieftain, for none of us are worthy of being chief
but her."[33]

When they left in the early afternoon, Sarah scarcely noticed that
a long time had passed since she last slept. At Antelope Springs they
caught up with Forsyth's command of 250 men. After a fruitless
search for Umapine, who had prudently absented himself, Natches de-
livered the speech of condemnation he had planned to shame the Cayuse chief and his companions before the officers. The officers assured
him that Howard would not allow Umapine to go scot-free and that
every prisoner held by Indian allies would be turned over to the army
after all the Bannocks and their Paiute allies had surrendered. In fact,
by the end of September, Col. Nelson A. Miles and others had killed or
captured the last of the Bannocks in Montana and Wyoming Territories, where they had fled. Umapine, despicable though he was, had
made himself too useful to the army to suffer unpleasant consequences, and nothing further was heard of the Paiute captives held by

the Umatillas. On 12 August, Oytes surrendered at Malheur. Tribal tradition holds that he took refuge in the mysticism of the Dreamers at his trial: "Do what you will with my body, because I will return and show you a much greater battle. More blood will be spilled."[34] He had misunderstood the spirit voices, for the Bannock War was the last major Indian uprising in the Northwest.

The Paiute party returned to Camp McDermit, with the exception of Lee, who remained with Sarah and his young wife as they accompanied Forsyth. On the next day's forty-mile march, many soldiers' horses collapsed in the waterless desert before they made camp in the deep canyon where the three forks of the Owyhee River converged. From their next camp near Silver City, Forsyth moved to Boise to replace Howard, who had gone north on 12 August to hold councils with the Umatillas and other tribes and to return to the headquarters of the Department of the Columbia at Fort Vancouver. Sarah was sent south with Captains Bernard and Winters to gather up the Paiutes in that region.[35]

At Duck Valley they found a band of Paiutes who welcomed Sarah joyfully. As Bernard directed, she told them all Paiutes had been ordered to Camp McDermit because the settlers might mistake them for Bannocks and kill them. The captain did not exaggerate, since the settlers angrily criticized the army for not slaughtering all the Indians they found. In the words of the *Idaho Statesman*, "It is idle to talk about mercy to such vile wretches, or to think of treating them when caught and forced to surrender as ordinary prisoners of war, and worse than idle to indulge any idea of another effort to bring them within the pale of civilization. Every consideration in which humanity has any interest requires that they should cease to exist under any circumstances, and that in their case an example shall be made which will be sufficient to deter others from a like course." Such attitudes so sickened Mason that he privately observed, "I am so disgusted with the vile, low people on the frontier — I have no heart to fight for them."[36]

After giving a letter of safe passage to the Paiutes at Duck Valley, Sarah returned to Boise, traveling the last stretch by stagecoach — no doubt a welcome change after so many weeks on horseback. When Forsyth asked her to talk with Shoshone prisoners in custody at the fort, Sarah spoke to them in Shoshone, but they maintained a stony silence — the first sign of how greatly Sarah's service to the army had damaged her standing among Indians. More than a century later, some of her own people blamed her still for the deaths of those who fell in the Bannock War. Among whites, by contrast, her celebrity had soared. A newspaper in Chicago eulogized her as a "heroic Indian woman" and praised her "great courage, her faithfulness to her promises to the whites, and her valuable services." The *New York Times* reported her remarkable exploits on the front page, under the headline "A BRAVE INDIAN SQUAW." Natches, as well, in the words of the *Silver State*, was "almost idolized" by the white settlers whose lives he had saved. They showered him with gifts that included a fine horse, a saddle and bridle, and a rifle.[37]

The army next requested Sarah to accompany Capt. Thomas McGregor's command to Camp Harney, now the repository for many Indian prisoners. They traveled by way of Baker City, and they had scarcely entered Canyon City, where Sarah anticipated a visit with Annie Parrish, when McGregor hustled her out of town. He explained that the sheriff wanted to detain her as a witness against Oytes at his forthcoming trial. At Harney, Sarah and Mattie went from one Indian camp to another showing the lost baby with her little yellow shirt and beads in the hope of finding her parents. When they encountered a young couple in deep mourning, their quest ended in joyful tears and the gratitude of parents, who said "everything that was beautiful" to Sarah and Mattie. The couple related that in their flight through the heavy timber, the baby had been thrown from her basket on a packhorse.[38]

On 12 July, when the war was still in progress, Natches had taken the wise step of journeying to San Francisco, accompanied by several Paiute leaders, to inform General McDowell that because no Paiutes outside Egan's and Oytes's bands had taken part in the war, these noncombatants should not be treated as prisoners. In September, an order directed that all Indians from the Malheur Reservation who were gathered at Camp McDermit should be moved to Camp Harney prior to wintering at Malheur. Sarah was sent with the two cavalry units under Captains McGregor and Wagner that the army detailed to effect this plan, evidently because resistance or flight were anticipated. One of the cavalrymen riding with her, Lewis H. Hopkins, was to play a large part in her future life. When she explained the order to the Paiutes at Camp McDermit, they sensed trouble: "We know there is something wrong. We don't like to go." Indeed, for some time Indian men in fear of being labeled prisoners of war and sent to a distant reservation had been slipping away from Camp McDermit in spite of Winnemucca's pleas to remain and assurances from Natches.[39]

Again and again they questioned Sarah, and she reassured them: "What need have you to be afraid? You have not done anything. . . . General Howard knows all about you. None of you have fought the whites. You have all done your duty to the whites during the campaign." She had no way of knowing that Generals Howard and McDowell had been debating their fate in an unusually sharp series of dispatches. When Howard sought to banish all Paiutes then at various army posts to the Indian Territory, McDowell responded, "You seem disposed to treat all Paiutes as hostile, and punish the innocent for the sins of the guilty." Many of them, he observed, "exerted themselves to save the lives and property of whites at personal risk."[40]

When Howard demanded an accounting of the number of Paiute prisoners at Camp McDermit, post commander Col. John D. Wilkins responded that none of the Paiutes subsisting at Camp McDermit had been sent there as prisoners. This should have settled the matter, but, unfortunately, it did not. Leggins, a subchief in Winnemucca's band, protested that if they returned to Malheur, which Rinehart still controlled, they would starve and more trouble would follow. At this point Wagner grew angry and told them that everyone, himself included, had no choice but to follow orders. If they would not go peacefully, he would be obliged to use force.[41]

With troubled hearts, Sarah's people reluctantly obeyed. Those ordered to Harney, 150 in all, left in early October. "Old and young were crying at parting with each other," Sarah remembered. Natches, always a comforting presence, traveled with them for two days before turning his horse toward his long-neglected ranch. The commander at Camp Harney treated the new arrivals kindly, but week after week slipped past. Autumn turned the grass on the mesas to the color of pale straw, snow would soon be falling, and no order arrived to travel to Malheur. Leggins repeatedly asked Sarah when they would leave, and she knew no more than he.[42]

Until a terrible premonition came to her in the night.

11
Yakama Reservation
"I am crying out to you for justice"

EW INDIANS of Sarah's day conceived of Indianness in the all-embracing terms of a common cause. Other tribes might be seen as allies or enemy nations, and they occupied varied positions in the pecking order: the Bannocks looked down on the Paiutes and the Paiutes thought themselves superior to the Washos. These deeply felt rivalries had enabled white men to control the West; the army could rely on the aid of Indian auxiliaries willing to oppose their tribal enemies. Problems often arose when different tribes were cast together on the same reservation, and even rivalries between various bands of the same tribe sometimes waxed intense.

When Sarah spoke of "my people," she usually meant all Paiutes. As she once wrote to the Paiutes of Inyo County, California: "You all know me; many of you are my uncles, aunts or cousins. We are of one race — your blood is my blood." But she felt special concern for Leggins's band because they were her people in the most intimate sense. Followers of her father, many of them were known to Sarah since childhood, and their leader was married to her cousin. Although the Winnemuccas might have denied the guilt of their own people in order to save them, they had strong evidence for their claim. True, Leggins's band had deserted Malheur, but it had taken no part in the pillaging and warfare, and, according to Leggins, his people had immediately taken refuge at McDermit. Indeed, even Rinehart attested to their innocence.[1]

On receiving a summons from the commanding officer at Camp Harney, Sarah obeyed, fearful and trembling. Not since the night when Egan's terrible death appeared before her in a dream had she felt so strong a premonition of impending disaster. The commander abjured her to silence until the orders just received had been confirmed and remarked that she looked as if she were "ready to die." Then he told her that her people would be taken to the Yakama Reservation, beyond the Columbia River. Their worst nightmare was upon them: exile in a far land.

"All my people?" was her first question.

Captain Cochran told her that the order covered all the Indians then held at Harney. That meant Leggins's band, along with the rest. When Sarah asked "What for?" the commander told her that he did not know why all should be treated as prisoners of war. The reason, apparently, lay in General Howard's unyielding insistence on chastisement. Facing stiff criticism from the public for his softness on Indians, the general had angrily denied these allegations as "utterly and wickedly false" and declared himself in favor of punishing all Indians who had abandoned Malheur, regardless of their innocence and the commitments made to them. He protested against General McDowell's proposal to return them to Malheur as "rewarding crime." McDowell, as staunch a friend to the Indians as Natches and Winnemucca believed him to be, acidly observed to Howard, "your protest will neither be forwarded nor entertained," but indiscriminate punishment of the Indians was the idea that carried the day in Washington.[2]

Sarah protested to Cochran, "My people have not done anything, and why should they be sent away from their own country?" She suggested that only Oytes and other guilty ones should be thus condemned, and then she finally dissolved in tears. "If you knew what I have promised my people, you would leave nothing undone but what you would try not to have them sent away. My people will never believe me again."[3]

Her loyal friend Mattie tried to cheer Sarah by reminding her that "we cannot help it if the white people won't keep their word." Being blameless gave Sarah no consolation, however, for she knew her people would think she had betrayed them for an army paycheck. She had aspired to lead, and among the Paiutes, where leadership rested on no hereditary right nor process of election, the shaman who could no longer cure found no patients (and might be killed) and the chief who could no longer influence events lost his followers. So would her failure turn them against her. Sick at heart by day and sleepless by night, she walked among them, heard them singing as they worked, and thought how soon their songs would turn to tears.[4]

When the commander sent for her a little before Christmas, her heart stood still. "I wish this was my last day in this cruel world," she said to Mattie. The strength that would move her feet to his office seemed to fail her, so Mattie drew her along. She must have looked a shadow of her usual self, with the vivacity drained away and the flashing black eyes dull and darkly circled. Cochran asked if she was ill, then told her he was "heartily sorry" but the order to move her people to Yakama was final. Even when all was lost, Sarah still protested, "What! In this cold winter and in all this snow, and my people have so many little children? . . . What can the President be thinking about? Tell me, what is he? Is he man or beast? Yes, he must be a beast."[5]

The army allowed the Indians a week to prepare for the journey to Yakama. During this period at Harney, Lee, Leggins, Sarah, and Mattie ostensibly continued to obey the officers' orders to bring Indians who tried to escape back to the post. In fact, Sarah had been trying to save as many as she could. More than a century later, the descendants of Pahvezo remembered that timely warnings from Sarah enabled their family and others to escape to Steens Mountain. Probably the pursuit of escapees brought surprisingly scanty results. On one of these rides, Mattie's horse jumped sideways and threw her. Seeing the blood ooze from her mouth, Sarah believed her dear friend could not live. Nonetheless, Mattie survived into the spring, dying "little by little" every day, in Sarah's words.[6]

Mattie's suffering was just one of Sarah's manifold sorrows. She had to announce the dreaded news that the army had condemned Leggins's band to exile. She told them that some hope remained that they might be allowed to return to Malheur in the spring, but both Lee and Leggins turned away and refused to speak to her. As one honored by Howard for her wartime service, Sarah might have left at this point to live wherever she pleased. Instead, she chose to share the sufferings of her people, every step of the way.[7]

So began the terrible northward trek of 350 miles in the depths of winter over mountains where deep snowdrifts prevented delivery of supplies at Malheur for the season and where snowshoes often offered the only means of travel. Soldiers dragged the women, screaming and fighting like wildcats, into wagons along with the children; Indian men walked, shackled in chains. Snow fell. Howard, somewhat defensively, proclaimed the enterprise a success in which casualties among nearly 550 Indians had been remarkably light. Sarah, by contrast, grieved for every body cast into the snow, including two babies born on the journey who could not survive the cold.[8]

On 2 February 1879 they reached Yakama and lingered for some ten days on the fringes of the reservation. Then, "as if we were so many horses or cattle," their army escort turned them over to Yakama agent James H. Wilbur, who had received only brief notice of their impending arrival. Their new agent housed them in a kind of cattle shed. "Oh, how we did suffer with the cold," Sarah remembered. "There was no wood, and the snow was waist-deep, and many died off just as cattle or horses do after traveling so long in the cold." Agent Wilbur described them as "in the most destitute condition of any Indians I have ever known in this, or any other country. Some of them were literally naked."[9]

Winnemucca, unwilling to accept the finality of the sentence passed upon his people, sent Natches to San Francisco in January 1879 to seek a reprieve from McDowell. The general, while appreciative of the Winnemuccas' loyalty and sympathetic to their needs, had already done all he could. In October he journeyed to Washington, conferred with the secretaries of War and the Interior, and urged the plan for creating small reservations for the bands of Winnemucca and Ochocho. It was by no means an unreasonable request. Had not the Shoshone chief Washakie received the Wind River Reservation in recognition of his loyalty? Unaware that the secretaries planned to abandon Malheur and exile the Indians who had lived there to a northern reservation, McDowell thought the idea of small reservations received the secretaries' approval. However, time passed and no directive arrived to create Winnemucca's reservation. After meetings with Natches and Winnemucca, McDowell again wrote to Washington inquiring where the reservation would be located. His efforts on behalf of the Paiutes succeeded only in bringing him official criticism for interfering with the prerogatives of the Interior Department.[10]

Thus the Paiutes remained at Yakama in the care of Wilbur, a Methodist Episcopalian and another of the "praying agents" at whose hands they had suffered so much. A clean-shaven man of sixty-seven, with thin, graying hair, a fierce expression, and the light of the fanatic in his pale eyes, Wilbur saw himself primarily as a missionary: "With feelings of profound gratitude to the Providence that has permitted me to witness the gradual progress of the people committed to my charge, from a state of degraded barbarism to comparative civilization, from the gross blackness of heathen corruption, to the glorious light and liberty of the Gospel of the Son of God, I can realize that from month to month, and from year to year, solid progress and improvement is being made." Wilbur had ruled as agent at Yakama for fifteen years with only brief interruption and brooked no challenges to his authority. One historian has concluded that his principal failing lay in "his religious intolerance and bigotry."[11]

It appears that Sarah became a Methodist at this time, which must have delighted both Wilbur and Howard. It is not clear whether her Methodism represented an imperfect engraftment upon traditional beliefs, as often occurred among Indians of her time. Or perhaps, like her claims to a convent education, the conversion was another item for her credentials in *taibo*'s world. Despite her childhood terror of white people's religion, she declared herself a Methodist, translated Wilbur's sermons into Paiute for the people, and reportedly played a part in the conversion of many. Though Wilbur enjoyed a reputation as a "forceful preacher," his sermons probably gained a good deal in Sarah's translation. "I know something about sermons myself," she observed with ill-concealed pride, "and can preach a better sermon than any of their ministers."[12]

At first, Sarah got along fairly well with the agent. She taught school at the reservation and reported in a letter to Natches that more had been done for Indian education under Wilbur's regime than had ever been accomplished at Malheur (an opinion she later rescinded). For his part, Wilbur praised her "noble work" in teaching and repeatedly requested an appointment for her, as she had been working for months without pay.[13]

Not much time passed, however, before life at Yakama began to take on a familiar cast. The Yakamas, resentful of these intruders on their land, abused the Paiutes and stole their few remaining horses, including Sarah's own prized horse, Meride. As an agency official later admitted, the "younger and more lawless" Yakamas saw the Paiutes as "fair game and miss no opportunity to show their contempt and dislike." Paiute children in the agency boarding school had to be constantly guarded to protect them from the Yakamas. Although Wilbur initially expressed satisfaction with the farming undertaken by the newcomers, Sarah thought the compensation inadequate and the clothing allotments almost farcical. "Another Rinehart!" the Paiutes began saying among themselves. "Don't you see he is the same? He looks up into the sky and says something, just like Rinehart. All white people like that are bad."[14]

Apart from these miseries, Sarah and the missionary agent were bound to clash head-on for a more fundamental reason: Sarah never lost sight of her overriding objective — the return of her people to their homeland. At the same time, Wilbur showed himself doggedly determined to keep them within his grip at Yakama. Unsympathetic to her petitions, Howard declared that if the Paiutes would simply settle down and farm the fertile, well-watered land of Yakama Reservation, they would be far better off than they had ever been in the inhospitable deserts. He failed to understand the depth of the Paiute attachment to their homeland. Even Sarah, accustomed to occasional absences, longed for at least a taste of home: the mealy sweetness of pinyon nuts and the spicy fragrance of the hot pitch that clung to the tiny dark brown shells. "Send as many as you can," she wrote to Natches. She also spoke of many deaths among her suffering people. Lee reported that they were "woefully heart sick and grieving to death; that many have already died and all the rest are sorely discouraged. . . . They are continually brooding over their wrongs and pining to come back to their native country. They can talk of nothing else." As he lay dying, one aged Paiute drifted into the delusion that he was making the journey home. He kept asking how much farther he must travel, and at the last he believed he could see the familiar Nevada *kahnees* and campfires just ahead.[15]

By the spring of 1879, it had dawned upon Rinehart that without any Indians residing at Malheur, or within one hundred miles of it, his position might soon be lost. First, he urged his superiors in Washington to coerce the Paiutes subsisting at McDermit to move to Malheur. As before, this letter produced no results. Next, Rinehart embarked on an effort to recruit some of the Indians he had formerly driven away. He journeyed to the town of Winnemucca for a meeting with the old chief, who kept him waiting for several days — apparently one of the means by which Winnemucca sometimes demonstrated his power and prestige. When he finally arrived, Winnemucca drove a bargain that secured his paramount aim: if Rinehart could bring Leggins's band back from Yakama, he would go to Malheur. Rinehart promised to have them back within six weeks, regrettably, a promise that he had no power to keep. He made strong pleas to Washington for their return and elucidated his theory that they had been taken by an error that could not be acknowledged because the expense of their removal to Yakama would be difficult to justify, but his words had no more effect on Washington bureaucrats than on Indians. Although Rinehart paid Natches one hundred dollars to persuade some Indians to go to Malheur, and also offered five dollars per head, no one would agree. To the last man, the Indians at Fort McDermit and Fort Bidwell, where Ochocho's band resided, refused to subject themselves to Rinehart's authority at Malheur.[16]

Recognizing the depth of Indian antipathy toward himself, Rinehart sent an unnamed emissary (evidently the contractor Jack Scott, whom Natches had saved from the Bannocks) in another attempt to bring some Indians to Malheur in the autumn. Scott first went to Fort McDermit for the dual purpose of seeing if he could catch the army giving rations to the Indians and bluffing the Indians into the belief that Washington had ordered them to Malheur, under military escort if necessary. The *Silver State* reported: "He was ordered by decent people to leave the place, and, it is said, narrowly escaped by a hasty retreat, contact with the toe of a boot."[17]

Scott next journeyed to Winnemucca, where Natches gathered the chiefs for a conference with him in the courthouse. The chiefs first questioned his credentials, then described their satisfaction and prosperity and subjected him to a little Paiute humor. The Indian "captains" thought their own clothes as good as his ("any Indian you can find naked will go with you"). Captain Jim observed that since he had a comfortable home with a stove and plenty of provisions he would be happy to board Scott for a year, an offer echoed by Natches. Buena Vista John remarked that as Scott had no wife, whereas he had four good ones (a hallmark of prosperity among the Paiutes), he would be happy to give one to Scott. Winnemucca, so feeble that he could barely walk, was able to summon the old eloquence to remind Scott of his debt to his Indian rescuers and to make a strong plea for the release of Leggins's band from captivity. The chiefs presented letters from local white notables urging that the Indians living among them should not be removed to Malheur. Not one would agree to live there. In the words of the "fine looking young savage" known as Captain Charley: "I have plenty to eat, plenty to wear. My people live at peace with the whites. . . . We do not want to go to Malheur to starve. I am done."[18]

By this time, Sarah had determined to leave her secure position at Yakama. Watching her people sicken and die grieved her beyond endurance, and she conceived a new effort to win their return to their homeland. Hopeless as their situation then appeared, Sarah still had two high cards in her hand: the Paiute leaders' gift for oratory, a skill as widely admired as their expert horsemanship and their proficiency in tracking, and the celebrity accorded to the Winnemuccas for their part in the Bannock War. Not only had Sarah been praised in newspapers from coast to coast but when Natches visited San Francisco, hundreds came to the house where he was staying to see the hero who had saved white men from death. Sarah had learned from harsh experience that appeals to state legislatures, army commanders, and emissaries from the Office of Indian Affairs brought no results, and she had been repeatedly told that since Washington had decreed the exile of Leggins's band, only an order from Washington could bring freedom. Very well, she would raise a clamor that Washington could not ignore. In November 1879 her lectures to San Francisco audiences began.[19]

Although other Indians made theatrical appearances in the Wild West Exhibition and in similar extravangazas, and Sarah herself had taken part in the family performances in 1864, her lecture series may have been one of the first sustained efforts by an Indian leader to win hearts and minds and to bring the pressure of public opinion to bear on the national government. Her lectures at Platt's Hall continued for a month, from 24 November until just before Christmas. The high point came when a distinguished audience packed the auditorium to laugh and weep with her, cheer her, and interrupt her with tumultuous applause. "Everybody wanted to see and hear this young woman," physician J. J. F. Haine remembered, and San Francisco newspapers ran descriptions of her lectures on the front page. Her costume changed little from one performance to another, and by the standards of the day, it was somewhat revealing. A reporter commented on her "beautifully-rounded brown" arms, and many eyes were drawn to the red leggings below the fringe of her knee-length buckskin dress, as well as to her voluptuous figure. Haine, on the other hand, who did admire her shapely legs, saw her wearing a black velvet costume decorated with gold bands. With her lively demeanor, her long, waist-

That she wears the medal presented to Natches after the Bannock War
and uses the signature "Winnemucca" (not "Hopkins") suggest that Sarah gave
this portrait to Natches in late 1879 or early 1880. Courtesy of the Nevada
Historical Society.

length black hair, her expressive black eyes, and her golden skin, he thought her "nearly beautiful."[20]

Both the cast and the content of her lectures varied. Once, she appeared alone. At other times, Natches, together with Jerry Long, Charlie Thacker, and another cousin, made up the supporting cast and sang a Paiute chant. Natches might give a short talk, translated by Sarah (although he spoke understandable English, he lacked his sister's supreme self-confidence). But Sarah was the real show. She would stride onto the stage with no trace of shyness and speak without notes in what reporters called "a spontaneous flow of eloquence," telling stories from Paiute history, from her childhood, and from her experiences in the Bannock War. Although Sarah's intense emotions sometimes tripped her grammar, one reporter admired her biblical cadences ("a striking similarity to the simple beauty of the style of some of the passages of the poetry of Holy Writ"). Her powerful charisma enhanced the effect of her words. Since many of her stories went into the book she wrote, it is likely that the Paiute plea for justice written there had been declaimed, by Sarah, with tears streaming down her face, during these appearances:[21]

Oh, for shame! You who are educated by a Christian government in the art of war. . . . Yes, you, who call yourselves the great civilization; you who have knelt upon Plymouth Rock, covenanting with God to make this land the home of the free and the brave. Ah, then you rise from your bended knees and seizing the welcoming hands of those who are the owners of this land, which you are not, your carbines rise upon the bleak shore, and your so-called civilization sweeps inland from the ocean wave; but, oh, my God! leaving its pathway marked by crimson lines of blood and strewed by the bones of two races, the inheritor and the invader; and I am crying out to you for justice — yes, pleading for [from?] the far-off plains of the West, for the dusky mourner.[22]

So strong was Sarah's hold over her audiences that they even cheered her indictment of whites and her plea for a Paiute reservation:

You take all the nations of the earth to your bosom but the poor Indian . . . who has lived for generations on the land which the good God has given to them, and you say he must be exterminated. [Thrice repeated, with deep passion, and received with tremendous applause.] The proverb says the big fish eat the little fishes, and we Indians are the little fish and you eat us all up and drive us from home. [Cheers.] Where can we poor Indians go if the government will not help us? If your people will help us, and you have good hearts, and can if you will, I will promise to educate my people and make them law-abiding citizens of the United States. [Loud applause.] It can be done — it can be done. [Cheers.] My father, Winnemucca, pleads with you that the guilty shall be punished, but that the innocent shall be permitted to live on their own lands in Nevada. . . . We want you to try us for four years, and if at the end of that time we don't learn, or don't work, or don't become good citizens, then you can do what you please. [Cheers.]

As literary scholars Brumble and Ruoff have noted, considerable art underlay the apparent simplicity of Sarah's lectures. Not only had she cleverly adapted Paiute oral conventions to white audiences but she also managed to excoriate white injustices without antagonizing her white listeners.[23]

Just as the emotional power of Sarah's presentations never altered, neither did the unrelenting fury of the public attack that she unleashed against Rinehart. "I will expose all the rascals. I will save nobody," she declared, and expose she did. She related how Rinehart had duped the Indians into working without recompense and how he had beaten them, threatened them with pistols, and withheld government supplies. What Rinehart might be doing with the plentiful supplies procured while no Indians resided on the reservation aroused her curiosity. The audience invariably exploded into laughter over her description of Rinehart as a man with a right arm longer than his left, beckoning them to be good, kind, and honest with one hand while the other was "busy grabbing behind their backs." Her presentation included what the *San Francisco Chronicle* termed "a summary of Mr. Rinehart's character with a bit of mischievous sarcasm that brought down the house," also noting that "there was little left of the redoubtable Christian agent when she finished him."[24]

In conjunction with her effort to arouse the public, Sarah sent a petition to Secretary of the Interior Carl Schurz detailing Rinehart's misdeeds, requesting the appointment of Parrish or some other humane agent at Malheur, and promising that the Paiutes would return to the reservation if this request was fulfilled. Winnemucca, Natches, and other Paiute leaders made their marks upon the petition. Several San Francisco journalists also signed, and newspaperman Frank Parker, whose suspicion of Sarah at the onset of the Bannock War had been transformed into wholehearted admiration, telegraphed his endorsement. When Sarah dispatched this missive to Washington, she probably had no inkling that Rinehart, poisonous as a rattlesnake, was coiled and ready to strike back.[25]

As Sarah prepared to leave San Francisco, she had a fateful meeting with an unidentified group of Boston dowagers in the railroad station. They urged her to lecture in Boston, where "you will meet a better class of people to aid you." For some time Sarah had been intending to take her lectures east, but these plans were superceded by an invitation to Washington from government officials, the first sign that her vocal criticism of Indian policy had struck its mark. As historian Katharine Turner has observed, the Office of Indian Affairs and the secretary of the Interior found the adverse publicity Sarah had aroused "intolerable." On the way, she returned to home ground, to the town of Winnemucca, where she gave her lecture (free to ladies) in Centennial Hall. Ironically, the *Silver State* found less to praise in her performance than the San Francisco newspapers and suggested that she drank too much afterward, a charge so infuriating to Sarah that she later threatened the editor.[26]

12

Washington DC

*"This which I hold in my hand
is our only hope"*

MOST PEOPLES have a myth about a hero who sets out to right a world gone wrong — a saga that embodies the hope that in desperate times a brave and resolute figure will rise to save them. Around Paiute campfires, this myth took the form of the battle between Tavu, the little rabbit, and the sun. In olden times, so the storytellers said, the days were so short that the people complained of having little time to hunt, and Tavu determined that he would conquer the sun. He journeyed far, crossing one basin and range after another, until at last he arrived at the eastern edge of the world, where the sun lived. From a hiding place behind a rock, he shot an arrow at the sun as soon as it rose, but, to his dismay, the arrow burned before it reached the target. He walked closer and closer, shooting arrows as he went, until only two remained. Then Tavu wept so much that his tears soaked the last arrows. The first came closer to the mark. With the last arrow he sent flying, he killed the sun. He rushed to the fallen enemy, cut it up with his flint knife, and cast its gall into the sky, saying, "Now go up higher and make the days longer."

As Tavu fled, the angry sun chased him, trying to burn him. Tavu hid in a hole, where the sun scorched him, then in the mud of a lake, and then in a thorny tree. At last the sun gave up the pursuit. When Tavu had watched the passage of the sun through the heavens, he could say with satisfaction, "Now the day is long enough."

On his way home, Tavu killed a squirrel who laughed at him and vanquished four enemy nations: the red ant nation, the louse nation, the chipmunk nation, and the vulture nation. His friends rejoiced over his victory and held a sun dance when he reached home. After the dance ended, some asked Tavu to fight the sun again so they could have daylight all the time. "That would not be well," said Tavu, in his wisdom. "I want you to have a part night, so that you may have time for sleep, and so the men may lie down by the women and not be ashamed, and so you can have dreams."[1]

In mid-January 1880, in the warmth of a false spring, the Winnemuccas and Captain Jim set out toward the east, across basin and range, on their own heroic journey to confront the powerful being who ruled them. From the late 1800s through the nineteenth century, Washington officials brought thousands of Indian dignitaries to Washington, usually for the purpose of impressing upon them the unconquerable numbers of white men and the futility of war (the same lesson that Winnemucca and Natches had hoped would sway the Bannock chiefs in San Francisco). On this occasion, the secretary of the Interior also attempted to impress, dispatching the Paiutes on what must have been the standard tour. Although Sarah politely told a *Washington National Republican* reporter that she thought Washington the "handsomest" city she had seen, the reminiscence she later wrote hardly palpitates with breathless admiration. "The Soldiers' Home is the only place we did *not* see" was her dry comment on the wonders of the capital. The secretary did not realize how sophisticated the Winnemuccas had become through long familiarity with San Francisco. Some thirty years had passed since a steamboat or a tall brick building could impress them.[2]

Sightseeing could not distract Sarah from her mission, which she pursued during two meetings with Secretary of the Interior Carl Schurz. The first commenced inauspiciously when a lower-ranking official accused her of trying to enrich herself by lecturing and laughed at her tears when she spoke of the troubles besetting her people. Nonetheless, the secretary received the Winnemuccas kindly. German-born, bespectacled, bushy-browed, and intense, with dark, wavy hair and a short, black beard, Carl Schurz reminded one ac-

quaintance of a "spindleshanked Mephistopheles." His political enemies might well have seconded the opinion. He had served commend-
ably in the Civil War, entered national politics as a senator from
Missouri, and gained political clout among Republicans through his
influence over German-American voters in the Midwest. When President Rutherford B. Hayes appointed him secretary of the Interior, it
seemed a daring step. Schurz had the reputation of a liberal and a reformer as those terms were defined in the 1870s — he favored civil service reform and hard money. Even after the Hayes administration's
feeble attempt at civil service reform had died on the vine, Schurz endeavored to enforce it in the notoriously corrupt Interior Department, with limited success.[3] Yet, ironically, this politician, still re-
vered as a reformer in a sink of political corruption, also presided
over some of the most unconscionable betrayals in nineteenth-
century Indian history: the avoidable tragedy of the Nez Percé War in
1877, the crushed flight of the Northern Cheyennes from Indian Territory in 1878, and the refusal to allow Poncas who had been forcibly removed to Indian Territory to return to their guaranteed reservation
on the Missouri River (already a cause célébrè among eastern reformers).[4]

If aware of how these tribes had fared in Schurz's hands, Sarah
must have approached the secretary with some trepidation. She put
up a bold front all the same. In an interview with the press that took
place upon her arrival in Washington, she issued a veiled threat that
unless Paiute demands received satisfaction, "general and specific
charges against the policy of the Indian bureau and the conduct of
past and present agents will be made and sustained."[5] Tavu had his
arrows; Sarah's weapon was her eloquent tongue.

At their initial meeting, Schurz asked Sarah for an account of the
Bannock War. At the second, Natches pled the Paiute cause through
Sarah's translation: "You, Great Father of the Mighty Nation, my people have all heard of you. We think you are the mightiest Father that
lives. . . . There is nothing you can't do if you wish to; and, therefore,
we one and all, pray of you to give us back what is of no value to you or

your people. Oh, good Father, it is not your gold, nor your silver, horses, cattle, lands, mountains we ask for. We beg of you to give us back our people, who are dying off like so many cattle, or beasts, at the Yakama Reservation." He went on to speak of the innocence of these Paiutes and his own wartime services to whites. One wonders if the secretary recalled that the previous summer the Bannocks, who instigated the war, had received his permission to return to their Fort Hall Reservation and receive land allotments.[6]

The result was what the *Silver State* termed the Paiute magna carta — an order from Secretary Schurz directing that the Paiutes at Yakama would be allowed to return to Malheur, where they would receive allotments of land in severalty. None of the Paiutes living and working among the settlers would be compelled to go to Malheur. Natches warmly expressed his gratitude.[7] Seemingly, the Paiute arrows had struck the sun.

Within two days of their arrival, the Winnemuccas also met with President Hayes at the White House. Once, in her anguish on learning that Leggins's band would be exiled to Yakama, Sarah had cried out, "I have never seen a president in my life and I want to know whether he is made of wood or rock, for I cannot for once think that he can be a human being. . . . Every night I imagined that I could see the thing called President. He had long ears, he had big eyes and long legs, and a head like a bull-frog."[8]

In fact, the president was composed of far more ordinary materials than wood or rock, and today is chiefly remembered for his questionable victory in the disputed election of 1876 and the mediocrity of his presidency. Kindly and agreeable, with a high forehead and neatly trimmed beard besprinkled with gray, he had served with distinction in the Civil War and risen through the ranks of Ohio Republicans. His sympathies for Indians were somewhat limited, however. He once confided to his diary that on listening to the recitation of a pathetic and witless poem on the decline of the Indian, "no longer able to restrain the powerful emotions that swelled my bosom, I burst into a — horse-laugh."[9]

Meeting Sarah, President Hayes benignly inquired if she had received "all you want for your people."

"Yes, sir, as far as I know," she responded. As far as I know. On that winter's day in Washington, it seemed that there was nothing more to be said.[10]

Sarah's celebrity as a lecturer brought many invitations to speak in Washington and other eastern cities. When she appeared likely to accept, Schurz hurriedly called her to his office and convinced her that it would be unethical to lecture in the East when she had traveled there at government expense. He again assured her that all she asked had been granted and added the additional promise that canvas tents would be distributed to her people at Lovelock, Nevada, as soon as she returned — a promise that sounds a good deal like a bribe for her silence. In the midst of a burgeoning scandal over the allegation that Commissioner Ernest Hayt had altered the boundary of an Arizona Indian reservation so as to omit a silver mine in which he was interested, the Office of Indian Affairs scarcely needed more bad publicity. As Turner points out, Schurz no doubt calculated that after this vocal Indian woman had been safely dispatched to the West, she would be unable to afford the long journey east.[11] Like many others, he underestimated Sarah.

It remained only for Sarah to charm the capital city, as her father had charmed the antelope, and Washington quickly succumbed. The *Washington Post* declared that "Dashing Sarah" in "deportment and appearance would compare favorably with most of her pale-faced sisters." A society reporter also admired her fashionable clothes, a sealskin sacque, silk dress, and dramatic hat. Despite the simultaneous presence of so many Indian delegations in Washington that the *Post* termed it a "paradise for Indians," Sarah stood out from the rest.[12]

At the same time that Sarah's gleaming smiles charmed Washington, Rinehart's campaign of character assassination against her was spreading venom behind the scenes. Dated 15 January and addressed to the commissioner of Indian Affairs, Rinehart's letter with enclosed petition and depositions may have reached Washington during the

Winnemuccas' visit. As he plainly stated, Rinehart aimed to counter the charges Sarah had made against him in her lectures (though he must have also sought to maintain his position). His strategy was not to provide evidence of his own successful management of Malheur but to generate scurrilous attacks against Sarah. In phraseology that varied only slightly, the letters raked her for "the vices of drunkenness, gambling, and common prostitution," one adding that she "could be bought for a bottle of whiskey," and all excoriated her as a "notorious liar and malicious schemer."[13]

In attacking her respectability as a woman, Rinehart unerringly struck Sarah at her most vulnerable point. Like virtually all her people, she sometimes gambled. She occasionally drank. She had loved a number of men, both husbands and otherwise (although her father, with his several wives, and other polygamous Paiute men evoked no adverse comment on such grounds). But the charge of prostitution cannot be seriously entertained. In the pages of the *Silver State*, where the most trivial act by the Winnemuccas always made news and the editor sometimes took a certain pleasure in criticizing the "Princess Sallie," any such activity would surely have been reported. Whether or not the other charges were true, all save lying were beside the point. Even if Sarah had been a drunkard, gambler, and prostitute as Rinehart and his friends declared, her account of his mistreatment of the Indians at Malheur had been in no way disproved.

Rinehart called his supporters the "best men in the country." Who were the twelve who agreed to blacken Sarah's name on his behalf? Insofar as they can be tracked today, the group included close business associates of Rinehart's, either contractors at Malheur or earlier connections from his Canyon City days, a Rinehart employee, a relative of Rinehart's wife, and signers of the 1878 petition that sought the abolition of Malheur in the interests of the encroaching settlers. In short, the "best men in the country" were biased. Either they had a financial relationship with Rinehart or they had gone on record as opponents of Indian interests. It is not known whether the Interior Department had as yet digested Rinehart's allegations, especially since Sarah arrived bearing letters filled with glowing recommendations from General Howard, Colonel Bernard, and other officers impressed by her heroism during the Bannock War, but it would soon become clear that Rinehart had succeeded all too well in damaging both Sarah's credibility and the Paiute cause.[14]

After demanding and receiving better accommodations for the railroad journey home and leaving Winnemucca and Captain Jim at Battle Mountain, Nevada, Sarah and Natches stepped triumphantly from the puffing train at Winnemucca on 2 February 1880. Both Indians and whites, who had been reading reports of their Washington mission in the *Silver State*, had gathered at the depot to greet them. Tavu himself could not have been more celebrated after his battle with the sun. Natches and Winnemucca would explain the terms of the Paiute magna carta, Natches to the Indians at Fort McDermit and Winnemucca to those in the Surprise Valley near Fort Bidwell. It remained for Sarah to carry the glad tidings to Yakama.[15]

She did not depart, however, before upsetting Charlie Thacker's household and embroiling herself in trouble with the editor of the *Silver State*. Thacker (probably the brother of the man rumor said she had briefly married in 1877) soon regretted inviting Sarah to stay with him in his *kahnee* across the river from Winnemucca, when his distinguished guest, who sometimes showed signs of concern for women's rights, began fomenting rebellion among his two wives. Thacker attempted to deal with this unaccustomed situation by tying the hands of one wife behind her and trying to gag Sarah. No one yet had successfully gagged Sarah, though many would have liked to. The rebellion culminated with a declaration of independence: Thacker's first wife left for a trip to Virginia City, and his second declared that she would no longer live with him unless the first returned.[16]

Sarah left (in Thacker's opinion, none too soon) for the distribution of tents at Lovelock, a small farming town on the Central Pacific Railroad line roughly seventy-five miles southwest of Winnemucca. Despite the February cold and snow, the people "came from far and near to hear of the wonderful father we had seen, how he looked and all about him" and to receive the tents. Winnemucca and Natches joined Sarah for the reading of Schurz's letter. Seeing the hunger that stalked her people, Sarah appealed to the secretary, wrongly believing him to be kindly disposed. He responded that rations would only be provided at Malheur. After waiting for some time, it was clear to all that no tents would arrive. Once again, the government's broken promises had humiliated Sarah and cast her as the betrayer of her people. "What could we say? We were only ashamed because we came and told them lies which the white people had told us."[17]

While many condemned Sarah over the tents, some understood and put little faith in the secretary of the Interior's other commitments. Sarah's uncle Captain John declared for all to hear: "My dear people, I have lived many years with white people. Yes, it is over thirty years, and I know a great many of them. I have never known one of them to do what they promised. . . . I would say to them, now or never, and if they don't, why it is because they never meant to do, but only to say so. These are your white brothers' ways, and they are a weak people."[18]

Perhaps Sarah's frustration over the tent fiasco and her dizzying fall from grace among her people contributed to her violent reaction when she belatedly learned that the *Silver State* had accused her of drinking heavily after her lecture in Winnemucca. She threatened the editor and challenged him to a duel with pistols or knives "just to show him how a drunken woman can shoot." Such temerity by an Indian could not be tolerated. The editor self-righteously declared, "A drunken savage, who threatens to take the life's blood of a white person, should be given to understand that there is such a thing as a jail in the community," and had her arrested. In court she denied rumors that white men had incited her to dispatch her challenge and insisted that it was all her own. She explained that the falsehood published about her and given wide coverage in the New York tabloids had aroused her anger. Apparently, the judge found her explanation satisfactory.[19]

Despite the questionable wisdom of putting Sarah and Rinehart within striking distance of each other, the commissioner of Indian Affairs had given Sarah an appointment as interpreter at Malheur, no doubt anticipating the return of Leggins's band. On receiving the commissioner's letter of appointment, Rinehart intensified his slanders. He wrote the commissioner that Sarah had been employed in a "public house of ill-fame" in Winnemucca and had been seen making love with an Indian man at Malheur. The possibility arises that Rinehart, who had also wrongly characterized the Paiute celebrations as "brothel dances," had grown obsessive on the subject of Indian sexuality and saw licentiousness wherever he looked. Presumably with clenched teeth, Sarah and Rinehart went through the formalities necessary for her appointment: she offered to take her post; he informed her that her services would not be needed since Malheur had no Indians. In fact, over the next few weeks, Sarah traveled around trying to persuade some of her people to go to Malheur. She may have realized that the reservation would be lost to the Indians if none resided there. But the Paiutes held fast to their refusal to go to Malheur until Schurz fulfilled his part of the bargain: the return of Leggins's band.[20]

At the end of April, when the ice-encrusted snows of an unusually heavy winter had retreated enough to allow the journey, Sarah and an unnamed companion she described as her sister set out on horseback from Pyramid to Yakama. "Sister" was an all-embracing term that could encompass a sister-in-law or a cousin, and Sarah never further identified the woman who rode at her side. Yet several signs suggest that the other woman might have been her only surviving sister, Elma. For some years Elma had been living in Montana with her white husband, John Smith, and may have already established a permanent home at Henry's Lake, Idaho, but she, like Sarah, had reportedly been visiting with her people at Pyramid Lake.[21]

Through four days of hard riding toward Steens Mountain, Sarah's heart soared with high hopes: "Just think how happy I was! to go for my poor, sick-hearted people. Yes, armed with a paper signed by Secretary Schurz. I thought I would not have anything to do but go there and get them." They passed the glittering mirror of Winnemucca

Lake, where their mother and her infant child had been massacred fifteen years earlier, and rode on, always heading north. They saw no one along the way and had nothing to eat beyond a little hard bread, but they found enough feed for their horses: "That was better than all, for I would rather any time have nothing to eat than have my horse go without anything."[22]

Late in the evening of the fourth day, they arrived at a ranch, where they were pleased to see one of the Winnemucca cousins working as a buckaroo. The rancher welcomed them hospitably, as was the custom when a traveler appeared at one of the isolated ranches of the region. A late spring snowstorm compelled them to remain for three days. When they swung onto their horses once more, their cousin rode with them to ensure their safety. He told them that cowboys at the next ranch had lassoed Indian women and done "terrible outrageous things" to them. Sarah took this warning very seriously: "If such an outrageous thing is to happen to me, it will not be done by one man or two, while there are two women with knives, for I know what an Indian woman can do. She can never be outraged by one man; but she may by two." We can guess that she fingered the handle of her knife.[23]

To Sarah's relief, when they reached the next ranch, she saw that the rancher was an old friend from Carson City. They spent the night there and "were treated beautifully." The next morning their cousin rode a little way with them before turning back. They had traveled about ten miles when they looked back to see three men rapidly pursuing them. Sarah could tell that the riders were Hispanics from the ranch (perhaps identifiable even at a distance by the brilliantly colored shirts and kerchiefs that the region's many Hispanic cowboys customarily wore). "We saw it was war then," Sarah remembered. "I said, 'Dear sister, we must ride for our dear lives.' Away we went, and they after us like wild men. We rode on till our horses seemed to drop from under us. At last we stopped, and I told sister what to do if the whole three of them overtook us. We could not do very much, but we must die fighting. If there were only two we were all right, —we would kill them." Sarah felt confident that they could handle just one. If he lassoed either of them, the other would cut the rope.[24]

The chase continued. Each time the pursuers fell back out of sight the women paused to rest their horses. At last, "to our great joy," they saw only one rider behind them. When the man overtook them, he attempted to make conversation, claiming acquaintance with Winnemucca and Natches. Sarah told him to "clear out" and refused to talk further. He offered fresh horses if the women would come with him to a house across the valley. They maintained an icy silence, so he finally turned away. After riding on for five miles to make sure he was truly gone, the two women paused to rest their horses. By the time they reached a warm spring at midafternoon, they felt safe enough to stop for a bath. In the late afternoon one of the horses gave out, and they had considerable difficulty reaching the next ranch. Here, on the southern end of shining, snow-clad Steens Mountain, they felt assured of a warm welcome because the rancher was married to one of the Winnemucca cousins, a circumstance that often provided Sarah with a supportive network during her travels.[25]

The next day they left the foundered horse behind and rode in the wagon of another traveler, leading Sarah's horse, for the next leg of their journey to the homestead belonging to G. W. ("Doc") Anderson. They passed scattered, reeking carcasses of cattle that had died unable to break through the ice-capped snow to feed during this unusually long, cruel winter. At Anderson's they felt uncertain of their reception. Indians had avoided the place for years, and the Bannocks had burned the homestead during the war. Although Anderson received them kindly in his rebuilt cabin and invited them to warm themselves by the large fireplace, Sarah felt nervous in the room full of strange men. As the bachelor Anderson and his eight cowboys began bedding down on the floor of the one room cabin, Sarah wondered where to sleep. Snow covered the ground outside, and the women had no blankets. When Anderson offered to give them his bed, they accepted, but Sarah's fears would not be stilled. "Oh, how my heart jumps!" she murmured to her sister, who shared her apprehensions. Once, years ago on the San Joaquin, Sarah had nestled close to her sister Mary, feeling Mary's heart beating wildly with terror. Now it was her own heart that pounded.[26]

At last she fell asleep. A hand touched her in the night, and a man's voice spoke her name. Sarah rose, striking him in the face, and cried, "Go away, or I will cut you to pieces." The man fled, mounted his horse, and rode away. When Anderson awoke and lit a candle, they saw blood on Sarah's hands, the side of the bed, and the floor. Probably she had given her assailant a nose bleed. Although Anderson left the candle burning for the rest of the night, the women slept no more. Andersen obligingly prepared a 4:00 A.M. breakfast so that they could depart early to traverse the fifty remaining miles to Fort Harney.[27]

By evening the wagon rumbled up to the familiar wooden buildings nestled beside the mesas at the edge of the mountains. The commanding officer and the three officers' wives at the post greeted them warmly. Invariably Sarah remembered and commented upon this because an Indian woman, no matter how celebrated, could never be certain how she would be received. Sometimes, she once said, white people "will not touch my fingers for fear of getting soiled." Since deep snow made the mountains impassable, they remained for several days. During this time Sarah wangled a loan and borrowed a second horse to continue the journey.[28]

Finally they rode on in spite of the weather: "Oh, such a time as we had going over! The snow was soft — our horses would go down and up again. If we walked we would go down too." Rain further softened the snow. The next day they had to swim their horses at one point before reaching Canyon City "almost frozen to death." While waiting three days for the buckboard that served as a stage, Sarah met with Charles Parrish and sadly told him the names of the children, once pupils taught by his wife at Malheur, who had died at Yakama. She felt certain that Annie would want to know. The remainder of the journey was uneventful by comparison.[29]

At Yakama, Sarah related news of the Nevada Paiutes to her people but delayed the joyous announcement of the Schurz letter for several days until she could arrange their departure with Wilbur. When she went to see the agent, her first question was, "Did you get a letter from Washington?" She had been promised that Wilbur would be sent instructions on the Paiute exodus and would provide a military escort if necessary. Wilbur denied receiving anything of the kind. After he read what Sarah called "the beautiful letter," she saw that he was angry. Handing the letter back to her, he told her not to reveal its contents to the Indians and offered her fifty dollars and a position as an interpreter for her silence. Although she pointedly remarked that he had paid her nothing for eight months of work teaching and interpreting at Yakama and she made him no promises, Sarah acceded to his wishes for several more days. At that point, the Paiutes demanded her presence in council. Through the invariably effective Indian grapevine, they had heard of the marvelous letter. Before the assembled people, Leggins denounced her with tears running down his face:

"You all see that our mother has sold us to Father Wilbur. You see that she does not want to let us know what our father Winnemucca has done for us. We are all told that she has a paper, which has been given to her by the mighty Big Father in Washington, and she has burnt it or hid it, so we won't know it. That way she has made her money, by selling us. She first sold us to the soldiers and had us brought here, and now she has sold us to this bad man to starve us. Oh, we shall never see our friends any more! Our paper is all gone, there is nobody to talk for us, we are all alone, we shall never get back to our sweet country."[30]

Lee sprang to her defense, telling them that Wilbur was the one who had sold them. Some of the women came forward and laid their hands on Sarah's head to show their support. Holding the letter she now saw as their last best hope high above her head, Sarah rose to speak:

My dear children, may the Great Father in the Spirit-land, will it so that you may see your husbands, and your children, and your daughters. I have said everything I could in your behalf, so did father and brother. I have suffered everything but death to come here with this paper. I don't know whether it speaks truth or not. You can say what you like about me. You have a right to say I have sold you. It looks so. I have told you many things which are not my own words, but the words of the agents and the soldiers. I know I have told you more lies than I have hair on my head. . . . They were the words of the white people, not mine. . . . You will never know until you go to the Spirit-land. This which I hold in my hand is our only hope. It came right from the Big Father you hear so much of. . . . If it is truth we will see our people in fifty days.[31]

When she had finished reading the letter, such jubilation reigned that Sarah later wrote "they all forgot they were grown people." They jumped about and ran to her with outstretched hands. Leggins declared that he would request an escort from Wilbur and asked how many wanted to leave. The response was unanimous, "We will all go, — yes, we will all go, if we have to crawl on our hands and knees." So great was their happiness that they even forgave Oytes, who sat weeping quietly with his hands over his face and wishing that he too might return to his homeland. One of the headmen, Paddy Cap, reminded him that when the Bannocks came "you were first on your horse" and "you got us all into trouble." Nonetheless, touched by his misery, Sarah declared that he should be allowed to go also, and the other Paiutes agreed that even the Dreamer chief should not be subjected to the misery of exile ("Why leave one behind?").[32]

The headmen wanted to request a military escort from Wilbur for protection from the virulent hatred of the settlers along the way. When he finally granted them an interview after considerable delay, fireworks exploded. Wilbur accused Sarah of "putting the devil into your people's heads" and threatened to "have you put in irons and in prison." At this, Sarah recalled, "I jumped upon my war-horse." "You have not got the first part of a Christian principle about you, or you would leave everything and see that my poor, broken-hearted people get home," she told him, among several other things. She accused him of keeping the Paiutes at Yakama for the money it brought him "not because you love us." She ringingly concluded, "Hell is full of just such Christians as you are."[33]

Wilbur again threatened, "Stop talking, or I will have you locked up."

Sarah defiantly told him, "I don't care how soon you have it done." At least, imprisonment would prove to her people that she had not sold out. With a final threat to lecture on his misdeeds — for by now she knew that the only power she possessed was the voice that would not be stilled — Sarah walked away, brushing aside the agent's attempts to detain her.[34]

In his report to Washington, Wilbur explained that he had "declined" to allow the Paiutes to leave Yakama without further instructions from the Interior Department. He insisted that the Paiutes would be "well content" to remain at the reservation if Sarah had not sown dissatisfaction among them. The few who wanted to leave had merely succumbed to "the desire for change, inherent in all savage natures." Above all, he argued that letters from General Howard and "prominent citizens of Eastern Oregon" had urged him to halt the exodus because it would lead to "bloodshed and murder." In a subsequent public statement, Wilbur acknowledged that the cause of the anticipated violence was the occupation by settlers of lands at Malheur. Preserving the peace by removing these illegal squatters instead of exiling the Indians from their own reservation does not appear to have been seriously considered by anyone in authority other than General McDowell. At the same time, Wilbur continued his offensive by other means, affording Lee some bitter amusement by offering him a bribe — land and a wagon — to stay at Yakama.[35]

For some two months Sarah and the headmen hoped and strove for departure on 3 July. Sarah appealed to Washington. Realizing that the matter of the military escort had become a sticking point, she attempted to counter the argument that the Paiute exodus would bring violence with a public statement published in the *Yakima Record* and signed by Lee, cousin Frank Winnemucca, Leggins, Paddy Cap, and Paiute Joe, who had been inexplicably sentenced to exile despite the great service he had done in killing Buffalo Horn. In the statement, Sarah announced that her people were "determined to return to their own country," with or without a military escort, and pledged her life for their "peaceful intentions and good conduct." Because so many of their horses had been taken by the Yakamas, about half would travel on foot. She declared that she did not believe the people of Oregon would kill them as they passed. No matter how great the danger, the Paiutes still wanted to go, "preferring to be killed quickly rather than encounter another season of lingering death." Sarah and Lee counted fifty-eight, thirty of them children, who had died over the past year at Yakama, so overcrowding the graveyard that Wilbur ordered bodies to be thrown in the river.[36]

All her efforts were to no avail. For the third time in her long fight for justice, an Indian agent evicted her from a reservation as a troublemaker. She had already discomfited Wilbur by her revelations to the Yakima City newspaper editor on the ragged, hungry condition of her people, and he knew well that her threatened lecture could arouse the public. He finally persuaded her to accept free transportation to the Dalles, where she could await the arrival of her people on the first part of their journey. They never came.[37]

Meanwhile, Wilbur had wired and written the commissioner of Indian Affairs for definite instructions, reiterating his arguments that the Paiute journey homeward would be "the signal for warfare" and that without Sarah's "disreputable intrigues" they would be satisfied to remain at Yakama. The Department of the Interior responded with the instructions he sought and also informed Sarah that due to reports from General Howard and others that the Paiute exodus would bring "great risk of life on the way, . . . the Secretary advised that your people remain at Yakama for the present."[38]

Why Schurz had reversed his written promise remains a matter of conjecture. Possibly his promise was only a political ploy to silence Sarah, one that he never intended to fulfill. Yet he appears to have been sincere at the time. In a private letter dated just after his interview with the Winnemuccas, he wrote that "it gave me the most heartfelt pleasure to comply with all their requests." Shortly afterward, Rine-hart's slanders on Sarah's character may have turned Schurz against the policies she championed. Even allowing for the glacial pace of action at the Interior Department, the passage of nearly four months without the dispatch of the necessary instructions to Yakama suggests as much. Or Wilbur's argument on the danger of further violence, with Howard's concurrence, may have been the final straw that changed the secretary's mind. Though crushingly defeated, Sarah had not given up, not then, not ever. As she left, she promised the Paiutes that she would work for them "while there was life in my body." And so she did.

As for the "beautiful letter" she had carried north with singing heart through snow and danger, believing it would free her people, now she knew its real value — "promises which, like the wind, were heard no more."[39]

13
Fort Vancouver

"For shame! For shame! You dare to cry out
liberty when you hold us in places
against our will"

RESURRECTION after defeat and death is a strong theme in
old Paiute stories. When Isha the hero wolf was killed in a
mighty battle in which he fought alone against an invad-
ing army, his younger brother, Itsa the coyote, disguised
himself as a woman, stole his brother's scalp from the enemy camp,
and buried it ceremoniously several times on his journey home. On
the sixth night, a mysterious voice ordered him to build a fire. After
reaching home, he heard the voice say, "My brother, come here," and
was surprised to see Isha loping toward him.

When Itsa caused the death of Koip, son of the mountain sheep,
Koip's wife restored him to life by greasing his bones each morning
and night. Alive again, Koip determined to put an end to this wicked
coyote, which had killed him and his parents before him, and he announced a contest to determine who was the greatest hunter. On a day
of heavy wind, he suggested that Itsa throw a big rock at the wind to
make it stop. Itsa hurled his rock again and again, enraged by his failure to halt the wind. Each time the wind cast his rock back with great
force, breaking his limbs, decapitating him, and finally tearing out
his heart.

Overjoyed by the death of Itsa, Koip called his friends together
and said, "Burn up this bones and this flesh. We will have no more
coyotes." This they did, but they could not find Itsa's heart because
the wind had blown it away. After they returned to their homes,
Itsa came trotting easily through the sagebrush, tail waving, ears
pricked, rust-colored tones in his gray fur gleaming in the sun, yel-

low eyes enigmatic. As long as his heart survived, Itsa could not be killed.[1]

So too would Sarah, her brave heart intact, rise again. At this point, she was financially destitute, defeated in all she had tried to accomplish, and discredited among her people. She might have resumed her lectures or returned to her family in Nevada, but she had reasons of her own for wanting to remain close to Yakama. She appealed to General Howard, and he, as hearty an admirer of Sarah as he was an opponent of freeing the exiled Paiutes, belatedly paid the reward promised her during the war. He also arranged a position for her at Fort Vancouver, military headquarters of the Department of the Columbia and at that time a prison for Indians defeated in a recent small engagement in the Northwest.[2]

In June 1879 false rumors of depredations by the Sheepeaters, a Shoshone subgroup so named because they often hunted the mountain sheep in the high ranges straddling the continental divide, had brought Captain Bernard and his command into the mountains of central Idaho. For an entire summer, one hundred soldiers failed to subdue fifty-one Sheepeaters. Of this number, only fifteen were warriors, most with antiquated firearms. With winter approaching, Bernard withdrew his command, leaving a contingent of Umatilla and Cayuse scouts (perhaps the same who had murdered Egan) to harry the Sheepeaters. So aggressive was their pursuit that the Sheepeaters had no chance to gather winter food supplies. When snow covered the ground, they finally surrendered rather than starve.[3]

Howard remembered that "Sarah Winnemucca ... as an interpreter rendered invaluable service in arriving at a better understanding of the Indian prisoners and their needs." This time Sarah was not interpreting her native language. Both Shoshone and Paiute belong to the Uto-Aztecan language family and, within that broad umbrella, to the Plateau Shoshonean language group. Though cross-influences can be traced in their vocabularies, the two remain distinct. Nonetheless, Sarah's fluent Shoshone enabled her to speak for the Sheepeaters. Their misery aroused her ready sympathies, and at their request she wrote to Washington appealing for land and living quarters for them at Fort Vancouver. She also began a school for the eighteen Sheepeater children. Under her gifted tutelage, they began learning English and pleased Sarah with their rapid progress in reading.[4]

President Hayes's fondness for traveling about the country afforded Sarah one more opportunity for a personal plea, reinforced by an appeal from Winnemucca and Natches, who had just journeyed to see the president during his visit to the California state fair. In the course of the October day that Rutherford and Lucy Hayes spent at Fort Vancouver, the president went to shake hands with Sarah and her pupils. Sarah followed him to his carriage and, in a trembling voice, so movingly described the sorrows of Paiute families separated by enforced exile at Yakama that tears welled from the eyes of the first lady. The president said, "I will see about it" — no doubt his standard response to importunities. But the sun sparkled on the river, gold and red spangled the forested heights of the Columbia River Gorge, the snowy peak of Mount Hood shone in the distance, and Lucy's tears were quickly forgotten amidst the beauty of the autumn scenery. "Nothing was ever done that I ever heard of," observed Sarah.[5]

Sarah spoke no less than the truth when she said the Paiutes were dying at Yakama. Fifteen more had died over the summer of 1880, and Sarah herself had lain ill and feverish for several weeks, possibly the onset of the malaria that later afflicted her. When malaria, probably brought on trading ships, first spread among the Northwest Indians in the 1830s, an estimated three-quarters of them died. The survivors and their descendants probably enjoyed a measure of genetic immunity to the disease that the Paiutes lacked. A recent study titled *Death Stalks the Yakama* describes the devastating effects on the reservation Indians of contagious diseases such as tuberculosis, pneumonia, smallpox, influenza, and malaria during the "Age of Pestilence and Famine." Measles also took a heavy toll. Of the 510 Paiutes who arrived at Yakama in 1879, only 440 could still be counted two years later. Because births had partially compensated for their decrease in number, it is clear that at least one-fifth of Sarah's exiled people died during those years of misery and grief, a loss exceeding the estimated number of Indians killed in the Bannock War. Instead of attempting to treat these patients, Kuykendall, the reservation physician, brushed aside Sarah's requests for medicine and instead gave them a little sugar so they would have "something good to eat before they die." Probably, like Sarah, they would have preferred the Paiute sugarcane, *pehave*. She wrote Natches to send her as much as possible, if shipment did not cost too much. She also pressed him to persuade some Indians to go to Malheur.[6]

It was the last time she could make that plea. The government soon afterward abolished Malheur Reservation, and the settlers who had been lusting for its lands moved in. Was there some basis for the suspicion that the sudden replacement of Parrish by Rinehart had been part of a conspiracy to drive the Indians from Malheur and acquire the lands on the west end for the settlers after their petition to emasculate the reservation had failed?[7]

Never willing to accept defeat, Sarah continued to work for the restoration of Malheur, but, in the meantime, she knew the Paiutes had to leave Yakama. Some might choose to live freely in northern Nevada as many of their kindred did; some might go to Pyramid; and some might find a place at Duck Valley, where the reservation long sought by Winnemucca had been created by executive order in the spring of 1877 for the Western Shoshones, at the request of their resident farmer. All these possibilities were surely on her mind while she was "doing duty" at Vancouver. The soldiers regarded this spot, with its wooden buildings against a backdrop of dense spruce forest and its green lawn sloping down to the great Columbia River, as the most pleasant of postings, and Sarah was considered so well situated in her own little house and her paid position that some saw it as a bribe to end her agitation.[8] Any who thought she could be thus corrupted had badly misread her.

The fulminations of Agent Wilbur make clear that Sarah had not ceased to strive for the freedom of her people. She had only turned to another method, in the best traditions of the adaptable Paiutes. From nearby Fort Vancouver, largely through Lee as a conduit, she remained in close communication with her people at Yakama and continually urged what may be roughly described as a strike. No matter how they blamed her for the broken promises of the past, they listened. Take no land, she told them. Refuse to farm. Build no houses. Do nothing that could be interpreted as a sign that you accept your situation at Yakama. All this they did, through hunger, cold, and misery. Only Oytes and his band broke ranks and cooperated with Wilbur. The rest persisted in their refusal, no matter how long it took, no matter how high the price. A special agent sent by the military in the winter of 1881 to investigate their condition reported, "A more destitute people I never met."[9]

In the end, they seized their freedom, though the end was long in coming. Leggins became so frenzied when Lee received permission to leave Yakama for a visit to relatives, without the others, that Wilbur locked him in prison, but even Wilbur realized that he had not prisons enough to hold them all. A group led by Sarah's cousin Frank Winnemucca had already escaped. Wilbur told the special agent that nothing short of military force could keep them. By November 1881 he was writing to his superior that to be rid of the Paiutes "would be an inexpressible relief to me." Yet he continued to hold them until Washington ordered their release. Washington remained adamant, and Howard, though transferred to the Department of the Platte, continued to insist that he had never promised Leggins's band that they might return home. "I never saw any people at any time so desperately homesick," wrote the reservation physician. "I thought of the Israelites when they were captive in Babylon."[10]

Freedom came only when Wilbur, in failing health, resigned and was replaced by Robert H. Milroy, a more humane authority with no interest in converting the Indians. The new agent, a valorous wounded veteran of the Civil War and a former superintendent of Indian Affairs, readily grasped the situation confronting him: "It is impossible to overcome their determination never to regard this Reservation as their home. Every method has been tried — they have been threatened and coaxed, but in vain. . . . They declare if brought back at one time, they will seize the next opportunity that offers, and that the only way they can be kept here, is to guard them at all times." He recommended relocating them with their kindred. What is more, he turned a blind eye as small groups of Paiutes began slipping away until, by the end of 1884, none remained at Yakama. It was wise that they had not delayed their departure. An agent so humane as Milroy would not last long at Yakama.[11]

Their flight exposed the falsity of Wilbur's claim that only a few malcontents wanted to leave, and the dire predictions that had provided an excuse for holding them at Yakama proved groundless. No depredations upon settlers occurred, nor did the settlers kill the Paiutes as they passed. Indeed, the settlers probably knew nothing of their passing, as the Paiutes kept to secret trails deep inside the wilderness. The only violence against them occurred when Paddy Cap's band tried to live in the Harney Valley. Wilbur's dark warning that the women and children would be unable to make the journey lost all credibility. This was, after all, a people accustomed to traveling with the smallest children and the most arthritic elders from the fishing grounds to the marshes, where the wild birds flocked, to the far mountains, where the pinyon nuts ripened, and during the Bannock War they had demonstrated how swiftly entire bands could travel. Lee and others went to Pyramid; Paddy Cap's band finally found a home at the new Duck Valley Reservation, which developed a mixed population of Paiutes and Shoshones; Leggins's band, starving and destitute, reached Fort McDermit late in the autumn of 1882. All returned in one way or another to "beat their tom-toms and dance and dream in their old haunts," as Howard wrote, with much displeasure.[12]

No doubt, the deerskin drum, punctuated with the clicking chatter of the rattle made from the dewclaws of deer, did sound at celebrations when their families welcomed them home at last. The Paiute singing masters knew many chants in praise of the beloved homeland from which the exiles had refused to be separated. Not all had survived to return — indeed, 510 had been herded to Yakama and by Leggins's count only 264, some born in exile, lived to escape — but the world had been set right. Their sacred connection with the land of their people had been restored. In this place at morning, for countless generations, Paiutes had cleansed their faces with cold water and turned to the rising sun to give thanks to Numina, the creator of all things, and pray for a good day. Now the days would be good again. They were home.[13]

Sarah had not been able to remain close to Yakama until the end. In July 1881 the government transferred the Sheepeaters to Fort Hall Reservation, Idaho, and asked her to accompany them as the interpreter. It is evident that she did not view the eventual return of the Yakama exiles as a success story, perhaps because it came so slowly and at so high a cost in lives. But Wilbur saw her as the catalyst. Until she brought "that unfortunate permission for her people to return to Malheur they had no expectation of returning," he reported. He felt positive that Sarah was the one who had launched the strike and kept it going: "Sarah Winnemucca finds frequent means to communicate with them, urging them to take no steps accept of nothing that can be construed into a prospect of accepting this reservation as their home." In the last analysis, she had succeeded better than she knew. Riding north with Schurz's promise, she had kindled the hope that would not die, and she had shown them the path that would finally lead to freedom.[14]

Soon after she accompanied the Sheepeaters to Fort Hall, Sarah's work with them ended, and so did the education of the children. War Jack, their chief, later sent her the discouraging news that in the absence of further schooling her pupils quickly forgot all that she had taught them. Though they had progressed well, she had not succeeded in instilling in them her own youthful determination to achieve literacy, the true source of white men's power.[15]

The written word, she now realized, could reach the people who would never hear her lectures. She was developing an interest in setting down her words on paper, perhaps prompted by the reprinting of her 1870 letter to the commissioner of Indian Affairs on the condition of the Paiutes in Helen Hunt Jackson's landmark denunciation of American Indian policy, *A Century of Dishonor*, in 1881. In September 1882 an article by Sarah on the Paiutes appeared in *The Californian*, but the date of its composition is probably earlier, perhaps 1880. The close of Sarah's article suggests that the ordeal of her people and the apparent failure of all she had fought for had plunged her into deep depression: "I see very well that all my race will die out. In a few short years there will be none left — no, not one Indian in the whole of America." She concluded with the bitter hope that some other race would drive out the white man as he had expelled the Indian. "Then I will say the Great Spirit is just, and that it is all right."[16]

Sarah's movements after leaving the Sheepeaters culminated in a late November reunion with Lewis H. Hopkins, a soldier discharged from the army at Fort Bowie, Arizona. She next appeared in the news when she married him on 5 December 1881 in Russ House, a fashionable San Francisco hotel. The 1906 earthquake and fire destroyed San Francisco marriage records, and it is not clear how this union could have been formalized under California's miscegenation law.[17] Indeed, that is one of several questions raised by the Hopkins marriage.

Lewis was the last of Sarah's white ne'er-do-well husbands. A small, slight man at five feet seven inches and 132 pounds, pale and gray-eyed, he sported a luxuriant light brown handlebar mustache. He was then thirty-one years old to Sarah's thirty-seven. He had been born in Memphis and may have acquired a smattering of the charm and soft accents of the South but no wife prior to Sarah. Upon his first enlistment in the army in Maryland in 1870, he described himself as a laborer, although he impressed people as well educated and genteel. The army brought him west and perhaps taught him a skill. At the time of his second enlistment in San Francisco in 1876, after a year out of the service, he called himself a musician. (One wonders if he blew the bugle that sounds the charge.) When he left the service upon the expiration of his enlistment in late November 1881, the army had evidently demoted him from sergeant to private, and his records contain the notation "no character," doubtless signifying that his superiors

Lewis Hopkins. Courtesy of the Nevada Historical Society.

considered him undeserving for a favorable character recommendation. As it turned out, "no character" was a pretty good description of Lewis Hopkins.[18]

Sarah never mentioned where she met Lewis, and clearly it must have been before his enlistment ended in Arizona. Though hilariously inaccurate in some respects, an article by Glenn Ranck, who claimed to have known Sarah at Fort Vancouver, may provide a clue. Accordingly to Ranck, they met during the Bannock War when Hopkins, a chief of Howard's scouts, rode by Sarah's side and performed deeds of "knightly valor" to win "glances of admiration" from her: "With . . . swinging sabre he led the charge driving the savages in terror before. The campaign was brief and bloody, and the hostiles were soon glad to lay down their arms." Hopkins then "gallantly handed her his bloodstained sword in token of his captivity," and she blushingly accepted it. "Thus did she plight her troth on the battlefield."[19]

That Sarah would have looked with favor upon a sword stained with the blood of "my own dear people" deserves no credence, but the suggestion that she met Lewis during the Bannock War is plausible. This information also appears in the newspaper report on their marriage. Company E, First Cavalry, the unit in which Lewis served after his second enlistment, participated in the Bannock War. Although the movements of each company within the First Cavalry are not always specified, Sarah and Lewis might have been at the same place at the same time at Birch Creek — would Lewis have sounded the charge on his bugle while Sarah stood transfixed with horror beside the Gatling gun? — and perhaps during Forsyth's pursuit through the desert.[20]

If they had not met before, they certainly came together on 30 September. A cavalryman's diary noted that Sarah arrived at Camp McDermit with Hopkins and others to escort the Paiute prisoners to Camp Harney. During the ensuing three months, they probably saw a good deal of each other at Harney, where Sarah remained with the Indian prisoners from McDermit at the same time that Company E, First Cavalry, was stationed there. Ranck remembered that at Fort Vancouver in 1880–81 she had been waiting for Lewis to complete his enlist-ment. Though still in what Ranck called "the full bloom and charm of womanhood" and as attractive to men as she had always been since the days when miners did their fanciest dancing to impress her in Dutch Nick's saloon, Sarah remained faithful once she had given her heart, even during a lengthy separation.[21]

Sarah once jokingly remarked that Indians liked epaulets, but her choice of another military husband probably reflected nothing more than her prolonged proximity with the young men of the army. Her affinity for white husbands poses a larger question. Of the three men she actually married (Bartlett, Satewaller, and Hopkins) and the three she reputedly married or had serious liaisons with (Snyder, the vari-ously named Indian, and Hamilton), only one was unquestionably In-dian. Doubtless, the attractions of the exotic were at work on both sides in her marriages to white men. Moreover, for Sarah, who always cared deeply about her acceptance by whites and felt her repeated re-jections so keenly, a white husband may have provided another item for her credentials, along with Methodism and her claim to a convent education. Perhaps most importantly, she had journeyed too far into *taibo*'s world to turn back. Few Paiute men of her day had become as acculturated as she. Marrying an Indian would have meant reversion to the role of a traditional Indian wife primarily occupied with gath-ering food for her family instead of pursuing the path of her own strong ambition. As she once told a newspaper reporter: "I would rather be with my people, but not to live with them as they live."[22]

Another feature of the traditional Paiute wife would have been a black-eyed, round-cheeked baby on the cradle board, with several other children tagging along behind. And Sarah had a way with chil-dren. One reporter noted how quickly she coaxed the shiest ones to her lap. Yet at thirty-seven, after several husbands and lovers, she had never borne a child. She may have simply been infertile. The possibil-ity can not be ruled out that Edward Bartlett, who had undergone treatment for gonorrhea before he met her, had not been fully cured by the often ineffective methods available in the nineteenth century and had transmitted the disease to her, thus damaging her fertility. Nonetheless, a more probable explanation for her childlessness lies in conscious choice. Sarah believed that Paiute women did not wish to bring children into a world of sorrow and peril: "My people have been so unhappy for a long time they wish now to *disincrease*, instead of multiply. The mothers are afraid to have more children, for fear they shall have daughters, who are not safe even in their mother's presence." Since a recent study has demonstrated unimpaired fertility among Paiute women on the Comstock, her assessment erred, but the key point was her implication that women could choose whether to bear children. It appears likely that Sarah had decided to forgo motherhood because it would interfere with the role she had chosen for herself. In this she placed herself at odds with her traditional culture in that the Paiutes always pitied a childless couple.[23]

A final question raised by Sarah's last marriage was her proclivity for ne'er-do-wells such as Bartlett, Hamilton, and Hopkins. She may well have suffered from the powerful woman's perennial problem in choosing a mate: a strong man with an important career of his own might have interfered with her independence to pursue her career, whereas a weakling could be bent to serve her purposes. This would prove to be the role for Lewis Hopkins, who had no detectable occupation after leaving the army and merely served as an aide to Sarah while she lectured.

In truth, Lewis may have been more an impediment than an aide as it became clear that he was uncontrollably addicted to gambling. During a visit by the couple to a settler's home near the Pyramid Reservation less than a month after their wedding, one participant recounted that the evening began pleasantly with "merry conversation, varied by humorous songs" and then progressed to poker. After a trivial loss, Lewis gave his place in the game to Sarah, only to see her quickly lose five dollars. "You can't play poker worth a damn," he chided her. It took no more to inflame Sarah's touchy pride. She asked him whose money she was playing and went on to remind him that he had gambled away 500 dollars of hers in an hour and a half in San

Francisco. Humiliated by this public tongue-lashing, Lewis swore he would no longer live with her, returned the jewelry she had given him for safekeeping, and walked out the door. Although Sarah returned to the game, a paroxysm of grief soon convulsed her. She snatched the money and beans from the table and threw them around the room, pointing to her heart and crying dramatically, "Oh, if I had a knife, I would place it here!" Shortly afterward she disappeared into the wintry night.

Following the sound of a low moan, men from the nearby settler's house where Lewis had bedded down for the night found her lying on the ground and bleeding from the nose and mouth. They carried her inside, and Lewis lay down beside her and pressed his cheek to hers, while the other men endeavored to revive her. Unable to detect a pulse, they pronounced her dead. As one of the onlookers wept in a corner, Lewis, overcome with grief, loudly cried and lamented, "Oh, don't tell me she is dead! Oh, my darling, don't die! Oh, why did I treat you so!" Then another man detected a faint throb in her wrist.

By the time the doctor arrived from the reservation, she had regained speech but appeared confused as to her whereabouts and the identity of her companions. The doctor seemed equally confused about the cause of her sudden illness. He gave her some medicine and tentatively pronounced it "hemorrhage of the lungs." So it may have been, if it was not a shaman's trance. Sarah appeared to fall asleep, softly singing as she slept a little song that went, "I won't go home till morning." One witness to the evening's events ironically observed that he hoped Hopkins would love her as well after her recovery as he had done "during the short time he thought her dead."[24]

Although Sarah had already announced plans for a series of lectures in the East, promising a frontal attack on Indian agents and a proposal for a system of Indian control, some time would pass before she actually reached Boston. After she spoke several times at Ogden, Utah, in February 1882, the Hopkinses apparently traveled north for a prolonged sojourn with Elma and her husband, John Smith, at Henry's Lake, Idaho. Sarah's movements during 1882 have not come to light. Perhaps she needed this year of prolonged honeymoon with the pale, slender, gray-eyed man she so dearly loved to regain the strength that would enable her to get on her warhorse once more and renew the fight for her people.[25]

While Sarah sojourned in the North, Winnemucca was dying. He who had once been so swift of foot that he seemed ubiquitous now promenaded in a slow and stately manner. At the train depots, passengers from the East gaped at the aged chief wearing his dark blue army coat with the brass buttons and his plumed hat with the brass eagle in front, and Winnemucca accepted money and cigars from them. Although other chiefs from Sitting Bull to Geronimo accepted similar tributes in their later years, some white men thought it beneath Winnemucca's dignity. The old chief, on the other hand, probably saw tourists as a new food source — and an easier one than charming antelope.[26]

Aside from this variation, Winnemucca followed his old pursuits in his last years. He still gambled recklessly, on one occasion losing all that he possessed down to the last pony and reducing himself to beggary. Despite his increasing feebleness, he continued to take an active part in political affairs. In the summer of 1881, he again protested to the press against the exile of the Paiutes at Yakama. Together with Natches, he intervened to prevent the tribe from taking vengeance on an Indian man accused of murder, Paiute Dick. Having long outlived all his wives, he still felt so full of the juice of life that in late July 1882 he married again, choosing a young widow with an infant child. Winnemucca had always thought a pretty young bride the prerogative of a chief. When Isaac Roop introduced him to his daughter on the streets of Virginia City many years earlier, Winnemucca jocularly remarked that he had presumed the seventeen-year-old girl a new bride of Roop's. Above all, Winnemucca remained beloved by his people. When the Paiutes learned that a report of his death in 1881 was false, they leapt about with such exuberant displays of joy that one reporter thought they had thoroughly disproved the novelists' cliches about Indian stoicism.[27]

The next news of his death would not be false. As summer turned to fall in 1882, Winnemucca rode north, passing Pyramid Lake Reservation. Never, in close to twenty years, had he broken his vow, made at the time of the Mud Lake Massacre, to live there no more. If he took the desert trail by present Gerlach, he would have passed a grassy upland, straw-colored by summer's end and cupped by gray hills. He would have skirted the southern tip of the Black Rock Desert, a white playa where flocks of black crows flew, and distant mountains swam in watery mirages. He would have wound his way through narrow passes, where the hills hug the trail. He would have crossed mile after mile of broad sagebrush plain until he arrived at the place where a wall of bare, flat-planed, lavender gray mesas — the Hayes Canyon Range — marked the boundary of the desert on the east side of the Surprise Valley. Rimmed by the Warner Mountains on the west, the valley was narrow and some thirty miles long. It contained three shallow alkaline lakes and many springs and marshes of dense, dark green tules taller than a man. This was the home of the Paiute band known as the golden marmot eaters, led by Chief Ochocho but watched carefully by the army at Fort Bidwell at the northern end of the valley. Toward the southern end of the valley near Coppersmith Station, Winnemucca made his last camp.[28]

After illness struck him down, death came slowly, as Winnemucca, unable to take nourishment, gradually starved and wasted away to a skeleton. His survival for nearly a month testifies to his great strength. Natches visited his father briefly, but Sarah and Elma did not go at all. By the time word of their father's illness reached them, they probably judged that they could not make so long a journey quickly enough to find him still alive. Although it is unclear whether Winnemucca and Hopkins ever met, there is also a ghost of a suspicion that the old chief disapproved of him for much the same reason that he rejected Bartlett, which means a new rift may have yawned between Sarah and her father. Whatever the reasons for her absence, the only close family members attending Winnemucca throughout were his two aged sisters and Lee.[29]

In his last years, Winnemucca had become prone to delusions springing from the ancient beliefs of his people. At one point, he complained that witches had caused his eyebrows to grow unnaturally long, obscuring his vision, and his nails to lengthen like the claws of a beast. Since the Paiutes attributed most illnesses to the malevolent spells of witches, it came as no surprise when Winnemucca dreamt that the witchcraft of his new bride had caused him to sicken and requested the death that old custom decreed for witches. Twice the unfortunate young woman ran away, and twice the Indians retrieved her. Once she tried to hang herself to avoid the horror ahead, but they cut her down.

Grizzly John, a half-breed, related what happened next. The women took her through the reeds, washed her in one of the springs, and covered her naked body with ashes. Then they brought her to a circle of fires atop one of the eastern bluffs and tethered her by the foot to a stump in the center, where she cowered, clasping her baby son to her breast. After a few moments of chanting and circling, an Indian stepped forward, ripped the child from the arms of his shrieking mother, and dashed his head on a rock, killing him instantly. The Paiutes continued to circle and chant, hurling stones at the crouched screaming woman until she lay on the ground, a mangled, bleeding mass. Her agony finally ended with a heavy rock that crushed her skull. They burned the bodies, but Winnemucca showed no improvement, and more than three weeks passed before he died on 21 October. With his last words, he urged his people to follow the path of righteousness and to live in peace with white men.[30]

In contrast to her long and heartrending account of Truckee's passing, Sarah never discussed her father's death. She had not, of course, witnessed it with her own eyes. Yet the larger reason may have been its entanglement with the horrible stoning of his bride. This might seriously hamper Sarah's efforts to win sympathy for the Paiutes and convince the public that they were not savages but a virtuous people well along the road to civilization. Natches also saw the need for damage control and told the press that the woman's threats to burn a white man's house had led Ochocho's band to stone her, though he later admitted the truth.[31]

Most of the Paiutes, overcome with sorrow for the old chief, cared little for *taibo*'s good opinion. They only knew that they had just seen the passing of the last of the great Paiute chiefs. They declared themselves too grief-stricken to decide upon a new chief, and a meeting convened for the purpose disbanded without a decision. At the last, Winnemucca had abjured them to choose a good man but did not indicate his preference. The whites then intervened to insist that the new chief must reside at Pyramid Reservation, which effectively eliminated Natches because he lived independently on his ranch near Lovelock. Evidently, agency officials wanted to elevate Dave Numana, a son of Sarah's cousin, the wise war chief who led during the Pyramid Lake War. Although Captain Dave headed the Indian police at Pyramid, Sarah would have received the notion of making him chief with distaste because she saw him as the Indian agent's puppet ("he has no character whatever, and could always be hired to do a wicked thing"). The issue of leadership remained unsettled.[32]

14

Boston

"I pray of you, I implore of you, I beseech of you,
hear our pitiful cry to you, sweep away
the agency system"

BOSTON, when the Hopkinses arrived in the spring of 1883, was more than rows of red brick houses, lengthy naves of old elms, the smooth, blue expanse of the Charles River at twilight, the silvery jangle of streetcar bells, and the bustle of crowds among the brightly lit shops, theaters, and hotels. Boston was the shrine of reform, indeed, "the national citadel of culture and moral purpose." And Boston was primed to take up the Indian cause.[1]

The ground had already been broken by the Omaha maiden Bright Eyes (Susette La Flesche), who, in company with her brother Frank and Chief Standing Bear, had lectured extensively in the area on behalf of the Ponca cause. So closely did Sarah follow Bright Eyes that they eventually blurred in the mind of one reporter, but no one who had seen both could have made that mistake. Granddaughter of a French trader and ten years younger than Sarah, Bright Eyes was petite, with small, delicate features, and had received a much better education through her attendance at both a reservation school and an eastern private school. Unlike Sarah, who spoke extemporaneously and never twice the same, Bright Eyes suffered agonies of shyness and always read her speech. Yet many found her modest sweetness engaging, and Henry Wadsworth Longfellow embraced her as the incarnation of his Minnehaha. It may have been Sarah's ill luck that she debuted too late to be the Boston reformers' first Minnehaha.[2]

Soon after her long-planned and much-delayed arrival, Sarah came under the aegis of two elderly Boston sisters, Elizabeth Palmer Peabody and Mary Mann, widow of the famed educator Horace Mann.

The appearance of the venerable Peabody in her old age, thinly fictionalized as "Miss Birdseye" in *The Bostonians,* has been masterfully described by Henry James: "She had a sad, soft, pale face, which (and it was the effect of her whole head) looked as if it had been soaked, blurred, and made vague by exposure to some slow dissolvent. The long practice of philanthropy had not given accent to her features; it had rubbed out their transitions, their meanings. The waves of sympathy, of enthusiasm, had wrought upon them in the same way in which the waves of time finally modify the surface of old marble busts, gradually washing away their sharpness, their details. In her large countenance her dim little smile scarcely showed." James saw Birdseye/Peabody as the last survivor of New England's heroic age, "an age of plain living and high thinking, of pure ideals and earnest effort, of moral passion and noble experiment." Of the many causes Peabody had championed in her long life, from Unitarian rationalism to the Kraitser theory of languages, the kindergarten movement had proven the most successful. As her biographer observes, she "found her greatest joy in the discovery of genius in others." Sarah was to be one of her last enthusiasms.[3]

Who exactly had invited Sarah to Boston, whether the dowagers encountered several years earlier in the San Francisco railroad station or the lecture bureau that engaged Bright Eyes, remains unclear. At some point Sarah was the houseguest of Mrs. Ole Bull, wife of the renowned Norwegian violinist, but she remained most of the summer and fall in the modest home of Peabody and Mann. During her stay, a bond of deep devotion developed between Peabody and Sarah. Peabody felt that she knew Sarah "more intimately than I ever knew anybody but my own sisters." Sarah, warmed by the old woman's sympathy, seems to have opened her heart to Peabody as she did to no one else. Peabody later said that during the following years I "have had constant intercourse with her when she was not with me — *by letter*" (letters which unfortunately have not yet been uncovered).[4]

No doubt, Sarah spent much of her time in the Peabody household writing at a furious pace, for as Peabody once observed, "A great pur-

Elizabeth Peabody. Courtesy of the Library of Congress.

pose must be accomplished in the first fervor of its conception, or it
will never be." Peabody, who has been called Boston's first woman
publisher, had written extensively and may have influenced, in her
strongly managerial style, Sarah's decision to set her words on paper,
while the equally supportive Mary Mann promised to correct Sarah's
difficulties with written English. Both sisters, however, credited Sa-

rah's idea to her "own deep impulse," originating in her wish to tell the whole story that she could only touch upon in the limited time of a single lecture. In Boston, where the very atmosphere palpitated with culture, what was more natural than to write a book?[5]

Life among the Piutes: Their Wrongs and Claims was published in 1883, a 268-page work that combines the history of the tribe and a description of Paiute culture with Sarah's autobiography and reprints a number of letters from her supporters. Needing only to set down on paper what she had been saying in her lectures, she had completed the manuscript in only a matter of months. Peabody's expertise in publishing ensured its prompt appearance in print. The book was above all a tract intended to win support and sympathy for the Paiutes at a time when abuses continued at the reservations and some exiles still remained at Yakama. Sarah also meant to clear her own name. Unlike modern Indian authors, she had no need to communicate with multiple audiences, being aware that few Indians would read her book. She aims her impassioned salvos directly at *taibo* and introduces him to Paiute life, remembered with love, sorrow, and pride. Sarah's choice of form had been partly influenced by her purpose, but it also conformed to the Indian view that relating one's personal story apart from the tribe is distasteful. Unable to conceive of herself as an entity apart from her people, she blended her own life with their saga to produce an ethnohistory. She may have also consciously intended to preserve the memory of her people, fulfilling the traditional role of an Indian woman as the keeper of knowledge for future generations.[6]

Life among the Piutes has been praised by Mann, among others, as the first book written by an Indian. This is not strictly accurate. Indians had been publishing for years, and if sermons, speeches, letters, short pamphlets, and the like are eliminated, Sarah's book appears to be the fifteenth. But it is the first written by an Indian woman, the first by an Indian west of the Rockies, and one of the earliest by an Indian west of the Mississippi. Mann recognized its significance at the time, "It is of the first importance to hear what only an Indian and an Indian woman can tell."[7]

Several issues arise in evaluating Sarah's book. Louise Tharp, biographer of the Peabody sisters, and others contend that Sarah did not write her own book, calling it an "as told to" effort actually composed by her editor, Mary Mann. Although no original manuscripts by Sarah are known to survive, it has been generally acknowledged, even by Sarah herself, that her writing skills lagged far behind her verbal accomplishments. A copy of an 1860 letter of hers shows considerable confusion, and Fanny Corbusier recalled helping her with her public letters in the Camp McDermit days. Thus it is likely that her manuscript required a good deal of editorial correction, as do many manuscripts, but this is a far cry from not composing her own book.[8]

An 1883 letter by Mary Mann definitively settles the issue: "I wish you could see her manuscript as a matter of curiosity. I don't think the English language ever got such a treatment before. I have to recur to her sometimes to know what a word is, as spelling is an unknown quantity to her. . . . She often takes syllables off of words & adds them or rather prefixes them to other words, but the story is heart-breaking, and told with a simplicity & an eloquence that cannot be described." This leaves no doubt that Mann was *working on a manuscript written by Sarah*, a conclusion also supported by Mann's comment in the editor's preface that she had confined her editing to spelling and punctuation because "I am confident that no one would desire that her [Sarah's] own original words should be altered." Furthermore, as anthropologist Catherine Fowler has rightly pointed out, pronunciation spellings such as "Acotrass" for "Alcatraz" and "Carochel" for "Churchill" in the published book are surely Sarah's own, unnoticed by Mann.[9]

A second issue raised by a book written almost entirely from memory is its accuracy. Sarah misstates the sizes of the Indian bands at Camp McDermit, either from imperfect recollection or from an effort to enhance the importance of the Paiutes. Also, she is sometimes inaccurate with dates, as when she places Truckee's death before the Pyramid Lake War. In the style of the traditional storyteller, she seems to have made no effort to sharpen her memory through research —

with one exception. She apparently read General Howard's official report on the Bannock War while she wrote. Her book is congruent with the report on many details such as dates and the number of people who surrendered. Moreover, her account of Forsyth's canyon battle (which she did not witness) is lifted almost word for word from Howard's report, as is her description of the journey north from Camp Lyon.[10]

Autobiographies have sometimes been characterized as the lives we wish we had led, and in Sarah's tract her political purpose intensified this tendency. Anything discreditable to Sarah or her people has been omitted, including all but two of her husbands and the stoning of Winnemucca's bride. But nearly all the events Sarah does describe that can be cross-checked elsewhere prove to be startlingly accurate. As Fowler notes, her recollections of the Carson Valley settlers and the McMarlin-Williams murders are substantiated by plat maps and other sources, even though at the time of these events, Sarah was just a youngster, present in the Ormsby household for no more than a few months. The disparity between Sarah's extraordinary memory for events and her unreliability with dates makes psychological as well as cultural sense. Psychologists now recognize that the two forms of memory — semantic memory for facts and episodic memory for events personally experienced — are distinct; a person may be richly endowed with one and deficient in the other.[11]

If the events in Sarah's book are accurately recalled, are the many conversations written as direct quotations, though presumably with some degree of reconstruction, also reliable? Certainly, none are implausible, and the rhetoric conforms with the Paiute speeches recorded at numerous conferences. Nonetheless, is it possible for anyone to remember conversations and speeches heard years earlier? Sarah, as one reporter phrased it, was "smart as a knife" and may have had the gift that some possess for recalling dialogue (Elizabeth Peabody also had a little of this talent). It is important to bear in mind that Sarah was reared in a culture of oral tradition in which people without a written language were trained to remember and memory was bolstered by repeating a tale many, many times — as Sarah did on stage and, in all likelihood, beside the campfires of her people. In Brumble's apt phrase, the book is "essentially an oral performance put down in writing." Anthropologist Jay Miller observes that among Great Basin cultures, the children of elite families were "specially trained to memorize," so this gift may have been particularly well developed in Sarah. Thus there is good reason to believe that voices otherwise dead and lost still speak to us through Sarah's writing.[12]

Today, *Life among the Piutes* remains a remarkable achievement. Once more in print, it is often read, frequently cited by historians, and carefully analyzed by literary scholars. Although some of the points these scholars make have been mentioned at various junctures in this book, several deserve further emphasis. Sarah's book attempts to establish her standing by recounting her great deeds as an Indian warrior would do. As Brumble points out, "she is the sum of her reputation." Insofar as she relates her own story, her areas of silence comport with a traditional concentration on deeds performed on behalf of the tribe. She mentions no cultural identity crisis, refrains from discussing her interior life and her experiences in the places where she lived apart from her people, remains completely silent on the subject of her Christian conversion (unlike some other Indian authors), and has little or nothing to say on the physical appearance of the places she had known, including the homeland that meant so much to the Paiutes.[13]

At the same time, she clearly perceives that establishing respectability in the face of Rinehart's slanders would be critical to the book's reception by the moralistic eastern reformers. She therefore includes not only a sizable number of letters attesting to her character but also what Brigitte Georgi-Findlay terms a "subtext of personal defense" underlying the recurrent theme of attempted rape in her narrative. On the issue of Sarah's attitude toward assimilation, Lape and Brumble are surely correct in observing that Sarah saw no essential differences between whites and Indians, only different customs and educational training. In this context, her recounting of the myth on the common ancestor who separated whites and Indians because they quarreled makes perfect sense.[14]

This recognition of *Life among the Piutes* by scholars underscores its importance. It is America's first portrait in English of an Indian woman written in her own words from her own point of view, and years would pass before other Indian women began telling their stories in print. Indeed, as late as 1987 the editors of an anthology of autobiographical writing by Indians experienced difficulty in securing contributions from Indian women, who evidently still found this mode of expression uncongenial. In ethnography, Sarah's book is no less valuable, because it covers a time period that predated anthropological research. As Fowler suggests, the general public in the 1880s probably learned more about Northern Paiute ethnography through Sarah's efforts "than has been known at any time since."[15]

In addition to her unquestionable influence on Sarah's book, Elizabeth Peabody embraced Sarah's cause with the gusto of an old warhorse hearing the trumpet of reform sound again. She tirelessly wrote letters on Sarah's behalf to influential friends and arranged talks for Sarah in the homes of Ralph Waldo Emerson, John Greenleaf Whittier, several congressmen, and other members of Boston's intellectual and social elite. Gratifying as it must have been for Sarah to be received by these distinguished people, the most momentous meeting came about as a result of her own letter to U.S. Senator Henry Dawes. In her letter she suggested improvements to his bill on the division of Indian lands in severalty, a plan to allot tribal lands to individual Indian families in an effort to turn the Indians into yeoman farmers and assimilate them. Sarah suggested that instead of allowing the secretary of the Interior in distant Washington to decide which Indians should obtain allotments, this authority should be given to the chiefs, who were in a better position to know which tribal members could benefit from receiving lands. In general, she argued that the government should deal directly with the chiefs and that the Indians themselves should select all agency employees, including, of course, the agents. Although the senator did not incorporate the changes that

Sarah suggested, her letter, which she had dictated to her husband, Lewis, impressed him. Moreover, Dawes's daughter, Anna, who heard Sarah speak on 2 October, probably gave him an enthusiastic account of the Paiute "princess."[16]

Dawes immediately invited Sarah and Peabody for an overnight visit on 5 October at his Massachusetts home, where, in Peabody's words, he "gave us the most affectionate hospitality": "After dinner when *he* heard her speak & shared in the great interest she excited — and in the evening after tea — he took her into his study & had a long talk with her — and said he should bring her before the Indian Committee of which he is chairman — & he told me to multiply occasions for her *to speak* as it was desirable that she should *stir hearts* as she did that day (& always does) to press on Congress the consideration of the Indian question."[17]

Lewis's whereabouts during these early months in Boston is not specified. He may have spent much of his time in Maryland, where he had enlisted in the army in 1870, visiting friends or relatives; author Canfield suggests that he might have done research for Sarah's book. Those who later saw the Hopkinses together thought them a devoted couple: "He evidently appreciated his wife's character and loved her. . . . I thought they were equally attached to each other." Yet, as subsequent events would show, the farther away was Lewis, the better.[18]

In the span of little more than a year, from the spring of 1883 to midsummer 1884, Sarah took the East by storm, lecturing more than three hundred times in Boston, New York, Pennsylvania, Baltimore, Washington, and throughout New England and collecting thousands of signatures for her petition to Congress. Her lecture at Christ Church in Philadelphia at the end of October 1883 was probably typical. Half an hour before the appointed time, crowds began to pack the entire church — galleries, aisles, and chancel steps included — with an audience estimated at fifteen hundred. After everyone joined in a hymn, the rector introduced Lewis, who briefly sketched Sarah's history. Then came Sarah — her straight, black hair flowing down her back, her strong, blunt, unmistakably Indian features visible in the farther reaches of the church. Doubtless she appeared in the same picturesque costume she later wore for her New York lectures: a beaded deerskin dress with an embroidered pouch at the waist, red leather leggings, and moccasins.[19]

Her telling of the Paiute story in a forty-five minute address captivated the audience. She told how unscrupulous agents calling themselves Christians robbed the Indians and often dramatized their behavior by rapaciously snatching up money cast onto the floor. She related how desperation had driven some of her people to join the Bannocks in the recent war. The solution she recommended was placing the Indians under the authority of the military, who could be trusted to deal fairly with them.[20]

Like any effective speaker, Sarah tailored her lectures to suit the interests of her audience, while always asserting her fundamental themes. Not unaware of the eastern reformers' interest in woman suffrage and the prevailing belief in the superior morality of women, she argued on some occasions that if the agent system must be continued, the agents should be women. When speaking to an audience of women, she stressed, perhaps a little fancifully, the virtue of Paiute courtship and marital practices and the role of the grandmothers in caring for the marriageable young. She told them how Paiutes raised their children with kindness and love instead of physical punishment (the whippings and ear-pullings that *taibo* inflicted on his children seemed appalling to the Indians). Peabody called this "a lecture which never failed to excite the moral enthusiasm of every woman that heard it, and seal their confidence in her own purity of character and purpose." Sarah also appealed to eastern pride by emphasizing American traditions of liberty and justice for all.[21]

Peabody, who heard Sarah speak some thirty times throughout the East, remained a devoted admirer: "She never repeated or contradicted herself once, though it was obvious that except in the choice of some particular subject to be made her theme, she took no previous thought as to what she should say, but trusted that the right words

245

Wearing a buckskin dress, red leggings, and moccasins, Sarah electrified
audiences at her lectures. Courtesy of the Nevada Historical Society.

would be given her by the 'Spirit Father,' whose special messenger she believed herself to be, and impressed her audiences to believe that she was."[22]

Nonetheless, Sarah's progress through the East was not an unmarred triumph. No matter how she stirred hearts "already all the organized sympathy for Indians in the East was pre-engaged," as Peabody put it. Otherwise said, the available charitable funding had already been committed to other aspects of the Indian cause, such as missionary work and the Carlisle boarding school. Although Sarah developed close ties to many church groups, especially in Baltimore, where the Hopkinses made their home for a while, she acquired an influential enemy at her first Boston lecture. According to Peabody, "She offended, by her story of the conduct of the Methodist agent Wilbur, a Methodist lady, who endeavored to bribe her to say no more about him, by promising her hospitality and other assistance." Sarah, unwilling to alter the truth no matter whom it affronted, predictably refused. "This started an opposition against herself at once, that succeeded in making the Woman's Association turn a cold shoulder to her." She had other enemies among the reformers. Herbert Welsh, a founder of the politically influential Indian Rights Association, and Charles Painter, the organization's energetic Washington lobbyist, not only rejected Sarah but endeavored to alienate her supporters.[23]

Sarah's ideas and those of the Indian reform organizations approached each other on one point — lands in severalty — but for very different reasons. The reformers envisaged the policy as a key element in assimilating the Indians; Sarah saw it as a means, though not the best one, of escaping the tyranny of reservation agents. Given the deep convictions of both Sarah and the reformers, their more fundamental differences left little room for compromise. Permeated by evangelical Christianity, the Women's National Indian Association, the Indian Rights Association, and other reformers who met annually at the Lake Mohonk conference saw the conversion of the Indians to Christianity as the essential step in civilizing and assimilating them. Sarah, in addition to ridiculing the conduct of missionary agents in

247

her lectures, sought only the selective adoption of certain useful features of *taibo*'s culture and once acidly remarked that the Indians needed practical help, not religious tracts from the missionary societies. The Indian reformers foresaw the breakup of the tribal organizations that blocked the civilizing process; Sarah wanted to strengthen traditional tribal authorities and never ceased to value Indian culture. Not least, Sarah had aligned herself with the losing side when she argued that army control of the reservations would be a better solution than continued abuse under the Interior Department. The idea of army control, which President Grant had initiated as part of a new order for Indian relations and then abandoned, was anathema to the reformers and to congressmen unwilling to relinquish patronage at the reservations.[24]

Even the rivalries between Indian reform organizations failed to benefit Sarah. Her belief in preserving traditional tribal authorities more closely approached the position eventually taken by Thomas Bland's National Indian Defense Association, a group heartily detested by the Indian Rights Association. But Bland had opposed Sarah since her first year in Boston. Peabody wrote of "the conspiracy against her of Dr. Bland and a woman who secretly acts with him and who have endeavored to destroy the reputation of her husband, and by the most subtle and cruel wickedness I ever knew of."[25]

It appears that the venom of an old enemy — Rinehart — had poisoned Sarah's cause in Bland's eyes (and likely in the eyes of the Indian Rights Association leaders as well). Shortly after her arrival in Boston, *Council Fire*, a publication of Bland's, promptly trotted out Rinehart's slanders, accusing her of lying and prostitution. Worse still, Bland attempted to quash publication of her book, a disaster averted only by the success of Peabody and Mann in raising a six-hundred-dollar subscription fund for *Life among the Piutes*. *Council Fire* characterized Sarah as a "tool of the army officers" seeking control of the reservations and concluded that "It is a great outrage on the respectable people of Boston for General Howard or any other officer of the army to foist such a woman of any race upon them."[26]

The general wanted no part of this controversy. A late summer effort by Mann to solicit a public letter from him in defense of Sarah's character shows that noxious rumors continued to circulate. Although Howard had already written a letter of recommendation for Sarah in the spring and would later praise her with fulsome verbiage in his books, he declined on this occasion, giving as his reasons a belief that "a lady's reputation" should not be discussed in the newspapers and his apprehension that "should I write I should lay myself open to be assailed by the same bad man, who is thoroughly wicked, and unscrupulous." "Agent Rhinehart," wrote Peabody in the margin of the letter. Rinehart's power to alarm a brigadier general illustrates just how formidable an enemy he was.[27]

When Sarah spoke in Norfolk in the spring of 1884, Rinehart's calumnies snapped at her heels again. One of her local supporters wrote to Mann, "It seemed to me melancholy that Winnemucca's influence in the Indian cause was totally undermined at the last minute by this insidious letter printed in an unsympathetic paper." The letter presented the Paiutes as "bloodthirsty and drunken" and described the stoning of Winnemucca's bride. Lewis attempted to explain the stoning as an execution carried out because the Paiutes suspected the woman of poisoning the chief. No doubt, he made his usual claim of intimate familiarity with the tribe through living with them for thirteen years (thirteen days would have been an exaggeration). Still, this effort may have been the only useful thing that Lewis ever did for Sarah, aside from introducing her lectures and handling orders for her books. The insidious letter went on to assert that "serious charges" had been filed against Sarah at the Indian Department — charges filed by Rinehart, of course. Sarah's supporter concluded with regret, "It is really unanswerable I believe, although it leaves such a bad taste in the mouth.... The Norfolk mind relapses into the estate in which Winnemucca found it or worse."[28]

Despite all the setbacks, Sarah's campaign to arouse public opinion throughout the East culminated in Washington in the spring of 1884. Washington in April, with its gleaming marble buildings, its locust blossoms, and its thousands of newly leafed green trees gracing broad avenues, showed Sarah a different aspect of the city than she saw in her winter visit of 1880. The men in power had changed, too. Secretary Schurz and President Hayes had departed, President James Garfield had succumbed to an assassin's bullets, and the "gentleman boss," Chester Arthur, had assumed the presidency, with former Colorado senator Henry Teller heading the Interior Department. Yet it would soon become clear that where those matters closest to Sarah's heart were concerned Washington had changed very little.

Sarah called upon President Arthur, Secretary Teller, and Indian Commissioner Hiram Price to plead the cause of the Paiutes, but she achieved even less success than in the era of the Hayes administration. She expected little of Teller, believing him "a Western man and put into office to serve the interests and passions of his constituents" rather than the Indians (in Peabody's paraphrase of Sarah's remarks). Her assessment proved correct. These politicians brushed her aside, vaguely telling her they would "see about it." But, as she said shortly afterward, "Their eyes aren't opened yet."[29]

This time, however, she had another arrow for her bow — Congress. In addition to urging Representative John D. Long, whom she deemed especially favorable, to champion the Paiute cause ("just such a thing as will fire your heart and glorify your Congressional life"), Peabody sent copies of a newspaper review of Sarah's book to all Republican congressmen. The petitions on which Sarah had gathered thousands of signatures the previous year had now been overtaken by events. But, if freedom for the Yakama exiles and the restoration of Malheur to the Indians had become moot points, the underlying issues — legal sanction for the escapees, so that they need never fear being driven back to Yakama, and an assured home for her people — remained critical as ever. The recent tragedy of the Northern Cheyennes had demonstrated the treatment that runaway Indians could expect. In 1878 the Cheyennes fled the Indian Territory for their old haunts in Montana; they endured great hardships and fought bravely. Those captured escaped anew until pursuing troops killed many of them and forced the rest to surrender. Leggins's band also endured much hardship in a flight for freedom that began late in the year. The Paiutes' desperate condition on reaching Fort McDermit led the Nevada legislature, scarcely noted for tenderheartedness toward Indians, to telegraph Congress for emergency provisions. The *Silver State* suggested that the greater part of the ensuing congressional appropriation disappeared into the Indian agency without benefit to the Indians.[30]

Sarah's petitions were presented to Congress, and the House Subcommittee on Indian Affairs chaired by Robert W. S. Stevens invited her to testify on 22 April 1884. At last, Peabody's confident hope that anyone who heard Sarah tell her story "in her artless but most touching and effective way" would be swayed seemed about to be realized. Sarah was accompanied by a delegation of supporters from Baltimore, where she had been invited to lecture more than thirty times during the preceding months.[31]

As always, Sarah spoke with passionate emotion and dramatic gestures interspersed with tears. She began her story with the brief, happy time at Malheur under Parrish, scathingly detailed the crimes of Rinehart (we could not live "on the air or the wind") and the government's broken promises, denied the participation of Paiutes other than Oytes's band in the Bannock War, and movingly described the forced journey through the winter snows and the exile at Yakama. Because the Paiutes had lost all belief that Malheur — where "the lion was lying there with his mouth open ready to shut his teeth down upon them" — might be restored after the settlers had taken over, she sought a reservation for them at Fort McDermit. It had long been anticipated that this army post would be abandoned: "So we have no reservation, no home, and now I ask you for my people to restore us and put us I do not care where as long as it is in our own home, in the home where we were born, and that is all." She explained that as a nomadic people the Paiutes had wandered over a wide area "before we were disturbed" and McDermit lay within that region. So poor was the land at McDermit that the Paiutes dared to hope white men would not covet it as they had Malheur.[32]

Lands in severalty, now three years away from congressional passage as the Dawes Act, was gathering momentum. Yet the issue received little attention in Sarah's testimony beyond her observation that if McDermit could not be turned over to the Paiutes, "anything is better than nothing." She emphatically rejected the idea of sending her people to the Indian Territory. Asked by Representative Melvin George of Oregon if the government had not appropriated funds to provision the Paiutes at Yakama, Sarah angrily demanded: "Why didn't they give it to them when they were there? They were there three or four years, three years and they didn't get it." Chairman Stevens, obviously sympathetic to Sarah, hurriedly changed the subject to McDermit.[33]

Indeed, Sarah's responses made it clear that she felt in no way awed by her august surroundings or the powerful men before her. When Representative George began to question her sharply in an attempt to salvage the reputations of Agents Rinehart and Wilbur and Judge George Curry (who had circulated the petition to open the west portion of Malheur to the encroaching settlers), she refused to back down an inch. "It is not a hidden thing that I am saying," she declared. Her charges had been openly stated in her book, and she would be only too glad to make them to the faces of the men concerned. What was more, she turned the tables and began to question George aggressively, "I would like to ask Mr. George concerning Mr. Rinehart, whether he does not know that Mr. Rinehart kept a saloon in Canyon City?"[34]

Although Sarah's congressional appearance with all her usual pride and fire betrayed no sign of inner turmoil, she must have been in deep distress. Lewis had been diagnosed with tuberculosis, usually a fatal disease in the nineteenth century. Moreover, he had disgraced them both by carrying his reckless gambling into the criminal zone. Not only had he incurred heavy gambling debts but he had also forged checks in the names of her Baltimore supporters, pocketed the money, and deserted her. She could only repay his thefts by depleting the fund intended for the Paiutes. Peabody kept faith with her, tactfully alluding to the "robbery" as "a tragic story of her private life that I must omit." Another of Sarah's New England admirers, Sylvia Delano, wrote from New Bedford to Peabody of her shock over the affair: "Poor dear Winnemucca, my heart aches for her, I fear that her husband's conduct will injure her *cause*. I hope that she . . . may find a quiet home under the protection of her brother out of the reach of her dishonest husband. I hope he will receive the imprisonment that his crime deserves that will make it impossible for him to follow her. . . . I fear her enemies will take advantage of his misconduct to prove that she is equally base & false."[35]

Doubtless, at this point many concluded that Sarah had served no larger cause than her own pocketbook and, believing her a charlatan, turned against her. Peabody thought that Secretary Teller refused to see Sarah any more because he assumed she had participated in the theft. According to Peabody, Sarah had never requested money in her many public appearances. She had asked only for "restored rights" for her people. Nonetheless, her audiences had made contributions, which she had banked for the assistance of the Paiutes upon her return. Thanks to Lewis's uncontrollable weakness, much of this fund had disappeared into what her enemies gleefully termed "low gambling dens." But no matter how he had damaged her own reputation and her cause, Sarah loved him still. Peabody related that his misconduct and his flight "nearly broke her heart." Sarah might remonstrate with him over his gambling, as she had done shortly after their marriage, but when all was said and done, she had no wish for a "quiet home" without him.[36]

By midsummer of 1884, Sarah was on the train heading west — alone. Hers had been a remarkable journey, walking out of the Stone Age where she was born into the parlors of the intellectual elite and the halls of Congress. In bringing the sufferings of a small and obscure Indian tribe to the attention of thousands, she had surely contributed to that sharp turn in American public opinion toward justice for Indians. Although she had not won all she hoped for, she had achieved a great deal beyond the barrels of old clothing that Mann collected for the Paiutes. Government permission for the Yakama escapees to go to Pyramid might seem a farce, because the reservation lacked the resources to support them. But the official end of their captivity at Yakama was the heart of the matter. Their terror of a forced return could be laid to rest, along with the nightmare of a new exile in Indian Territory. Despite several years' delay caused by the army's unwillingness to relinquish McDermit, the post eventually became a reservation — no small victory at a time when government policy sought to consolidate Indians in large units such as Indian Territory instead of creating new reservations.[37]

Now the cheering crowds, the fashionable teas, and the days of summoning the eloquence of the Winnemuccas to speak for her people were behind her. She was going home to be once more the simple schoolteacher she had been in the days of helping Annie Parrish at Malheur, before the whirlwind of events swept her away. Or so she believed.

15

Lovelock

"Education has done it all"

THE SACRED LAKE, in its circlet of desert hills, reflected the deep blue of late summer skies. All Paiute children learned early that they must bless and respect Kuyuiwai — Pyramid Lake in *taibo*'s tongue. Beneath its waters lurked evil powers, the Paohas, wicked mermaids who might devour a baby or sink their sharp teeth in the breast of a nursing mother, monsters who might drag the disrespectful down to their doom. Storms can blow up in a trice, catching the unwary boatman. Yet the lake also sends visions, chants of healing, and messages of hope to the shamans. Near the shore stands a rock formation of pale gray tufa that resembles a woman with a basket — the stone mother. The legends on why she weeps vary: she cries for her lost sons; she laments for her children, who quarreled so much that she had to send them away; she mourns for her people, who traveled on and left her behind. But all agree on this: the lake was formed by the tears of a grieving woman.[1]

Here Sarah meant to return when she alit from the train at Wadsworth in early September 1884. Although she had visited briefly, she had not lived at her ancestral home since 1868, when Natches and she rode forth with the army to Camp McDermit. The rich fisheries where the Truckee River flowed into the lake still sustained her people, but *taibo* continued to encroach. His illegal commercial fishing operations depleted the catch and competed with Paiute fishermen; his cattle grazed on reservation lands, consuming the scanty grass in the sagebrush hills that rightly belonged to Paiute stockmen; his land seizures had consumed all of the river bottomland beyond the immediate vicinity of the agency buildings. "I find everything just as I left it, two years ago — nothing better yet," she wrote Elizabeth Peabody on 4 September.[2]

Although conditions at Pyramid cast Sarah into "utter despair," they came as no surprise. The greater change that darkened the world she once knew was the loss of her father. No longer would she be surrounded by his prestige as with the protective warmth of a rabbit-skin robe. Less than two months earlier, at a large gathering of Paiutes, the rivalries preceding the election of a new chief in the autumn had turned nasty. Natches and Sarah had been accused of seeking to return the exiles to Yakama. Some muttered ugly threats to kill Natches and Lee, charging that Natches had hired soldiers to drive all the Paiutes from their homeland. Natches and his followers from the Humboldt had been ordered to leave shortly before the gathering broke up in an angry argument. These things would not have happened while Winnemucca lived.[3]

Upon her arrival, Sarah expected a paid position as a teacher at the Pyramid Reservation school, where she hoped to put her ideas on education into effect. Commissioner of Indian Affairs Hiram Price had written Mary Mann that his office was "ready to cooperate with all her definite plans for education" — surely a promise. Moreover, Sarah's credentials as a teacher were impeccable, despite her difficulties in writing English. Not only had she taught with notably good results at Malheur and Yakama but she had also established and taught the school for the Sheepeater children at Fort Vancouver with great success. Yet once again Washington's commitment turned into a promise which, like the wind, was heard no more.[4]

The reason was Nevada's Indian agent, William D. C. Gibson. A saloonkeeper on the Comstock, Gibson belonged to a type described by Mark Twain with as much truth as humor: "The cheapest and easiest way to become an influential man and be looked up to by the community at large was to stand behind a bar, wear a cluster-diamond pin, and sell whiskey. I am not sure but that the saloonkeeper held a shade higher rank than any other member of society. His opinion had weight. It was his privilege to say how the elections should go. No great movement could succeed without the countenance and direction of the saloonkeepers." Having well served U.S. Senator John P. Jones at election time, Gibson received his reward in the form of the patronage appointment of Nevada Indian agent.[5]

Sarah had initially been favorably disposed toward Gibson, believing that a "square gambler" would be preferable to "a preacher with a bottle in one pocket and a Bible in the other." She had not scalded Gibson in her tirades against Indian agents, but he may have anticipated joining her roster of villains once she became better acquainted with his methods of running the agency. A political appointee himself, Gibson saw all agency positions as sinecures for relatives and associates — including the position of teacher, which he refused to Sarah. In an interview with a San Francisco newspaper, Sarah bitterly and publicly criticized the performance of these appointees: "They never do anything for the Indians. They live in idleness and draw their salaries regularly. The carpenter has not driven a nail for months; the teachers [have] never given a lesson; the blacksmith rarely lights a fire in his forge, and the farmer ploughs only for the white people."[6]

Sarah's immediate necessity was money. Her finances, already depleted by Lewis's misdeeds, had further dwindled when she visited Natches on her way to Pyramid and learned that he was in danger of being jailed over a false claim on a debt. Of course she helped. Once bereft of the position she had counted on, she had no income beyond the small amounts Peabody sent from sales of her book and occasional donations from eastern supporters. But she knew that if she could raise money she might be able to realize a dream that had been hatching in her mind for some time — her own school. Peabody, who, in addition to bringing the kindergarten movement to America, had run small schools in her home as a young woman, provided inspiration and encouragement. Sarah would not need a great deal of money to set up an independent school at Pyramid Reservation. Not yet defeated, she took to the lecture hall once more.[7]

Sarah began in mid-September with a Reno lecture arranged by her advance agent. In addition to her usual themes, she spoke about her sojourn in the East and openly criticized the Indian missionary societies. One newspaper reported that "She said these zealous societies had only one idea in view — that of administering to the spiritual wants, which they proposed to cater to through missionaries, tracts, books, etc., which were of no avail, for the reason that her people could not read, and that religious teaching would not go far on an empty stomach. What was wanting was food, clothing, farming implements, practical teaching, their rights to be recognized in courts, and hold the title to lands." Sarah's impatience with Christian proselytizing underscored her dissent from the policy of eradicating Indian culture to assimilate the Indians.[8]

Her next lecture in Carson City attracted an audience of less than twenty. To one who had achieved the kind of celebrity that packed large auditoriums on both coasts, the sight of all those empty seats in the town she had known since girlhood must have been painful. Nonetheless, she managed to make a joke of it, and, at one point shaded her eyes to peer around the hall for the missing audience. Her dramatic portrayal of an Indian agent praying with one hand lifted to heaven while the other rummaged in a money sack was particularly savage that night, and it aroused a good deal of laughter. The *Carson Appeal* declared that those who failed to attend Sarah's lecture had "missed a treat."[9] During her visit to Carson, an admiring crowd of Washo women followed Sarah through the streets and waited in front of her hotel to catch a glimpse of her when she emerged to give her lecture. They were delighted when she paused to speak a few kind words to each one (probably in Washo).[10]

The adulation of the Washo women must have been a balm to Sarah's sore heart, as she found herself estranged from many of her people. While obviously intended to discredit her, the newspaper story that her people had come to regard her with suspicion contained a measure of truth. As a Winnemucca, she could not avoid the virulent band rivalries that had broken out after the death of her father. As a

Paiute, she had broken tribal custom by making herself into something different and apart from the rest, and she had revealed secrets known only to them when she spoke with General Howard and led his army to the hidden watering holes in the southeast Oregon deserts. As a spokesman for her people, she had served as "the mouthpiece for so many lying promises" from *taibo* — her own explanation for the Paiutes' loss of confidence in her. Within the first year of her return, she would renounce with sorrow and anger her place as champion of her people, a position to which she had aspired for most of her life: "As recent events have shown that they [the Paiutes] are not disposed to stand by me in the fight, I shall relinquish it. As they will not help themselves, no one can help them. . . . I have worked for freedom. I have labored to give my race a voice in the affairs of the nation, but they prefer to be slaves so let it be."[11]

Yet, in spite of this estrangement, Sarah's people still listened to her in a crisis. In mid-October, Sarah walked into a crowd of angry Paiutes and prevented a pogrom in Carson's Chinatown. Paiute relations with the Chinese had long been somewhat strained. Liquor sales by Chinese to Indians had worried Natches, and the Paiutes had evicted a colony of Chinese from Winnemucca Lake because they attempted to seize part of the commercial fishing business on which the Indians depended. Sarah's protest in an 1879 San Francisco lecture that Chinese people received more favorable treatment than Indians hints at resentment, but she could not countenance a massacre by Paiutes inflamed over an especially gruesome murder.[12]

When the facts of the crime at last came to light, Sarah's intervention proved especially fortunate because the Chinese were innocent. The Paiute had been murdered by a Washo. While the two tribes hovered on the brink of war, a hopeful development for the Washos occurred: the Paiutes elected Natches their chief. Since Natches had gone to the mountains to gather pinyon nuts, they elected him in absentia. Despite his previous resignation from the chieftaincy and *taibo*'s insistence on electing a chief who resided at Pyramid, Natches accepted and at once began exerting his influence in the direction of

259

peace and compassion, as he had always done. Natches first suggested that the Washo surrender the murderer to be executed according to *taibo*'s laws; the Washos instead offered a large payment, which the victim's father refused. Natches then arranged for the imprisonment of the guilty party at Alcatraz, and the incident faded away without further bloodshed.[13]

Sarah ended her Nevada lectures with an appearance in Virginia City, but the public probably took more interest in a fresh scandal that presently landed her in the news, courtesy of Agent Gibson. Where the truth lay is difficult to determine. A Bannock visiting at Pyramid charged that when he gambled with Sarah and several Paiutes, they robbed him of eighteen dollars and struck him. He said Sarah had encouraged him to drink whiskey and egged on his assailants. Sarah claimed that the Bannock robbed her and that she simply reclaimed her money; she further declared that she had struck him herself "in a fit of ungovernable passion." (As she admitted in the incident of the would-be rapist who bled on the floor and fled into the night, Sarah's blows were no light taps.) Natches, whose reputation for honesty and integrity carried great weight, flew to corroborate her.[14]

Regardless of who played the coyote, the incident appears trivial. Gibson's letters, however, reveal that he hoped to try and jail Sarah on the charge, a scheme that would have silenced her effectively. In this he did not succeed, but he brought the story to the newspapers, where it damaged her reputation. He also reported the charge to Washington in what Peabody called his "atrocious despatches," though it is doubtful that he could harm Sarah more in the Office of Indian Affairs than Rinehart had already done.[15]

Realizing that there could be no accommodation with Gibson, Sarah fought back with all the weapons of her fiery nature. She took her version of the incident to the newspapers, and in interviews and an early February lecture in San Francisco, she raked Gibson for his patronage appointments and for the poverty of the Paiutes under his care: "My people are famishing in the snow. . . . They have been driven like wild beasts from place to place and forced back from the meadows and the banks of rivers and streams into the mountains that are barren and wholly destitute of game." Stung by her charges as a blow to the honor of the state, Nevada newspapers affirmed Gibson's glowing reports on the condition of the Paiutes: "They are 'rolling fat' and as sleek as high-salaried preachers in a hot climate."[16]

More than twenty years had passed since San Franciscans first saw Sarah on stage in crude dramatic tableaux with her father and brothers. As one observer put it, she was no longer the "gay young thing" who used to dance at Dutch Nick's and ride so dashingly into the McDermit parade ground, but a mature woman of forty. Although her voluptuous figure had grown somewhat heavier and the strong line of her jaw seemed more pronounced than ever, a reporter from the *San Francisco Call* admired her command of forceful colloquial English, her glossy black hair fashionably styled in a Grecian coil, and her "large and expressive" dark eyes.[17]

Over these twenty years her performance had evolved into a virtual one woman show, for the only other person on stage with her was one of Natches's young sons. At the same time that the exotic appeal of colorful Indian customs was drawing crowds to Wild West shows, Sarah had stripped those elements from her presentation, trading he beaded deerskin dress and red leggings for a gown "in the civilized American fashion." All now depended on her power to stir hearts by words alone. Newspaper stories suggest that she still had great impact on an audience, but, apparently, she stopped emphasizing the policy alternatives she once hoped would create a groundswell of public opinion that Washington would be unable to ignore. Instead, she turned to black humor: "If she possessed the wealth of several rich ladies whom she mentioned, she would place all the Indians of Nevada on the ships in our harbor, take them to New York and land them there as immigrants, that they might be received with open arms, blessed with the blessing of universal suffrage, and thus placed beyond the necessity of reservation help and out of the reach of Indian agents."[18]

Although Sarah's performance appeared undiminished, she failed to generate enough interest for more than one San Francisco lecture, and her Nevada engagements earned just enough to pay her expenses. For obscure reasons, the day of the Indian lecturer had passed; Bright Eyes was also less in demand after her tour in England. By 1885 Sarah's celebrity as the heroine of the Bannock War had faded. After the Indian wars ended, Indians had lost much of the dangerous glamour formerly attributed to them. With the Dawes Act inching toward approval and the Yakama exiles at liberty, Indian policy had ceased to be a burning issue. The public had lost interest in Sarah unless she appeared as a dime novel redskin in Wild West shows, and she chose not to. So far as we know, her February 1885 lecture in San Francisco was her last public appearance.[19]

Sarah returned to Natches's ranch. Indeed, she had few options, as Gibson, predictably, refused to allow her to open an independent school at Pyramid. Months of misery ensued, a continuation of the time Peabody described as "a martyrdom from starvation, cold, and the resulting sickness, for her splendid health succumbed the first time under all her strain of mind and body." The death of Natches's eight-year-old son, Kit Carson, in mid-March saddened them all.[20]

Sorrow heaped upon sorrow when news came in late May that Sarah's older brother Tom lay seriously ill at Pyramid. When she reached Tom's farm, Sarah found him lying in an open sagebrush corral, where the shamans had declared they could treat him best, despite chilly weather that veered back toward winter. Nine years older than Sarah, Tom had shared her childhood journey to California with Truckee and afterward farmed at Pyramid for most of his adult life. Lacking the stubborn independence of Sarah, Natches, and Elma, this Winnemucca had been a "good Indian" from the agent's point of view: obedient and industrious. Although before he died Tom thanked Sarah for the financial aid that had helped him to eke out a meager living, Sarah believed he paid a high price for being her brother. "Instead of fighting me," she wrote in a public letter, "They cowardly fought him." The business of hauling supplies from the railroad to the agency had earned Tom a little money until the agent stopped his participation because "your sister has been talking about me."[21]

None of the shaman's chanting could halt Tom's death. His burial spiked Sarah's tears with rage at Gibson's lack of concern for one who had worked so long and hard at the reservation. The Paiutes had recently started to abandon the old practice of laying a body in a stone cairn and destroying the home and possessions of the deceased. Instead, they buried the dead in *taibo*'s style as a mark of love and special respect. When Sarah requested a proper coffin for Tom and offered to pay for it, Gibson insultingly sent a crude pine box. At least Sarah saw to it that the death of this quiet, hardworking brother who had never asked for anything and Gibson's cheap coffin received plenty of newspaper attention in Nevada, and even San Francisco. "He was only an Indian, a pine box was good enough for him."[22]

Lovelock lay seventy-five miles southwest of Winnemucca on the Central Pacific Railroad line in the long valley of the Humboldt Sink. It was bounded on the southeast by the West Humboldt Range and on the northwest by the low barren ranges of the Trinity Mountains — brushed with pastel shades of rose, lavender, and cream — that hugged the valley in what the Paiutes called a "sacred circle." Unlike Winnemucca, which grew because it served as the transportation point for a large area, Lovelock remained so tiny that "town" was almost a misnomer. But enough ranchers had moved into the Big Meadows to greatly change the land where Sarah was born. As they drained away the water to grow alfalfa and grain in the deep rich soil, the broad lake where this peculiar inland river had its ending steadily diminished. Sheets of flame lit the night skies as ranchers burned the tules where the Paiutes had once plied their light reed boats.[23]

The Paiute band native to the Big Meadows called themselves the Ground Squirrel Eaters (Kibidika-a). They stayed on mainly because they had always lived there. Most were descendents of Winnemucca's brother Wahe, the spirit chief, and thus relatives of Sarah and Natches. They had neither reservation nor land, although Natches employed as many as he could on his ranch, and they led an increasingly marginal existence. They found seasonal work on the ranches when they could, gathered pinyon nuts in the mountains, camped on the outskirts of Lovelock, and begged at the railroad depot. The antelope they once hunted in the Trinities had nearly disappeared, but at least in 1885 they did not go hungry, thanks to an unexplained explosion in the jackrabbit population. It was said that the rabbits reached such large numbers that when they bounded together over the plain they raised a cloud of dust like a herd of sheep. Indian men rode through town with circlets of freshly killed jackrabbits around their waists.[24]

The one hopeful development in Sarah's spring season of many miseries came in early May, when railroad baron Stanford sold Natches the 160-acre ranch on railroad lands about two miles south of Lovelock that Natches had worked for years. However, the four-hundred-dollar price probably exhausted Natches and Sarah's funds and landed them in debt. With his usual generosity, Natches readily acceded to Sarah's wish to start a school on the ranch. Of course, they lacked a schoolhouse, and a regrettable squabble with Tom's widow over the ownership of two houses on the farm at Pyramid evidently failed to bring one from that source. Perhaps they hoped eastern supporters would donate money for a building now that Natches's ownership of the ranch was assured. Or they might build adobes. But no matter. *Taibo* might think he needed a building to have a school. Sarah knew that many of her people still lived in *kahnees* and that their children would hardly mind going to school in a brush shelter. She could not wait to begin.[25]

Judge Bonnifield (Sarah's former attorney) reported to Peabody that Sarah was on the ranch in late June and preparing to open a school for "all the Piute children in the neighborhood." With soaring optimism, he told Sarah and Natches that if they could succeed with their enterprise, the president would probably make them the agents for all their people and within a few years every industrious Indian would receive land and citizenship. Ambitious and enthusiastic as she was, Sarah may not have dared to hope for so much. She had earlier cautioned Peabody that after Gibson's appointment "all your hopes are knocked in the head of my brother getting to be appointed agent." Still, Peabody continued to lobby for the plan. The arrival of Special Indian Agent Folsom in early July to consult with Sarah on Indian matters seemed an encouraging sign.[26]

Sarah's "model school," as Peabody called it, was innovative in more essential ways than its initial location in a brush shelter. U.S. Indian policy in this period aimed to eradicate Indian culture and "civilize" Indians by "education for extinction," in the apt phrase of historian David W. Adams. Conversion to Christianity was the keystone, and the minds and hearts of the young were the battleground. Boarding schools, preferably far removed from tribal culture, would accomplish their assimilation. As a commencement speaker at Carlisle boarding school in Pennsylvania put it: "The Indian is DEAD in you. Let all that is Indian within you die! ... You cannot become truly American citizens, industrious, intelligent, cultured, civilized until the INDIAN within you is DEAD."[27]

Sarah has been called an assimilationist, and to the extent that she did not advocate resistance in the mountains until the last man fell, this was true. It does not, however, convey the nuances of her position. Like old Truckee, in his delight over his rag friend and its almost magical powers, she saw literacy in English as a technology the Paiutes had to acquire, much in the same way some Indians saw guns. In her lectures, she spoke of "civilizing" Indians — and she was well aware that no other language could generate *taibo*'s support — but she meant only selective adoption of some of *taibo*'s innovations. Never did she favor the eradication of the Paiute culture she so profoundly valued. Changes such as the introduction of divorce and the shamans' new practice of charging for treatment as white doctors did saddened her. In her eyes, Indians were morally superior in many ways to whites, with their "cursed whiskey and selfishness and greed," as well as their lying and stealing.[28]

The most innovative feature of Sarah's school, as Peabody penetratingly noted, was that "instead of being, as usual, a passive reception of civilizing influences proffered by white men who look down upon the

Indian as a spiritual, moral, and intellectual inferior, it is a spontaneous movement, made by the Indian himself, *from himself*, in full consciousness of free agency, for the education that is to civilize him."
Moreover, at a time when Indian children in government schools
often learned a few hymns by rote and failed to master English, it presented a model for education. First, the children learned to understand and speak English by speaking to Sarah in Paiute and learning
her English translation. Then they learned to read and write—and became so excited about it that they scrawled the new words all over the
fences of Lovelock. Sarah believed that a good interpreter was critical:
"The most necessary thing for the success of an Indian school is a
good interpreter, a perfect interpreter, a true interpreter, one that can
and will do. . . . I attribute the success of my school not to my being a
scholar and a good teacher but because I am my own Interpreter, and
my heart is in my work." Sarah hoped that some students would teach
their new skills to their parents and, in time, become teachers themselves in a school system of, by, and for Indians. Arithmetic, hymns,
drills for exercise, and industrial training in sewing and other skills
also played a part in the curriculum. Peabody, drawing on her long experience as a teacher, sent lesson plans for reading and arithmetic. In
the Paiute way, Sarah taught with kindness, her pupils responded eagerly, and punishment was unnecessary.[29]

To have a school, there must be pupils—far from a foregone conclusion at the government schools. At a time when agents scoured the
hills where Indians hid their children, threatened Indian mothers
that they must give one child to boarding school or lose the family rations, jailed stubborn fathers, and shipped orphans, who had no families to conceal them, to Carlisle, Paiute parents willingly sent their
children to Sarah's school. Sarah subsequently set forth a strong argument for education in a letter to Paiutes in Inyo County, California,
who wanted to start a school like hers:

*Your children can learn much more than I know, and much easier, and it is
your duty to see that they go to school. There is no excuse for ignorance. Schools*

are being built. . . . All they ask you to do is to send your children. You are not asked to give money or horses — only to send your children to school. The teacher will do the rest. He or she will fit your little ones for the battle of life, so that they can attend to their own affairs instead of having to call in a white man. A few years ago you owned this great country; to-day the white man owns it all, and you own nothing. Do you know what did it? Education. You see the miles and miles of railroad, the locomotive, the Mint in Carson where they make money. Education has done it all. Now, what it has done for one man it will do for another. . . . I entreat you to take hold of this school, and give your support by sending your children, old and young, to it, and when they grow up to manhood and womanhood they will bless you.[30]

In the Big Meadows, Sarah's strongest argument to the Paiutes remained unstated, but well understood: unlike the government schools, Sarah's would make no effort to separate the children from their families and erase their identity as Indians. They would not be whipped for speaking their native language as they often were in the government schools. Within a year she had twenty-four pupils, while the government school at Pyramid had only twenty-eight to thirty-four, and Indian parents at Pyramid began making inquiries about sending their children to Sarah's school.[31]

Mary Dave, who attended Sarah's school as a little girl, told her granddaughter what a wonderful teacher Sarah had been. She taught them English, naming each thing in Paiute and English. When she said "up," the boys jumped up gleefully to show they understood by lifting the roof of the brush shelter, and Sarah laughed as merrily as they did. At the word "down," they flattened themselves on the ground. When Sarah taught them to write, little Mary Dave puzzled over the letter "Q." She could understand making the "O" well enough. But how could you get that tail in the "Q"? It seemed a great mystery until Sarah showed her how.[32]

Through the roasting days of an unusually hot summer in which the temperature often soared above one hundred degrees, Sarah taught, and the children knelt on the hard-packed earth in the brush shelter to use their benches as desks while they learned to write. Natches worked at clearing, fencing, and planting his land, aided by a wagon and team supplied by Peabody and her friends. Despite this brave beginning, future necessities pressed on them. Sarah would need a school building by the time the cold and storms of winter swept over the Big Meadows. It was also increasingly evident that some boarding facilities would allow the children to stay in school when their parents left for seasonal work or headed into the mountains for the pinyon harvest. To make a success of his ranch, Natches had to have water because the land he bought from Stanford did not include water rights, and crops in the arid Great Basin required irrigation. A well could provide an assured water supply for the school and ranch, but sinking one would take money. That was the question that perpetually plagued them: Would government funds or charitable donations provide them with the small amount of support they so badly needed?[33]

It would come, if Peabody had anything to say about it. As Mann observed, Peabody spent a "very perturbed summer" working for the Paiute cause — and, indeed, also a perturbed spring, fall, and winter. During two months of lobbying in Washington, she believed that she had gained the ear of the newly elected president, Grover Cleveland, through his youngest sister Rose Elizabeth, who served as mistress of the White House prior to the president's marriage. She handed Rose Elizabeth a letter from Sarah to give to the president, accompanied by some diplomatic suasion on behalf of the Paiutes (this letter has not been uncovered among the Cleveland papers). Peabody also visited the president and the commissioner of Indian Affairs, John D. C. Atkins, afterward telling the press that she had enjoyed "as satisfactory an interview as I could desire" and received assurance that Atkins recognized the slanders against Sarah for what they were. She also believed she had his promise of funding for the school, but, evidently, as politicians had done before, they humored the distinguished old woman and took no action. In the end, she brought away nothing more substantial than Rose Elizabeth's vague belief that "the thing that ought to happen is the thing that will happen in the long run."[34]

Nothing daunted Peabody, and, as passionately committed as ever to "Sarah Winnemucca's Sacred Cause," she turned to the press and to the many personal connections she had gained in a lifetime of assiduous philanthropy. A newspaperman replied, whether in weariness or admiration is hard to say, "you have never grown tired in well doing." She succeeded in generating enough donations for supplies, as well as for the construction of a small schoolhouse, for which Sarah scrupulously sent the receipted bills. Half of the fourteen hundred dollars raised for Sarah had come from Peabody's own pocket, and the old woman declared, "If I had it or could get it by begging I should advance $1,000 more."[35]

By and large, however, the results of her canvass were disappointing. Senator Dawes apparently failed to provide the testimonial to Sarah that she sought. Peabody found most charitable donations for Indians already committed to the missionary societies and reform groups or to pre-existing schools such as Hampton and Carlisle. Only those who had themselves heard Sarah's stirring lectures proved susceptible to her appeals, and even in this group, many had turned against Sarah. One correspondent told her: "As I think Mr. Hopkins behaved so badly here it would be unwise to make any extended appeal, for aid in her [Sarah's] behalf." The commissioner of Indian Affairs had made it known that "if any of 100 affadavits in his office were trustworthy, Sarah Winnemucca was not a proper person to associate with good people," and Herbert Welsh, director of the powerful Indian Rights Association, and its lobbyist, Charles Painter, lost no opportunity to spread the news. One hundred affidavits, of course, was gross exaggeration: only nine had signed the petition attacking Sarah's character generated by Rinehart, and the depositions reached a grand total of three.[36]

Sarah's powerful enemies, the professional reformers Welsh and Painter, emerge still more clearly in another letter: "Mr. Welsh wished me to put you on your guard against the woman you spoke of yesterday. He says Prof. Painter has had evidence of the most indisputable character, that she has been engaged in transactions disreputable, and is unworthy of trust." Some five years later it was abundantly clear how lastingly Rinehart's slanders had poisoned the well. Peabody perceived the situation clearly in one of the letters she wrote to a Massachusetts congressman on behalf of Sarah and the Paiutes: "A subtle but powerful influence from the Indian office *opposes her* taking the form of unfavorable insinuations against her personally & sometimes open accusations — *which can all be answered.*"[37]

Despite Sarah's precarious finances, the school, now christened the Peabody Institute over Peabody's modest objections, appeared to be doing well in the summer of 1886, after the first year of its existence. Sarah was able to provide meals and clothing for her students and continue their schooling during the summer for those able to remain. A number of western newspapers applauded the enterprise and urged the government to support facilities equal to Sarah's "energy and her noble spirit." For instance, *Alta California* declared: "We cannot help feeling that such a woman deserves help. . . . We believe that the Indian Department should found an Indian school in Nevada and put Sarah at the head of it. The cost would be small compared with the value of the experiment, and surely it would command the support of all right-thinking people."[38]

Visitors also uniformly praised the school. The *Silver State* especially commended Sarah's pupils for their spelling and arithmetic and noted that the little girls looked "quite cute" in their Mother Hubbard dresses. Alice Chapin, an experienced Indiana teacher and close friend of Peabody's, came to Lovelock to report on Sarah's novel undertaking in education. The commissioner of Indian Affairs assured Peabody that if this competent examiner gave a favorable report, government funding would soon follow. Chapin found Sarah's pupils from ages six to sixteen "decidedly superior to white children of the same age" and "so interested and zealous to learn that they were perfectly obedient." Peabody could leaf through the samples of their writing and artwork that Chapin mailed her and be pleased by the results of her intensive campaign for the school. Chapin thought the children's industrial training in agriculture and housekeeping (a standard part of the curriculum in Indian schools) equally impressive.[39]

Yet outside the schoolhouse Chapin observed looming problems. Sarah suffered from neuralgia and rheumatism and frequently lay prostrated by an unspecified malady that sounds a good deal like malaria, which she may have contracted at Yakama. Chapin plied her with quinine. Peabody, learning of Sarah's hardships, admired her all the more: "All that we did for her still left her with broken health and numberless hardships to contend with, which would have crushed any less heroic spirit."[40]

Although Natches was raising a good wheat crop, he still lacked money to sink a well. He thought he had made a satisfactory arrangement when he agreed to take an allotment of water from the white ranchers' irrigation ditch that crossed his land in exchange for Indian labor on the ditch. But the agreement foundered within a short time, possibly because the irrigation system proved so costly that the profit margin narrowed. The ranchers insisted that the ranch gate must be kept open so they would have access to the ditch, and Natches stationed an elderly Paiute at the gate to prevent cattle from wandering in to devour his wheat. The ranchers seized upon the old watchman's apparent idleness as proof that Indians were too lazy to deserve a share of the irrigation water — the perfect excuse for denying water to Natches. "I tried to explain," wrote Chapin, perplexed by the intensity of western conflicts over water, "but it is not permitted to explain things here." Apparently, Natches did secure water by some means, since he reaped a crop that fall.[41]

Paradoxically, in the same year they nearly denied water to the Winnemuccas' ranch, Lovelockers had joined the chorus of unanimous praise for Sarah's school. Louisa Marzen, of Lovelock's most influential ranching family, and a group of friends decided to visit the school in late February 1886. They extolled it even more warmly than Chapin: "When we neared the school shouts of merry laughter rang upon our ears, and little dark and sunburnt faces smiled a dim approval of our visitation." In her letter to Peabody, Marzen went on to describe the amazing accomplishments of Sarah's pupils:

Speaking in her native tongue, the Princess requested the children to name all the visible objects, repeat the days of the week and months of the year, and calculate to the thousands, which they did in a most exemplary manner. Then she asked them to give a manifestation of their knowledge upon the blackboard, each in turn printing his name and spelling aloud. It is needless to say, Miss Peabody, that we were spellbound at the disclosure. Nothing but the most assiduous labor could have accomplished this work. But most amazingly did I rudely stare (and most of our party were guilty of the same sin) when these seemingly ragged and untutored beings began singing gospel hymns with precise melody, accurate time, and distinct pronunciation. The blending of their voices in unison was grand, and an exceedingly sweet treat. We look upon it as a marvelous progression; and so gratified were we that we concluded to send this testimonial containing the names of those present, in order that you may know of the good work the Princess is trying to consummate.[42]

Why, when Sarah's school had won the support of the press, the local community, and the Indian parents as well as the praise of every visitor who came to investigate, did the government refuse to support it? Peabody had no doubt of the reason: "It is plain that jealousy and opposition were excited to madness by the very success of Sarah's unexampled enterprise." Gibson had refused funds from the money reserved for Indian education, and the enmity of Welsh, Painter, and the commissioner of Indian Affairs ensured that no support would be forthcoming from Washington. Beyond the jealousy, the subtle influence at the Indian Department, and the unending debate over Sarah's personal virtues lay a fundamental difference in policy that would have probably doomed her hopes for government funding even if she had been a vestal virgin who never criticized the reservation system. The government's aim was total assimilation, and the white-run boarding school far removed from tribal influences was its preferred method. What Peabody saw as the essential strength of Sarah's school — its creation by an Indian — made it unacceptable to government officials. In the words of historian Adams, "As savages, Indians were incapable of determining what was in their own best interests."[43]

While Sarah struggled, the drive to assimilate Indian children in boarding schools moved relentlessly forward, but not without resistance, and sometimes with tragic results. Many Indian parents saw the government boarding schools as a virtual death sentence — and not wrongly. Diseases such as scarlet fever and measles, to which the Indians had little immunity, could sweep through a school with fatal results; of twenty-one Spokane children sent to eastern boarding schools, sixteen died. Some children resisted their captivity. Suspicious fires broke out at the boarding schools. Another alternative was flight. Three runaway Kiowa boys froze to death when caught in a blizzard as they tried to make their way home. Others were more fortunate: kindergartners at the Fort Mohave boarding school battered down the door to the jail where other kindergartners were being confined for intractability, and all made a break for the river bottoms. To reach their home in the Verde Valley, several Yavapai boys made an epic journey of over one hundred miles in cold winter weather with no provisions.[44]

When an official from the government boarding school in Colorado attempted to round up Paiute children in the spring of 1887, over the protests of their shrieking mothers, Sarah refused to let them take any of her pupils without the consent of their parents. She then made public her opinions on the government boarding schools: the "right place" to teach children was in their homeland amid familiar surroundings with their parents nearby, not among strangers in a distant land. If treated well, they would learn rapidly in any school. She dismissed as "all nonsense" the theory that children would change physically when civilized in a government boarding school. Experience, she said, had taught her what young people need. Despite the urgings of Buena Vista John and Dave Numana, the superintendent of the Colorado school finally settled for only a dozen children for the boarding school from a population of nearly three thousand Paiutes. All but one of these were from reservation families living under the thumb of the agents. (That little boy never returned, and his family could get no information on what had happened to him.) Three children, including a son of Lee (then absent in California for medical treatment), were kidnapped without the knowledge or consent of their parents.⁴⁵

During the period preceding this confrontation, some signs indicate that Sarah was regaining her stature among Paiutes. Her school, a happy alternative to the government boarding school, had their warm support, and her presence among them had helped to restore her to her old place. This was shown in the 1886 trial of Willow Creek Charley, a Paiute who killed his adulterous wife when so drunk that he claimed to have been unable to remember the act until a month had elapsed. He was tried by Paiutes in the Paiute way, with some admixture of *taibo*'s judicial practices, and Sarah was the only woman present, clearly a mark of honor.⁴⁶

It was a cold but sunny January day, with Shutaiyunana, the north wind, who is a horned monster with a huge mouth, blowing through a crack in the sky. In the Winnemucca courthouse yard, shielded from the wind by the brick wall, the Paiutes sat, wrapped in blankets and steadily smoking a prodigious amount of tobacco supplied by the defendant. The jury consisted of six friends and relatives of Willow Creek Charley, who sat facing six impartial figures. Natches, Lee, and other leaders made eloquent speeches in Paiute, followed by Sarah, who summarized the evidence in English, partly for the benefit of white observers. Her presentation placed Charley in a sympathetic light as one driven to drink by the infidelities of a woman who had made him her lover when he was still a boy.⁴⁷

When Sarah finished speaking, all agreed that "firewater" was a curse to the tribe and urged the young men to avoid it. The jury then acquitted Willow Creek Charley, and each juror, in turn, lectured him on the evils of drink. As long as no witchcraft figured in the crime, Paiute justice tended to be forgiving and aimed less toward punishment than toward the rehabilitation of the transgressor.⁴⁸

The next Paiute trial for homicide was a very different affair because this time the victim was a white emigrant from Germany, but Sarah again played a part, showing her concern with individual cases as well as larger, more general causes. In August 1886, Andrew Kinnegar, a middle-aged German storekeeper in Willow Creek (evidently not the safest place to live), was shot as he sat in his chair, and a witness implicated the Indian known as One Arm Jim. *Silver State* reported both Sarah and Natches involved in the investigation. The newspaper does not state exactly what Sarah did, though it is likely that she persuaded witnesses to speak. Initially, doubts had been voiced that the Paiute women on whose testimony much depended would be willing to bear witness in *taibo*'s court, where Jim was to be tried.[49]

As it turned out, One Arm Jim confessed, but the jury deliberated at some length because two jurors found his claim that a white man had paid him to kill Kinnegar disturbing. Nonetheless, they finally convicted One Arm Jim of first-degree murder. An effort immediately ensued in which ten jurors and many settlers petitioned to have his execution commuted to life imprisonment, the sentence favored by the Paiutes. It was believed to be the first trial in a northern Nevada court of an Indian for killing a white man and the first scheduled execution of an Indian for such an offense. Regardless of One Arm Jim's obvious guilt, the settlers feared Indian unrest because the severity of the punishment exceeded normal Paiute practice. Although no source explicitly declares as much, Sarah and Natches may have played a role in calming these tensions. The wheels of *taibo*'s justice ground slowly, but One Arm Jim's sentence was eventually commuted in January 1888. Confounding expectations that he would die quickly because Indians could not bear confinement, he lived on in the state prison at Carson City for many years.[50]

That Sarah and Natches concerned themselves with the fate of One Arm Jim and the fears of the settlers demonstrates how strongly they felt the obligations of leadership because in the summer and fall of 1886, troubles of their own engulfed them. Natches's little daughter Delia was dying of tuberculosis and would not survive the autumn.

Natches had suffered a painful accident when his team bolted and threw him from the wagon. Worse yet, he had been accused of cattle theft, ever a dangerous matter in the early West. On her warhorse once again, Sarah thundered to his defense in a public letter: "If any one knows anything about it let him come forward and tell it face to face like a man. If he has seen him kill [beef] or can prove anything, let him prove it in court. But if there is no proof, except that he is an Indian, and it is safe to slander him, then those who value their words will not say what they have no proof of." After the Bannock War, grateful northern Nevada settlers had presented Natches with a silver medal embossed with the hands of an Indian and a white man clasped in friendship and inscribed with the words "Presented to Chief Nachez by Humboldt County." Eight years later their debt to him appeared to be rapidly fading from memory.[51]

The financial crisis in which the school and ranch were floundering is one of the murkier episodes in Sarah's story. In August she suspended the school, explaining to Peabody that she must have rest and the children's help would be needed with the harvest. Although the chronology is confused, it appears that Sarah then urged her benefactor to "rest from her labors." The reason lay in a letter to Sarah written by one of Peabody's friends telling her that Peabody had been giving money from her savings that she could ill afford and that Peabody had been working harder for Sarah at her advanced age than Sarah had ever worked "in her life." "I need not say," wrote Peabody, "that this was accompanied with a passionate entreaty that I would never send her another cent, and suspend all further care for her work." Peabody at once responded "that this letter was false in every point; that the provision for my old age was untouched, and that the work I was doing for her was the greatest pleasure I had ever enjoyed in my life." In fact, Peabody had indeed sought a loan to cover the unpaid pledges of private funds for Sarah's school and offered her own small savings as security.[52]

By then, Sarah and Natches had left the ranch to earn some money as best they could — Sarah by housework and Natches as a ranch hand.

In late September, Sarah wired Peabody from Elko to send her two hundred dollars at once. Having no means to comply, the good old woman passed along the request to Warren Delano, Sarah's other main benefactor. Delano not only refused this sudden and unexplained appeal but also lost much of his confidence in Sarah: "Is it *possible* that there is truth in some of the scandalous reports of vicious habits: of drinking and gambling &c. &c. which have been so positively urged? I am too sorry to think . . . indeed I do not believe these reports are true, or that there is any good foundation for them — but they have been made and we cannot easily shut our eyes to them."[53]

At length, Sarah's explanation of their "ill luck" reached Peabody. Some inimical white ranchers spread a rumor that Peabody had sent Natches and Sarah cash to pay the Indian harvesters instead of the payment in grain that they had been promised. To meet the harvesters' demand for immediate cash, Sarah sought the two-hundred-dollar loan. When that was not forthcoming, Natches was forced to sell the wheat crop immediately for little more than half the usual price, earning a sum that served only to pay their debts. "I could not feed on love, so could not renew the school; and I was perfectly discouraged and worn out," Sarah concluded.[54]

To Peabody, in distant Boston, this explanation seemed entirely satisfactory. During her visit, Chapin had noted the "general hostility of the frontiersmen to Indians, and their disposition to crush their attempts at self-subsistence, intensified by every degree of Indian success." It is therefore possible that as the Paiute ranch turned into an ambitious undertaking and more settlers sought land in the Big Meadows, Natches's land became increasingly attractive. Also, the sudden demand from Paiutes of Natches's own band, despite their long relationship with him, was more plausible than Sarah's eastern friends could know. Natches had enemies among the Paiutes, enemies who had threatened to kill him at the gathering only two years before and would turn to violence against him in the future. Perhaps, if the ill will of these rival bands had infected his own group, he was so injured by his accident and so grieved by the impending death of his little daughter that he could not muster his persuasive powers as he had so often done before.[55]

As for Sarah, loss of confidence in her, which she had only recently overcome, might have been revived by this fresh rumor of wealth, a rumor that would have taken root in fertile ground. Natches's new wagon, gaily painted in green and yellow, created an impression of riches, as did the story still surviving among the Lovelock Paiutes that Sarah had been seen in the railroad station with bags of money and that coins had scattered all over the platform when she struck someone who angered her over the head with one of the bags. In the Paiute way of thinking, having wealth without sharing was a great sin.[56]

All the same, Sarah's explanation contains some troublesome points. Delano wondered why her request for money to pay the harvesters should come from Elko (220 miles east of Lovelock). Her previous request in the spring for a loan from him in exactly the same amount (which he refused) suggests a pressing debt that preceded the harvest by several months. Nor can Delano's suspicion of gambling be entirely dismissed. Sarah did gamble on occasion, and it would have been difficult for the daughter of so famous a gambler as Winnemucca to see the time-honored Paiute pastime as a vice. As she once told Peabody, "Everybody gambles here in this country, and it is not considered wrong." Nearly a thousand Indians had gathered for a grand fandango near Reno at the beginning of September. They had prayed, they had feasted, they had raced their ponies, they had danced each night by the light of many fires, and they had played cards.[57] Sarah might have been tempted, seeing the familiar circle of Paiutes sitting with cards in their hands, to be one of the people again and sink back into the old ways, as the Paiute baby nestles into the soft swan's down–lining of his cradle board. She might have hoped to win so much that she would no longer need to struggle to make ends meet with meager donations from a dwindling number of supporters. It would have been so easy to fall.

Peabody entertained none of the doubts that crept into more skep-

Indian gamblers in Reno. Courtesy of the Nevada Historical Society.

tical minds. In her eyes, Sarah glowed with an aura of grandeur as a heroine for the ages: "Sarah Winnemucca is one of those characters that make eras in history — like Isabella of Spain — & Elizabeth of England — and a greater than they — and it seems to me that all my own life has been a special preparation to enable me to understand and help her." Peabody's absolute faith that "my dear Sarah" would revive the school proved well placed. Late in 1886 Peabody told Sarah that she had located two hundred more copies of *Life among the Piutes* that could be sold to support the school. Sarah accepted twenty-one pupils at once, and the Peabody Institute resumed. Peabody wrote enthusiastically: "The *temporary* despair & relinquishment of her great work *proved* reactionary — and *rested* the long overstrained nerves. She felt in better health than for nearly two years."[58]

Indeed, in the early months of 1887 the school appeared to be thriving more than ever. Peabody successfully solicited funds to support twelve boarders and published two pamphlets singing the praises of

Sarah and her school, *Sarah Winnemucca's Practical Solution of the Indian Problem* (1886) and *Second Report of the Model School of Sarah Winnemucca, 1886–87* (1887). By late January, Sarah reported forty-five enthusiastic children in attendance. Mann, in one of her last letters before her death on 11 February 1887, related that her sister was "quite happy about her pet Indian who is doing wonders." Although Mary had described herself as "not so much of the fanatic" over Sarah as her sister and sometimes betrayed a hint of resentment toward Elizabeth's obsession with the pet Indian, she was sufficiently devoted to Sarah to leave her a small legacy in her will. Some of this funding Sarah set aside to buy irrigation water for the ranch, for she knew that one day when aid disappeared the ranch would have to support the school.[59]

Nearly eighty-three, almost blind, in failing health, and saddened by the loss of her sister's companionship, Peabody chose to believe that Sarah's project was well launched. That she had managed to do so much for the school despite feeling the "weight" of her years was remarkable. Being a woman of such severe moral rectitude that she forbade her sister Sophia to read Byron, and worried much over the personal morality of the novelist George Eliot, she might have been disturbed if she had believed in Sarah's occasional carousing and what the press had termed her "extensive and diversified matrimonial experience." Instead, she chose to see only Sarah's "noble spirit." She still interested herself in good causes such as woman suffrage and universal peace, but she finally acquiesced, with only occasional relapses, to Sarah's insistence that she rest from her labors on behalf of the school: "Sarah Winnemucca's great experiment is so far *accomplished* that it needs no further bolstering up — all the conditions of independance of self support & the education of their children *within themselves* attained — on a small scale as to numbers indeed — but making a *vital seed* of an *ideal future!*" Sarah had promised to write "while I live."[60]

After the novelty wore off, items on Sarah's school rarely appeared in the newspapers, and its fortunes after the spring of 1887 become difficult to trace. Fearing that their children might be kidnapped and sent to a distant government boarding school, the parents of four hundred children applied for places in Sarah's boarding school. This far exceeded the small number she could accommodate, but Sarah had always responded to the needs of her people. At the beginning of June, she announced a new plan: she would go east and rally her supporters there to pressure the government into funding an industrial school to be constructed on forty acres of land that Natches would donate to the cause. Government policymakers and the powerful Indian reform associations had become enamored of industrial training to teach Indians the work skills that would make them economically self-sufficient. Why shouldn't the government support a school that conformed to the latest ideas and promised to be a great success because Sarah enjoyed the support of Indian parents?[61]

That Sarah actually journeyed east in the summer of 1887 remains in doubt. Paiute legend ridicules those who repeatedly attempt the impossible. As a child, she had no doubt giggled with the rest around the campfire when the old ones told how Coyote repeatedly tried and failed to run across a stick between two rocks, hoping to prove to his wolf brother that he was ready to be a warrior. Foolish Coyote! Perhaps Sarah dropped the plan when she realized her past failures had shown she could no more secure government funding than Coyote could balance himself on a stick. No evidence has emerged that she visited Peabody, though to go east without calling upon the ailing old woman to whom she owed so much would seem terribly heartless. No new funding from eastern supporters or government action came to her hand. The only sign that she made the journey, as author Canfield points out, was the sudden reappearance of Lewis Hopkins, pale, spectral, feeble, glassy-eyed, and coughing, his voice a mere whisper. Unless he simply turned up at the ranch, Sarah, loving him still, may have gone east not for money but for him.[62]

Natches and Warren Delano thought that Lewis faked his illness in order to squeeze money from Sarah by arousing her pity ("when he has got her last dollar the fellow will be himself again and up to some

Paiute harvesters near Lovelock. Lone Mountain rises at left rear. Courtesy of the Nevada Historical Society.

mischief"); Sarah believed he was dying. None were entirely wrong: Lewis was truly on the point of death, but he roused himself for one last monstrous act. Though Natches did not want Lewis on the ranch, he reluctantly acceded to Sarah's insistence. It was harvesttime then. The fine crops of wheat, oats, and barley that Natches had raised rippled golden in the fields and the Paiute harvesters, including women, in their traditional role as seed gatherers, were threshing industriously. They filled four hundred sacks with grain, and the hope that none among them would go hungry and the ranch could help support the school seemed on the point of fulfillment. Then Lewis appropriated the harvest money and departed for San Francisco, offering Natches a niggardly fifty dollars, which Natches angrily refused. An awful breach yawned between Sarah and Natches, who may have felt that despite her assistance in developing the ranch her ambition and her misplaced attachment had ruined them.[63]

It was the deathblow for the ranch and school, though the final writhing agonies were not yet finished. Lewis succumbed first. The medical treatment that Sarah arranged for him in the Bay Area failed to improve his tuberculosis, and he returned to her to die. On 18 October 1887, at the age of thirty-eight, he breathed his last. Following *taibo*'s customs, Sarah ordered memorial cards with a sentimental poem expressing her feelings for him:

'Tis hard to break the tender cord,
When love has bound the heart,
'Tis hard, so hard, to speak the words,
We must forever part.
Dearest loved one, we must lay thee,
In the peaceful grave's embrace,
But thy memory will be cherished,
'Till we see thy heavenly face.

Newspaper obituaries described Lewis as genteel and well educated but a "peculiar character," perhaps alluding to his relation to an Indian woman.[64]

Far across the desert plain from the little settlement and isolated from the rest of the Trinity Range stands Lone Mountain, a triangular peak with eroded terraces, tipped with a slide of mulberry-colored scree. In the Lone Mountain cemetery at its base, Sarah mourned the thief who was probably the last and surely the most calamitous of her several loves.

16

Henry's Lake

"Let my name die out and be forgotten"

A NEW POWER and an old dream were rising in the land. In the Mason Valley, far south of Lovelock and beyond the Walker River Reservation, a Paiute named Wovoka, or Jack Wilson, heard a great roaring on the mountain. Sinking into a deep trance, he saw a vision, and he began to preach to the people. They must do the dance he showed them, the Ghost Dance, slowly shuffling and chanting in a circle. Then they too would fall into trances in which they might visit the land of the dead and see again the loved ones they had lost. In time, if they performed the dance as Wovoka told them, Numina, the power who rules all, would bring the Indian dead back to life and restore the world to the Indians. As Wovoka's fame spread, emissaries from tribes as far as the Sioux came to hear him preach, watch him perform miracles, and learn the sacred dance.[1]

But not Sarah and Natches. They had never followed the Dreamers. Almost twenty years earlier they stood aside while the devotees of Wodziwob painted themselves and danced. Time had shown Sarah right, for no armies of resurrected warriors poured from the rays of the rising sun as Wodziwob had promised. Later, at Malheur, Sarah had feared Oytes but never followed him. She had heard how Agent Parrish disproved his boast of invulnerability to bullets and reduced him to subservience. When a newspaper reporter asked Sarah's opinion of the latest Paiute messiah, she laughed and called Wovoka's predictions "nonsense."[2]

Sarah's movements in the years following 1887 are hard to follow.

After the pamphlets and the voluminous correspondence of Elizabeth Peabody ceased, Sarah lost the Boswell who had reported on her activities and sometimes quoted from her letters during the four-year period after her book appeared. Nor did Sarah herself speak out in public letters, lengthy interviews, lectures, or testimony to governmental committees any longer. Once, when her cousin Jerry Long urged her to ignore the grievances of her people and maintain a tactful silence in Rinehart's presence, she had defiantly declared, "I am going to talk for them just as long as I live." Now her people had wrapped themselves in the Ghost Dance dreams of Wovoka and no longer wanted her to speak for them.[3]

Bereft of government support, private charity, or harvest money, Sarah kept the school going somehow, but she evidently lapsed into reckless desperation at times. In February 1888 the press reported her gambling at cards, losing, and fighting over a disputed pot. When General Howard came to visit in late March 1888, he could offer no assistance for the school. However, he anticipated the abandonment of Fort McDermit as a military post within the year and promised to recommend that its lands be divided in severalty among the Paiutes as the Winnemuccas wished. In fact, the executive order making McDermit a reservation came in 1889, and Paiutes received allotments in 1892. Although Sarah had long fought for this reservation, no one, Indian or white, apparently gave her any part of the credit for its establishment. When a shaman ceased to be effective, when a chief lost his influence over events and the people came to believe his power had deserted him, it had always been their way to abandon him for a new leader. Now it was Wovoka.[4]

In February 1889 Sarah's school was still limping along with fifteen or sixteen pupils, but in March a new prediction from Wovoka jeopardized its survival. He promised that when the dead Indian warriors returned to earth they would not only exterminate the whites but also all Indians who could speak or write English, a strong incentive for the messiah's followers to withdraw their children from Sarah's school. Although this promise is not usually considered part of Wovoka's message — and it is not clear what would happen to the messiah himself, who spoke some English — much variation occurred in the dissemination of his teachings, and despite Sarah's ridicule, this rumored prophecy evidently gained credence in Lovelock. How rapidly Sarah's schoolhouse emptied is not known. Nonetheless, as the Ghost Dance excitement intensified, some losses surely took place, and no further newspaper reports on the school appeared. Sarah probably closed the door of the schoolhouse for the last time in the summer of 1889.[5]

The dream of a school of her own, where children would be taught with kindness by one who understood their native tongue, had died, and this crowning loss wounded Sarah terribly. Yet even four years of schooling for these children had made a difference. Mary Dave had learned to speak English quite well, much better than another little girl who had not been allowed to attend the school. Even limited English could make the difference between life and death. The Lovelock Paiutes still tell of the Indian man who was killed when he lacked the words to explain the nuggets and the gun in his possession (he had picked up the rocks, thinking them pretty). Some of their band had died, unable to read the sign white men had posted beside a watering hole poisoned to kill rabbits. As Sarah, and her grandfather before her, had seen, education was the key to the altered world in which they must live. Eighteen years would pass before the government finally opened a school for the Paiute children at Lovelock, and another twenty years before Paiutes were permitted to attend a public school with white children.[6]

It is likely that, along with the loss and grief, these last years contained some good times. Sarah continued to enjoy riding horseback with the old panache. She had gone pinyon nutting with Natches and his family in 1885, and each October when the nights turned frosty and the sunlight took on a golden autumnal cast she probably joined them again. Peabody had pitied these poor Indians because they depended upon nuts for their food, and it was true that for a people who lived so close to the bone as they did, pinyon nuts were necessary to

Indian women preparing pinyon nuts. Courtesy of the Nevada Historical Society.

subsist. But a Bostonian like Peabody could not understand that going pinyon nutting also meant a happy gathering of the clan.[7]

In a merry cavalcade, they would ride through the pass amidst the pastel undulations of the West Humboldts to the higher mountains of the Stillwater Range. In these canyons, the old, rounded pinyon trees grew thick and blue with small, brown cones bursting with nuts nestled among their needles. The Paiutes would speak to the mountain, asking for strength, for a cool night breeze when they slept, for permission to drink the water that was its juice, and for the gift of its pinyon nuts. Boys dashed ahead to scout the best trees; men beat a shower of cones from the pinyons and hooked down the last cones with long forked sticks; women piled cones in baskets; girls carried the laden baskets back to camp, where the grandmothers roasted the nuts.[8]

First, the old women cleaned debris from the tiny brown nuts and tossed them with hot coals in broad platter-like winnowing baskets. Then, with hands long skilled in a delicate operation, they placed the nuts on a board or stone and rubbed a stone huller over them, just hard enough to crack the shells without crushing the sweet, transparent nuts within. They then returned the nuts to the baskets for winnowing, and if the wind did not answer their prayer for his help as they rhythmically flipped the baskets, they blew the last shells away. A second roasting and winnowing followed, and, after a cleaning with nut flour, the mountain harvest was ready for storage. In the evening, when the canyons turned blue in the fading light, there would be plenty of pinyon nut soup to eat and many stories to be told around the campfires.[9]

Yet, unavoidably, the time came to leave the mountains. The few shards of evidence on the Winnemuccas that survive today suggest deepening crisis and increasing hostility from tribal enemies. Another Paiute murdered Charlie Winnemucca (possibly a half-brother of Sarah's) at Pyramid in June 1888. In the same month, other Paiutes beat Natches so unmercifully that his survival seemed doubtful. At the same time, his ranch was foundering. Eighteen-eighty-eight began with such a severe drought that the *Silver State* reported Humboldt Lake shrunken to a "mere pond" soon to become "dry as a powder horn." Without the lake, nothing would cool the hot blasts of wind from the Stillwater and Hot Springs Deserts that scorched all the vegetation in the valleys. Ranchers anxiously scanned the skies in vain, and the next winter brought no relief.[10]

Even when crops were stillborn, Natches still had a few cattle. The following year, after he had set off to drive them to the mountains for summer grazing, his home went up in flames, with his blankets, his gun, and all his provisions inside. Whether an arsonist set the blaze is not known, nor, if so, whether the deed was done by settlers who coveted his land or by Indians. Captain John, an ambitious rival, had sworn from the beginning that Natches's ranch must fail. If arson it was, it succeeded. Natches spiraled downward into despondency.[11]

The one event that brightened the summer of 1889 when Sarah had lost the school and Natches had come to believe he soon must lose the ranch was the arrival of a long lost cousin, William Ferguson. As a youngster, Ferguson had traveled with Sarah and Natches in the Indian party that Truckee took to California, and he had remained there living and working for some forty years. He returned to Nevada in search of his relatives. Although wealthy by Paiute standards, with eight hundred dollars in savings that Sarah deposited for him in the bank, he went to work at one of the large Lovelock ranches. It is perhaps unfortunate that Sarah had not sooner been reunited with this successful cousin, no doubt considerably acculturated by his long immersion in *taibo*'s world, four years older than she — and unmarried. But she may not have seen the last of him.[12]

In late September Sarah traveled east to Elko to mediate between the Indian and white worlds on the fate of another Indian murderer, Tuscarora Jack. She had performed this service before in the cases of Willow Creek Charley and One Arm Jim but always for her own people. Now the Shoshone had called on her to speak for them, even though relations between the Paiutes and the Shoshones living in eastern Nevada had not always been particularly cordial. Settlers reported that the Paiutes had tyrannized the Shoshones, encroaching on their territory and stealing horses and women. Whatever their past differences, the Shoshones set them aside to secure Sarah's assistance. The adulation of the Washo women had already shown how much the neighboring tribes admired her.[13]

From *taibo*'s point of view, alarm over the Ghost Dance formed the subtext of the matter. The obvious agitation among the Indians, rumors of warlike prophecies from Wovoka, and parties of Indians racing their ponies to join a large gathering may have aroused fears of an Indian rising. Sarah reassured them. She told the white authorities that the Indians had not convened for a Ghost Dance but to settle the fate of Tuscarora Jack, who had killed two Indians and possibly a Chinese in a drunken rage. His family had offered ponies and money to the victims' families and promised to vouch for his future good behavior. The headmen had nonetheless decided that he should face white society's justice as an example to others, be it hanging or the state prison. It is not unlikely that Sarah had a voice in their decision.[14]

When several people recognized "the Princess" taking a "hand-out breakfast" with Natches and other Indians in a railroad station hotel kitchen, she explained with embarrassment that she followed the customs of her people when she was with them. Despite the poverty she could not conceal, Sarah seemed as impressive as ever in her last appearance as a spokeswoman for Indians in a matter of public concern. Some white women had come to meet the famous Paiute princess at the hotel, and Sarah conversed with them with her old vivacity, telling of her eventful life. A newspaperman thought her still a handsome woman, younger-looking than her years. Her clothing symbolized the life she led in two different worlds. Among whites she garbed herself as fashionably as any lady of the late 1880s; among Indians she dressed as they did, probably in loose-fitting calico.[15]

The drought ended that winter in a season of heavy storms, which Wovoka's followers credited to his powers over the weather. For Natches, the snows came too late. Thirteen years had passed since he and the young men of his band started clearing the land on the understanding of eventual ownership. It had been a bold dream, a prime ranch owned by Indians proving that they could work and succeed without a reservation agent's supervision — a dream perhaps too bold for the times. Even thirty years later no Indian owned a ranch in the Big Meadows, and whites throughout the western frontier often failed as well in their agricultural enterprises. Research on four California counties, with lands less harsh and difficult than Nevada's, has shown that 40 to 60 percent of the farmers there could not last a decade. Beset by the difficulties inherent in frontier ranching and continually enticed by white ranchers who had been trying to buy him out since at least 1886, Natches finally decided to sell.[16]

Sarah refused to accept the final end of the dream so bravely begun. In November she published a notice in the newspaper declaring that because she held an interest in it, the ranch could not be sold without her agreement. Her stubborn refusal succeeded in blocking the sale as long as she lived. Natches had made up his mind all the same. He moved to Pyramid with his family, and J. H. Thies, the white

Sarah wore this black velvet costume as early as 1879,
but the mature lines of her face suggest that this is one of the later photos
taken of her. Courtesy of the Nevada Historical Society.

rancher and mine owner who eventually bought the ranch, began paying taxes on it in 1890 and doubtless worked the fields under a private agreement with Natches.[17]

Although Sarah and Natches are believed to have fought angrily over the disposition of the ranch, the quarrel did not — could not — last. Natches was the one person who had stood steadfastly beside her through all the vicissitudes of the years. Moreover, tribal elder Helen Williams explains: "Indian people don't stay mad forever you know. You're mad for awhile, and it goes away, and you can be friends again."[18]

Henry's Lake spread over a slight concavity just west of Yellowstone Park and south of the Montana-Idaho border. It was a shallow lake, with floating marshy islands, that often turned chocolate-colored when wind-whipped waves stirred silt from its bottom. To the east, silver ribbon rivulets slid down the green, wooded escarpment to feed the lake; southward, a sea of waist-high grass on the flats waved in the wind; southwest, beyond aspen groves, thunder clouds boiled over Rea and Sawtell Peaks, the eastern heights of the Centennial Range. In the canyon along the base of the mountains, Red Rock Pass, scarcely more than a trail, led west and eventually to other roads and towns.[19]

So isolated was Henry's Lake that it remained a paradise of wildlife, almost unchanged since Lewis and Clark crossed the Continental Divide. The lake teemed with fish; flocks of ducks bobbed on its waters; elk grazed in the deep grass; bears lumbered heavily through the woods; wolves, including the huge, hunchbacked, almost mythic black wolf, howled in the night; hawks and eagles soared above; and herds of antelope flicked their white tails and bounded over the sage hills north of the lake.[20]

The human landscape, by contrast, was much sparser. The Great Bannock Trail ran just south of the lake, across the mountains, through Yellowstone, and into the buffalo country. Although the Bannocks had been strictly confined to reservations since the war, an occasional party still traveled the old route. The few frontiersmen in the area lived mainly by fishing and hunting and raised a few cattle or sheep. Carrie Strahorn, an early visitor to Yellowstone who arrived by stage in 1880, was told that no woman lived within thirty-five miles of Henry's Lake and believed herself the first woman whose voice had ever floated across its surface. Strahorn's informant evidently took no account of Indian women, for Sarah's sister Elma and her white husband, John Smith, are believed to have lived at Henry's Lake since at least 1880.[21]

Elma remains the most enigmatic among the Winnemuccas. Although it is difficult to judge by photos taken in her old age, she appears smaller and thinner than the others, with sharper features, more conventionally pretty than Sarah but without the large expressive dark eyes. Through a long period spent with a white family in Marysville, California, she had learned English and grown accustomed to *taibo*'s ways. Unlike Sarah, with her several unlucky loves, she had stayed married to one man for most of her adult life and jokingly called herself "Pokey," in reference to the story of Pocahontas and John Smith. The name stuck, and those at Henry's Lake, where she served as the local midwife, generally called her Pokey Smith. The two children she bore to John Smith both died, and the couple informally adopted Will and Ed Staley, two white boys whose parents had been killed by Indians.[22]

In 1889 Elma's husband died suddenly. Joseph Sherwood, the settler who took the place of a coroner, declared that the cause was "too much chokecherry wine." Sherwood, of course, had no medical knowledge beyond the practical experience of a frontiersman accustomed to coping with emergencies. The accuracy of his conclusion would later emerge as a question of some importance.[23]

Winters were fierce at Henry's Lake. Strong winds blew from the west; five to twelve feet of snow blanketed the region; temperatures often fell to fifty or sixty degrees below zero. Those not inclined to venture out by snowshoe, dogsled, or sleigh stayed holed up in their cabins. More often, settlers left for the winter, leading the cow behind the wagon. Elma sometimes wintered in Nevada, as she did in 1889–90 after the death of her husband.[24]

Long separation and the very different lives they led precluded Sarah and Elma from being close, but they had stayed in touch through occasional visits. Although Sarah evidently did not feel the same warm affection for Elma that she had shown for Mattie, blood ties counted heavily among the Paiutes. Heartsick, believing that she had won little for her people in all her years of struggle, Sarah decided to leave for Henry's Lake with Elma in the spring. Once, in anger, she had said that she would no longer speak for the Paiutes, but she fought on all the same. This time, however, the passionate voice of the Paiutes was stilled at last. She would depart in silence.

In late April, as the snows receded from Henry's Lake, mud clogged the trails, and spring wildflowers bloomed in the valleys, the sisters journeyed to Elma's place. We catch a few glimpses of them over the following months. They planted a large, ambitious vegetable garden, where Sarah kept watch with a gun to prevent the depredations of ground squirrels. When settlers gathered from far and wide to celebrate the most important holiday on the pioneer calendar — the Fourth of July — Sarah and Elma amazed and delighted all present with their spirited performance of intricate Mexican dances, which they no doubt learned many years earlier in California.[25]

Sighting a party of Bannock riders on the old trail not long afterward, Sarah responded with the hospitality traditional for the daughter of a chief and invited all of them to dinner. As the Paiutes tell it, Sarah later said "there was one man in the bunch stared at her, looked at her, had a big scar on his face. She said he was a real fierce looking man." After the Bannocks left, night fell and an owl spoke to Sarah, warning her of danger and telling her to leave the house at once. While the sisters hid in a haystack, the Bannocks returned to burn the house. In mid-July a news report from Henry's Lake included an item on the construction of a new house for Elma.[26]

Again the sisters wintered in Nevada. They found the Ghost Dance frenzy at its zenith because Wovoka had promised that the long-awaited day was at hand. With the coming of spring, the dead would live again, the old would become young, and Numina would return the world to the Indians. The unrest culminated on 29 December 1890, when the U.S. cavalry killed nearly two hundred Sioux men, women, and children at Wounded Knee Creek, South Dakota.[27]

Quickly grasping how easily a similar tragedy could occur in Nevada, the messiah's homeland and the place where excitement among the believers reached a high level of intensity, Sarah attempted to cool the agitation by warning the Ghost Dancers against provoking whites to violence. She spoke with some authority, for not only did her English enable her to read newspaper accounts of Wounded Knee but also she knew the commanding officer, Col. James W. Forsyth, having served beside him during the final phase of the Bannock War in the eastern Oregon desert. Her words so alarmed the Lovelock band that Indians rode about on guard all night, expecting the arrival of the army. Again, whites saw Sarah as a troublemaker. Outraged by the idea that Indians needed a warning against whites, the *Silver State* sarcastically suggested that she should "pack up her duds and Winter pine nuts and go east on a lecturing tour." At the same time, Indians reacted even more negatively to the stance taken by Sarah and Natches. "Because of our warnings and not believing what they say of a crazy preacher, we have made our own people hate us," she wrote. Thanks to a happy confluence of circumstances—wise and restrained leadership on both sides and the absence of a military force on the scene—violence did not explode in Nevada.[28]

Spring came, the millennium promised by Wovoka failed to materialize (as Sarah had anticipated), and the sisters returned to Henry's Lake by way of Monida and Red Rock Pass, supping along the way with Lillian Culver, a Centennial Valley settler. William Ferguson, the lost cousin recently returned from California, may have accompanied them. He homesteaded lands just north of Henry's Lake in 1900, and it is likely that he had been occupying them for some time prior to that.[29]

Summer warmed Henry's Lake. Goldenrod, white yarrow, blue lupine, and orange Indian paintbrush bloomed amidst the grasses. Sarah traveled to Bozeman, Montana, to serve as companion to a New York woman tourist visiting the area. The sisters picked chokecherries, from which Elma made her chokecherry wine.[30] Nights turned frosty, and autumn arrived in a blaze of color. Golden aspen groves contrasted with the dark green of pines, sumac flamed a brilliant red, and grassy meadows turned yellow and brown. The sisters had to leave soon or they would be caught in the first lasting snow that usually fell at the end of October. Then, on 16 October, Sarah ate a large dinner with chokecherry wine, doubled up in pain with severe stomach cramps, gasped, collapsed, and died. She was only forty-seven years old, came of a long-lived family, and no hint of failing health had recently been reported. The cause of her death has never been established.[31]

One of Sarah's biographers has suggested that she died of tuberculosis contracted from Lewis before his death four years earlier. This is, of course, possible but does not seem likely. Sarah, the spirited performer of Mexican dances and companion to the woman tourist, showed no sign of serious illness. Moreover, those on the scene saw her death as a sudden, unforeseen event. Lillian Culver believed it a suicide. Given Sarah's character, her zest for life, her brave heart, and her stubborn persistence in the face of all obstacles, this, too, seems unlikely.[32]

Unofficial coroner Joe Sherwood, when called to Elma's house, attributed Sarah's death to "too much chokecherry wine" — the same conclusion he had reached following the death of Elma's husband in 1889, almost two years earlier. Although this may have simply been Sherwood's standard explanation for mysterious deaths, it better fits the suddenness of the event than tuberculosis. Too much wine does not, however, jibe with the violent stomach cramps that Sarah suffered. Could it, then, have been bad wine, perhaps a bottle left over from the batch that killed John Smith? Or a flaw in Elma's winemaking process that produced contamination and food poisoning? This could explain both the cramps and the suddenness of her death.

If Sarah had been wasting away over a long period in the later stages of tuberculosis, both Sherwood and Culver would have noticed. Yet there is one difficulty with the supposition of bad wine. If Sarah and Elma drank the wine together with their meal, as would seem probable, why had only Sarah died?[33]

This leads to the wildest theory that can be spun on Sarah's death, one uncovered by author Patricia Stewart more than twenty years ago when the rumors at Henry's Lake were much fresher than today. Elma, so it was said, poisoned Sarah because both had fallen in love with the same man. This would explain all the anomalies: the suddenness of death, the violent cramps, and Elma's survival. Although as a trusted midwife Elma had friends among the settlers, some clearly had their doubts about her. These misgivings climaxed less than a year later when her adopted son Will Staley disappeared and Elma stood trial for murder before Judge McMinn. The matter ended inconclusively: Will Staley was never seen again, nor was his body found; the lack of evidence against her brought Elma's release; Will's brother, Ed, remained devoted to Elma and cared for her until her death many years later in 1920. He believed unquestionably in her innocence. The suspicions about Elma might be written off as racism or transference: these frontiersmen, who often acted violently, may have projected their own tendencies onto Elma.[34]

And yet there had been two mysterious deaths and one disappearance at Elma's home in less than three years, and those who had long lived near her knew something of her. Apparently, some believed her capable of ruthlessly murdering her own kin. If she was indeed the woman they believed her to be, who was the man the Winnemucca sisters vied for? Could he have been their prosperous cousin William Ferguson, who remained at Henry's Lake until he froze to death in a blizzard in 1915? He left all he possessed to Elma.[35]

How do the Paiutes think Sarah died? "Somebody witched her probably," says Helen Williams. "Put the curse on her."[36]

Sarah lies in an unmarked grave, its location as uncertain as the cause of her death. The assumption that she was buried in the Targhee cemetery appears erroneous because the cemetery had not yet been created, and all the known graves inside it (including Elma's and Ferguson's) are dated later. Probably the most reliable information comes from the reminiscence of one of Sherwood's daughters. She relates that Sarah lies alone outside the cemetery on the slope below the old Richards ranch house on the east side of the lake.[37] There may be a certain symbolic rightness in this because for much of her life Sarah had been an outsider, both in *taibo*'s world, where she was never fully accepted, and in her own, where many of her people had finally turned away from her. It is said that some of the Bannocks came to her burial. She may have been an enemy they had tried to kill, but she was also a worthy opponent and the daughter of a chief. Her passing needed to be observed with due ceremony.[38]

Natches also came for a final leave-taking, although the season was late and he could not make the journey in time to see her laid to rest. Snow would already have whitened the peaks of the Centennial Mountains. He must have stood amidst the brown grass and scattered sage on the slope, with leafless aspens white as skeletons against the pines behind him. Looking over the glimmer of the lake and the snowy peaks to the southwest, he may have thought of the long journey he and this well-loved sister had made together and of the child who wept and screamed in her terror of *taibo* when they first rode to California.

The insignificance of her grave, no more than a wedge of dirt beside his feet, would not have troubled him greatly, for the Paiutes know that earthly remains do not matter much. The spirit that flies out through the nose with the last breath is what matters. Spirits of wicked people return to roam the Nevada deserts as whirlwinds, but Sarah would not be one of these. Buzzard would lift the firmament so that she might pass between the meeting place of earth and sky, and her brave spirit would travel the starry path of the milky way. Then she would reach Panukwit, the Land of the Sunny South, where the good spirits live forever.[39]

Epilogue

Sarah Today

MORE THAN A CENTURY after her death, the old controversies over Sarah have not yet been laid to their final rest. This was demonstrated in 1994 at the naming of the Sarah Winnemucca elementary school in Reno. After the name had been accepted by the school board, several parents who favored naming the school Suncrest after a nearby housing development secured reconsideration. Georgia Hedrick, a former Daughter of Charity, a teacher, and a warm admirer of Sarah's, rallied her forces, and each side drew in Paiutes to bolster its position. The Inter-Tribal Council of Nevada and the Nevada Indian Commission both supported naming the school for Sarah.[1]

The battle culminated in an overflow meeting with all seats taken and people standing in the back of the room and in the entryway. Invited to explain the context, Nevada State Archivist Guy L. Rocha pointed out that nearly all public figures are controversial and that the old rivalries between different Paiute bands continue to play out in the present. Sarah's opponents had generated a response to school board members from Paiutes that confirmed these divisions in the Paiute community. Some sensed an undercurrent of racism on both sides beneath the specious argument that the school might be confused with the town of Winnemucca: white parents opposed naming the school for an Indian; and for equally racist reasons, their Paiute allies rejected Sarah as a turncoat who married white men and favored assimilation. Two families threatened to withdraw their children if the school were named for her.[2]

Those in favor of Sarah carried the day. Speaking with "contained fury," Hedrick phrased her speech as a series of rhetorical questions ("Did you know Sarah Winnemucca was the first Indian woman to write a book?"). It soon became clear that the audience had no conception of Sarah's achievements. The meeting culminated when Alexandra Voorhees, the young Paiute performance artist who portrays Sarah at chatauquas and other events and shares much of the gift of the original to "stir hearts," rose to speak on the theme of Sarah's belief in education. By the time Voorhees finished, people in the audience were crying and clapping. The school was named Sarah Winnemucca. In several subsequent portrayals of Sarah at the school, it heartened Voorhees to see that the children had studied Sarah's life and took "a great deal of pride and joy in their school." If you tried to change the school name today, says school board member Dan Coppa, "they would run you out of town on a rail."[3]

Measured against what she had tried to achieve, Sarah's only real failures were not matters of personal morality but victories she could not win for her people — and their welfare was always foremost in her thoughts. Freedom for the Yakama exiles had been long delayed. The effort to tap the public appetite for Indian spectacle had brought returns too meager to alleviate Paiute poverty. Malheur had been lost. Yet, caught up as she was in immediately responding to desperately urgent problems, some of Sarah's solutions seem almost visionary today. Her school had failed — yet it left a vision of how Indian children might be taught with kindness and respect for their culture, their traditions, and their language. This is now seen as the right path, while education to eradicate Indian culture is recognized as a monstrous mistake.

Of the battles she could not win, the struggle to change the reservation system concerned her most. She had neither succeeded in ridding her people of the tyrannical Indian agents who mistreated them nor in changing the system to one of reservations without agents, with agents chosen by the Indians, or — most revolutionary of all — with Indians as agents. She had finally endorsed lands in severalty as a lesser evil than the existing system but still vainly sought to restore the authority of the Indians' own traditional leaders. Here as well, Sarah saw the right path a century too soon, as Indians have finally gained authority on their own reservations. To alter the course of public policy so fundamentally would surely have been beyond the powers of any Indian leader of Sarah's day. Yet Washington's apparent commitments raised a vision of Nevada as it might have been that still echoes among the Paiutes today.[4]

Win or lose, the causes Sarah championed showed her wisdom and courage. In view of the forces arrayed against her, the losses seem scarcely surprising, and the marvel is that she achieved so much. She gave a voice to the voiceless. She made the plight of an obscure Indian tribe a matter of public concern. By her example, she disproved the racist notion that Indians were subhuman and could not be taught. Her school demonstrated a better model for Indian education under Indian auspices. In the words of Voorhees, she performed "the first duty of a Paiute" when she saved her family during the Bannock War. More broadly, she affected the lives of her people in many ways: she played a part in freeing the Yakama exiles and winning the McDermit Reservation; she improved the lives of those she taught; she mediated and interpreted between the Indian and white worlds; and above all, she preserved the heritage of her people in her book.[5]

Even with the benefit of hindsight it is difficult to conceive what methods the Winnemuccas might have used to more effectively influence events. Winnemucca's tactics were varied and ingenious: the visits to powerful persons, the attempt at legal action, the diplomatic maneuvering over a possible return to Malheur, the theatrical performance to raise money, the appeal to public charity, the threat of force — and more than threat in the Pyramid Lake War. Sarah's tactics, by contrast, drew more heavily on the traditional role of the Paiute leader who sways the assemblage with eloquence, a role that she adapted to *taibo*'s world in sophisticated ways. She personally brought the Paiute cause to presidents, secretaries of the interior, army generals and other officers, legislators, senators, and Indian agents. She testified before Congress. She appealed to popular opinion through interviews, newspaper statements, and her many impassioned lectures in theaters, churches, and parlors on both coasts. She strove to reach both the public and influential politicians through her book, and that, too, was talking. As her people had said so long ago, it was "talking on paper."

Sarah remains remarkable among Indian leaders of her day in that she did not advocate resisting white encroachment with warfare, with flight to a more distant region, or, as the only remaining option, with acceptance of a disadvantageous treaty. Instead, she attempted to change white policies through peaceful means by working through the system of white society. Although her belief that the mighty juggernaut of American Indian policy could be turned if the desperate situation of the Paiutes became known may seem naive, it made a good deal of sense in the aftermath of the Civil War. After all, the agitation of northern reformers had played a large role in ending slavery. Sarah, though apparently not well read, showed a keen awareness of where potential supporters for the Paiute cause might be found. She knew better than to seek them among the settlers of the interior West, since many of these settlers coveted reservation lands and harbored hatred for Indians. However, in the big cities on both coasts, where fear of Indians had long since died and Indian lands offered no temptation, reformers might be persuaded to take up the Indian cause. The publication of Helen Hunt Jackson's influential *A Century of Dishonor* (with Sarah's contribution) in 1881, two years before Sarah's book, seemed to signify growing momentum for the reform of Indian policy, with a place for the Paiutes on the agenda.

Although the time was ripe, Sarah never gained the allies who might have helped realize her ideas. The Women's National Indian Association had already committed itself to a policy centered on Christianizing the Indians, and Sarah's refusal to soften her criticism of Agent Wilbur raised an additional obstacle to an accommodation. Such prominent figures in Indian policy reform as Herbert Welsh, Charles Painter, and Thomas Bland not only rejected Sarah on the basis of Rinehart's slanders but actively worked to discredit her. "She has no weapons of defense against such foes," wrote Peabody to Senator Dawes, "and can only say like Christ in whose spirit she lives & speaks, 'I come to testify to the truth — he that [has] ears to hear let him hear.' "[6] Senator Dawes listened to Sarah sympathetically but made no alterations in his bill in accordance with her suggestions. Realizing that lands in severalty had blotted out all other proposals, Sarah bowed to the inevitable in her congressional testimony and argued primarily for the more limited objectives of McDermit Reservation and assured freedom for the Yakama escapees. Beyond generating public interest in the plight of the Indians, Sarah bore no responsibility for the reform de jour — the Dawes Act — nor any for the failure within a few years of what would be widely acknowledged as a mistaken policy. Not until long after her death would America catch up with Sarah's ideas.

In this and all she undertook, Sarah's willingness to assume large tasks on her own initiative commands respect. Volunteering to lead her father's band to safety during the Bannock War, a mission that Major Mason believed impossible, offers an instance involving great hardship and physical danger. When the Office of Indian Affairs refused to support her school or employ her as a teacher, Sarah started her own school. The repeated cry "It can be done!" that won her cheers from a San Francisco audience was one that she applied above all to herself.

In relation to the Paiutes, Sarah had an important but circumscribed role buttressed by the prestige of her family. As a woman, she could not be a chief like her father and brother nor was she chosen by consensus or election as they were. Rather, she became a leader for the more narrow function of spokeswoman, interpreter, and mediator, analogous to a shaman or a rabbit boss, who also have important but limited functions. As the shaman heeds the voice of the spirits and declares his calling, Sarah chose her role (with a considerable push from her grandfather) and prepared herself for it by studying English so assiduously that she apparently became the most fluent among her people. She never mastered *taibo*'s methods of political manipulation along with his language, however, and to the end she remained the traditional Paiute leader who rises to sway listeners by persuasive oratory and force of personality.

Her fall from grace also occurred in the Paiute way. Like the shaman whose patients die or the rabbit boss who drives few rabbits into the net, Sarah lost the confidence of her people when she failed to deliver results. From their standpoint, either nothing changed, as in the nondelivery of the promised tents or the continuance of hated Indian agents in office, or they found it difficult to discern Sarah's part in an eventual favorable outcome, as in the validation of freedom for the Yakama exiles and the creation of McDermit Reservation. Sarah recognized, with how much pain can only be imagined, that her people turned away from her because she had too often served as the messenger for white men's broken promises. Moreover, the partial adoption of white men's ways that had enabled her to straddle both worlds in her role as spokeswoman and mediator also alienated her from her people.

"Those who maligned me have not known me," Sarah once wrote, a truth confirmed by the Sarah Winnemucca school hearing, where none who voiced opposition had read *Life among the Piutes*.[7] Unless seeking ammunition at a school naming, few whites still malign Sarah. Although she may not be as well known as military leaders such as Crazy Horse and Geronimo (whose luster may in part reflect the military values of American society), she is easily one of the three most famous pre–twentieth century Indian women, along with Sacajawea and Pocahontas. The main criticisms voiced — and they are rare — turn on her private life, not her public role. As her star ascends, enemies such as Rinehart and Wilbur sink into obscurity to become mere footnotes to history, remembered only because their lives touched hers. She has been the subject of television documentaries and several biographies that unanimously praise her.

Among her own people, by contrast, her reputation is mixed. As Voorhees puts it, any gathering of Paiutes will be "divided in their devotions." Some erroneously condemn her as an assimilationist who married white men. Those who do not realize that she was obliged to couch her appeals in the language of the day blame her because she spoke of "civilizing" Indians. Her critics often do not realize that she also spoke of the moral superiority of Paiute culture. Some see her as a "traitor" who sold out her people during the Bannock War and even cost Paiute lives (a conclusion difficult to sustain in close study of the Bannock War). Critics who would not go so far condemn her for revealing to white people Indian secrets such as the hidden springs in the desert. At least one man has publicly charged her with prostitution (not, says Voorhees, "a Paiute argument"). The old band rivalries of which Rocha spoke at the school board hearing are sometimes explicitly stated.[8]

More fundamentally, we may guess that for a people determined to maintain their identity at the close of the twentieth century, some of Sarah's achievements have been devalued. True, she learned English, lectured on both coasts, and wrote a book, but in so doing she violated tribal norms by making herself different and better than others, and by her leaving, she diminished the strength of the community and made her people die a little more. There is no going home again. Some will never accept the one who tries to return, even over the distance of a century.[9]

But there are many among Sarah's people to whom, in Hedrick's words, "her name is gold." Voorhees calls Sarah's book her bible, opens it at random, takes the passage she sees as her text, steps before an audience, Paiute or white or both, and speaks spontaneously as Sarah did. The old yet ever-new story of the Paiute struggle for survival and of justice betrayed reduces many to tears — as when Sarah told it. Sarah still inspires. Says tribal elder Marjorie Dupée, Sarah's brave life helps us "hold to our pride."[10]

Notes

Abbreviations

AAG   Assistant Adjutant General
AG   Adjutant General
CIA   Commissioner of Indian Affairs
HR   *Humboldt Register*
LR   Letters Received
OIA   Office of Indian Affairs
SS   *Silver State*

PROLOGUE

1. Woodward, *Pocahontas*, e.g., 99, 117; H. P. Howard, *Sacajawea*, 17.

2. Woodward, *Pocahontas*, 72–73, 81–82, 153–59, 172–73, ch. 15; H. P. Howard, *Sacajawea*, 18–19; Ruoff, "American Indian Autobiographers," 261–62.

3. Woodward, *Pocahontas*, 162, 189; H. P. Howard, *Sacajawea*, 29–30, 49–50, 98, 114, 117, 129.

4. Ambrose, *Crazy Horse and Custer*, 134; J. Miller, "Basin Religion and Theology," 76. On the strong vindication element, see Brumble, *American Indian Autobiography*, 66. Doubts on the reliability of the book appear in Sands, "Personal Narrative," 278.

1. THE WORLD OF THE PAIUTES

1. Hopkins, *Life*, 11–12. This incident is difficult to date. Sarah's younger sister, Elma, believed she was born in 1850 (U.S. manuscript census, Idaho, 1900). If she was right — or nearly so — and if she was the younger sibling Tuboitony carried, the event may have taken place in 1849 or 1850; however, the events Sarah links with the incident, and the way she describes her size and behavior, suggest an earlier date, perhaps 1848.

2. Hopkins, *Life*, 11–12.

3. Hopkins, *Life*, 5, 20.

4. Knack and Stewart, *As Long*, 28; C. S. Fowler, *Park's Notes*, 9.

5. Knack and Stewart, *As Long*, 13–15.

6. Spence and Jackson, *Expeditions*, 2:26.

7. Wheat, *Survival Arts*, 5. Scholars disagree on the exact number of bands

(see Knack and Stewart, *As Long*, 16), and Steward and Wheeler-Voegelin deny that territorial bands existed in the aboriginal period (see *Paiute Indians*, 293).

8. Knack and Stewart, *As Long*, 15.

9. Knack and Stewart, *As Long*, 26–27; C. S. Fowler, *Park's Notes*, 134; Hopkins, *Life*, 53; Steward and Wheeler-Voegelin, *Paiute Indians*, 305 (quote).

10. C. S. Fowler, *Park's Notes*, 133 n.2; Hopkins, *Life*, 55–57; Knack and Stewart, *As Long*, 26–27.

11. On woman's work, see Wheat, *Survival Arts*, 6–11, 16.

12. Hopkins, *Life*, 46–48.

13. Wheat, *Survival Arts*, 15. For other versions of Paiute marriage customs, see Scott, *Karnee*, 18–19, and Hopkins, *Life*, 49.

14. On storytelling, see Wheat, *Survival Arts*, 16. On shamans, see Park, "Paviotso Shamanism," 99–106.

15. On pinyon ceremonies, see Wheat, *Survival Arts*, 12. On abandonment, see Spence and Jackson, *Expeditions*, 2:25. Unless otherwise noted, Paiute vocabulary is drawn from Fowler and Fowler, *Anthropology*.

16. Knack and Stewart, *As Long*, 31, 56; Scott, *Karnee*, 6.

17. Scott, *Karnee*, 9–12; Gilbert, *Westering Man*, 130–31. The number of Paiutes involved in the encounter that resulted in the first Humboldt Sink massacre has been variously estimated at 200 (Scott) and 400–900 by sources in the Walker party (Gilbert). Scott's figure seems more plausible.

18. Knack and Stewart, *As Long*, 38; Gilbert, *Westering Man*, 146–47.

19. Hopkins, *Life*, 5–7.

20. Hopkins, *Life*, 8–9; Scott, *Karnee*, 25–26.

21. Heizer, "Notes on Some Paviotso Personalities," 1–2. Sarah states that the name Truckee was bestowed on her grandfather by Frémont. Frémont is also said to have named the river after Truckee; however, this seems unlikely because Frémont specifically states that he named the river the Salmon Trout. Sarah probably is correct on the meaning of Truckee. In Scott's version, the hat is a dinner plate on Winnemucca's head. See Hopkins, *Life*, 8–9; Scott, *Karnee*, 25–26; and Spence and Jackson, *Expeditions*, 1:610. On the Stevens party, see Stewart, *California Trail*, esp. 67–69, 81. On another expedition guided by Truckee, see Hermann, *Paiutes*, 66.

22. Spence and Jackson, *Expeditions*, 1:601, 609–10. Sarah places the Truckee-Frémont meeting in summer, but Frémont's first Great Basin trip occurred in January and the second in autumn. See Hopkins, *Life*, 9, 22; Bry-

ant, *What I Saw*, 228; and Spence and Jackson, *Expeditions*, 2:xxxiii–iv, 27–28.

23. Spence and Jackson, *Expeditions*, 2:28; Knack and Stewart, *As Long*, 42–47.

24. Knack and Stewart, *As Long*, 42–44.

25. Hopkins, *Life*, 12–16; Knack and Stewart, *As Long*, 43–47, 83.

26. Hopkins, *Life*, 13–16. The races may well have been an extraordinary display of athletic prowess. Edwin Bryant, who traveled across the Great Basin on mule-back in 1846, admired the speed and endurance of the Great Basin Indians. Not only could Indian runners keep up beside a trotting mule for as long as four hours without showing any strain but they could run with speed "greater than could be achieved by any of the animals we were riding"; see Bryant, *What I Saw*, 194, 205–6.

27. Hopkins, *Life*, 13–16.

28. Hopkins, *Life*, 13–16.

2. THE SAN JOAQUIN

1. Hopkins, *Life*, 5; Brimlow, "Life of Sarah Winnemucca," 105. On the mud hen hunt, see Wheat, *Survival Arts*, 11; C. S. Fowler, *Park's Notes*, 56–57; and Scott, *Karnee*, 23–25. The latter two place the annual mud hen hunt in early fall.

2. Wheat, *Survival Arts*, 11, 85, 97–102; Hopkins, *Life*, 49–50.

3. Heizer, "Notes," 1–2; Hopkins, *Life*, 9. Another version of the meaning of Winnemucca's name was "one moccasin." Because Indian names can change over time to reflect outstanding characteristics or experiences, he reportedly also had other names, including Mubetawaka for an ornamental bone in his nose, Puidok for his deep-set eyes, and Po-i-to. For these accounts, see Heizer, "Notes," and Fowler and Fowler, *Anthropology*, 230.

4. Hopkins, *Life*, 11–13.

5. Hopkins, *Life*, 17–18.

6. Hopkins, *Life*, 18.

7. Hopkins, *Life*, 18–19. While Truckee's presence in the Bear Flag Revolt has been questioned, Bryant's statement that he met Truckee in the Great Basin and later saw the old chief with the California battalion (*What I Saw*, 211, 228) confirms Truckee's account.

8. Hopkins, *Life*, 19. On the Saidukas, see Fowler and Fowler, *Anthropology*, 218.

9. Hopkins, *Life*, 20–21. On burial customs, see Fowler and Fowler, *Anthropol-*

ogy, 248, and Fallon Paiute-Shoshone, *After the Drying*. The Fowlers suggest that graves may not have been dug in aboriginal times (see 285 n.78).

10. Hopkins, *Life*, 20.

11. Hopkins, *Life*, 10, 21. An 1851 date for the trip also fits with Sarah's own tentative chronology (*Life* 58). The 1852 death of Bonsall, whom Sarah remembered, rules out a later date. Her reference to climbing three times in a "red stone" building, if it denotes three stories rather than a staircase with landings, is confusing because the taller red brick buildings evidently were constructed later. On Stockton, see Martin, *Stockton Album*, 23, 120, and Hubert H. Bancroft, *History of California*, 467. Sarah is not consistent in her description of the kinfolk who remained behind: at this point she mentions only one aunt and her family but later relates that two of her mother's sisters and their families died in an epidemic over the winter; see also Canfield, *Sarah*, 6.

12. Hopkins, *Life*, 21–22.

13. Hopkins, *Life*, 22–23. The locale of this encounter is unclear. Sarah places it at "the head of the Carson River" about fifteen miles south of Carson City, but the distance to the heads of both the east and west forks of the Carson River is much farther than fifteen miles. On the Washo, see Knack and Stewart, *As Long*, 70.

14. Hopkins, *Life*, 23–24. On the witch woman, see Wheat, *Survival Arts*, 11–12.

15. Hopkins, *Life*, 24–25. On the Toya Numu, see Fowler and Fowler, *Anthropology*, 241.

16. Hopkins, *Life*, 25–27. Kilcup observes that Sarah "disarms" white readers with the humorous pie plate story that shows the innocence of her people (introduction, xv).

17. Hopkins, *Life*, 27–28.

18. Hopkins, *Life*, 29; Hubert H. Bancroft, *History*, 467–69; Martin, *Stockton Album*, 24.

19. Hopkins, *Life*, 29–30. Sarah writes of thinking of the kindly woman as an "angel," but since angels did not figure in Paiute mythology, she probably used a term she thought would be understandable to white readers.

20. Hopkins, *Life*, 33–34. This is the first instance of the recurring "theme of sexual violence" that Georgi-Findlay observes in Sarah's narrative — see "Frontiers," 236. On early Stockton, see Taylor, *Eldorado*, 56–59.

21. Hopkins, *Life*, 34–38.

22. Hopkins, *Life*, 35–38.

23. Hopkins, *Life*, 37–39.

24. Hopkins, *Life*, 39–40. On the Paiutes and the horse, see Steward and Wheeler-Voegelin, *Paiute Indians*, 295; Clemmer, "The Tail of the Elephant," 281–87; Layton, "From Potage to Portage," 243–57; Scott, *Karnee*, 32; and Fowler and Fowler, *Anthropology*, 212.

25. Hopkins, *Life*, 40–41.

26. Hopkins, *Life*, 33, 41–43.

27. Hopkins, *Life*, 42–44. On the cholera epidemic, see Groh, *Gold Fever*, 215–24, 233, and Bayer, *Profit*, 10, 14.

3. GENOA

1. Spence and Jackson, *Expeditions*, 1:599–601; Bryant, *What I Saw*, 217; Simpson, *Report*, 48, 79, 87; Hopkins, *Life*, 40. As Brumble notes, Sarah is curiously silent on the appearance of the homeland that meant so much to her people (*American Indian Autobiography*, 64).

2. Knack and Stewart, *As Long*, 65; Hopkins, *Life*, 58. Because the 1851–52 epidemic predated accurate records on Nevada Indians, losses can only be estimated; however, Lowry was told that "half or more" of the Paiutes died in the epidemic; see Scott, *Karnee*, 26.

3. Bayer, *Profit*, 71.

4. Bayer, *Profit*, 63, 100; Griffith, "What's Nevada's Oldest Town?" 13.

5. Rocha, "Nevada's Emergence," 257–59, 273–74 n.10; Bayer, *Profit*, 46–47, 63.

6. Bayer, *Profit*, 67, 70, 120.

7. Rocha, "Nevada's Emergence," 257–59; Bayer, *Profit*, 54–61, 85–89.

8. Bayer, *Profit*, 47; Hopkins, *Life*, 58, 64.

9. Simpson, *Report*, 56, 463; Spence and Jackson, *Expeditions*, 1:599.

10. Thompson, *Tennessee Letters*, 3; Bayer, *Profit*, 89. Though Sarah does not name the sister accompanying her, she once alludes to "my poor little sister" (Hopkins, *Life*, 64), so I have assumed the sister was Elma.

11. Thompson, *Tennessee Letters*, 40; Bayer, *Profit*, 22, 49–50, 115.

12. Hopkins, *Life*, 45, 58; Pedersen, "Ormsby Gown," 79; Mathews, *Ten Years in Nevada*, 287. Sarah's statement (*Life*, 45) on the absence of swearing in Paiute is confirmed by Riddell in "Honey Lake Paiute Ethnography," 88.

13. On schools, see Thompson, *Tennessee Letters*, 17, and Angel, *History*, 37.

14. Pedersen, "Ormsby Gown," 77.

15. Bayer, *Profit*, 68–69.

16. Hopkins, *Life*, 60. On war paint, see C. S. Fowler, *Park's Notes*, 138.

17. Bayer, *Profit*, 70, 74; Angel, *History*, 147. The discrepancies are not resolved by the Washos, as the incident is not mentioned in their tribal history; see Inter-Tribal Council of Nevada, *Wa She Shu*. During this period, Genoa had a monthly newspaper of sorts — the handwritten *Scorpion* — but no issues survive; see Lingenfelter and Gash, *Newspapers*, 89.

18. Hopkins, *Life*, 60–62; Bayer, *Profit*, 72. On Captain Jim's band, see Inter-Tribal Council of Nevada, *Wa She Shu*, 51.

19. Hopkins, *Life*, 60–62; Bayer, *Profit*, 72.

20. Hopkins, *Life*, 63–65. Sarah uses the phrase "the Great Spirit," probably in an attempt to use a term familiar to her readers, rather than more correctly translating the Washo term as "the Maker." Unless she is embroidering her tale, her account raises questions about how she could understand Washo so well, as it was a language unrelated to Paiute. Given her linguistic abilities, it is possible that she had picked up Washo from Washo workers she met in Genoa.

21. Hopkins, *Life*, 61.

22. Hopkins, *Life*, 58, 64; Bayer, *Profit*, 99–103.

23. De Quille, *Bonanza*, 11, 23. On the early Comstock, see Smith, *Comstock Lode*, 3–18, and James, *The Roar*, ch. 1–3. Since De Quille had not yet arrived on the Comstock, he must have heard this from others. As Mary is not mentioned at the dances, despite her presence in Johntown, one wonders if she thought them too risky in view of her California experiences; see Hutcheson, "Before the Comstock," 14.

24. Thompson, *Tennessee Letters*, 22, 45, 49–50.

25. *San Francisco Daily Evening Bulletin*, 3 Sept. 1858, 3. The winter of 1858–59 seems the most likely date for Sarah's first encounter with Methodism because on her first trip she did not yet understand English and on later trips (without Tuboitony) she was too old to react in the childlike way she describes; see Hopkins, *Life*, 54–55.

26. Thompson, *Tennessee Letters*, 49, 102–3, 112.

27. Knack and Stewart, *As Long*, 67–68 (*Enterprise* quote); Thompson, *Tennessee Letters*, 49.

28. Hopkins, *Life*, 10. On begging and sharing, see Downs, "Differential Response," 121.

29. Hopkins, *Life*, 10. As Lape notes in "Cultural Liminality," Sarah's parody of the term "savage" completely reverses its meaning (274–75).

4. THE PINE NUT MOUNTAINS

1. W. C. Miller, "Indian War," 1:52.

2. Thompson, *Tennessee Letters*, 54–55, 57; Bayer, *Profit*, 12–23.

3. Thompson, *Tennessee Letters*, 57, 88–89, 140; De Quille, *Bonanza*, 32.

4. Thompson, *Tennessee Letters*, 45, 49–50. Allen was writing of the Washo in the previous winter, but his remarks show the settlers' attitude. On settler attitudes toward military action, see Downs, "Differential Response," 128.

5. Knack and Stewart, *As Long*, 67; Angel, *History*, 149–50.

6. Knack and Stewart, *As Long*, 69; Angel, *History*, 149 (quote); Bayer, *Profit*, 143.

7. Angel, *History*, 150–51. Angel's account is especially valuable because he sent a team to interview Indian participants in the council and the war.

8. Angel, *History*, 151 (quote); Egan, *Sand*, 264–65. It is doubtful that Numaga used the term "Nevada," a name not yet established; see Rocha, "Nevada's Emergence," 265–72.

9. Hopkins, *Life*, 70–71.

10. Hopkins, *Life*, 70–71. On gun sales to Indians, see Thompson, *Tennessee Letters*, 30. Accounts of the events at Williams Station vary: one gives the trade as the cause of the trouble; another relates that the Williamses raped Indian women and compelled their husbands to watch. Because her brother was involved in the killings, Sarah's account is considerably more credible. See also De Quille, *Bonanza*, 81–82; W. C. Miller, "Indian War," 2:107; Thompson, *Tennessee Letters*, 159–60.

11. W. C. Miller, "Indian War," 1:38; Hopkins, *Life*, 71.

12. Angel, *History*, 151.

13. W. C. Miller, "Indian War," 2:102–7; Thompson, *Tennessee Letters*, 135–36.

14. Bayer, *Profit*, 149, 152; Hopkins, *Life*, 72.

15. Angel, *History*, 153; De Quille, *Bonanza*, 77; Bayer, *Profit*, 149.

16. Angel, *History*, 153–54; Thompson, *Tennessee Letters*, 140; Egan, *Sand*, 133, 142.

17. Angel, *History*, 154–55.

18. Hopkins, *Life*, 72; Angel, *History*, 158. Angel relates a different version of Ormsby's death (157), and unless she was misquoted, Sarah told an interviewer an almost identical story about a man named Clayton (*Alta California*, 26 Nov. 1879). Casualty counts vary widely; this figure is from Egan, *Sand*, 155.

19. Thompson, *Tennessee Letters*, 139; De Quille, *Bonanza*, 79.

20. W. C. Miller, "Indian War," 1:46–52; Egan, *Sand*, 234–46 (quote).

21. Egan, *Sand*, 154, 217; De Quille, *Bonanza*, 82–84.

22. Knack and Stewart, *As Long*, 72–73; Egan, *Sand*, 256–59.

23. Thompson, *Tennessee Letters*, 145–46 (quote); Knack and Stewart, *As Long*, 72.

24. Knack and Stewart, *As Long*, 74, 89–93; Downs, "Differential Response," 128–29.

25. Thompson, *Tennessee Letters*, 161.

26. Thompson, *Tennessee Letters*, 160–61; De Quille, *Bonanza*, 81.

27. Hopkins, *Life*, 66–68; De Quille, *Bonanza*, 200. Sarah erroneously reverses the order of Truckee's death and the Pyramid Lake War, perhaps because her deep emotions over the loss of her grandfather led her to give that event greater weight and place it first. Sarah also places Bonsall with Scott in Truckee's request. If it is not simply her own mistake, Truckee may have been unaware that Bonsall had died in 1852; see Martin, *Stockton Album*, 78.

28. Hopkins, *Life*, 66–68.

29. Hopkins, *Life*, 66–70.

30. De Quille, *Bonanza*, 201 (quote); Hopkins, *Life*, 70; *Alta California*, 10 May 1875, 2. On Captain John's rivalry with the Winnemuccas, see Scott, *Karnee*, 16.

31. De Quille, *Bonanza*, 201 (quote); Hopkins, *Life*, 69. On bonding with grandparents, see Wheat, *Survival Arts*, 97.

5. WINNEMUCCA LAKE

1. Hopkins, *Life*, 12; *Nevada State Journal*, 12 Feb. 1873; Canfield, *Sarah*, 266–67 n.12. Although Sarah mentions both Scott and Bonsall, Bonsall had died in 1852. See Martin, *Stockton Album*, 78. De Quille relates that she attended the Santa Cruz mission school (*Bonanza*, 202).

2. *Nevada State Journal*, 12 Feb. 1873; Hopkins, *Life*, 70.

3. Angel, *History*, 168–69; Canfield, *Sarah*, 33–34; Egan, "Warren Wasson," 4–5. On the marriage offer, see the *Battle Mountain Scout*, 29 Oct. 1921.

4. *Gold Hill News*, 18 Mar. 1865; Angel, *History*, 168–69.

5. De Quille, *Bonanza*, 12, 202; *Nevada State Journal*, 12 Feb. 1873. On the creation myth, see Fallon Paiute-Shoshone, *After the Drying*.

6. De Quille, *Bonanza*, 197–201.

7. De Quille, *Bonanza*, 197–201.

8. Hopkins, *Life*, 67; De Quille, *Bonanza*, 202. On miscegenation laws, see Earl, "Nevada's Miscegenation Laws," 1–3.

9. *Gold Hill News*, 22 Sept. 1864.

10. On Sitting Bull, see Utley, *The Lance*, 262–65; on the importance of the family, see Steward and Wheeler-Voegelin, *Paiute Indians*, 283, 306–7.

11. On the Comstock in this period, see Smith, *Comstock Lode*, 28, 48–49, 58–60, and the *Virginia Daily Union*, 4–8 Oct. 1864.

12. On Paiutes on the Comstock, see Mathews, *Ten Years*, 286–91, and De Quille, *Bonanza*, 212–19.

13. Bancroft Scraps, 10.

14. Angel, *History*, 165; Egan, "Warren Wasson," 7–8; Helen Williams, Paiute tribal elder, interviews by author, 8 Apr. 1998 (telephone) and 29 Apr. 1998 (Lovelock NV). Winnemucca's daughters were identified in the press as Sallie (a diminutive of Sarah) and Maria (presumably Mary). I have assumed that Sarah gave the interview and served as interpreter, since that was usually her role.

15. On Comstock entertainment, see Watson, *Silver Theater*.

16. Stoddard, *Sam Knew Them*, 59. Davis did not witness the events he described but rather heard them secondhand, which probably accounts for the wrong date and other discrepancies, but the story is authentically his work (Professor Lawrence I. Berkove, letter to author, 16 Jan. 1998).

17. *Virginia Daily Union*, 5 Oct. 1864, 3; Lape, "Cultural Liminality," 270. On scalp dances, see Riddell, "Honey Lake," 87.

18. Stoddard, *Sam Knew Them*, 59–60.

19. *Alta California*, 22–23 Oct. 1864; *Virginia Daily Union*, 4–5 Oct. 1864; Bancroft Scraps, 27.

20. *Alta California*, 22–23 Oct. 1864. On the Pocahontas drama, see Watson, *Silver Theater*, 82. On the Plains Indians as models, see Downs, "Differential Response," 129, 134.

21. *Alta California*, 23 Oct. 1864; *Virginia Daily Union*, 7 Oct. 1864.

22. Stoddard, *Sam Knew Them*, 60–61.

23. *Virginia Daily Union*, 16 Mar. 1865; *Gold Hill News*, 16 Mar. 1865; HR, 18 Mar. 1865; Wheeler, *Nevada Desert*, 62, 163.

24. Hopkins, *Life*, 78; Wheeler, *Nevada Desert*, 62–64. An 1860 map already designated the site as Winnemucca Lake (see Carlson, *Nevada Place Names*, 248), but Mud Lake was the name usually used in newspaper reports on

the massacre. On the lake, see Lt. J. M. Lee to Henry Douglas, 20 Dec. 1869, OIA, LR, NV Superintendency, roll 539.

25. Wheeler, *Nevada Desert*, 62–64; Hopkins, *Life*, 78.

26. Hopkins, *Life*, 77–78; Knack and Stewart, *As Long*, 79, 371; Bancroft Scraps, 28.

27. HR, 8 Apr. 1865, 2 Mar. 1865, 18 Mar. 1865; *Virginia Daily Union*, 17 Mar. 1865; 22 Mar. 1865; 26 Mar. 1865; 30 Mar. 1865; *Gold Hill News*, 18 Mar. 1865; Wheeler, *Nevada Desert*, 66. Military archives have no record of an investigation; see Wheeler, *Nevada Desert*, 163.

28. *Virginia Daily Union*, 3 Jan. 1866; HR, 3 Feb. 1866.

29. *Virginia Daily Union*, 23–26 Mar. 1865; Myles, *Nevada's Governors*, 12–13. Although he confirmed the deaths of Winnemucca's wives, Numaga did not believe that any of Truckee's daughters died at Mud Lake. Sarah is inconsistent on these points: in a letter written three years after the event, she states that Winnemucca's wives and her sisters died in the massacre (we know that Elma survived); in her book, she indicates that Tuboitony and Mary died soon afterward, see Knack and Stewart, *As Long*, 79, 371, and Hopkins, *Life*, 77–79.

30. *Virginia Daily Union*, 25 Mar. 1865.

31. *Virginia Daily Union*, 25 Mar. 1865.

32. *Virginia Daily Union*, 25 Mar. 1865.

33. Wheeler, *Nevada Desert*, 60; Hopkins, *Life*, 78; *Virginia Daily Union*, 25 Mar. 1865.

34. HR, 8 Apr. 1865, 20 Jan. 1866.

35. HR, 17 Mar. 1866; Williams, interviews.

36. Wheeler, *Nevada Desert*, 77–78, 80, 165; Angel, *History*, 150; HR, 10 Feb. 1866. As Wheeler points out, casualty figures in military and newspaper reports do not always agree.

37. *Virginia Union*, 3 Jan. 1866 (quote); Wheeler, *Nevada Desert*, 72, 165; Wasson to CIA, 11 Sept. 1865, U.S. Congress, Report of the Joint Special Committee, 520.

38. Hopkins, *Life*, 78. On atrocities, see Wheeler, *Nevada Desert*, 71–72.

39. Hopkins, *Life*, 79.

40. Hopkins, *Life*, 86.

41. Hopkins, *Life*, 86–87. Canfield dates this issue in 1873; see *Sarah*, 76–77.

42. Hopkins, *Life*, 87.

43. Hopkins, *Life*, 87–88.

44. C. S. Fowler, "Sarah," 33; Knack and Stewart, *As Long*, 53–54. Although Winnemucca allegedly expressed a wish to live at Pyramid in 1867, this was apparently a mere diplomatic ploy, see the HR, 1 June 1867.

45. HR, 5 May 1866; Wheeler, *Nevada Desert*, 62 (last quote); Angel, *History*, 150.

46. On Pyramid, see Knack and Stewart, *As Long*, esp. chs. 6 and 7, 179–81.

47. Knack and Stewart, *As Long*, 104, 180–82.

48. *Reese River Reveille*, 8 July 1867; Knack and Stewart, *As Long*, 182 (quote); Hopkins, *Life*, 78.

6. CAMP MCDERMIT

1. J. Miller, "Basin Religion," 70; Steward, "Two Paiute Autobiographies," 424.

2. Hopkins, *Life*, 79. On Wodziwob, see Thornton, *We Shall Live*, 1–6. As Thornton notes, the 1870 Ghost Dance movement had many variations.

3. Hopkins, *Life*, 79–80.

4. Hopkins, *Life*, 79–80. The attack on Coffman's Station is briefly mentioned in the *Territorial Enterprise*, 30 May 1868, and in the HR, 6 June 1868, with some differences (one man mortally wounded, not one dead and one about to die, as in Sarah's account). Lieutenant Jerome was then at Pyramid on detached service from Camp McDermit; see U.S. Military Post Returns, June 1868–July 1868, roll 666.

5. Hopkins, *Life*, 80–81. On the Indian agents' powers, see Knack and Stewart, *As Long*, 94.

6. Hopkins, *Life*, 82.

7. Hopkins, *Life*, 82–83.

8. Hopkins, *Life*, 83–84.

9. Hopkins, *Life*, 85.

10. Hopkins, *Life*, 85.

11. *Winnemucca Argent*, 22 Oct. 1868; *Nevada State Journal* clipping, 25 Oct. 1959, box 1, Wheat Papers. Due to similarity of names (Numaga was often termed Young Winnemucca or, simply, Winnemucca), it is not clear whether this is the same 1867 incident in which a visiting chief of this name was jailed "for safe keeping" while the Honey Lakers unsuccessfully attempted to shoot the members of his hunting party, but mention of a permission letter from the agent at Pyramid suggests that the latter was a separate incident involving Numaga. See the *Territorial Enterprise*, 29 Aug. 1867.

12. Hopkins, *Life*, 85–86, 99.

13. Steward and Voegelin, *California and Basin-Plateau Indians*, 217–23, 258–62; Bischoff, "Aspects of Punishment," 269–70.

14. Schmitt, *General George Crook*, 142–54. On Crook's campaign, also see Utley, *Frontier Regulars*, 179–80.

15. Kober, *Reminiscences*, 257; Steward and Voegelin, *California and Basin-Plateau Indians*, 261; Summerhayes, *Vanished Arizona*, 213; Meacham, *Wigwam and War-Path*, ch. 14. On government policy, see Prucha, *American Indian Policy*, 18.

16. Summerhayes, *Vanished Arizona*, 212; Corbusier, *Verde to San Carlos*, 90, 93, 104–5.

17. Corbusier, *Verde to San Carlos*, 93, 97–98; Summerhayes, *Vanished Arizona*, 210; Hopkins, *Life*, 101 (last quote).

18. Hopkins, *Life*, 101–2.

19. Hopkins, *Life*, 90–91, 128; *Humboldt Star*, 2 Feb. 1914. On Oregon stock raising, see Rinehart MS, part 2. McDermit post returns show two periods when the number of Indian prisoners increased prior to the abandonment of Camp C. F. Smith: March 1869 and autumn 1868. The 22 Oct. 1868 *Winnemucca Argent* also mentions an Indian exodus from Smith, and a false report of Winnemucca's death suggests that his whereabouts were not then known. Thus, 1868 appears the most probable date for the arrival of the Paiutes from Smith, and 1869 for the arrival of Winnemucca and his followers. The number of Indians at McDermit appearing in post returns is far smaller than those recalled by Sarah. I have considered the post returns more reliable; see U.S. Military Post Returns, Jan. 1868–July, 1870, roll 666.

20. Hopkins, *Life*, 90–91.

21. Hopkins, *Life*, 99–100.

22. Summerhayes, *Vanished Arizona*, 213; Kober, *Reminiscences*, 257–58. On Winnemucca's wanderings, see Wagner to AAG, 18 Feb. 1878, OIA, LR, OR Superintendency, roll 626.

23. Corbusier, *Verde to San Carlos*, 95–96; Kober, *Reminiscences*, 244.

24. Summerhayes, *Vanished Arizona*, 213; Kober, *Reminiscences*, 252–53, 279.

25. Kober, *Reminiscences*, 257–58.

26. Kober, *Reminiscences*, 243, 252, 257; Hopkins, *Life*, 92.

27. Hopkins, *Life*, 100; Corbusier, *Verde to San Carlos*, 94; U.S. Military Post Returns, Dec. 1869, roll 666. On the role of interpreters, see Kawashima,

"Forest Diplomats," 1. In "Cultural Liminality," Lape notes the interpreter's dilemma of being blamed for the "false language" of whites (266–67).

28. Hopkins, *Life*, 93; U.S. Military Post Returns, 30 June 1870, roll 666.

29. Kober, *Reminiscences*, 258–59; *Gold Hill News*, 28 Apr. 1870; Jackson, *Century of Dishonor*, 395–96.

30. Kober, *Reminiscences*, 258–59.

31. HR, 21 May 1870, 28 May 1870.

32. Forbes, *Nevada Indians*, 98–99; Prucha, *American Indian Policy*, ch. 3.

33. Forbes, *Nevada Indians*, 105–8; E. O. C. Ord, Report, 50.

34. Forbes, *Nevada Indians*, 99–100.

35. Ranck, "A Pacific Coast Pocahontas," 44

36. Corbusier, *Verde to San Carlos*, 94.

37. Hopkins, *Life*, 101–3; Bancroft Scraps, 11

38. Corbusier, *Verde to San Carlos*, 94–95; De Quille, *Bonanza*, 196; C. S. Fowler, *Park's Notes*, 103.

39. Corbusier, *Verde to San Carlos*, 94. The variety of football played by the Camp McDermit Indian women was probably *wutsimu*. The game featured a four-hundred-yard course and a round buckskin ball filled with deer hair, which players kicked from starting point to goal. On *wutsimu*, see Riddell, "Honey Lake," 90.

40. Kober, *Reminiscences*, 238–39, 240–43.

41. Corbusier, *Verde to San Carlos*, 95; *San Francisco Call*, 22 Jan. 1885.

42. Corbusier, *Verde to San Carlos*, 94, 107; *Nevada State Journal*, 12 Feb. 1873; IIR, 15 Oct. 1870; Hein, *Memories*, 67.

43. Corbusier, *Verde to San Carlos*, 95; Kober, *Reminiscences*, 243; Davison, "The Bannock-Piute War," 133; Edward C. Bartlett veterans' pension file and military service records, esp. "first endorsement," 18 July 1879, and William H. C. Bartlett to Gen. E. D. Townsend, 17 Dec. 1871.

44. Edward C. Bartlett veterans' pension file and military service records; Sarah Bartlett v. Edward C. Bartlett divorce file, 21 Sept. 1876, Grant County Courthouse, Canyon City OR. In her 12 Feb. 1873 *Nevada State Journal* interview, Sarah misstated the marriage date or was misquoted, but the marriage certificate presented at her divorce hearing, together with other evidence, fixes it at 29 Jan. 1872. See also the HR, 9 Mar. 1872, and SS, 27 Jan. 1872.

45. HR, 9 Mar. 1872, 3.

46. *Nevada State Journal*, 12 Feb. 1873; Edward C. Bartlett veterans' pension file and military service records, esp. Capt. James Egan to AAG, 28 Sept. 1870.

47. *Nevada State Journal*, 12 Feb. 1873. Gossip appears in Davison, "Bannock-Piute War," 133.
48. *Nevada State Journal*, 12 Feb. 1873; HR, 8 June 1872. In *American Indian Autobiography*, Brumble notes the importance of reputation in Indian culture and its particular importance to Sarah (66).
49. HR, 22 June 1872.
50. *Nevada State Journal*, 12 Feb. 1873.
51. *Idaho Statesman*, 4 July 1872, 2; HR, 15 Oct. 1872; *Nevada State Journal*, 12 Feb. 1873.
52. *Nevada State Journal*, 12 Feb. 1873. Sarah had evidently heard a false report of the death of her cousin Jerry Long, who was still demonstrably alive several years later. On the Modoc War, see Brady, *Northwestern Fights*, 229–56.
53. *Nevada State Journal*, 12 Feb. 1873; Brady, *Northwestern Fights*, 229–56.
54. *Nevada State Journal*, 12 Feb. 1873.
55. *Reno Crescent*, 20 Feb. 1873.

7. WINNEMUCCA

1. HR, 30 Jan. 1874
2. HR, 30 Jan. 1874. On Delano's plan, see Prucha, *American Indian Policy*, 106–11.
3. HR, 30 Jan. 1874; Hopkins, *Life*, 89.
4. *Nevada State Journal*, 28 Dec. 1875; SS, 8 Dec. 1881; U.S. manuscript census, 1870, Nevada.
5. HR, 13 Feb. 1874.
6. HR, 7 Aug. 1874; U.S. Department of the Interior, *Report*, 1868–69, 818.
7. HR, 7 Aug. 1874.
8. *Territorial Enterprise*, 1 Jan. 1875, 5 Jan. 1875; HR, 1 Mar. 1873, 17 May 1873. The *Register* reported that Sarah planned to visit Bartlett in Salt Lake City, but Bartlett had long since deserted her.
9. SS, 5 Feb. 1875; *Sacramento Record*, 16 Jan. 1875.
10. *Sacramento Record*, 16 Jan. 1875; Bancroft Scraps, 55.
11. *Carson Appeal*, 14 Jan. 1875; SS, 5 Feb. 1875.
12. Nevada Legislature, *Journal of the Senate*, 1875, 44, 59, 66, 89; Nevada Legislature, *Journal of the Assembly*, 1875, 70, 77; HR, 5 Feb. 1875.
13. Hopkins, *Life*, 90. On Jones, see Smith, *Comstock Lode*, 134–35.
14. SS, 15 Jan. 1875, 12 Feb. 1875; Kober, *Reminiscences*, 249–50.

15. Kober, *Reminiscences*, 248–50, 252. On Paiute food prohibitions, see Wheat, *Survival Arts*, 15. There is some disagreement on crows. Wheat states that Paiute custom prohibited them; Corbusier (*Verde to San Carlos*, 93) relates that both Indians and soldiers at McDermit ate them.

16. Kober, *Reminiscences*, 250.

17. HR, 26 Feb. 1875.

18. SS, 8 Feb. 1875. On Civil War charity, see Angel, *History*, 268.

19. Prucha, *American Indian Policy*, 30–32; Hopkins, *Life*, 87.

20. Douglas to CIA, 30 Nov. 1870, OIA, LR, NV Superintendency, roll 539. On the effort to start a school at McDermit, see Bancroft Scraps, 54.

21. On simultaneous adherence to several religions, see Stewart, "Three Gods for Joe."

22. *Sacramento Record*, 16 Jan. 1875.

23. SS, 16 Mar. 1875; HR, 19 Mar. 1875.

24. Angel, *History*, 459–60 (first quote); Kober, *Reminiscences*, 236. I have estimated Winnemucca's population at the midpoint between the U.S. censuses of 1870 (290) and 1880 (763).

25. *Nevada State Journal*, 28 Mar. 1875; SS, 27 Mar. 1875. The latter source placed the incident on the sidewalk in front of the Winnemucca Hotel.

26. *Humboldt Star*, 16 July 1913; *Humboldt National*, 25 Sept. 1869.

27. SS, 29 Mar. 1875. On the Humboldt County Courthouse, see James, *Temples of Justice*, 87–88.

28. *Nevada State Journal*, 11 Apr. 1875; SS, 20 Apr. 1975, 28 Apr. 1875.

8. MALHEUR RESERVATION

1. Brimlow, *Harney County*, 90, 150, 247. On cattle empires, also see *An Illustrated History*, 401. Sources disagree on the size of the French herd, though all estimates are large. On Indians, see Liljeblad, "The Indians of Idaho," 28.

2. Brimlow, *Harney County*, 96; Hopkins, *Life*, 105–6, 108; Parrish to CIA, 7 Feb. 1874, OIA, LR, OR Superintendency, roll 620.

3. Hopkins, *Life*, 106–7; O. O. Howard, *Famous Indian Chiefs*, 259–67.

4. Brimlow, *Harney County*, 91; Otis to AAG, 15 Mar. 1874, OIA, LR, OR Superintendency, roll 620; Parrish to CIA, 3 Mar. 1876, OIA, LR, OR Superintendency, roll 622, and 25 Nov. 1875, roll 622.

5. Hopkins, *Life*, 106–7.

6. Hopkins, *Life*, 108; Brimlow, *Harney County*, 96–97.

7. Brimlow, *Harney County*, 97; Hopkins, *Life*, 110–14; O. O. Howard, *Famous Indian Chiefs*, 266; Parrish to CIA, 12 Apr. 1875 and 26 Apr. 1875, OIA, LR, OR Superintendency, roll 621. On Dreamer beliefs, see Ekland, "'Indian Problem,'" 123–24.

8. Hopkins, *Life*, 112–13.

9. Hopkins, *Life*, 114–15; O. O. Howard, *Famous Indian Chiefs*, 266–67. Although Howard probably heard about these incidents from Sarah, he may have also drawn information from his own observations at Malheur and from other Indians he knew well, such as Egan and Mattie.

   Oytes may have reverted to threats at the time Sarah indicates, but Otis's letter of 15 Mar. 1874 suggests that Sarah incorporated an incident she had not actually witnessed in her story. In the letter he relates that at an earlier date "Oytz attempted some trouble, which was quelled on the spot by Mr. Parrish in such a firm and decisive way that Oytz has feared him ever since." See Otis to AAG, LR, OIA, OR Superintendency, roll 620, and T. Wilson and Lyman Daman to CIA, 13 July 1874 on the same roll. Also see Hopkins, *Life*, 115–16.

10. Hopkins, *Life*, 115–16; O. O. Howard, *Famous Indian Chiefs*, 258. This is probably the petition mentioned in Currey's 30 June 1875 cover letter to the CIA (OIA, LR, OR Superintendency, roll 620). The document itself, presumably distinct from the one on the same subject dated 13 May 1878, has not been preserved with these records. It is probably the one discussed by Parrish in his letter to the CIA of 25 Nov. 1875, OIA, LR, OR Superintendency, roll 622. Also see Green to CIA, 25 Nov. 1875, roll 622. On the reservation's agricultural potential, see William Vandever to CIA, 13 Sept. 1874, OIA, LR, OR Superintendency, roll 620.

11. Hopkins, *Life*, 115–16. Sources conflict on Leggins's position. Special Agent William Turner calls him a subchief in Winnemucca's band, a statement that comports with Sarah's extreme concern for his group and his eventual return to Nevada. See Turner to Rinehart, 10 Sept. 1877, OIA, LR, OR Superintendency, roll 624. But Rinehart places him in Egan's band, along with Sarah's cousin Jerry Long. See Rinehart to CIA, 24 July 1877, roll 624.

12. Hopkins, *Life*, 116; Parrish to CIA, 4 Apr. 1876, OIA, LR, OR Superintendency, roll 623; O. O. Howard, *Famous Indian Chiefs*, 258.

13. Hopkins, *Life*, 117.

14. Brimlow, *Harney County*, 98; Hopkins, *Life*, 118.

15. Hopkins, *Life*, 119.

16. O. O. Howard, *Famous Indian Chiefs*, 254, 264–65, 270; Hopkins, *Life*, 121–22. O. O. Howard to AAG, 8 June 1876 and Green to AAG 26 May 1876, both in OIA, LR, OR Superintendency, roll 622.

17. Rinehart to Mrs. F. F. Victor, 6 Mar. 1874, and MS; O. O. Howard, *Famous Indian Chiefs*, 273; Hopkins, *Life*, 117, 123, and congressional testimony 22 Apr. 1884, in the privately held Georgia Hedrick papers. Also see the Malheur Reservation accounts for the third and fourth quarters of 1873 and the first and second quarters of 1874, OIA, LR, OR Superintendency, roll 621.

18. Hopkins, *Life*, 123–24; O. O. Howard, *Famous Indian Chiefs*, 273.

19. Hopkins, *Life*, 124–26; Rinehart MS; O. O. Howard, *Famous Indian Chiefs*, 273.

20. Hopkins, *Life*, 126–27. On Egan's homeland, see Parrish to CIA, 26 Apr. 1875, OIA, LR, OR Superintendency, roll 621.

21. Hopkins, *Life*, 127–30.

22. Hopkins, *Life*, 131–33.

23. Hopkins, *Life*, 112, 133–34.

24. Hopkins, *Life*, 134; Rinehart to O. O. Howard, 23 Dec. 1876, OIA, LR, OR Superintendency, roll 624.

25. Green to AAG, 20 Dec. 1876, OIA, "Case of Sarah Winnemucca"; Green to AAG, 16 Nov. 1876, OIA, LR, OR Superintendency, roll 624.

26. Rinehart MS; O. O. Howard, *Famous Indian Chiefs*, 134; Turner to Rinehart, 10 Sept. 1877, OIA, LR, OR Superintendency, roll 624, and Thompson to AAG, 11 Feb. 1878, roll 626; Wagner to AAG, 18 Feb. 1878, OIA, LR, OR Superintendency, roll 626.

27. Rinehart to CIA, 14 Apr. 1877, 21 Nov. 1877, 17 Dec. 1877, 23 Mar. 1878, OIA, "Case of Sarah Winnemucca"; Capt. E. F. Thompson to AAG, 16 May 1878, OIA, LR, OR Superintendency, roll 626.

28. Hopkins, *Life*, 134–36.

29. Rinehart MS; O. O. Howard to CIA, 30 Dec. 1876, roll 623; Otis to AAG, 15 Mar. 1874, LR, OR Superintendency, roll 620; John J. Burke to Sen. Newton Booth, 22 Mar. 1878, LR, OR Superintendency, roll 625; Harrison Linville to CIA, 1 Apr. 1874, LR, OR Superintendency, roll 619.

30. Sarah Bartlett v. E. C. Bartlett divorce file, 21 Sept. 1876; Grant County marriage records, book 1, Canyon City OR; Edward C. Bartlett veterans' pension files and military service records.

31. Satewaller's absence from the Grant County grantor-grantee index, which shows property transactions, is another indication of mobility.

32. Patricia Stewart, "Sarah Winnemucca," 27; Hopkins, *Life*, 136–37; Rinehart to O. O. Howard, OIA, 23 Dec. 1876, LR, OR Superintendency, roll 624. A source cited by Canfield places Sarah's marriage to an Indian in 1873 and calls the husband D. R. Jones, see *Sarah*, 81–82. This seems less likely in view of Sarah's activities in that year and her married status.

33. SS, 24 Feb. 1877, 16 Apr. 1877, 2 Jan. 1886; Bowling to Frank Winnemucca, 6 Feb. 1878, OIA, "Case of Sarah Winnemucca." On Paiute marital customs, see Steward, *Basin-Plateau Aboriginal Sociopolitical Groups*," esp. ch. 8.

34. SS, 5 Mar. 1878; Hopkins, *Life*, 137.

35. SS, 27 Nov. 1876, 8 Feb. 1877; Thompson to AAG, 11 Feb. 1878, OIA, LR OR Superintendency, roll 626.

36. *Idaho Statesman*, 6 Dec. 1877; SS, 22 June 1877, 26 June 1877, 12 Dec. 1877.

9. THE BANNOCK WAR BEGINS

1. Madsen, *The Bannock*, 32–34, 216; Brimlow, *Harney County*, 102.

2. Madsen, *The Bannock*, 19, 21–24, 27, 33; Brimlow, *Harney County*, 5; *An Illustrated History*, 744. Liljeblad argues that the Bannocks were never an independent tribe and designates them as Paiutes in the process of acculturation into the Shoshones. However, they seem distinctively different from either tribe; see Liljeblad, "Indians of Idaho," 27.

3. O. O. Howard, *My Life*, 370; Madsen, *The Bannock*, 203–9; Hopkins, *Life*, 138–39;

4. Forbes, *Nevada Indians*, 126; Madsen, *The Bannock*, 183, 212–14, 227–28. For the Crook interview, see the *New York Times*, 23 June 1878, 5.

5. SS, 4 May 1878, 1 June 1878, 8 June 1878.

6. Brimlow, *Harney County*, 104–5; *An Illustrated History*, 744; O. O. Howard, Report, 211. O. O. Howard to AAG, 21 Oct. 1878, OIA, LR, OR Superintendency, roll 626.

7. Gregg, *Pioneer Days*, 134–35; *An Illustrated History*, 745.

8. Hopkins, *Life*, 137–38; *Idaho Statesman*, 7 Aug. 1932.

9. Hopkins, *Life*, 138–40. Sarah gave the Mortons' original destination as Malheur City, Oregon. They later changed it to Silver City, Idaho, from where she planned to continue to Elko.

10. Hopkins, *Life*, 141–46. Some chronological discrepancies emerge here: Sarah places the meeting with Egan at Malheur on 7 June, while Rinehart reports all Indians had left the agency by that date (Rinehart to CIA, 28 June 1878, OIA, LR, OR Superintendency, roll 626). Although Sarah was often in-

accurate on dates, those she gives during the war usually jibe with probable travel times and other sources, so it is hard to determine who was in error. Another possibility is that Egan and the others were still on the reservation on 7 June but that Rinehart, whose relations with them were hardly close, did not know their whereabouts. Parker confirms her presence at Malheur and her consultation with Egan; see the *Weekly Gazette and Stockman*, 26 Nov. 1891.

11. Hopkins, *Life*, 146–47, 151.

12. Hopkins, *Life*, 146–47, 151; ss, 24 June 1878; *Idaho Statesman*, 1 June 1878.

13. Hopkins, *Life*, 147; *Idaho Statesman*, 8 June 1878. On Stone House, see Fretwell-Johnson, *In Times Past*, 169.

14. Hopkins, *Life*, 147–49, 178; Brimlow, *Harney County*, 106–7; Glassley, *Indian Wars*, 229–30. As late as 12 June, Oliver O. Howard remained unaware that Buffalo Horn had been shot. See O. O. Howard to AAG, 12 June 1878, Secretary of War, *Annual Report*, 1878, 147.

15. ss, 13 June 1878; Hopkins, *Life*, 149.

16. Hopkins, *Life*, 149–50.

17. Hopkins, *Life*, 150–52. On Sheep Ranch, see Fretwell-Johnson, *In Times Past*, 19, 47–50.

18. Hopkins, *Life*, 152–53; O. O. Howard, *My Life*, 388. Winnemucca's unwilling presence in the Bannock camp was less anomalous than it appears. Agent N. A. Cornoyer at the Umatilla Reservation wrote of his concern that his reservation Indians might be compelled to join the hostiles. See Hines, "Indian Agent's Letter Book," 10.

19. O. O. Howard, *My Life*, 387–88; Davison, "Bannock-Piute War," 130–31; Hopkins, *Life*, 153–54.

20. Hopkins, *Life*, 154–55; O. O. Howard, *My Life*, 392. Bringing scalps into camp on poles suggests a dance; see the *Idaho Statesman*, 20 June 1878. On Buffalo Horn's survival for two days, see Glassley, *Indian Wars*, 230, and the narrative of Birdie Blackhawk Calico in Gibson, *Family History*.

21. Hopkins, *Life*, 155.

22. Hopkins, *Life*, 156. On two of the Harney Valley ranchers murdered by Indians, see McArthur, "Early Scenes," 127.

23. Hopkins, *Life*, 157.

24. O. O. Howard, *My Life*, 392–93; Hopkins, *Life*, 157–58; ss, 21 June 1878, 6 Nov. 1879; Rinehart to CIA, 12 May 1879, OIA, "Case of Sarah Winnemucca." Having lost the Crowleys' affidavit, Rinehart recounted their story from memory.

25. Hopkins, *Life*, 157–58.
26. Hopkins, *Life*, 158–59.
27. Hopkins, *Life*, 158–59.
28. Hopkins, *Life*, 158–61.
29. O. O. Howard, *My Life*, 394; Hopkins, *Life*, 159–61.
30. Hopkins, *Life*, 161–62.
31. O. O. Howard, *My Life*, 394; Hopkins, *Life*, 161–62. According to Sarah, the rider also related that Egan and his band had been recaptured when they attempted to escape, but in view of Egan's subsequent role as war chief, this is doubtful.
32. Hopkins, *Life*, 162–63.
33. Hopkins, *Life*, 163. O. O. Howard relates this episode with a minor difference. He includes George and John in Sarah and Mattie's ride in the vanguard. See *My Life*, 395.
34. O. O. Howard, *My Life*, 391, 395, and Report, 214; Hopkins, *Life*, 163; Forbes, *Nevada Indians*, 146.
35. Utley, introduction, x–xvii.
36. Utley, introduction, x–xvii.
37. O. O. Howard, *My Life*, 395–96 and Report, 208. On the functions of Indian scouts, see Dunlay, *Wolves*, 8–9.
38. O. O. Howard, *Famous Indian Chiefs*, 238–58.
39. O. O. Howard, *My Life*, 396, and Report, 214; SS, 21 June 1878. Howard was not the only general to base some decisions on the reports of Indian scouts. Crook also did so; see Dunlay, *Wolves*, 95.
40. Hopkins, *Life*, 165. On Camp Lyon, see Fretwell-Johnson, "Cavalry Days," 12–13.
41. Hopkins, *Life*, 165–66.
42. Parker, 18 June 1878 letter in the *Idaho Statesman*, 20 June 1878; Hopkins, *Life*, 165–66.
43. SS, 27 June 1878.
44. O. O. Howard, *My Life*, 399, and Report, 216; Hopkins, *Life*, 166–67; Davison, "Bannock-Piute War," 131 (quote).
45. Hopkins, *Life*, 167–68.
46. Hopkins, *Life*, 168–69.
47. *Idaho Statesman*, 6 June 1878; Hopkins, *Life*, 169, 260.
48. Brimlow, *Bannock War*, 98–100.
49. O. O. Howard, *My Life*, 399. On the Malheur census, see Rinehart to O. O. Howard, OIA, 23 Dec. 1876, LR, OR Superintendency, roll 624.

50. *Idaho Statesman*, 29 June 1878 (quote). Brimlow, *Bannock Indian War*, 87. On this and other battles in the Bannock War, see Utley, *Frontier Regulars*, 325–29.

51. *Idaho Statesman*, 29 June 1878; Brimlow, *Harney County*, 118–20.

10. THE BANNOCK WAR

1. Hopkins, *Life*, 169–70; *Idaho Statesman*, 29 June 1878.

2. Hopkins, *Life*, 170; Davison, "Bannock-Piute War," 132; *Idaho Statesman*, 13 June 1878; Brimlow, *Harney County*, 120.

3. Hopkins, *Life*, 170–71. Mason's usual position was inspector general, but he served as chief of staff during the campaign. See Davison, "Bannock-Piute War," 128.

4. O. O. Howard, *My Life*, 400–401, and Report, 219; Davison, "Bannock-Piute War," 132; Hopkins, *Life*, 171–72; Brimlow, *Bannock Indian War*, 127.

5. Davison, "Bannock-Piute War," 132; Hopkins, *Life*, 172–73; O. O. Howard, *My Life*, 402.

6. Rinehart to CIA, OIA, 6 June 1878 and 1 July 1878, LR, OR Superintendency, roll 626; Brimlow, *Harney County*, 123.

7. Davison, "Bannock-Piute War," 133.

8. Davison, "Bannock-Piute War," 133.

9. O. O. Howard, *My Life*, 530–31.

10. O. O. Howard, *My Life*, 530–31.

11. Hopkins, *Life*, 173; Davison, "Bannock-Piute War," 130, 133; O. O. Howard, Report, 219.

12. Davison, "Bannock-Piute War," 133.

13. *An Illustrated History*, 749–51; Glassley, *Indian Wars*, 234; Brimlow, *Bannock Indian War*, 86. Dunlay notes that Indians often intentionally limited casualties in warfare; see *Wolves*, 124.

14. Davison, "Bannock-Piute War," 134–36.

15. Hopkins, *Life*, 174–75; O. O. Howard, *My Life*, 404; Davison, "Bannock-Piute War," 136–37.

16. O. O. Howard, *Famous Chiefs*, 243–44; Hopkins, *Life*, 175–76; Morgan, *My Story*, 12. On battle songs, see the Birdie Blackhawk Calico narrative in Gibson, *Family History*.

17. O. O. Howard, *My Life*, 406; *Idaho Statesman*, 7 July 1878, 11 July 1878, 16 July 1878; Hopkins, *Life*, 176; Davison, "Bannock-Piute War," 136.

18. O. O. Howard, *My Life*, 408–10; *Idaho Statesman*, 11 July 1878, 23 July 1878;

Dunlay, *Wolves*, 121 and ch. 5; Utley, *Frontier Regulars*, 327; Brimlow, *Bannock Indian War*, 136–39. On Natches, see ss, 24 June 1878.

19. Hopkins, *Life*, 184; *Idaho Statesman*, 23 July 1878, 25 July 1878, 27 July 1878; *Washington Standard*, 27 July, 1878; O. O. Howard, *My Life*, 410; Gregg, *Pioneer Days*, 141. Col. Frank Wheaton unequivocally states that the Umatillas brought in Egan's head; see Wheaton to McDowell, oia, 20 July 1878 (wire), lr, or Superintendency, roll 626. For other versions, see Brimlow, *Bannock Indian War*, 151–54, and Santee, "Egan," 20–24. A. H. Robie, who placed the reward on Egan's head, died shortly afterward without paying it, see the *Idaho Statesman*, 30 July 1878.

20. ss, 1 Aug. 1878; Hopkins, *Life*, 182–84; O. O. Howard, *My Life*, 416–17.

21. O. O. Howard, *My Life*, 413; Davison, "Bannock-Piute War," 141; *Idaho Statesman*, 25 July 1878; O. O. Howard, Report, 229–30; Utley, *Frontier Regulars*, 327; Hopkins, *Life*, 176.

22. Hopkins, *Life*, 178–80; *Idaho Statesman*, 6 Aug. 1878; O. O. Howard, Report, 228. Sarah's description of this engagement was copied nearly word for word from Forsyth's report. This reinforces the possibility that she was with Howard.

23. Davison, "Bannock-Piute War," 139–40; Hopkins, *Life*, 180–81.

24. Hopkins, *Life*, 178–81. Davison writes on 25 July of finding the baby after the "last attack"; see "Bannock-Piute War," 140. Sarah's mention of orders given by O. O. Howard for the baby's care indicates that she was with Howard, not Forsyth, at this point.

25. Hopkins, *Life*, 181; Davison, "Bannock-Piute War," 140; Morgan, *My Story*, 12; O. O. Howard, Report, 229.

26. Hopkins, *Life*, 178, 182.

27. O. O. Howard, *My Life*, 414, and Report, 230; Hopkins, *Life*, 182.

28. O. O. Howard, *Famous Indian Chiefs*, 237; Davison, "Bannock-Piute War," 138.

29. Davison, "Bannock-Piute War," 141; Hopkins, *Life*, 185–86.

30. Hopkins, *Life*, 185–87; Davison, "Bannock-Piute War," 141; O. O. Howard, Report, 232.

31. Hopkins, *Life*, 188–89

32. Hopkins, *Life*, 189–91; the *Idaho Statesman*, 20 July 1878, confirms the capture of women and children by the Umatillas, as does a telegram from Wheaton to McDowell; see McDowell to Secretary of War, oia, 19 July 1878, lr, or Superintendency, roll 626. Also see Gregg, *Pioneer Days*, 142. At

Sarah's arrival, the resemblance noted by Brumble to a traditional coup tale is especially strong; see Brumble, *American Indian Autobiography*, 66.

33. Hopkins, *Life*, 193–94.

34. Hopkins, *Life*, 193–95; Madsen, *Bannock*, 224–26. Brimlow confirms Umapine's presence with Forsyth's force (*Bannock Indian War*, 155), and O. O. Howard recounts Natches's speech of condemnation, (*My Life*, 410–11). On Oytes, see Louie, "History," in *A Lively Little History*, 5.

35. Hopkins, *Life*, 195–96; Brimlow, *Bannock Indian War*, 165–66; O. O. Howard, Report, 232–34.

36. *Idaho Statesman*, 30 July 1878; Davison, "Bannock-Piute War," 142; Hopkins, *Life*, 196.

37. Hopkins, *Life*, 197–99; ss, 27 June 1878, 10 July 1878; *New York Times*, 17 June 1878, 1.

38. Hopkins, *Life*, 198–99.

39. Hopkins, *Life*, 200; *Idaho Statesman*, 13 Aug. 1878; Brimlow, "Two Cavalrymen's Diaries," 251–52; McDowell to Secretary of War, oia, 12 July 1878, lr, or Superintendency, roll 626; aag to Commanding Officer, 10 Sept. 1878 and 12 Sept. 1878; O. O. Howard to aag, 13 Sept. 1878, in Secretary of War, *Annual Report*, 191–92.

40. Hopkins, *Life*, 200; O. O. Howard to aag, 10 Aug. 1878, 23 Aug. 1878, and 29 Aug. 1878, aag to O. O. Howard, 21 Aug. 1878 and 28 Aug. 1878, and McDowell to O. O. Howard, 23 Aug. 1878, 24 Aug. 1878, and 30 Aug. 1878, in Secretary of War, *Annual Report*, 185–90.

41. Hopkins, *Life*, 200–201; Wilkins to ag, oia, 28 Sept. 1878, lr, or Superintendency, roll 626.

42. Hopkins, *Life*, 201; aag to McDowell, oia, 4 Oct. 1878, lr, or Superintendency, roll 626.

11. YAKAMA RESERVATION

1. Rinehart to cia, 12 May 1879 and 31 May 1880, oia, "Case of Sarah Winnemucca"; Hopkins, *Life*, 190; *Territorial Enterprise*, 7 July 1886. Lewis to cia, 22 Dec. 1886, in Gibson, *Family History*.

2. Hopkins, *Life*, 203; O. O. Howard to McDowell, 23 Aug. 1878, and McDowell to O. O. Howard, 23 Aug. 1878, in Secretary of War, *Annual Report*, 187–88; *Idaho Statesman*, 15 Aug. 1878.

3. Hopkins, *Life*, 203–4.

4. Hopkins, *Life*, 204.

5. Hopkins, *Life*, 204–5.

6. Hopkins, *Life*, 205–7, 209; Inter-Tribal Council of Nevada, *Numa*, 46.

7. Hopkins, *Life*, 208.

8. Morgan, *My Story*, 11; Louie, "History," in *A Lively Little History*, 5; O. O. Howard, *My Life*, 414; Hopkins, *Life*, 209.

9. Hopkins, *Life*, 209–10; Wilbur to CIA, 25 Aug. 1879, *Exec. Documents*, 46th Cong., 2nd Sess., 1879–80, 9:264; Turner, *Red Men*, 165.

10. ss, 22 Jan. 1879; esp. see McDowell to AG, 21 Oct. 1878 and 27 June 1879, OIA, "Case of Sarah Winnemucca."

11. Wilbur to CIA, 31 May 1880, OIA, "Case of Sarah Winnemucca."

12. Van Arsdol, "Sarah," 3; O. O. Howard, *My Life*, 418; Hopkins, *Life*, 54–55, 215–16; Winnemucca, "Pah-Utes," 256 (quote). O. O. Howard's letter of 7 Nov. 1879 (qtd. in Hopkins, *Life*, 261) also supports the idea of Sarah's conversion at Yakama.

13. ss, 6 Sept, 1879; Wilbur to CIA, 25 Aug. 1879, Department of the Interior, *Report*, 1879–80, 9:264–65; Turner, *Red Men*, 166;

14. Hopkins, *Life*, 210–13; Milroy to CIA, 11 Aug. 1880, OIA, "Case of Sarah Winnemucca"; Wilbur to CIA, 25 Aug. 1879, Department of the Interior, *Report*, 1879–80, 9:264. On the stolen horses, see Lewis to CIA, 22 Dec. 1886, in Gibson, *Family History*.

15. O. O. Howard, *My Life*, 420; ss, 15 July 1879; Rinehart to CIA, 10 July 1881, OIA, "Case of Sarah Winnemucca"; Van Arsdol, "Sarah," 3.

16. Rinehart to CIA, 3 Mar. 1879 and 12 May 1879, OIA, "Case of Sarah Winnemucca"; ss, 12 June 1879, 6 Nov. 1879. Camps McDermit, Harney, and Bidwell were designated forts on 5 Apr. 1879.

17. ss, 6 Nov. 1879.

18. ss, 6 Nov. 1879. Two Captain Charleys spoke at the conference; the one quoted lived permanently in Paradise Valley.

19. On Natches, see ss, 13 July 1878; on Indian oratory, see O. O. Howard, *My Life*, 561–62.

20. *Alta California*, 26 Nov. 1879, 4 Dec. 1879; ss, 28 Nov. 1879 (reprint of article originally printed in *San Francisco Chronicle*); Haine, "A Belgian in the Gold Rush," 153–54. In his 1883 talk, Haine alludes to lectures Sarah gave "some ten years ago," but he clearly means her 1879 lectures, since he goes on to state that she afterward went to Washington DC with her family to seek justice for the Indians.

21. *Alta California*, 26 Nov. 1879, 4 Dec. 1879, 24 Dec. 1879; ss, 28 Nov. 1879 (re-

print of article originally printed in *San Francisco Chronicle*). None of Sarah's lectures were reprinted in their entirety, but liberal quotations appeared in the San Francisco newspapers.

22. Hopkins, *Life*, 207.

23. *Alta California*, 4 Dec. 1879; Brumble, *American Indian Autobiography*, 69; Ruoff, "American Indian Autobiographers," 252.

24. *Alta California* 26 Nov. 1879, 24 Dec. 1879; ss, 28 Nov. 1879 (reprint of article originally printed in *San Francisco Chronicle*).

25. ss, 16 Dec. 1879.

26. ss, 5 Jan. 1880, 16 Feb. 1880; *Alta California*, 24 Dec. 1879; Hopkins, *Life*, 217, 261–63.

12. WASHINGTON DC

1. Fowler and Fowler, *Anthropology*, 227–29, possibly narrated (and in more detail) by Natches, who related many of the Paiute myths to Powell.

2. ss, 14 Jan. 1880, 31 Jan. 1880; Turner, *Red Men*, xiv–xv; Hopkins, *Life*, 219, 222.

3. Trefousse, *Carl Schurz*, 230–35; 240–45; Hopkins, *Life*, 218–19.

4. Trefousse, *Carl Schurz*, 242–47; James Howard, *Ponca Tribe*, 32–39. Senator Dawes, among others prominent in the reform of Indian policy, sharply criticized Schurz; see Frederic Bancroft and Dunning, *Reminiscences of Carl Schurz*, 3:392. For a positive assessment of Schurz's Indian policy, see Schafer, *Carl Schurz: Militant Liberal*, 218–22 and n.99.

5. *Washington Post*, 20 Jan. 1880.

6. Hopkins, *Life*, 219–20; Brimlow, *Bannock Indian War*, 191.

7. The Schurz letter (misdated) is reprinted in Hopkins, *Life*, 223–24. Also see ss, 2 Feb. 1880.

8. Hopkins, *Life*, 205.

9. Hoogenboom, *Hayes*, 447–54; Williams, *Diary of Hayes*, 59.

10. Hopkins, *Life*, 221–22.

11. Turner, *Red Men*, 168; Hopkins, *Life*, 221. Brumble notes that Schurz's behavior offers convincing proof of the effectiveness of Sarah's lectures; see Brumble, *American Indian Autobiography*, 70. On Hayt, see the *Washington Post*, 30 Jan. 1880 and 31 Jan. 1880, and the *Washington Evening Star*, 30 Jan. 1880.

12. *Washington Post*, 20 Jan. 1880; ss, 31 Jan. 1880.

13. Rinehart to CIA, with enclosed petition and depositions, 15 Jan. 1880, OIA,

"Case of Sarah Winnemucca." Depositions were made by William Curry, Thomas O'Keefe, and W. W. Johnson.

14. Among these deposers and petition signers were John Muldrick, who had received a large contract from Rinehart for Malheur supplies; D. G. Overholt, who was a partner in the Canyon City Overholt and Muldrick firm that shared a common partner with Rinehart's firm; W. W. Johnson, who was a blacksmith employed at Malheur; J. H. Wood, J. W. Church, John Muldrick, Phil Metschan, F. C. Sels, and D. G. Overholt, all of whom had all signed the 1878 petition; William and Edwin Hall, who may have been related to Halls with different first names on the 1878 petition, as is also true of William Curry, who was perhaps related to the prime mover on that petition, George Curry. See esp. the petitions of 13 May 1878, and Mitchell to CIA 20 Feb. 1878, OIA, LR, OR Superintendency, roll 625. Sarah's letters of recommendation are reprinted in Hopkins, *Life*, 259–63. On the issue of Sarah's respectability, see Georgi-Findlay, "Frontiers," 229–30.

15. SS, 2 Feb. 1880, 18 Feb. 1880; Hopkins, *Life*, 223.

16. SS, 13 Feb. 1880.

17. Hopkins, *Life*, 224–25.

18. Hopkins, *Life*, 225.

19. SS, 16 Feb. 1880.

20. Rinehart to CIA, 20 Mar. 1880, OIA, "Case of Sarah Winnemucca"; Winnemucca to Rinehart, 4 Apr. 1880, same roll; Hopkins, *Life*, 226.

21. Hopkins, *Life*, 226. According to McKenna, author of "Wonderful Winnemucca Sisters," Sarah visited Elma in Montana in 1880 and Elma went to Pyramid with her. If Sarah went to Montana between mid-February and April and Elma then went to Pyramid and rode north with Sarah, this would fit the chronology of Sarah's known 1880 movements.

22. Hopkins, *Life*, 226. Although Sarah placed her departure in early April, her dates were often inaccurate, and the late April date given in SS (5 May 1880), which comports with the date Wilbur gave for her arrival at Yakama (Wilbur to CIA, 31 May 1880, OIA, "Case of Sarah Winnemucca"), is more probably accurate.

23. Hopkins, *Life*, 227–28.

24. Hopkins, *Life*, 228–29. On Hispanic cowboys in the area, see Brimlow, *Harney County*, 54.

25. Hopkins, *Life*, 230. Sarah calls this rancher James Beby. The closest name in early local histories is E. L. Beede; see Brimlow, *Harney County*, 216.

26. Hopkins, *Life*, 231. On Anderson, see Brimlow, *Harney County*, 61–62, 111.
27. Hopkins, *Life*, 231–32.
28. Hopkins, *Life*, 232; *Alta California*, 24 Dec. 1879.
29. Hopkins, *Life*, 234–35. On that year's harsh weather, see Brimlow, *Harney County*, 136, and Wilbur's reference to the unusual cold of April and May, Wilbur to CIA, 31 May 1880, OIA, "Case of Sarah Winnemucca."
30. Hopkins, *Life*, 234–35.
31. Hopkins, *Life*, 236.
32. Hopkins, *Life*, 237–38.
33. Hopkins, *Life*, 238–39.
34. Hopkins, *Life*, 239–40.
35. Wilbur to CIA, 31 May 1880, OIA, "Case of Sarah Winnemucca"; AAG to O. O. Howard, 28 Aug. 1878, in Secretary of War, *Annual Report*, 188; Hopkins, *Life*, 240.
36. SS, 10 July 1880; Hopkins, *Life*, 240–41.
37. Turner, *Red Men*, 171–74.
38. Turner, *Red Men*, 171–74.
39. Frederic Bancroft, *Speeches*, 3:501; Hopkins, *Life*, 221, 241. Schurz had, however, endorsed the CIA's recommendation to send the "ring leaders" to Yakama instead of imprisoning them at Alcatraz as O. O. Howard preferred; see Schurz to Secretary of War, 23 July 1879, in Gibson, *Family History*.

13. FORT VANCOUVER

1. Fowler and Fowler, *Anthropology*, 222–24.
2. Hopkins, *Life*, 241.
3. Liljeblad, *Idaho Indians*, 37–39; Dunlay, *Wolves*, 88.
4. O. O. Howard, *My Life*, 432; Hopkins, *Life*, 241, 244–45. Although Sarah writes of both Sheepeater and Weiser prisoners, Liljeblad, *Idaho Indians* (36–39), makes clear that this group was Sheepeater. On linguistics, see Liljeblad, "Indian Peoples," 37–38.
5. Hoogenboom, *Hayes*, 303; SS, 20 Sept. 1880; Turner, *Red Men*, 175; Geer, *First Lady*, 227; Hopkins, *Life*, 246.
6. SS, 9 Oct. 1880; Hopkins, *Life*, 213–14; Nelson A. Miles to Secretary of War, 21 Nov. 1881, and Arthur Chapman to Miles, 6 Dec. 1881, OIA, "Case of Sarah Winnemucca"; Brimlow, *Bannock Indian War*, 198; Trafzer, *Death Stalks*, 69, 91; Cook, *Epidemic of 1830–1833*; Helland, *There Were Giants*, 147; Lewis to CIA, 22 Dec. 1886, in Gibson, *Family History*.

7. Bischoff, "Aspects of Punishment," 278. On the suspicion, see Peabody to Mrs. Booth, 1882 or 1883, Massachusetts Historical Society, and Forbes, *Nevada Indians Speak*, 133.

8. SS, 2 Aug. 1880, 9 Oct. 1880; Van Arsdol, "Vancouver Barracks," 85, 104, 108, 115. On Duck Valley, see Crum, *The Road*, 35.

9. Wilbur to CIA, 27 Oct. 1881, and Chapman to Miles, 6 Dec. 1881, OIA, "Case of Sarah Winnemucca." Apparently, communication between the Interior and War Departments was poor, and the War Department appeared unaware that the Schurz letter had been rescinded; thus, Chapman's mission included arranging the departure of the Indians.

10. Chapman to Miles, 6 Dec. 1881 and 19 Dec. 1881; Wilbur to CIA, 27 Oct. 1881; OIA to Secretary of the Interior, 18 Nov. 1881; Rinehart to CIA, 10 July 1881; CIA to Secretary of the Interior; O. O. Howard to AG, 16 Dec. 1882. All in OIA, "Case of Sarah Winnemucca"; SS, 23 July 1881; Helland, *There Were Giants*, 147 (last quote). On Wilbur's treatment of disobedient Indians, see a misdated account of his arrest of the religious leader Smohalla, in Coe, "Indian Agent's Experience," 65–67.

11. Milroy to CIA, 11 Aug. 1883, OIA, "Case of Sarah Winnemucca"; Bishoff, "Aspects of Punishment," 279; Indian Rights Association, *Proceedings of the Mohonk Lake Conference*, 1886, 13; Helland, *There Were Giants*, 171–72, 181; Whitner, "Grant's Peace Policy," 53; Fenton, "Father Wilbur," 16. The narrative of Clara Thompson also relates how the Paiutes "secretly snuck" out of Yakama, see Gibson, *Family History*.

12. Wilbur to CIA, 27 Oct. 1881, OIA, "Case of Sarah Winnemucca"; O. O. Howard, *My Life*, 420; SS, 8 Dec. 1884; Fenton, "Father Wilbur," 21. On the Harney Valley violence and the Paddy Caps band, see Crum, *The Road*, 47, and SS, 3 Feb. 1885, 25 June 1885, and 18 July 1885.

13. On morning prayers, see Inter-Tribal Council of Nevada, *Numa*, 3–4; on Leggins's count, see Lewis to CIA, 22 Dec. 1886, in Gibson, *Family History*.

14. Wilbur to CIA, 27 Oct. 1881, OIA, "Case of Sarah Winnemucca"; SS, 12 July 1881.

15. Hopkins, *Life*, 242; SS, 12 July 1881.

16. Sarah's protest against the army's failure to pay her for her services during the Bannock War suggests that the article was written prior to her stint at Vancouver, which began in the summer of 1880. Her mention of appeals to fellow Methodists in San Francisco places it after her 1879 lectures there. Signing herself as Winnemucca, which she would not have

done after her Dec. 1881 marriage to Hopkins, sets it before that date. See Sarah Winnemucca, "The Pah-Utes," 252–56 and Jackson, *A Century*, 395–96 (also in the *Gold Hill News*, 28 Apr. 1870).

17. Hopkins military service records; ss, 8 Dec. 1881. The *Helena Daily Herald*, however, stated at the time of Sarah's death that the Hopkinses married in Helena; see 4 Nov. 1891.

18. Hopkins military service records. A slight age discrepancy between Hopkins's two enlistments leaves it unclear whether he was born in 1849 or 1850. On Hopkins's previous rank, see Brimlow, "Two Cavalrymen's Diaries," 252 n.149. See also *Reese River Reveille*, 21 Oct. 1887.

19. Ranck, "Pacific Coast Pocahontas," 44.

20. ss, 8 Dec. 1881; Hopkins military service records; O. O. Howard, Report, 222, 227–29.

21. O. O. Howard, Report, 235; Ranck, "Pacific Coast Pocahontas," 44; Brimlow, "Two Cavalrymen's Diaries," 251–52. Although the slanderous letters generated by Rinehart must be skeptically viewed, it should be noted that one accused Sarah of living with an enlisted man other than Hopkins at Harney, as well as of prostitution; see undated affidavit of Thomas O'Keefe, OIA, "Case of Sarah Winnemucca."

22. Bancroft scraps, 54. On epaulets, see *Alta California*, 24 Dec. 1879.

23. Edward C. Bartlett veterans' pensions file and military service records; *San Francisco Chronicle*, 23 Nov. 1879; Hattori, "Swear Like Pirates," 236–38; Hopkins, *Life*, 48. On Paiute culture, see Wheat, *Survival Arts*, 97. Despite the possible effects of gonorrhea, Bartlett fathered two children during his second marriage; see Edward C. Bartlett veterans' pension file and military records.

24. ss, 9 Jan. 1882.

25. *Dillon (ID) Tribune*, 25 Feb. 1882.

26. ss, 19 Sept. 1879, 22 Oct. 1881, 10 Dec. 1881.

27. ss, 15 Sept. 1880, 21 June 1881, 22 Oct. 1881, 15 Dec. 1881, 7 Aug. 1882, 27 Sept. 1882; *Paradise (NV) Reporter*, 30 Aug. 1879; *Nevada State Journal*, 25 Oct. 1959, in Wheat Papers.

28. For historic descriptions of the Surprise Valley, see Steward and Wheeler-Voegelin, *Paiute Indians*, 159–60. On the habitats of Paiute bands, see C. S. Fowler, *Park's Notes*, 1–4.

29. ss, 9 Oct. 1882, 27 Oct. 1882.

30. ss, 16 Sept. 1882, 27 Sept. 1882, 31 Oct. 1882; *Reno Evening Gazette*, 11 Nov. 1882.

31. ss, 27 Sept. 1882, 31 Oct. 1882.

32. ss, 31 Oct. 1882, 4 Nov. 1882, 23 Dec. 1882; Hopkins, *Life*, 96–98; Inter-Tribal Council of Nevada, *Numa*, 68–69.

14. BOSTON

1. Peabody, *Practical Solution*, 24; O'Connell, *Boston*, 1. On the centrality of Boston in Indian reform, see Dippie, *Vanishing American*, 155.

2. Wilson, *Bright Eyes*, esp. 210, 219, 227–41, 266–82; Franks, "La Flesche Family," 324–27.

3. James, *Bostonians*, 20, 147; Tharp, *Peabody Sisters*, 213, 321. The identification of Peabody with Birdseye is discussed by Ronda (*Letters*, 396).

4. Tharp, *Peabody Sisters*, 138; Peabody to Bacon, [1883], Straker Collection; Morrison, *Chief Sarah*, 141; Peabody to [?], 25 May 1886, Peabody Letters.

5. Peabody, *Practical Solution*, 27 n.1 (quote). Mann's mention of a "dying charge" from Winnemucca to write the book is dubious. Winnemucca may have expressed this wish but not during his final illness when, so far as we know, Sarah was not present; see Mann's preface to Hopkins, *Life*.

6. Swann and Krupat, introduction, ix; Sands, "Personal Narrative," 269. On multiple audiences, see Velie and Vizenor, introduction, 8–9. On the vindication element, see Ruoff, "American Indian Autobiographers," 262–63. Brumble takes note of Sarah's "tribal sense of self," (*American Indian Autobiography*, 66); Winnemucca, "Pah-Utes," 256.

7. Mann's preface to Hopkins, *Life*; Hirschfelder, *American Indian and Eskimo Authors*. Sarah's chronological place in the roster of authors will of course vary with what is classified as a book.

8. Tharp, *Peabody Sisters*, 327; Sarah Winnemucca, 1860, letter (copy held in the Nevada Historical Society); Corbusier, *Verde to San Carlos*, 94.

9. C. S. Fowler, "Sarah Winnemucca," 40–41; Mann to Eleanor Lewis, 25 Apr. 1883, Straker Collection.

10. Hopkins, *Life*, ch. 4, 166; O. O. Howard, Report, 216, 227–28.

11. C. S. Fowler, "Sarah Winnemucca," 40. On different forms of memory, see Schacter, *Searching for Memory*. The principal incident in Sarah's narrative that I could not confirm was the Joe Lindsay affair (Hopkins, *Life*, 103–4). Lindsay did commit a murder, but the victim was not Indian. Apparently, Sarah mistakenly transposed his name to another incident.

12. J. Miller, "Basin Religion," 76; Brumble, *American Indian Autobiography*, 71. Ruoff notes that dialogue strengthens Sarah's case by enabling her to use

the testimony of witnesses ("American Indian Autobiographers," 264), and, as Brumble points out, witnesses are an important part of the coup tale that Sarah's narrative resembles (*American Indian Autobiography*, 26–27, 72).

13. Ruoff, "American Indian Autobiographers," 263; Brumble, *American Indian Autobiography*, 64–66; Georgi-Findlay, "Frontiers," 238.

14. Lape, "Cultural Liminality," 274–75; Brumble, *American Indian Autobiography*, 64; Georgi-Findlay, "Frontiers," 229. On myth as an integral part of personal and tribal history, see Ruoff, "American Indian Autobiographers," 257.

15. Swann and Krupat, introduction, xii; C. S. Fowler, "Sarah Winnemucca," 40. As Sands notes, autobiography "is not an indigenous form of literature" for Indians, "Personal Narrative," 270–71.

16. Peabody to Edwin M. Bacon, [1883], Straker Collection; C. S. Fowler, "Sarah Winnemucca," 38; Anna L. Dawes diary, 2–6 Oct. 1883, and Peabody to Dawes, 12 Nov. 1883 and 2 Mar. 1886, Dawes Papers.

17. Peabody to Bacon, [1883], Straker Collection.

18. Sylvia H. Delano to Peabody, 21 June 1884, Straker Collection (quote); Hopkins military service records.

19. C. S. Fowler, "Sarah Winnemucca," 38; ss, 7 Nov. 1883, 5 Dec. 1883.

20. ss, 7 Nov. 1883; Wren, *History*, 306.

21. Peabody, *Practical Solution*, 5, 28, and *Second Report*, 5; ss, 5 Dec. 1883.

22. Peabody, *Practical Solution*, 25.

23. ss, 5 Dec. 1883; Peabody, *Practical Solution*, 16, 24; Canfield, *Sarah*, 234–35; Elizabeth P. Bond to Peabody, 9 Dec. 1885, Straker Collection.

24. On the reform organizations, see Prucha, *Great Father*, ch. 24. On Grant's policy, see Levine, "Indian Fighters," 336–42, and Dippie, *Vanishing American*, 144–48.

25. Peabody to Dawes, 12 Nov. 1883, Dawes Papers. On Bland, see Prucha, *Great Father*, ch. 24.

26. Hopkins testimony, 22 Apr. 1884, Hedrick Papers; Canfield, *Sarah*, 204. Also see Peabody to Dawes, 12 Nov. 1883, Dawes Papers (quote). On Bland, see Prucha, *Great Father*, 628.

27. O. O. Howard to Mann, 13 Sept. 1883, Straker Collection; Canfield, *Sarah*, 205.

28. M. Jarvis to Mann, 17 Apr. 1884, Straker Collection; ss, 5 Dec. 1883.

29. Hopkins testimony, 22 Apr. 1884; Peabody to Dawes, 12 Nov. 1883, Dawes Papers (quote).

30. Hopkins testimony, 22 Apr. 1884; Mann to Lewis, 17 Nov. 1883 and 24 Dec. 1883, Straker Collection; Hopkins, *Life*, 247; SS, 8 Dec. 1884; Nevada Legislature, *Journal of the Senate*, 1883, 176–77; Peabody to John D. Long, [27] Mar. 1884, Long Papers, courtesy of the Massachusetts Historical Society (quote). On the Cheyennes, see Josephy, *Indian Heritage*, 342.

31. Hopkins testimony, 22 Apr. 1884; SS, 12 May 1884; *Washington Post*, 23 Apr. 1884, 2; Peabody to Long, [27] Mar. 1884, Long Papers (quote).

32. Hopkins testimony, 22 Apr. 1884.

33. Hopkins testimony, 22 Apr. 1884.

34. Hopkins testimony, 22 Apr. 1884.

35. Peabody, *Second Report*, 10; S. H. Delano to Peabody, 21 June 1884, Straker Collection; Canfield, *Sarah*, 215; Peabody to Dawes, [9] Nov. 1884, Dawes Papers.

36. Peabody, *Second Report*, 8; Peabody to Dawes, [9] Nov. 1884, Dawes Papers.

37. Peabody, *Second Report*, 10; Hopkins testimony, 22 Apr. 1884. On Fort McDermit, see Inter-Tribal Council of Nevada, *Numa*, 48–49. On Paiute fears of a return to Yakama, see SS, 14 July 1884. For a very different assessment of Sarah's success, see Canfield, *Sarah*, 214–15.

15. LOVELOCK

1. Inter-Tribal Council of Nevada, *Numa*, 62; Fowler and Fowler, *Anthropology*, 224–25; Hermann, *Paiutes*, 224–29; Cerveri, *The Ways*, 86, 99.

2. SS, 30 Aug. 1884; Knack and Stewart, *As Long*, 149–56, 167–75, 192; Sarah Winnemucca to Peabody, qtd. in Peabody to Dawes, [9] Nov. 1884, Dawes Papers.

3. SS, 14 July 1884; Peabody to Dawes, 9 Nov. 1884, Dawes Papers.

4. Peabody, *Second Report*, 9–11.

5. Twain, *Roughing It*, 255; McKaskia S. Bonnifield to Peabody, 1 July 1885, OIA, "Case of Sarah Winnemucca."

6. *San Francisco Call*, 22 Feb. 1885.

7. Peabody, *Second Report*, 10; SS, 11 Sept. 1884; Tharp, *Peabody Sisters*, 26, 35.

8. SS, 11 Sept. 1884; *Reese River Reveille*, 6 Sept. 1884.

9. *Carson Appeal*, 16 Sept. 1884.

10. *Reese River Reveille*, 17 Sept. 1884.

11. SS, 24 June 1885; *Reese River Reveille*, 12 Dec. 1884; Peabody, *Practical Solution*, 35 n.1; Williams, interviews; Marjorie Dupée, tribal elder, interview by author, 29 Apr. 1998 (Lovelock NV). See also the statements against Sa-

rah allegedly made by Pyramid Reservation Indians to Indian Inspector Robert Gardner, in the *Nevada State Journal*, 28 Feb. 1885. Bright Eyes was also ostracized by her people after her return; see Wilson, *Bright Eyes*, 315.

12. *Reese River Reveille*, 20 Nov. 1884; *Alta California*, 4 Dec. 1879; Inter-Tribal Council of Nevada, *Numa*, 69; ss, 17 Oct. 1884. On Chinese liquor sales, see, for example, ss, 12 May 1876.

13. ss, 1 Nov. 1884, 11 Nov. 1884, 15 Nov. 1884, 26 Nov. 1884.

14. William D. C. Gibson to Judge Pearson, 30 Dec. 1884 and to CIA, 31 Jan. 1885, both in OIA, "Case of Sarah Winnemucca"; *San Francisco Call*, 22 Feb. 1885; ss, 24 Feb. 1885.

15. Gibson to Pearson, 30 Dec. 1884 and to CIA, 31 Jan. 1885, both in OIA, "Case of Sarah Winnemucca"; Peabody to Dawes, 10 Mar. 1885, Dawes Papers.

16. *San Francisco Call*, 22 Feb. 1885; ss, 26 Jan. 1885, 11 Mar. 1885; *Nevada State Journal*, 1 Feb. 1885.

17. *San Francisco Call*, 22 Jan. 1885; *Reese River Reveille*, 12 Dec. 1884.

18. *San Francisco Call*, 4 Feb. 1885; ss, 6 Feb. 1885.

19. Wilson, *Bright Eyes*, esp. 314–17; Peabody to Dawes, [9] Nov. 1884, Dawes Papers.

20. Peabody, *Second Report*, 10–11; ss, 12 Mar. 1885.

21. *San Francisco Call*, 24 May 1885; ss, 24 June 1885.

22. *San Francisco Call*, 24 May 1885; ss, 24 June 1885. On changing burial practices, see for instance, the burial of Buena Vista John's daughter, ss, 3 Sept. 1884.

23. John T. Reid and J. R. Hunter, "Humboldt County," in Davis, *History*, II, 893–95; ss, 6 Jan. 1885; Williams, interviews.

24. Inter-Tribal Council of Nevada, *Numa*, 39–43; ss, 9 Nov. 1885, 10 Dec. 1885; Williams, interviews. Tribal members interviewed by Brimlow ("Life of Sarah Winnemucca," 118) described the relationship differently and, in my view, less plausibly; however, in both versions, Sarah was related to leading members of the Lovelock band.

25. ss, 7 May 1885, 17 Aug. 1885; Bonnifield to Peabody, 1 July 1885, OIA, "Case of Sarah Winnemucca." Although Peabody believed the ranch had been given to Natches, the deed and the newspaper report on the sale indicate that he purchased it; see Humboldt County, *Deeds*, 14 May 1885, book 26, 254–58, and ss, 7 May 1885.

26. Bonnifield to Peabody, 1 July 1885, OIA, "Case of Sarah Winnemucca"; Peabody to Dawes, [9] Nov. 1884 and ca. 19 Mar. 1885, Dawes Papers.

27. Adams, *Education for Extinction*, 21–24, 214.

28. C. S. Fowler, "Sarah Winnemucca," 33, 41; Winnemucca, "Pah-Utes," 255–56.

29. Peabody, *Practical Solution*, 1, 3, and *Second Report*, 2, 13; SS, 9 July 1886; Peabody to Dawes, 9 Mar. 1886, Dawes Papers.

30. Adams, *Education for Extinction*, 211–15; *Territorial Enterprise*, 7 July 1886.

31. Adams, *Education for Extinction*, 213; SS, 17 May 1886; Gibson to CIA, 31 Jan. 1885, OIA, "Case of Sarah Winnemucca."

32. Williams, interviews.

33. *Nevada State Journal*, 24 Oct. 1885; SS, 26 June 1885, 4 Aug. 1885.

34. Mann to Lewis, 25 May 1885 and 7 Sept. 1885; *Nevada State Journal*, 7 May 1885; Peabody to Stuart, 13 May [?], Mrs. E. G. Stuart Papers; Rose E. Cleveland to Peabody, 18 Nov. 1885, Straker Collection. In her 25 May letter, Mann mentions a "huge gift of seeds" for Natches's spring planting from "Ben" in the Agricultural Bureau, but it is not clear whether this was assistance from the federal government.

35. George W. Curtis to Peabody, 22 Nov. 1885, and Warren Delano to Peabody, 2 Nov. 1885, Straker Collection. Peabody to Dawes, 2 Mar. 1886, Dawes Papers, and to [?] 21 May 1886, Peabody Letters.

36. Amelia B. James to Peabody, 18 Dec. 1885; Bond to Peabody, 9 Dec. 1885 and 19 Dec. 1885, both in the Straker Collection; Peabody to Long, [27] Mar. 1884, Long Papers.

37. Bond to Peabody, 9 Dec. 1885, Straker Collection (first quote); Peabody to Long, Mar. 1884, Long Papers (second quote).

38. Peabody, *Practical Solution*, 4–7 (quote); SS, 14 Apr. 1886, 6 July 1886, 28 July 1886.

39. SS, 6 July 1886, 18 July 1886; Peabody, *Practical Solution*, 17–18 (quote).

40. Peabody, *Practical Solution*, 9, 17.

41. Peabody, *Practical Solution*, 20–21; SS, 3 Nov. 1885, 20 Feb. 1886.

42. Peabody, *Practical Solution*, 10–11.

43. Peabody, *Practical Solution*, 1, 22. On government policy, see Adams, *Education for Extinction*, 21, 55–59.

44. Adams, *Education for Extinction*, 214, 217–18, 224–25, 228–31; Child, *Boarding School Seasons*, 6, 13; Lomawaima, *Prairie Light*, 121.

45. SS, 25 Apr. 1887, 27 Apr. 1887, 29 Apr. 1887, 6 June 1887; Canfield, *Sarah*, 289 n.20; Dupée, interview. The 1880 census carried out under Natches's direction counted 2,965 Paiutes and did not include mixed-blood Paiute/

Shoshones; see ss, 11 June 1880. On Paiute resistance to the Colorado boarding school, see Knack and Stewart, *As Long*, 98–99.

46. ss, 5 Jan. 1886.

47. ss, 5 Jan. 1886. On the north wind, see Fowler and Fowler, *Anthropology*, 243.

48. ss, 5 Jan. 1886.

49. ss, 17 Aug. 1886, 20 Aug. 1886, 25 Aug. 1886, 28 Aug. 1886, 30 Aug. 1886, 2 Sept. 1886.

50. ss: 1 Dec. 1886, 4 Dec. 1886, 6 Jan. 1887, 19 Apr. 1887, 22 Apr. 1887, 21 Oct. 1887, 2 Dec. 1887, 9 Dec. 1887; 7 Jan. 1888, 12 Jan. 1888, 23 Jan. 1888.

51. *Reese River Reveille*, 2 Aug. 1886 (quote); ss, 21 Aug. 1886; Peabody, *Practical Solution*, 34. On the medal, see the *San Francisco Chronicle*, 23 Nov. 1879.

52. Peabody, *Practical Solution*, 32–33 (quote); Peabody to Stuart, 13 May and undated fragment, Mrs. E. G. Stuart Papers.

53. Peabody, *Practical Solution*, 34; W. Delano to Peabody, 27 Sept. 1886, Straker Collection.

54. Peabody, *Practical Solution*, 33–34.

55. Peabody, *Practical Solution*, 17.

56. Williams, interviews; ss, 6 June 1885.

57. W. Delano to Peabody, 27 Sept. 1886, and to Winnemucca, (Peabody's copy) 6 May 1886, Straker Collection; Peabody to Dawes, [9] Nov. 1884, Dawes Papers (quote); *Nevada State Journal*, 2 Sept. 1886.

58. Peabody to Stuart, undated fragment, Mrs. E. G. Stuart Papers (first quote); Peabody to Anna C. Lowell, 26 Dec. 1886, in Ronda, *Letters*, 438–40 (second quote); Peabody, *Practical Solution*, 35–36.

59. Peabody to Lowell, 26 Dec. 1886, in Ronda, *Letters*, 438–40; Mann to Lewis, Nov. 1886, 26 Jan. 1887, Straker Collection; Peabody to Dawes, Mar. 1887, Dawes Papers; Canfield, *Sarah*, 248; Peabody, *Second Report*, 15.

60. Tharp, *Peabody Sisters*, 27, 338; Peabody to Ednah D. Cheney, May 1887 (quote), and Peabody to Ellen D. Conway, 28 June 1880, in Ronda, *Letters*, 443–44; Peabody to Long, May 1884, Long Papers; Peabody, *Practical Solution*, 34.

61. Peabody, *First Report*, 16; ss, 3 June 1887. On industrial training, see Adams, *Education for Extinction*, 149, and "Proceedings of informal Indian meeting," 7 July 1885, Dawes Papers. Since Sarah's school already included the elements of industrial training, the proposed school would have been a change only in name and scale.

62. W. Delano to Peabody, 12 Oct. 1887, Straker Collection; Canfield, *Sarah*, 250. On Coyote, see Fowler and Fowler, *Anthropology*, 222.

63. SS, 18 July 1887, 21 Sept. 1887, 26 Sept. 1887; W. Delano to Peabody, 12 Oct. 1887, Straker Collection. A letter signed "Pale Face," probably generated or written by Sarah, claimed that Natches had no right to a crop on which he had done no work, (see SS, 26 Sept. 1887), but given the many crops Natches had raised on his land over the years, this is hardly credible. The letter mainly demonstrates the bitter feeling between Sarah and Natches.

64. SS, 20 Oct. 1887; Canfield, *Sarah*, 253–54; *Reese River Reveille*, 21 Oct. 1887. Lewis's name does not appear on the cemetery list of remaining tombstones.

16. HENRY'S LAKE

1. In his careful dating of the Ghost Dance, Hittman concludes that ceremonies began in December, 1888 prior to Wovoka's "great revelation" on 1 Jan. 1889 (*Wovoka*, 65–66). Also see Mooney, *Ghost Dance*, 134, and Zanjani, *Ghost Dance Winter*, 26.

2. SS, 16 Mar. 1889. Hittman notes that Wodziwob's message was far more militant than Wovoka's, see *Wovoka*, 97–98.

3. Hopkins, *Life*, 129.

4. SS, 25 Feb. 1888, 26 Mar. 1888. On McDermit, see Inter-Tribal Council, *Numa*, 48.

5. SS, 13 Feb. 1889, 16 Mar. 1889. On Wovoka's message, see Hittman, *Wovoka*, esp. 101–2, and Mooney, *Ghost Dance*, 139–46. On variations, see Hittman, *Wovoka*, 98, and Smith, *Moon of Popping Trees*, esp. 74. Evidently, many believed that Wovoka was predicting the destruction of Indians who "tried to be on the whites' side," perhaps sometimes interpreted to mean English speakers. The only evidence that Sarah's school operated into 1889 is slight: an SS reprint of an *Idaho Statesman* item that apparently conflates Sarah (who never wrote and illustrated stories, as Bright Eyes did) with Bright Eyes (who taught in the 1870s but never operated her own school).

6. Williams, interviews; Dupée, interview; Inter-Tribal Council, *Numa*, 40–41.

7. Williams, interviews; Peabody to Dawes, 2 Feb. 1886, Dawes Papers.

8. Williams, interviews. On pinyon nutting, see Wheat, *Survival Arts*, 29–31.

9. Wheat, *Survival Arts*, 29–37.

10. SS, 2 Apr. 1888, 13 June 1888, 16 June 1888.

11. ss, 23 Dec. 1876, 3 June 1889.

12. ss, 3 July 1889. Although ss refers to Ferguson as a brother of Sarah, other sources make clear that he was a cousin; the 1900 and 1910 U.S. censuses for Idaho list his age differently but the 1840 birth date best fits his presence on the California trip.

13. On Paiute-Shoshone relations, see *Reese River Reveille* clippings, 3 July 1869, 17 Aug. 1871, box 4, Wheat Papers.

14. *Elko Free Press*, 5 Oct. 1889. On alarm among Nevada settlers over the Ghost Dance, see Zanjani, *Ghost Dance Winter*, 25–38.

15. *Elko Independent*, 30 Sept. 1889.

16. ss, 27 Nov. 1876; U.S. census for Nevada, 1920; Dupée, interview; Peabody to Dawes, 2 Mar. 1886, Dawes Papers. On California farms, see Burchell, "Opportunity and the Frontier," 189–90. One of the Lovelock Paiutes believed that Natches had lost his ranch in gambling, but considering his lack of reputation as a gambler and his known difficulties, this seems unlikely; see Inter-Tribal Council, *Numa*, 40. On Wovoka's powers over weather and the severe winter of 1889–90, see Hittman, *Wovoka*, 67–68.

17. ss, 16 Nov. 1889. See Humboldt County, *Deeds*, book 30, 254, *Mortgages*, book E, 318, 353, and the Humboldt County tax records. Natches appears in these records as Natches Overton. I am much indebted to Ruth Danner, Deputy Humboldt County Clerk, for tracing these records.

18. Williams, interviews.

19. Strahorn, *Fifteen Thousand Miles*, 1:256; Jane Daniels, Island Park Historical Society archivist, interviews, 7 Aug. 1997 and 13 Aug. 1997.

20. Strahorn, *Fifteen Thousand Miles*, 1:256, 258; Tamra Cikaitoga, "Family Fills Museum" clipping, Island Park Historical Society archives.

21. Strahorn, *Fifteen Thousand Miles*, 1:258.

22. U.S. census, Idaho, 1900; Daniels, interviews; McKenna, "Winnemucca Sisters."

23. McKenna, "Winnemucca Sisters."

24. Daniels, interviews.

25. Lillian Culver diary, 13 June 1890, 4 [July] 1890, privately held.

26. Williams, interviews; Culver diary, [14 July 1890].

27. On Wounded Knee, see Smith, *Moon of Popping Trees*.

28. ss, 9 Jan. 1891; Taylor Dalton, letter, 6 Jan. 1891 in the *Nevada State Journal*, 8 Jan. 1891; *Chloride Belt*, 7 Jan. 1891. On the Ghost Dance in Nevada, see Zanjani, *Ghost Dance Winter*, 25–41.

29. Culver diary, 27 Apr. 1891.

30. Culver diary, 6 Aug. 1891.

31. Stewart, "Sarah," 39; Canfield, *Sarah*, 259; *Bozeman Chronicle*, 28 Oct. 1891. On the longevity of Sarah's family: Tuboitony had died in a massacre; Mary had died young of unknown causes; Tom's age at death is not known; but Natches, Lee, and Elma all lived to be much older than Sarah, and Truckee and Winnemucca died at very advanced ages.

32. Morrison, *Chief Sarah*, 158; Culver diary, 17 Oct. 1891.

33. On Sherwood's verdict, see Canfield, *Sarah*, 259.

34. Stewart, "Sarah," 39; Culver diary, 16 Aug. 1892.

35. U.S. Census for Idaho, 1910. On Ferguson's death, see the Island Park Historical Society archives.

36. Williams, interviews.

37. Ainsworth reminiscence. Ainsworth's meaning when she says "below" the Richards house is not clear: I have taken her to mean farther down the slope, but it is possible that she means underneath the house.

38. Canfield, *Sarah*, 259.

39. On Paiute beliefs, see Fowler and Fowler, *Anthropology*, 242, 246.

EPILOGUE

1. Alexandra Voorhees, interview by author, Reno NV, 9 Jan. 1998; Phillip I. Earl, interviews by author, Reno NV, 28 Aug. 1997 and 21 Jan. 1998; Daryl Crawford to Bob Bentley, 16 May 1994; anonymous letter to "Neighbors," 11 May 1994, in the Hedrick Papers.

2. Guy L. Rocha, telephone interview by author, 7 Jan. 1998; Dan Coppa, interview by author, Reno NV, 24 Sept. 1998; Voorhees, interview; Georgia Hedrick, telephone interviews by author, 17 Jan. 1998 and 21 Jan. 1998.

3. Voorhees, interview; Coppa, interview; Hedrick, interviews.

4. Voorhees, interview; Dupée, interview.

5. Voorhees, interview.

6. Peabody to Dawes, 12 Nov. 1883, Dawes Papers.

7. Hopkins, *Life*, 258–59.

8. Earl, interviews; Voorhees, interview; Rusty Crook, telephone interview by author, 9 Sept. 1998; John Collins to Steve Mulvenon, n.d. and Debbie [?] to Steve [Mulvenon], n.d., Hedrick Papers. On the "taste of the age," see Ruoff, "American Indian Autobiographers," 269.

9. I am indebted to Peggy Lear Bowen, former chairman of the Nevada In-

dian Commission, for her insights on current attitudes (interview with author, Reno NV, 31 Jan. 1998). Sands observes that the Indian woman who writes a book risks tribal censure; see "Personal Narrative," 273.

10. Voorhees, interview; Hedrick, interviews; Dupée, interview.

Bibliography

MANUSCRIPT MATERIALS AND GOVERNMENT DOCUMENTS

Ainsworth, Rosetta. Reminiscence. Idaho State Historical Society, Boise.

Bancroft Scraps (scrapbook). Vol. 93. Bancroft Library, University of California, Berkeley.

Bartlett, Edward C. Veterans pension file and military service records. RG 94. National Archives, Washington DC.

Dawes, Henry L. Papers. Manuscript Division. Library of Congress.

Hopkins, Lewis H. Military service records. RG 94. National Archives, Washington DC.

Howard, Oliver O. Report. In Secretary of War, *Annual Report for the Year* 1878. Vol. 1. 45th Cong., 3rd sess. Washington DC: GPO, 1878. 207–36.

Hutcheson, Austin E. "Before the Comstock, 1857–1858: Memoirs of William Hickman Doleman." Special Collections. University of Nevada, Reno, Libraries.

Island Park Historical Society Archives, Island Park ID.

Long, John Davis. Papers. Massachusetts Historical Society, Boston.

Nevada Legislature. *Journal of the Assembly,* 1875. Carson City NV, 1875.

——. *Journal of the Senate,* 1875. Carson City NV, 1875.

——. *Journal of the Senate,* 1883. Carson City NV, 1883.

Ord, Edward O. C. Report. In Secretary of War, *Annual Report,* 1870–1871. Vol. 1. 41st Cong., 3rd. sess. Washington DC: GPO, 1871.

Peabody, Elizabeth P. Letters. Special Collections. Owen D. Young Library, St. Lawrence University, Canton NY.

Record of Events in Post Returns, Fort McDermit, Aug. 1865–Dec. 1875. National Archives Microfilm Publication M617. Returns of U.S. Military Posts, 1800–1916. Roll 666.

Rinehart, William V. Unpublished manuscript and correspondence. Bancroft Library, University of California, Berkeley.

Secretary of War. *Annual Report for the Year* 1878. 45th Cong., 3rd sess. Washington DC: GPO, 1878.

Straker, Robert L. Straker Collection. Antiochiana. Antioch College, Yellow Springs OH.

Stuart, Mrs. E. G. Papers. Schlesinger Library, Radcliffe College, Cambridge MA.

347

Bibliography

U.S. Congress. Report of the Joint Special Committee. *Condition of the Indian Tribes.* 39th Cong., 2nd sess. Washington DC: GPO, 1867.

U.S. Department of the Interior. *Report,* 1868–69. 40th Cong., 3rd sess. Washington DC: GPO, 1869.

U.S. Department of the Interior. *Report,* 1879–80. 46th Cong., 2nd sess. Washington DC: GPO, 1880.

U.S. Office of Indian Affairs. "The Case of Sarah Winnemucca." Nevada Superintendency. Special files. Roll 74, file 268. National Archives, Washington DC.

———. Letters Received. Nevada Superintendency. RG 75, M234. National Archives, Washington DC.

———. Letters Received. Oregon Superintendency. RG75, M234. National Archives, Washington DC.

Van Arsdol, Ted. "Vancouver Barracks," 85–121. Pacific Northwest Collection, University of Washington Libraries, Seattle.

Wheat, Margaret. Papers. Special Collections. University of Nevada, Reno, Libraries.

BOOKS AND ARTICLES

Adams, David Wallace. *Education for Extinction: American Indians and the Boarding School Experience,* 1875–1928. Lawrence: University Press of Kansas, 1995.

Ambrose, Stephen E. *Crazy Horse and Custer: The Parallel Lives of Two American Warriors.* New York: Doubleday, 1975.

Angel, Myron, ed. *History of Nevada.* Oakland: Thompson and West, 1881.

Bancroft, Frederic, ed. *Speeches, Correspondence, and Political Papers of Carl Schurz.* 6 vols. New York: G. P. Putnam's Sons, 1913.

Bancroft, Frederic, and William A. Dunning, eds. *The Reminiscences of Carl Schurz.* 3 vols. New York: Doubleday, 1908.

Bancroft, Hubert H. *History of California.* Vol. 6. San Francisco: History Company, 1888.

Bayer, C. W. *Profit, Plots, and Lynching.* Carson City NV: Privately printed, 1995.

Bischoff, Matt. "Aspects of Punishment: Indian Removal in Northern Nevada." *Nevada Historical Society Quarterly* 37 (winter 1994): 263–81.

Brady, Cyrus T. *Northwestern Fights and Fighters.* 1907. Reprint, Lincoln: University of Nebraska Press, 1979.

Brimlow, George F. *The Bannock Indian War of 1878.* Caldwell ID: Caxton, 1938.

Bibliography

——. *Harney County, Oregon and Its Range Land.* Burns OR: Harney County Historical Society, 1980.

——. "The Life of Sarah Winnemucca: The Formative Years." *Oregon Historical Quarterly* 53 (June 1952): 103–34.

——. "Two Cavalrymen's Diaries of the Bannock War, 1878: I. Lt. William Carey Brown." *Oregon Historical Quarterly* 68 (Sept. 1967): 221–58.

——. "Two Cavalrymen's Diaries of the Bannock War, 1878: II. Pvt. Frederick W. Mayer." *Oregon Historical Quarterly* 68 (Dec. 1967): 293–316.

Brumble, H. David, III. *American Indian Autobiography.* Berkeley: University of California Press, 1988.

Bryant, Edwin. *What I Saw in California.* 1848. Reprint, Minneapolis: Ross and Haines, 1967.

Burchell, Robert A. "Opportunity and the Frontier: Wealth-Holding in Twenty-Six Northern California Counties, 1848–1880." *Western Historical Quarterly* 18 (Apr. 1987): 177–96.

Canfield, Gae Whitney. *Sarah Winnemucca of the Northern Paiutes.* Norman: University of Oklahoma Press, 1983.

Carlson, Helen F. *Nevada Place Names.* Reno: University of Nevada Press, 1974.

Cerveri, Doris. *The Ways of an Indian.* Elko NV: Nostalgia Press, 1989.

Child, Brenda J. *Boarding School Seasons: American Indian Families, 1900–1940.* Lincoln: University of Nebraska Press, 1998.

Clemmer, Richard O. "The Tail of the Elephant: Indians in Emigrant Diaries, 1844–1862." *Nevada Historical Society Quarterly* 30 (winter 1987): 269–90.

Coe, Henry C. "An Indian Agent's Experience in the War of 1886." *Oregon Historical Society Quarterly* 14 (Mar. 1913): 65–67.

Cook, S. F. *The Epidemic of 1830–1833 in California and Oregon.* Publications in American Archeology and Ethnology, vol. 43. Berkeley: University of California Press, 1955. 303–26

Corbusier, William T. *Verde to San Carlos.* Tucson AZ: Dale Stuart King, 1968.

Crum, Steven J. *The Road on Which We Came: A History of the Western Shoshone.* Salt Lake City: University of Utah Press, 1994.

Dalton, Taylor. Letter. *Nevada State Journal,* 8 Jan. 1891.

Davison, Stanley R., ed. "The Bannock-Piute War of 1878: Letters of Major Edwin C. Mason." *Journal of the West* 11 (Jan. 1972): 128–42.

De Quille, Dan (William Wright). *The Big Bonanza.* 1876. Reprint, New York: Alfred A. Knopf, 1947.

Dippie, Brian W. *The Vanishing American: White Attitudes and U.S. Indian Policy.* Middletown CT: Wesleyan University Press, 1982.

Downs, James F. "Differential Response to White Contact: Paiute and Washo." In *The Washo Indians of California and Nevada*, ed. Warren L. d'Azevedo. *Anthropological Papers* 67. Salt Lake City: University of Utah Press, 1963. 115–37.

Dunlay, Thomas W. *Wolves for the Blue Soldiers: Indian Scouts and Auxiliaries with the United States Army, 1860–90.* Lincoln: University of Nebraska Press, 1982.

Earl, Phillip I. "Nevada's Miscegenation Laws and the Marriage of Mr. and Mrs. Harry Bridges." *Nevada Historical Society Quarterly* 37 (spring 1994): 1–17.

Egan, Ferol. "Letters of Warren Wasson, Indian Agent." *Nevada Historical Society Quarterly* 12 (fall 1969): 4–26.

——. *Sand in a Whirlwind: The Paiute Indian War of 1860.* Garden City NY: Doubleday, 1972.

Ekland, Roy E. "The 'Indian Problem': Pacific Northwest, 1879." *Oregon Historical Quarterly* 70 (June 1969): 101–37.

Fallon Paiute-Shoshone. *After the Drying up of the Water.* Fallon NV: Duck Down Press, 1977.

Fenton, William D. "Father Wilbur and His Work." *Oregon Historical Society Quarterly* 10 (June 1909): 16–30.

Forbes, Jack D. *Nevada Indians Speak.* Reno: University of Nevada Press, 1967.

Fowler, Catherine S. "Sarah Winnemucca." In *American Indian Intellectuals*, ed. Margot Liberty. St. Paul MN: West Publishing, 1978.

Fowler, Catherine S., ed. *Willard Z. Park's Ethnographic Notes on the Northern Paiutes of Western Nevada, 1933–1940.* Salt Lake City: University of Utah Press, 1989.

Fowler, Don D., and Catherine S. Fowler, eds. *Anthropology of the Numa: John Wesley Powell's Manuscripts on the Numic Peoples of Western North America, 1868–1880.* Washington DC: Smithsonian Institution Press, 1971.

Franks, Kenny A. "La Flesche Family." In *Encyclopedia of North American Indians*, ed. Frederick E. Hoxie. New York: Houghton Mifflin, 1996.

Fretwell-Johnson, Hazel. "Cavalry Days of Yore." *Owyhee Outpost* 23 (May 1992): 1–33.

——. *In Times Past.* Filer ID: Privately printed, 1990.

Geer, Emily Apt. *First Lady: The Life of Lucy Webb Hayes.* Kent OH: Kent State University Press, 1984.

Georgi-Findlay, Brigitte. "The Frontiers of Native American Women's Writing: Sarah Winnemucca's *Life among the Piutes*." In *New Voices in Native American Literary Criticism*, ed. Arnold Krupat. Washington DC: Smithsonian Institution Press, 1993.

Gibson, Benson. *The Family History of Hank Thomas, Nora Tavashee (Williams) Thomas Dorsey, Maggie Ellen (Williams) Thomas Crow Roberts*. Duck Valley Reservation: privately printed, 1986.

Gilbert, Bil. *Westering Man: The Life of Joseph Walker*. New York: Atheneum, 1983.

Glassley, Ray H. *Indian Wars of the Pacific Northwest*. 2nd ed. Portland OR: Binfords and Mort, 1972.

Gregg, Jacob R. *Pioneer Days in Malheur County*. Los Angeles: Lorrin R. Morrison, 1950.

Griffith, Martin. "What's Nevada's Oldest Town?" *Nevada* 58 (Sept./Oct. 1998): 10–15, 77.

Groh, George W. *Gold Fever*. New York: William Morrow, 1966.

Haine, J. J. F. "A Belgian in the Gold Rush: California Indians." *California Historical Quarterly* 38 (June 1959): 141–55.

Hattori, Eugene M. " 'And Some of Them Swear like Pirates': Acculturation of American Indian Women in Nineteenth-Century Virginia City." In *Comstock Women: The Making of a Mining Community*, ed. Ronald M. James and C. Elizabeth Raymond. Reno: University of Nevada Press, 1997.

Hein, O. L. *Memories of Long Ago*. New York: G. P. Putnam's Sons, 1925.

Heizer, Robert F. "Notes on Some Paviotso Personalities and Material Culture." *Anthropological Papers* 2. Carson City: Nevada State Museum, 1960. 1–15.

Helland, Maurice. *There Were Giants*. Yakima WA: Privately printed, 1980.

Hermann, Ruth. *The Paiutes of Pyramid Lake*. San Jose CA: Harlan-Young Press, 1972.

Hines, Clarence. "Indian Agent's Letter-Book." *Oregon Historical Quarterly* 39 (Mar. 1938): 8–15.

Hirschfelder, Arlene B. *American Indian and Eskimo Authors: A Comprehensive Bibliography*. New York: Association on American Indian Affairs, 1973.

Hittman, Michael. *Wovoka and the Ghost Dance*. Lincoln: University of Nebraska Press, 1997.

Hoogenboom, Ari. *Rutherford B. Hayes: Warrior and President*. Lawrence: University Press of Kansas, 1995.

Hopkins, Sarah Winnemucca. *Life among the Piutes: Their Wrongs and Claims*. 1883. Reprint, Bishop CA: Sierra Media, 1969.

Bibliography

Howard, Harold P. *Sacajawea*. 1971. In *Three American Indian Women*. New York: MJF Books, 1995.

Howard, James H. *The Ponca Tribe*. 1965. Reprint, Lincoln: University of Nebraska Press, 1995.

Howard, Oliver O. *Famous Indian Chiefs I Have Known*. New York: Century, 1912.

———. *My Life and Experiences among Our Hostile Indians*. 1907. Reprint, New York: Da Capo Press, 1972.

An Illustrated History of Baker, Grant, Malheur and Harney Counties. Western Historical Publishing Company, 1902.

Indian Rights Association. *Proceedings of the Mohonk Lake Conference, 1886*. Indian Rights Association, 1887.

Inter-Tribal Council of Nevada. *Numa: A Northern Paiute History*. Salt Lake City: University of Utah Printing Service, 1976.

———. *Wa She Shu: A Washo Tribal History*. Salt Lake City: University of Utah Printing Service, 1976.

Jackson, Helen Hunt. *A Century of Dishonor*. 1881. Reprint, Minneapolis: Ross and Haines, 1964.

James, Henry. *The Bostonians*. 1886. Reprint, Cutchogue NY: Buccaneer Books, 1976.

James, Ronald M. *The Roar and the Silence: A History of Virginia City and the Comstock Lode*. Reno: University of Nevada Press, 1998.

———. *Temples of Justice: County Courthouses of Nevada*. Reno: University of Nevada Press, 1994.

Josephy, Alvin M. *The Indian Heritage of America*. New York: Bantam, 1969.

Kawashima, Yasuhide. "Forest Diplomats: The Role of Interpreters in Indian-White Relations on the Early American Frontier." *American Indian Quarterly* 13 (winter 1989): 1–14.

Kilcup, Karen L., ed. Introduction to *Nineteenth-Century American Women Writers: An Anthology*. Oxford: Blackwell, 1997.

Knack, Martha C., and Omer C. Stewart. *As Long as the River Shall Run: An Ethnohistory of Pyramid Lake Indian Reservation*. Berkeley: University of California Press, 1984.

Kober, George M. *Reminiscences*. Washington DC: Kober Foundation, 1930.

Lape, Noreen Grover. " 'I Would Rather Be with My People, but Not Live with Them as They Live': Cultural Liminality and Double Consciousness in Sarah Winnemucca Hopkins's *Life among the Piutes: Their Wrongs and Claims*." *American Indian Quarterly* 22 (summer 1998): 259–79.

Layton, Thomas N. "From Potage to Portage: A Perspective on Aboriginal Horse Use in the Northern Great Basin Prior to 1850." *Nevada Historical Society Quarterly* 21 (winter 1978): 243–57.

Levine, Richard R. "Indian Fighters and Indian Reformers: Grant's Indian Peace Policy and the Conservative Consensus." *Civil War History* 31 (Dec. 1985), 329–52.

Liljeblad, Sven. *Idaho Indians in Transition, 1805–1960.* Pocatello: Idaho State University Museum, 1972.

———. "The Indians of Idaho." *Idaho Yesterdays* 4 (fall 1960): 22–28.

———. "Indian Peoples in Idaho." In *The History of Idaho*, ed. Merrill D. Beal and Merle W. Wells. New York: Lewis Historical Publishing, 1959.

Lingenfelter, Richard E. and Karen Rix Gash. *The Newspapers of Nevada: A History and Bibliography, 1854–1979.* Reno: University of Nevada Press, 1984.

Lomawaima, K. Tsianina. *They Called It Prairie Light: The Story of Chilocco Indian School.* Lincoln: University of Nebraska Press, 1994.

Louie, Marion. "History of the Malheur Paiutes." In *A Lively Little History of Harney County.* Burns OR: Harney County Chamber of Commerce, 1989.

Madsen, Brigham D. *The Bannock of Idaho.* 1958. Reprint, Moscow: University of Idaho Press, 1996.

Martin, V. Covert. *Stockton Album through the Years.* Stockton: n.p., 1959.

Mathews, Mary McNair. *Ten Years in Nevada.* 1880. Reprint, Lincoln: University of Nebraska Press, 1995.

McArthur, Lewis A. "Early Scenes in Harney Valley." *Oregon Historical Quarterly* 32 (June 1931): 125–29.

McKenna, Sue. "The Wonderful Winnemucca Sisters." Island Park ID: Island Park Historical Society Publication, [1993].

Meacham, A. B. *Wigwam and War-Path.* Boston: John P. Dale, 1875.

Miller, Jay. "Basin Religion and Theology: A Comparative Study of Power (*Puha*)." *Journal of California and Great Basin Anthropology* 5 (summer/winter 1983): 66–86.

Miller, William C. "The Pyramid Lake Indian War of 1860 (Part 1)." *Nevada Historical Society Quarterly* 1 (Sept. 1957): 35–53.

———. "The Pyramid Lake Indian War of 1860 (Part 2)." *Nevada Historical Society Quarterly* 1 (Nov. 1957): 99–113.

Mooney, James. *The Ghost Dance.* 1896. Reprint, North Dighton MA: JG Press, 1996.

Morgan, Thomas. *My Story of the Last Indian War in the Northwest.* N. p.: Privately printed, 1954.

Morrison, Dorothy N. *Chief Sarah: Sarah Winnemucca's Fight for Indian Rights.* 2nd ed. Portland: Oregon Historical Society Press, 1990.

O'Connell, Shaun. *Imagining Boston: A Literary Landscape.* Boston: Beacon Press, 1990.

Park, Willard Z. "Paviotso Shamanism." *American Anthropologist* 36 (Jan./Mar., 1934): 99–113.

Peabody, Elizabeth P. *Sarah Winnemucca's Practical Solution of the Indian Problem.* Cambridge MA: John Wilson and Son, 1886.

———. *Second Report of the Model School of Sarah Winnemucca, 1886–87.* Cambridge MA: John Wilson and Son, 1887.

Pederson, Elaine L. "Deciphering the Ormsby Gown: What Does It Tell?" *Nevada Historical Society Quarterly* 38 (summer 1995): 75–88.

Prucha, Francis Paul. *American Indian Policy in Crisis: Christian Reformers and the Indian, 1865–1900.* Norman: University of Oklahoma Press, 1976.

———. *The Great Father: The United States Government and the American Indians.* 2 vols. Lincoln: University of Nebraska Press, 1984.

Reid, John T., and J. R. Hunter. "Humboldt County." In *History of Nevada.* Vol. 2, ed. Sam P. Davis. Los Angeles: Elms Publishing, 1913.

Riddell, Francis A. "Honey Lake Paiute Ethnography." *Occasional Papers* 3. Carson City: Nevada State Museum, 1978. 1–116.

Rocha, Guy Louis. "Nevada's Emergence in the American Great Basin: Territory and State." *Nevada Historical Society Quarterly* 38 (winter 1995): 255–80.

Ronda, Bruce A., ed. *Letters of Elizabeth Palmer Peabody.* Middletown CT: Wesleyan University Press, 1984.

Ruoff, A. LaVonne Brown. "Three Nineteenth-Century American Indian Autobiographers." In *Redefining American Literary History,* ed. A. LaVonne Brown Ruoff and Jerry W. Ward Jr. New York: Modern Language Association of America, 1990.

Sands, Kathleen M. "Indian Women's Personal Narrative: Voices Past and Present." In *American Women's Autobiography: Fea(s)ts of Memory,* ed. Margo Culley. Madison: University of Wisconsin Press, 1992.

Santee, J. F. "Egan of the Piutes." *Washington Historical Quarterly* 26 (Jan. 1935): 16–25.

Schacter, Daniel L. *Searching for Memory: The Brain, the Mind, and the Past.* New York: Basic Books, 1996.

Schafer, Joseph. *Carl Schurz: Militant Liberal.* Evansville WI: Antes Press, 1930.

Bibliography

Schmitt, Martin F., ed. *General George Crook: His Autobiography.* Norman: University of Oklahoma Press, 1946.

Scott, Lalla. *Karnee: A Paiute Narrative.* Reno: University of Nevada Press, 1966.

Simpson, James H. *Report of Explorations across the Great Basin of the Territory of Utah.* 1876. Reprint, Reno: University of Nevada Press, 1983.

Smith, Grant H. *The History of the Comstock Lode,* 1850–1920. University of Nevada Bulletin 37 (1 July 1943). Reno: Nevada State Bureau of Mines and the Mackay School of Mines, 1943.

Smith, Rex Allen. *Moon of Popping Trees.* New York: Reader's Digest Press, 1975.

Spence, Mary Lee, and Donald Jackson, eds. *The Expeditions of John Charles Frémont.* 2 vols. Urbana: University of Illinois Press, 1973.

Steward, Julian H. *Basin-Plateau Aboriginal Sociopolitical Groups.* Bureau of American Ethnology Bulletin 120. Washington DC: GPO, 1938.

——. "Two Paiute Autobiographies." *Publications in American Archeology and Ethnology 33.* Berkeley: University of California Press, 1934. 423–38.

Steward, Julian H., and Erminie Wheeler-Voegelin. *The Northern Paiute Indians.* United States Indian Claims Commission. American Indian Ethnohistory Series, *Paiute Indians,* vol. 3. New York: Garland Publishing, 1974.

Stewart, George R. *The California Trail.* American Trails Series. New York: McGraw-Hill, 1962.

Stewart, Omer C. "Three Gods for Joe." *Tomorrow* 4 (1956): 71–76.

Stewart, Patricia. "Sarah Winnemucca." *Nevada Historical Society Quarterly* 14 (winter 1971): 23–38.

——. "Sarah Winnemucca: Paiute Princess." *Nevada* 38 (Apr./June 1978): 36–39.

Stoddard, Sylvia C. *Sam Knew Them When.* Reno: Great Basin Press, 1996.

Strahorn, Carrie A. *Fifteen Thousand Miles by Stage.* 2 vols. 1911. Reprint, Lincoln: University of Nebraska Press, 1988.

Summerhayes, Martha. *Vanished Arizona: Recollections of My Army Life.* 1908. Reprint, Philadelphia: J. B. Lippincott, 1963.

Swann, Brian, and Arnold Krupat, eds. Introduction to *I Tell You Now.* Lincoln: University of Nebraska Press, 1987.

Taylor, Bayard. *Eldorado.* 1850. Reprint, New York: Alfred A. Knopf, 1949.

Tharp, Louise Hall. *The Peabody Sisters of Salem.* Boston: Little, Brown, 1950.

Thompson, David. *The Tennessee Letters from Carson Valley,* 1857–1860. Reno NV: Grace Dangberg Foundation, 1983.

Thornton, Russell. *We Shall Live Again.* Cambridge: Cambridge University Press, 1986.

Bibliography

Trafzer, Clifford E. *Death Stalks the Yakama*. East Lansing: Michigan State University Press, 1997.

Trefousse, Hans L. *Carl Schurz*. Knoxville: University of Tennessee Press, 1982.

Turner, Katharine C. *Red Men Calling on the Great White Father*. Norman: University of Oklahoma Press, 1951.

Twain, Mark (Samuel Clemens). *Roughing It*. 1871. Reprint, New York: Harper and Row, 1962.

Utley, Robert M. *Frontier Regulars: The United States Army and the Indian 1866–1891*. New York: Macmillan, 1973.

———. Introduction to *My Life and Experiences among Our Hostile Indians*, by Oliver O. Howard. New York: Da Capo Press, 1972.

———. *The Lance and the Shield: The Life and Times of Sitting Bull*. New York: Ballantine Books, 1993.

Velie, Alan R., and Gerald Vizenor. Introduction to *Native American Perspectives on Literature and History*, ed. Alan R. Velie. Norman: University of Oklahoma Press, 1994.

Watson, Margaret G. *Silver Theater: Amusements of Nevada's Mining Frontier, 1850–1864*. Glendale CA: Arthur H. Clark, 1964.

Wheat, Margaret M. *Survival Arts of the Primitive Paiutes*. Reno: University of Nevada Press, 1967.

Wheeler, Sessions S. *The Nevada Desert*. Caldwell ID: Caxton, 1972.

Whitner, Robert L. "Grant's Peace Policy on the Yakima Reservation, 1870–82." In *The Western American Indian: Case Studies in Tribal History*, ed. Richard N. Ellis. Lincoln: University of Nebraska Press, 1972.

Williams, Charles R., ed. *Diary and Letters of Rutherford Birchard Hayes, Nineteenth President of the United States*. 5 vols. Columbus: Ohio State Archeological and Historical Society, 1922.

Wilson, Dorothy C. *Bright Eyes*. New York: McGraw-Hill, 1974.

Winnemucca, Sarah. "The Pah-Utes." *The Californian* 6 (Sept. 1882): 252–56. (see also Hopkins)

Woodward, Grace Steele. *Pocahontas*. 1969. In *Three American Indian Women*. New York: MJF Books, 1995.

Wren, Thomas C. *A History of the State of Nevada*. New York: Lewis, 1904.

Zanjani, Sally. *Ghost Dance Winter and Other Tales of the Frontier*. Reno: Nevada Historical Society, 1994.

Index

"Sarah Winnemucca" has been abbreviated as sw in the index.

Adams, David W., 265, 273
Alcatraz (CA), 115
Allen, Richard N. "Tennessee," 46, 52, 64–65
Alta California (San Francisco), 76, 270
Ambrose, Stephen E., 4
Anderson, G. W. "Doc," 212–13
Angel, Myron, 74
Argasse, Julius, 126, 321 n.25
Arthur, Chester, 250
assimilation, of Indians, 46–47, 88, 124, 258, 299
Atkins, John D. C., 268

Baltimore, 244, 247, 251
Bannocks, 7, 65, 74, 84, 94, 121, 189, 212, 260; description of, 146–47, 324 n.2; at Henry's Lake, 294, 298
Bannock War, 2–3, 146, 177, 204–5, 228, 251; and battle at Birch Creek, 175–76, 228; and battle at Silver Creek, 167; and battle at South Mountain, 151; causes of, 147; end of, 178, 181–83; escape of Winnemucca's band from, 157–60; and Forsyth's fight, 179–80; map of, 168; and Miles's fight, 176; murder of Egan in, 177–78; numbers in, 166
Barren Valley (OR), 149, 155
Bartlett, Edward C., 106–7, 172, 229, 220, 233; background and description of, 109–10, 335 n.23; divorce from sw of, 142–43; marriage to Louisa Butler of, 142–43; marriage to sw of, 108–10; military record of, 109–10
Bateman, Calvin, 85–86, 114–16, 118, 123–24
battles: Birch Creek, 175–76; Fish Creek Valley, 82; Forsyth's fight, 179–80; the Infernal Caverns, 95; Miles's fight, 176; Pyramid Lake, 61–62; Rock Canyon, 82–

84; Silver Creek, 167; South Mountain, 151
Bear Flag Revolt, 17, 30
Bernard, Reuben F., 150, 152–54, 164, 167, 171, 175–76, 178, 185, 208, 220
The Big Bonanza (De Quille), 51, 70, 83
Big George, 81
Birch Creek, Battle of, 175–76
Black Rock Desert (NV), 57, 63–64, 69
Black Rock War, 82–85, 94; and Battle of Fish Creek Valley, 82; and Battle of Rock Canyon, 82–84
Bland, Thomas, 248, 302
Blasdel, Henry G., 77, 80, 84
Boise City News, 103
Boise ID, mentioned, 150, 154, 182, 185
Bonnifield, McKaskia S. "Mac," 126–27, 145, 264
Bonsall, Jacob, 33, 314 n.27
Boston, 236, 237
The Bostonians (James), 237
Brayman, Mason, 145
Breckenridge (chief), 116
Bright Eyes (Susette La Flesche), 236, 237, 262, 339 n.11
Brimlow, George F., 174
Brumble, H. David, III, 200, 242, 307 n.4, 311 n.1, 320 n.48, 328–29 n. 32, 331 n.11, 336 n.6, 337 n.12
Bryant, Edwin, 42, 309 n.36
Buena Vista John (chief), 116, 196, 273
Buffalo Brush (Paulina), 94
Buffalo Horn, 147–48, 151, 154
Bull, Mrs. Ole, 237
Butler, Louisa, 142–43

The Californian, 226
Camas Prairie (ID), 147, 162
Camps: Bidwell, 141; C. F. Smith, 97–98, 182, 318 n.19; Harney, 128, 135, 140, 156,

Camps *(cont.)*
164–65, 169, 187–88, 228; Lyon, 162, 241;
McDermit, 92, 94–95, 96, 97–109, 119–21,
141, 144–45, 152–53, 183, 185, 187, 189,
240. *See also* Forts: Bidwell, Harney, McDer-
mit *after* 5 *Apr.* 1879
Canfield, Gae W., 244, 281
cannibalism, Paiutes' fear of, 22
Canyon City OR, 133, 137, 142–43, 186, 207,
213; during Bannock War, 171–72, 180
Captain Charley, 196, 330 n.18
Captain Jim, 116, 196, 203, 208
Captain Jim (Washo), 50–51
Captain John, 13, 66–67, 118, 209, 288
Captain Soo (Moguanoga), 57, 60, 84, 87–88
Carlisle Indian School, 247, 265, 266
Carson Appeal (Carson City), 48, 120, 258
Carson City NV, mentioned, 61, 120, 211, 258,
259, 267
Carson Pass (CA), 28
Carson River (NV), 26, 47, 57, 59, 71
Carson Valley (NV), 7, 27, 44–45, 48, 241
Cayuses, 129, 148, 177. *See also* Umapine
Central Pacific Railroad, 208, 263
A Century of Dishonor (Jackson), 103, 226, 302
Chapin, Alice, 270–71, 277
Charbonneau, Toussaint, 1
chieftainship, 43, 87–88, 235, 303
Chinese, 125, 289; and crisis with Paiutes,
259–60
cholera epidemic, 39–40, 311 n.2
Clark, William, 2
Cleveland, Grover, 268
Cleveland, Rose Elizabeth, 268–69
Cochran, Captain, 190–91
Coffman's Station (NV), 91–92, 317 n.4
Columbia River, 169–70, 176, 190
Comstock, Henry, 51
Comstock region (NV), 43, 51
conferences: at Camp Harney, 95; at Camp
McDermit, 105, 121–23; at Winnemucca,
196
Congress (U.S.), 250–51
Corbusier, Fanny, 106–8, 240
Council Fire (Bland), 248

Crane, James M., 45
Crook, George, 99; 1868 campaign of, 95–96;
conference with Winnemucca of, 95;
opinions of, 95, 147–48
Crowley, Greenwood, 149, 156, 325 n.24
Crowley, James, 149, 156
Culver, Lillian, 295, 296, 297
Currey, George B., 133
Curry, George, 116

Dave, Mary, 267, 286
Davis, Sam P., 75, 315 n.16
Dawes, Anna, 244
Dawes, Henry L., 243, 269, 303
Dawes Act, 252, 262, 303
Death Stalks the Yakama (Trafzer), 221
Delano, Columbus, 114
Delano, Sylvia, 253
Delano, Warren, 277, 278, 282
Demming, Dexter, 56
Department of the Interior. *See* United States
Interior Department
De Quille, Dan (William Wright), 51–52, 61,
63, 65, 69–71, 83, 312 n.23
Dodge, Frederick, 43, 55–56, 64
Donner party, 22
Douglas, Henry, 102, 105
Dunlay, Thomas W., 176
Dupée, Marjorie, 305
"Dutch Nick's" saloon, 52

Egan (Ehegante), 162; death of, 177–78, 183,
328 n.19; description of, 129; at Malheur
Reservation, 131, 133–35, 137, 139–40,
148–50; as war chief, 165–67, 171, 174, 326
n.31
Elko NV, 277–78, 289
Emerson, Ralph Waldo, 243

factionalism, among Paiutes, 256, 277, 299
Ferguson, William, 288, 295, 297
Fish Creek Valley, Battle of, 82
Fleming, Alec, 88–89
La Flesche, Frank, 236
La Flesche, Susette. *See* Bright Eyes

Folsom, Special Agent, 265

Forbes, Jack, 105

Forsyth, James W., 178, 186; desert campaign by, 182–85; at Forsyth's fight, 179–80; at Wounded Knee Creek (SD), 295

Forsyth's fight, 179–80

Fort Bridger Treaty, 147

Forts: Bidwell, 195–96, 208, 233; Churchill, 63–65, 74, 80, 89; Hall, 146, 205, 225; Harney, 213; McDermit, 208, 251–52, 254, 285; Mohave, 273; Vancouver, 185, 220, 221, 256; Walla Walla, 176. *See also* Camps: Bidwell, Harney, *and* McDermit *prior to* 5 *Apr.* 1879

Forty Mile Desert (NV), 13

Fowler, Catherine, 240–41, 243

Frémont, John Charles, 8, 16–17, 22, 30, 33, 42, 46, 308 n.22

French, Peter, 128

Garfield, James, 250

Gates (rancher), 88–89

Genoa NV (earlier Mormon Station), 44–47, 50–51, 55

George (chief), 116

George (Paiute companion to SW), 153–56

George, Melvin, 252

Georgi-Findlay, Brigitte, 242, 310 n.20, 332 n.14

Ghost Dance, 90, 112, 284–86, 289–90

Gibson, William D. C., 256–57, 260–64, 272

Gold Canyon (NV), 43, 45

Gold Hill News, 69, 78

Grande Ronde River, 178

Grant, Ulysses S., 248; peace policy of, 124

Grass Valley Bob, 116

Green, John, 133, 135, 140

Grizzly John, 234

Haine, J. J. F., 197, 199, 330 n.20

Hamilton, Charles B., 115, 229–30,

Hamilton, E. E., 107

Harper's magazine, 102–3

Hayes, Lucy, 221

Hayes, Rutherford B., 204–6, 221, 250

Hays, Jack, 63

Hayt, Ernest, 206

Hazabok, 58

Hedrick, Georgia, 299, 300, 305

Henry's Lake (ID), 210; description of, 292–93, 295–96

Homeli, 184

Honey Lake (CA), 8, 43, 56–57, 69, 77–78

Hope Valley (CA), 28, 39

Hopkins, Lewis H., 228, 233, 244, 249, 252, 269, 281–83, 296; background and description of, 226–28, 335 n.18; death of 283; gambling and financial misdeeds of, 230–31, 252–53, 257, 282; marriage to SW of, 226, 228–29

horses, late adoption of, 37–38

House Subcommittee on Indian Affairs, 251

Howard, Oliver O., 99, 135–36, 208, 216, 220, 223–24, 248–49, 259, 285; description and background of, 161, 160; account of Indian-white marriage by, 173; in Bannock War, 147, 152, 241; battle plans of, 161–62, 166, 170; on postwar disposition of Paiutes, 187, 190, 192, 194, 217, 222, 224, 333 n.39; wartime association with SW of, 154, 160, 162–64, 170, 172, 175, 181–82

Hozia, 57

Humboldt County (NV): petitions of settlers in, 87, 116, 120, 275; tolerance develops in, 145

Humboldt Register (Winnemucca NV), 78–79, 82–84, 103, 114, 123

Humboldt River (NV), 5, 12, 24, 39, 43, 77, 110

Idaho Statesman (Boise), 112, 180, 185

Indian policy (U.S.). *See* United States Indian policy

Indian reform organizations, 247, 302

Indian Rights Association, 247–48, 269

Indians. *See individual tribal names (e.g., Paiutes, Shoshones)*

Indian Territory, 204, 250, 252, 254

Infernal Caverns, Battle of, mentioned, 95

Ingalls, G. W., 114

Interior Department. *See* United States Interior Department

Intertribal Council of Nevada, 299

interpreters, function of, 101–2

Inyo County (CA), 189, 266

Jackson, Helen Hunt, 103, 226, 302

James, Henry, 237

Jamestown, 1

Jerome, Aaron, 92–94

Joaquin Ben, 81

John (Paiute companion to SW), 153, 156

John Day River (OR), 173, 174; north fork of, 180; south fork of, 173–74; valley of, 144, 149, 174

Johntown NV, 51–52

Jones, John P., 119, 121, 257

Juniper Lake (OR), 155, 157–58

Kammidika-a, 8

Kearny, Stephen W., 22

Kelley, E. D., 123

Kibidika-a, 8, 263

Kinnegar, Andrew, 275

Kiowas, 273

Knack, Martha C., 57, 89

Kober, George, 99–101, 109, 122, 126

Kuykendall, Dr., 222

Kuyuidika-a, 8, 14, 16–17, 21–22, 24–25, 39, 47, 78

Lake Mohonk Conference, 247

Lander, Frederick W., 64

lands in severalty. *See* Dawes Act

Lape, Noreen Grover, 75, 242, 312 n.29

Lassen, Peter, 55

Leggins, 133, 187, 191, 214–16, 322 n.11; band of, 189–90, 205, 210, 223–24, 251

Lewis and Clark expedition, 2

Lewis, Meriwether, 2

Life among the Piutes: Their Wrongs and Claims (Hopkins), 3–4, 125, 239–43, 279, 304; accuracy of, 4, 240–42, 314 n.27, 336 n.11; analysis of, 239–43; composition of, 240; publication of, 239

Linville, Harrison, 129–30

Long, Jerry (Riding Down Hill with Hair Standing on End,) 134, 138, 149, 248, 285, 320 n.52

Long, John D., 250

Longfellow, Henry Wadsworth, 236

Lovelock NV, 206; description of, 208, 263; Indian band at, 208–209

Lowry, Annie, 12–13

lynching, 50–51, 94

Madsen, Brigham, 147

Malheur Lake (OR), 155

Malheur Reservation (OR), 132–140, 142, 148, 171, 181, 195–96, 205, 207, 209, 210, 213, 250, 257; abolition of, 222; description of, 128–29, 165; establishment of, 128; Indian population at, 131, 166; settlers' petition on, 133. *See also* Parrish, Samuel B.; Rinehart, William V.

Malheur River (OR), 129

Malheur City OR, 164

Mann, Horace, 236

Mann, Mary, 236–40, 248–49, 253, 256, 268, 280

Marysville CA, mentioned, 45, 293

Marzen, Louisa, 271–72

Mason, Edwin C., 164, 171, 175, 179, 185; observations on SW by, 154, 170, 172, 174, 182

massacres. *See under individual names (e.g., Mud Lake, Wounded Knee Creek)*

McDermit, Charles, 78, 80–81, 84

McDermit Reservation, 285, 304

McDowell, Irvin, 145, 186–87, 190, 192–93, 216

McElroy, James N., 98

McGregor, Thomas, 164, 186–87

McMarlin, John, 49

McMinn, Judge, 297

Meacham, A. B., 95

Meek, Joe, 12

Mexicans, 30

Miles, Evan, 176

Miles, Nelson A., 184

Index

Miles's fight, 176

Miller, James, 76–77

Miller, Jay, 242

Milroy, Robert H., 223–24

miscegenation laws, 71, 110

Modoc Indians, in war, 112–13, 122, 176. *See also* Snake River Sal

Moguanoga. *See* Captain Soo

Mormon Station NV (later Genoa), 39, 41, 47

Morton, Mr., 149–50

Morton, Rosie, 149–50

Moses, (chief), mentioned, 169

Mud Lake (NV; also Winnemucca Lake), described, 78, 315–16 n.24; massacre at, 78–82, 233, 316 n.29

Murphy's Station (NV), 79

My Life and Experiences among Our Hostile Indians (Howard), 173

National Indian Defense Association, 248

Nevada Indian Commission, 299

Nevada legislature, 80, 120–21, 251

Nevada politics, early period of, 44–45; legislature in, 80, 120–21, role of saloonkeepers in, 256–57

Nevada State Journal, 111–13

New York Times, 186

Nez Percés, 147, 204

Nick (chief), 116

Nojomud, 57

Northern Cheyennes, 204, 250

Nugent, Hugh, 90–93

Numaga ("Young Winnemucca"), 49, 56, 58–59, 62, 64, 81, 317 n.11

Numana, Dave (Captain Dave), 235, 273

Nye, James W., 69, 121

Ochocho, 141, 233, 235

Office of Indian Affairs. *See* United States Office of Indian Affairs

Ogden, Peter Skene, 12

Ogden UT, mentioned, 231

Omahas, 236

One Arm Jim, 275

Ormsby, Lizzie Jane, 46, 48–49

Ormsby, Margaret Trumbo, 44, 47–48, 50

Ormsby, William: background of, 44–45, death of, 62, 313 n.18; political activity of, 45; in Pyramid Lake War, 61–62

Otis, Elmer, 131

Overton, Natches. *See* Winnemucca, Natches

Owens Valley CA, 8

Owyhee River, 141, 154, 182, 185

Oytes, 156, 158, 166, 169, 172, 183, 185–86, 251; at Battle of Birch Creek, 175; at Malheur Reservation, 129, 132–35, 137–38, 141, 148, 322 n.9; prophecies of, 148, 185; religion of, 132; at Yakama Reservation, 215, 223

"Pacific Republic," 45

Paddy Cap, 215–16, 224

Pahvezo, 191

Painter, Charles, 247, 269–70, 272, 302

Paiute Joe, 151, 160, 216

Paiutes, 49, 189, 259; bands of, 8–9, 307–8 n.7; culture of, 7–12, 20–21, 37–38, 107, 319 n.39; early contact with whites of, 5–6, 12–19, 24, 308 n.17; employment of, 46–47, 73, 282; escape from Yakama Reservation by, 224, 334 n.11; exile to Yakama Reservation of, 190, 192; factions among, 256, 277, 299; food sources of, 8–10, 20, 37, 43, 288, 286–88, 321 n.15; gambling by, 107, 279; and Ghost Dance, 284–85; illnesses of, 39–40, 121, 221–22; language of, 220; and legal inequities, 81, 105; myths of, 14, 28–29, 70, 202–3, 219–20, 255, 274, 281, 298; population of, 116; social and political organization of, 8–9, 43, 87–88; settlers' attitudes toward, 46, 65, 69, 120; starvation among, 17, 43, 52–54, 64, 84, 105, 121–22; territory of, 8; traditional religious practices of, 24–25, 39–40, 224–25, 298; women's role among, 9–11, 303. *See also* Bannock War, Black Rock War, Malheur Reservation, Pyramid Lake Reservation, Pyramid Lake War, Yakama Reservation

Parker, Frank, 150, 163

Parrish, Annie, 134, 143, 213, 254

Parrish, Charles, 143, 213, 251

Parrish, Samuel B., 128–30, 180; background of, 129; in confrontation with Oytes, 132–33, 322 n.9; loss of position by, 134–35, 222; at Malheur Reservation, 131–34

Payne, Edward, 88–89

Peabody, Elizabeth Palmer: background and description of, 237, 238, 336 n.3; financial aid from, 268–69, 276, 279; lobbying by, 243, 250, 268, 280; and publication and sales of *Life among the Piutes*, 237–39; on sw, 245–47, 252–53, 262, 265–66, 270, 272–73, 278–81, 303; as sw's hostess, 236–37, 244

Peabody Institute, 270

Pendleton OR, in Bannock War, 174

Pocahontas, 1–2, 182, 304

"Po-ca-hon-tas; or Ye Gentle Savage" (play), 76

Poncas, 204, 236

Price, Hiram, 250, 256

Prucha, Frances Paul, 124

Pyramid Lake (NV), 8, 14, 16, 42–43, 55, 57, 78

Pyramid Lake Reservation (NV), 90, 103, 114, 233, 235, 257; establishment of, 64; life at, 85–86; settlers' encroachments on, 88, 103, 255–56; school at, 256–57, 262, 267

Pyramid Lake War, 55–63, 235, 240, 301

Qudazoboeat, 57

Quinn River Valley, 96; Paiute band in, 96–97, 105

Ranck, Glenn, 228–29

rape: attempts upon Mary Winnemucca, 33–34; attempts upon sw, 126, 181, 213; as cause of Bannock War, 147; of Indian women, 106; at Williams Station, 59–60

religion: Dreamers (*see* Oytes: religion of); eclectic, 124–25; Episcopalianism, 125; evangelical Christianity, 247; Ghost Dance, 90, 112, 284–86, 289; Methodism, 52, 124, 193, 247; Peyoteism, 125. *See also* Paiutes: traditional religious practices of

Reno Crescent, 113

Reno NV, 111, 115, 258, 299

reservations; Duck Valley, 222, 224; Fort Hall, 114, 225; Fort McDermit, 224, 303–4; Indian Territory, 114; Klamath, 94; Pyramid Lake, 64, 85–86, 88, 90, 114, 123–24, 222, 224; Umatilla, 176; Walker River, 114; Warm Springs, 143–44, 176; Wind River, 193. *See also* Malheur Reservation, Yakama Reservation

Rinehart, William V., 143, 187, 189, 222, 252, 285, 304; background and description of, 136–37; in Bannock War, 163–64, 171–72; maltreatment of Indians by, 137–40, 142, 148, 251; requests for Indians' return by, 141–42, 195; slanders on Winnemuccas by, 139–41, 206–8, 210, 218, 242, 248–49, 260, 269–70, 303, 332 n.14

Roach, Mrs., 68

Rocha, Guy Louis, 299, 305

Rock Canyon, Battle of, 82–84

Rogers, William ("Uncle Billy"), 44, 49–50

Rolfe, John, 2

Roop, Isaac, 53, 57, 232

Roop, Susan, 94

Ruoff, A. LaVonne, 2, 200, 336–37 n.12 n.14

Saaba, 57

Sacajawea, 1–2, 182, 304

Sacramento CA, mentioned, 119

Sacramento Record, 119–20

Salt Lake City UT, mentioned, 44, 109, 118

Sanford, Maj., 178

San Francisco CA, 76–77, 105, 115, 145, 148, 186, 197–201, 203

San Francisco Call, 261

San Francisco Chronicle, 200

San Francisco Herald, 46, 49, 52–53, 56, 60

San Joaquin River (CA), 30, 52

Sarah Winnemucca school (Reno NV), 299, 304

Sarah Winnemucca's Practical Solution of the Indian Problem (Peabody), 280

Satewaller, Joseph, 143, 229

Sawadabebo, 57

Schofield, John M. 105, 109, 115–16, 119, 122

schools: Indian boarding schools, 265, 272–74; Peabody Institute, 270; at Pyramid Lake, 256–57, 262, 267; Sarah Winnemucca school (Reno), 299–300, 304. *See also* Winnemucca, Sarah: teaching and school of

Schurz, Carl, 250; background and description of, 203–4; broken commitments of, 208–9, 213–14, 217–18; at meeting with Winnemuccas, 204–6; policies of, 204–6, 331 n.4, 333 n.39

Scott, Hiram, 33–36, 66, 68

Scott, Jack, 156

Second Report of the Model School of Sarah Winnemucca (Peabody), 280

secretary of the interior, 192–93, 201, 250, 253. *See also* Schurz, Carl

secretary of war, 192–93

Sequinata ("Chiquito Winnemucca"), 57, 62

settlers, in early period: attitudes toward Indians of, 46, 52–53, 56, 65, 69, 87, 78–80; employment of Paiutes by, 46–47, 73; encroachment on Paiute lands by; 17, 64–65, 84, 88; in violent encounters with Paiutes, 24–25, 77–79, 85, 88–89

Sheepeaters, 220–21, 225; children of, 221, 225, 256

Sheep Ranch (OR), 152–54, 159

Shenkah, 162

Sherwood, Joseph, 296–97

Shoshones, 7, 13, 57, 65, 84, 86, 116, 121, 148, 186, 220, 289

Silver City ID, 150–51, 185

Silver Creek, Battle of, 167

Silver State (Winnemucca), 123, 152, 163–64, 178, 186, 205, 207–9, 251, 270, 275, 288, 295

Sioux, 284

Sitting Bull, 72, 170

Smith, Elma. *See* Winnemucca, Elma

Smith, Jedediah, 12

Smith, John, 88, 210, 231, 293, 296

Smoke Creek Desert (NV), 57, 69

Smoke Creek Sam, 69

Snake River Sal, 125–26

Snyder ("White Winnemucca"), 66–68, 229

Southern Paiutes, 7

South Mountain, Battle of, 151

Spencer, James, 86

Spokanes, 273

Staley, Ed, 293, 297

Staley, Will, 293, 297

Standing Bear, 236

Stanford, Leland, 145, 264, 268

Steamer Bulletin (San Francisco), 63

Steens Mountain (OR), 87, 112, 123, 140, 154–58, 162, 166, 182, 191, 210, 212

Stevens, Robert W. S., 251–52

Stevens party, 16

Steward, Julian, 9

Stewart, Omer C., 57

Stewart, Patricia, 297

Stockton CA, 30

Strahorn, Carrie, 293

Summerhayes, Martha, 97, 99

Susanville CA, 57, 94

tactics, of Indians, 61–62, 167, 170, 176, 220; of United States army, 78–79, 161–62, 166, 170

Tambiago, 147

Teller, Henry, 250, 253

Territorial Enterprise (Virginia City NV), 45, 53, 79, 118

Thacker, Bob, 144

Thacker, Charlie, 208–9

Tharp, Louise, 240

theater appearances, of the Winnemuccas, 72–77

Thies, J. H., 290

Thocmetony. *See* Winnemucca, Sarah

Thorington, William ("Lucky Bill") 44, 51

Toidika-a, 8

Truckee, 21–22, 45, 47, 58; in Bear Flag Revolt, 17; on California trips, 17, 25–33, 36–41; death of, 65–67, 234, 240; as guide, 16; on meeting whites, 14–15; peace policy of, 14–16

Truckee John, 88–89

Truckee Meadows (NV), 7
Truckee River, 16, 61, 78, 255
Tuboitony. *See* Winnemucca, Tuboitony
Turner, Katharine, 201, 206
Tuscarora Jack, 289
Twain, Mark, 256

Umapine, 177–78, 179, 183–84
Umatillas, 148, 169, 176–77, 183–85, 220, 325
    n.18; reservation of, 169–70, 174, 176
United States Congress, 250–51; House Sub-
    committee on Indian Affairs of, 251–52
United States Indian policy: and Dawes Act,
    252, 262, 303; in Delano consolidation
    plan, 114; in Grant's peace policy, 124
United States Interior Department, 207, 248,
    250; secretary of, 192–93, 201, 250, 253.
    See also Carl Schurz
United States Office of Indian Affairs, 88,
    133, 136, 201, 206, 260
United States War Department, Secretary
    of, 192–93
Utley, Robert, 160

Varian, C. S., 120
Virginia Chronicle (Virginia City NV), 120
Virginia City NV, 56–57, 61–62, 73, 79, 208,
    232, 260
Virginia Daily Union (Virginia City NV), 76, 79,
    81–82
Voorhees, Alexandra, 300–301, 304–5

Wadsworth NV, mentioned, 16, 255
Wagner, Henry: and arrest of Natches, 115;
    background of, 108; as Camp McDermit
    commander, 108, 122; at Paiute removal
    to Camp Harney, 187
Wahe, 74
Walker, Joseph Reddeford, 13
Walker, William, 45
Walker River (NV), 56, 74, 77
Walker River Reservation, 64, 90, 114, 284
Walter, Max, 75
War Jack, 225
Washakie, 193

Washington DC, 203–4, 206, 214, 249–50,
    256, 260–61, 268
Washington National Republican, 203
Washington Post, 206
Washos, 7, 27, 44, 258, 312 n.20, 313 n.4; and
    McMarlin-Williams homicide, 49–51, 312
    n.17; and Paiute homicide, 259–60
Wasson, Warren, 69, 74, 84–85
Watkins, Richard, 62
Weawea, 95
Wells, Almond B., 78–79, 84
Welsh, Herbert, 247, 269–70, 272, 302
Wheeler, Sessions, 82
Wheeler-Voegelin, Erminie, 9
Whittier, John Greenleaf, 243
Wilbur, James H., 247, 252, 303–4; attitude
    toward Indians of, 193, 334 n.10; descrip-
    tion of, 193; and Paiute captivity, 192,
    223–24; resignation and death of, 223;
    and SW, 194, 214–15, 217, 222, 225
Wilkins, John D., 187
Wilkinson, Melville C., 164–65, 181
Williams brothers, 59–61
Williams, Helen, 297
Williams, James, 49
Williams Station (NV), 59–60, 313 n.10
Willow Creek Charley, 274
Wilson, Jack. *See* Wovoka (Jack Wilson)
Winnemucca NV, 110–11, 115–16, 118, 123,
    208–9, 263, 299; description of, 126
Winnemucca (chief): appeals to army offi-
    cers by, 119, 135; attitude toward Bartlett
    marriage of, 110, 112, 119; at Camp McDer-
    mit, 99–102, 318 n.19; at conferences, 43,
    65, 80–82, 95, 121; death of, 233–35;
    descriptions of, 99, 100, 118, 145, 308 n.3;
    early California journey of, 52; escape
    from Bannock War of, 157–60; gambling
    by, 107, 232; last years of, 232; at Malheur
    Reservation, 129, 131, 135; peace efforts
    by, 55–56, 65, 81–82; 145, 148–49; philo-
    sophical quest by, 87, 99–101; tactics of,
    57, 123, 141, 195, 301; theatrical appear-
    ances by, 72–77; after Truckee John's mur-
    der, 89; in Washington DC, 203

Winnemucca, Charlie, 288

Winnemucca, Delia, 275

Winnemucca, Elma (Mrs. John Smith), 66, 125, 210, 233, 262; birth of, 21–22; at Henry's Lake, 231, 293–94, 296–97; in Ormsby household, 45–46; trial of, 297

Winnemucca, Frank, 216, 223

Winnemucca, Lee, 128–29, 138, 162, 192, 233, 256, 274; at Camp McDermit, 98, 102; at escape from Bannock War, 156–60; at Yakama Reservation, 192, 216–17, 223

Winnemucca, Mary, 21, 28, 33–39, 51, 312 n.23, 316 n.29

Winnemucca, Mattie (Mrs. Lee Winnemucca), 190; in Bannock War, 158–60, 169–70, 172–73, 175, 181–82, 186; death of, 191; description of, 162

Winnemucca, Natches (Natches Overton), 38, 117; appeals to army officers by, 119, 145, 186, 192; arrest of, 114–16; at Camp McDermit, 97–98; census by, 116; as chief, 259–60; at conferences, 104–5, 196; deaths of children of, 262, 275; denunciation of Umatillas by, 184; dream of, 91; and factionalism, 256, 277, 288; following McMarlin-Williams homicides, 49–51; as mediator in murder trial, 275; peace efforts of, 148–49; at Pyramid Lake Reservation, 85, 88, 91–94; at Pyramid Lake War and Williams Station, 60, 62; ranching by, 145, 148, 235, 263–64, 268, 271, 276–78, 282–83, 288, 290, 292, 343 n.16; rescue of white captives by, 153, 156; in Washington DC, 203–5

Winnemucca, Sarah: achievements of, 2–3, 253–54, 286, 300–301; aims of, 4, 119, 124–25, 243, 245, 251–52, 258, 265–67, 300–301; appeals to army officers by, 105, 119, 135, 140; attempted assaults upon, 126, 181, 211–13; as author, 3, 6–7, 102–4, 125, 226, 239–43, 302, 328 n.22 n.24, 334–35 n.16; in Bannock War, 153–82, 166; birth of, 6, 20; in Boston, 236–37; at Camp Harney, 128, 189–91; at Camp McDermit, 97–110; childhood of, 5, 26–41, 307 n.1,

310 n.11 n.13 n.19; comparison to Sacajawea and Pocahontas of, 1–2; at conferences, 104–5, 121–23; criticism of Indian agents by, 85–86, 257–58, 260–63; death of, 296–98, 344 n.37; descriptions of, 52, 70, 113, 120, 198, 246, 291; divorce by, 142–43; education of, 46–48, 66, 68; family of, 21, 344 n.31; fiction about, 107–8; fracases of, 111, 125–26; gambling by, 207, 230–31, 260, 278, 285; and Ghost Dance, 284–86, 295; at Henry's Lake, 294–98; illnesses and injuries of, 31–32, 111, 121, 127, 231, 262, 271; and Indian reform organizations, 247–48; as an interpreter, 101–2, 108, 121, 128–29, 210, 225; interviews with, 74, 111–13, 119–20, 123, 257, 260; journeys to Yakama Reservation of, 192, 210–13, 332 n.21 n.22; lectures by, 197–201, 231, 244–45, 247, 258, 260–62; at Malheur Reservation, 129, 131–40, 142, 324–25 n.10; marriages and liasons of, 69–71, 108–10, 115, 118, 143–44, 319 n.44, 324 n.32; as mediator in murder trials, 274–75, 289; in Ormsby household, 45–51; present opinions on, 299–300, 304–5; religion of, 52, 193–94, 312 n.25, 330 n.12; Rinehart's campaign of slander against, 206–8, 249, 269–70, 331–32 n.13, 332 n.14; tactics of, 301–2; teaching and school of, 124, 134, 194, 221, 265–73, 276, 280–81, 285–86, 300, 342 n.5; testimony of, 251–52; theatrical appearances of, 72–77; trials of, 127, 209; vision of, 177; in Washington DC, 203–8, 249–52; white attitudes toward, 103–4, 109, 113, 164–65, 299–300, 304; at Yakama Reservation, 192–95, 223

Winnemucca, Tom, 51, 119

Winnemucca, Tuboitony, 5, 20–23, 25–26, 28–29, 31–40, 52, 79

Winnemucca Argent, 94

Winnemucca Lake. *See* Mud Lake

Wodziwob, 90, 284

Wolverton, Lieutenant, 82

women: attitudes toward sw of, 164–65, 213–14, 258; role among Paiutes of, 9–11, 303; sw's lecture to, 245

Women's National Indian Association, 247, 261

Wounded Knee Creek (SD), 295

Wovoka (Jack Wilson), 284–85, 289, 294, 295

Wright, William. *See* De Quille, Dan

Yakima Record, 216

Yakama Reservation, 190, 192, 205, 213, 223–24, 250, 256; Paiute mortality at, 221–22

Yakamas, 194

Yavapais, 273

"Young Winnemucca" (Numaga), 49, 56, 58–59, 62, 64, 81, 317 n.11

Youth's Companion, 107–8

Yurdy, 57

In the *American Indian Lives* series

I Stand in the Center of the Good
Interviews with Contemporary Native American Artists
Edited by Lawrence Abbott

Authentic Alaska
Voices of Its Native Writers
Edited by Susan B. Andrews and John Creed

Dreaming the Dawn
Conversations with Native Artists and Activists
By E. K. Caldwell
Introduction by Elizabeth Woody

Chief
The Life History of Eugene Delorme, Imprisoned Santee Sioux
Edited by Inéz Cardozo-Freeman

Winged Words
American Indian Writers Speak
Edited by Laura Coltelli

Life, Letters and Speeches
By George Copway (Kahgegagahbowh)
Edited by A. LaVonne Brown Ruoff and Donald B. Smith

Life Lived Like a Story
Life Stories of Three Yukon Native Elders
By Julie Cruikshank in collaboration with Angela Sidney,
Kitty Smith, and Annie Ned

LaDonna Harris
A Comanche Life
By LaDonna Harris
Edited by H. Henrietta Stockel

Essie's Story
The Life and Legacy of a Shoshone Teacher
By Esther Burnett Horne and Sally McBeth

Song of Rita Joe
Autobiography of a Mi'kmaq Poet
By Rita Joe

Catch Colt
By Sidner J. Larson

Alex Posey
Creek Poet, Journalist, and Humorist
By Daniel F. Littlefield Jr.

Mourning Dove
A Salishan Autobiography
Edited by Jay Miller

John Rollin Ridge
His Life and Works
By James W. Parins

Singing an Indian Song
A Biography of D'Arcy McNickle
By Dorothy R. Parker

Crashing Thunder
The Autobiography of an American Indian
Edited by Paul Radin

Telling a Good One
The Process of a Native American Collaborative Biography
By Theodore Rios and Kathleen Mullen Sands

Sacred Feathers
The Reverend Peter Jones (Kahkewaquonaby) and the Mississauga Indians
By Donald B. Smith

Grandmother's Grandchild
My Crow Indian Life
By Alma Hogan Snell
Edited by Becky Matthews
Foreword by Peter Nabokov

Blue Jacket
Warrior of the Shawnees
By John Sugden

I Tell You Now
Autobiographical Essays by Native American Writers
Edited by Brian Swann and Arnold Krupat

Postindian Conversations
By Gerald Vizenor and A. Robert Lee

Chainbreaker
The Revolutionary War Memoirs of Governor Blacksnake
As told to Benjamin Williams
Edited by Thomas S. Abler

Standing in the Light
A Lakota Way of Seeing
By Severt Young Bear and R. D. Theisz

Sarah Winnemucca
By Sally Zanjani